Oracle:
A Beginner's
Guide

Oracle:
A Beginner's
Guide

Michael Abbey
Michael J. Corey

Osborne **McGraw-Hill**

Berkeley New York St. Louis San Francisco
Auckland Bogotá Hamburg London Madrid
Mexico City Milan Montreal New Delhi Panama City
Paris São Paulo Singapore Sydney Tokyo Toronto

Osborne **McGraw-Hill**
2600 Tenth Street
Berkeley, California 94710
U.S.A.

For information on translations or book distributors outside the U.S.A., or to
arrange bulk purchase discounts for sales promotions, premiums, or fundraisers,
please contact Osborne **McGraw-Hill** at the above address.

Oracle: A Beginner's Guide

1234567890 DOC 998765

ISBN 0-07-882122-3

Publisher
  Lawrence Levitsky

Aquisitions Editor
  Joanne Cuthbertson

Project Editor
  Wendy Rinaldi

Technical Editor
  Dave Teplow

Copy Editor
  Kathryn Hashimoto

Proofreader
  India Echo

Computer Designer
  Peter Hancik

Illustrator
  Rhys Elliott

Series Design
  Jani Beckwith

Cover Design
  Ted Mader Associates

Quality Control Specialist
  Joe Scuderi

Contents At A Glance

PART III
Developer Bells and Whistles

PART IV
So You're the New DBA

Contents

PART I
Startup

PART II
Developer Basics

PART III
Developer Bells and Whistles

PART IV
So You're the New DBA

Foreword

Over a decade has past since the introduction of desktop computers as personal productivity workcenters. In the early to mid 1980s, power users of these new computers explored the intricacies and challenges of stand-alone spreadsheet and simple text-based decision support applications. Those on the forefront moved into the world of shared data, local area networks and data transfer protocols. Early networked applications left end users and developers battling over issues involving system performance, user interfaces, security and data integrity. At the same time, their colleagues working on larger midrange and mainframe computers began to exploit the benefits of a special breed of database management system, DBMS, based on a relational data model. As with their peers on the new desktop computers, developers using new relational databases started exploring the new technology by building simplistic decision support applications.

In the early 1980s, data management on the desktop consisted of simplistic list managers storing information in stand-alone files. End users and developers toyed with these structured data files, frustrated by their inadequate capability in applications requiring shared data, remote data access and complex data relationships. They envisioned mainframe class applications and data migrated to the desktop but needed far better data management tools and methods.

Fortunately, help was on its way. Already a leader in database technology since the late 1970s, in 1984, Oracle successfully ported its Version 4 relational database management system, RDBMS, to the personal desktop computing environment. Oracle's next release, Version 5, awakened the desktop community to the possibilities of distributed data and client/server architecture and downsized mainframe applications. Few realize that Oracle Version 5 was the first MS-DOS product to operate beyond the 640k memory barrier, running simultaneously in both real and extended memory. Industrial strength RDBMS computing on the new desktop technologies was becoming a reality.

It seems fitting that the second decade of both desktop computing and the relational database, be enabled by the availability of database power that was previously only available on more complex, powerful and expensive computers. Using Oracle7, Oracle Corporation's newest RDBMS, today's user of personal and desktop computing resources can perform tasks that previously required the industrial strength resources of the expensive computers and peripherals of the seventies and eighties. Connectivity and portability between desktop, midrange and mainframe computing environments have never been more attainable and cost effective. While capitalizing on these advances in technology and economies, end users and developers are realizing that even though their specific technology requirements are diverse, they share an important fundamental functional need. Developers seek construction tools, database engines and expertise that will allow them to build functionally rich applications that will run on any combination of stand-alone, client/server or networked host-based computer environments. End users search for intuitive methods and visually oriented tools to access massive amounts of data with ease. Both share the common desire to move away from the restraints of the highly controlled, centralized data centers of the previous decades and move quickly towards distributed, interactive information-on-demand environments. The legacy applications and data of older mainframe-based applications require updating and migration to today's more cost effective and end-user accessible computing environments. Computing environments of the 1990s are focusing on a mixture of personal productivity applications operating on stand-alone desktop computers, workgroup computing applications where functional departments operate networked, shared data applications without MIS resources or expertise and enterprise-wide computing involving vast amounts of data across heterogeneous computing environments and networks. To address these needs, Oracle has developed scalable and portable data management servers, tools and applications that can transparently cross the technical and expertise chasms that naturally exists between individual, workgroup and enterprise-wide computing.

As this book will explain in considerable detail, Oracle, with its commitment to open, portable and scalable DBMS architecture, has positioned itself as the sole provider of data management servers, tools, applications and services that enable the simultaneous use of personal, workgroup and enterprise-wide computing environments. End users will find this book to be a road map to understanding and harnessing Oracle's power to efficiently store massive amounts of data containing complex interrelationships. Application developers will find this book to provide great insight into capitalizing on an environment where applications can be prototyped, developed and deployed onto the computing platform of choice with virtually no change to code or functionality. The authors, both experienced application developers and database administrators, clearly show a simple but effective approach to understanding Oracle and it's vast capabilities.

Time will tell whether new technologies like multimedia, wireless networking, or the current advancements in data management will make a lasting impact on future generations of computing. Leveraging the synergy that exists between these advancing technologies will undoubtedly yield the most effective results. Enterprise-wide, mission-critical applications of the 21st century will find their start during this decade using powerful, stand-alone desktop computers, exciting new application development tools and innovative, functionally rich data management systems like Oracle7. This book will be the introduction for many end users, developers and managers seeking a reliable route to more effective use of their computing environment and information technology investments. Oracle would like to thank the authors for providing a great starting point that will help many new developers and end users of Oracle7 enabled applications.

Gary E. Damiano
Senior Marketing Director
Oracle Corporation

Acknowledgments

Michael Abbey

This book is dedicated to my four wonderful children: Jordan Noah, Nathan Mordecai, Ben James, and Naomi Liba. I fantasize about how wonderful it is going to be to meet my childrens' children.

I would also like to thank the countless number of people who have helped get this work out the door. My friend Dianne Henderson for her patience. Thanks to my fellow author Mike Corey. Thanks to Darryl Smith for writing the chapter on Oracle Forms. Mike Teske helped with some VMS commands in a few areas where my VAX skills were deficient. I enjoyed working with Wendy Rinaldi, Kelly Vogel and Joanne Cuthbertson at Osborne McGraw-Hill. Other names that come to mind: Sydney and Rhoda Abbey, Dave Teplow (your friendly neighborhood technical editor), Kevin Canady, Dave Kreines, Per Brondum, Jamie Best, Gary Damiano, Nancy Taslitz, Carl Dudley, Zoran Stojanov, Ira Greenblatt, Buff Emslie - thanks!

I would also like to mention the late Herman Wong who worked for Oracle Corporation in Toronto—a wonderful man who "held my hand" through many sessions wrestling with the Oracle software. The kind of guy you meet once and feel you've known all your life—only the good die young.

Michael J. Corey

Now having co-authored two books, it is very clear to me why most acknowledgments start off with "Thanks to my wife and family....." It is true, the family suffers the most. Writing a book has the ability to drain all your time, your personal time, your friends' time, your associates' time and anyone else around you. Well, to bring this book to press required a lot of time and effort from a lot of people. This list does not begin to do it justice.

A special thanks to my wife Juliann (a woman with a lot of understanding), and my children John, Annmarie and Michael. Special thanks to Michael Abbey, my co-author. This book would not have been possible without his many phone calls/emails night after night. This book is a great example of the technology highway at work. You have one author in Hingham, MA USA, the other in Ottawa, Canada, and the publisher in Berkeley, CA USA—each able to communicate electronically.

I would also like to thank my friend and partner (at Database Technologies Inc., Newton, MA USA) David Teplow. I consider myself very fortunate to be associated with David both professionally and personally. I was even more fortunate when David agreed to be our technical editor for this book. David has been using Oracle since version 2.0. He is probably the best application developer in all of New England. Please do not blame David for spelling errors, he was told not to correct spelling or grammar as part of the technical review.

Another associate of mine at Database Technologies Inc. deserves special mention: Darryl Smith. He was the key source of talent for our Oracle Forms 4.5 chapter. One of the things you realize after working with Oracle as long as I have—you can't know all the answers. When I first started working with the product, there were three manuals. Now I could easily fill a book case and have. So when we decided to do this book, we looked to the best Forms developer I know to help us. Well, judge for yourself.

I would also like to extend a special thanks to all my colleagues at Database Technologies. Don Briffett has nicknamed me "Hurricane man," as I have been known to send my office into a whirlwind when I arrive. Thanks to all for their patience.

Thanks to my many friends at Oracle whose talents and capabilities never fail to amaze me. Here is a short but in no way complete list: Ray Lane (Mr. Blues), Andy Laursen (Mr. Parallel Server/Media Server), Mark Porter (Video Lad), Scott Martin (Mr. SQL*TRAX), Rama Velpuri (Mr. Backup/Recovery), Stephanie Herle (Miss Events), Gail Peterson (Miss Road Block Breaker), David Anderson (a True Californian), Judy Boyle, (Miss Usergroup 93), Joe Didonato (Mr. Education).

A special thanks to a friend/associate at Oracle Corporation, Gary Damiano. Not only has Gary helped me greatly professionally, but was kind enough to write the foreword to this book.

Thanks to my many friends at the Oracle Users Groups. Here is a small but incomplete list: Dave Kreines, Marty Greenfield, Geoff Girvin, Merrilee Nohr, Buff Emslie, Bert Spencer, Warren Capps, Julie Silverstein, Emily Bersin, Chris Wooldridge (WIZOP on CompuServe), Mark Farnham (great comments on *Tuning Oracle*) and so many more.

Thanks to the people at Osborne McGraw-Hill; without them you would never have received the finished product. A Special Thanks to Joanne Cuthbertson. Her numerous comments have been critical. A special thanks to everyone who purchased *Tuning Oracle*. Your comments and encouragement have been tremendous.

Introduction

This book is designed to be an introduction to Oracle and its tools. We cover, in everyday language, everything you need to know to work with and understand Oracle and its technology. On first inspection, Oracle seems to be a complex product that is next to impossible to understand. The authors' combined experience of 18 years of working with Oracle and its technology are in this book. This book is the perfect introduction to Oracle and its technology or a great complement for the seasoned veteran.With some guidance, and some help zeroing in on the important parts, learning Oracle's technology can be likened to learning to ski. Don't bite off more than you can chew when getting started. Go slowly, and assure yourself all along the way that you are on top of things. We are your ski instructors; we have been to the top and back down many times over. You have an advantage—you can learn from our mistakes and expertise, and avoid some of the pitfalls you encounter when setting out on your own to master Oracle—the company, and Oracle—the software. Yes, there can be some pretty nasty spills along the way; but *Oracle: A Beginner's Guide* is there for you. We intend to help you get started, and point you in the right direction. When you know all there is to know (and yes there is quite a bit in this book), give yourself a pat on the back—you did it!

In the beginning, Oracle created . . . . let's start things off with four chapters rolled together into the "Startup" section. We'll set the groundwork for material covered throughout the book. We'll discuss Oracle, the company, and Oracle, the software, then show you how Oracle has architected its software. We'll take you on a guided tour of the objects Oracle stores in the database, and how they are used. Getting the software onto your machine, regardless of the machine size, is a good place to start; that gets covered in Chapter 4.

And then along comes the four "Developer Basics" chapters. This section provides you with material on the industry standard structured query language (SQL), Oracle's procedural SQL (PL/SQL), Oracle Forms, Oracle Reports, and finally Oracle Loader. Armed with the material in this section, you will know the basics and begin to see how Oracle's electronic solutions can solve your continued business requirements.

"Developer Basics" will no doubt whet your appetite; you'll be hungry for more advanced material—(drum roll) "Developer Bells and Whistles." In the following three chapters, we discuss the basics of application tuning and lead you through some advanced material on SQL. This section wraps up with some advanced application tuning information. This section will leave you panting, looking for some more exciting technical information to satisfy your voracious appetite; not only will you be interested, but you won't be able to put this book down. Get an extra copy for work—once your colleagues see this section, you may never see the book again!

We finish with "So You're the New DBA." This section will take you to places you have never tread before; you will explore the technical catacombs of the Oracle software as a database administrator. Should you decide to accept this mission, you will learn how to work with Oracle through two chapters on database administration. We will show you how to use Oracle's export and import utilities, do some basic database tuning, then discuss backup and recovery.

We believe Oracle is a habit you and your company cannot afford to be without another second. If you want to be part of it, this book is for you. So read on; you will be able to understand what Oracle is, how it works, and how you can use it. We do have one thought to leave you with before you start your descent into Oracle-land.

(Sirens, flashing lights, bugle fanfare...)

WARNING
Learning more about Oracle and using Oracle's software can be addictive.

PART 1

Startup

CHAPTER 1

What Is Oracle?

Why bother to learn Oracle or even read this book? Perhaps you have picked up this book because you keep seeing the big O word, Oracle. This is the same word you keep seeing in the help wanted section of your local newspaper. This is also the same word you keep seeing in your favorite trade journal. Seeing this word makes you think about the big C word, Career. Of course all this thinking links up with the big M word, Money.

You have your reasons—career and money, for instance, or you just want to be part of the current technology movement. You have interest areas—be it rightsizing, client/server, or even video on demand. One thing is very clear: Oracle Corporation and its technology is a major player in today's technology movement and will be an even bigger player tomorrow.

This chapter introduces Oracle and its tools. We will first discuss the basics of the database model Oracle has implemented and its core development tools (SQL*Plus, Oracle Forms, Oracle Reports, Oracle Book, and Oracle Loader). We will then discuss how Oracle has grown. We'll introduce you to SQL*Connect, the tool that allows Oracle to talk to other data sources. We'll also explain how Oracle started to use its own tools to build applications that cater to customers' standard business requirements. We will then move on to Oracle the company today, highlighting the advancement and various flavors of the core database, ending with an overview of Oracle user groups. So here we go—you will learn what Oracle is, how it works, and how you can use it.

Terminology

The following definitions will arm you with the technical jargon to make it through this chapter.

- *Oracle Applications* is a suite of off-the-shelf programs written by Oracle that provide electronic solutions to clients' business requirements. Applications satisfy Oracle customers' needs in areas such as financial management, human resources, and inventory.

- A *master file* is used by computer systems to store information that is used across multiple applications. In a billing system, the name, address, and other contact information may be stored in a master file and used by accounts receivable, inventory, and accounts payable.

- *Client server* computing has three components. Users work with a PC (client), and communicate with a larger central computer (server). An assortment of network software is the third component, allowing communication between the two computers.

- *Rightsizing* is an exercise companies go through when they assess their existing computer hardware and software, and decide on future direction. Given the direction the industry is taking towards smaller, more powerful computers, a great deal of rightsizing exercises end up choosing a flavor of client server computing.

- Programs are *event-driven* when portions of code initiate special activities when a certain event happens. For example, when exiting your favorite word processor, there is an event mapped to Exit. When the event occurs, the software checks to see if your document should be saved, and brings up the Save dialog box, if necessary.

- Programs are *function key/keypad-driven* when pressing certain function keys or keys on the number keypad initiate special activities.

- Applications are called *turnkey* when they do everything the users ever wanted and then some. They are easy to learn and can be used with little or no training. The metaphor refers to turning the key in an automobile's ignition and the car (or application in this case) springs to life.

What Is Oracle?

What a great question! We wish this question had been asked when we first started working with the product in version 4, when the entire documentation set for Oracle consisted of three or four books. Back then, Oracle was primarily a database company with little or no services. In addition, Oracle had no canned applications. Today, the picture is quite different. This multibillion-dollar company has lots of products, lots of services, and even more applications. To help you understand Oracle the company, we will go back to its roots and its foundation—the database. From there, we will move forward to Oracle the company and how it is structured today.

In the Beginning

In the beginning, Oracle was just a database company—a relational database company, to be specific. At that time, relational databases were a new way of thinking about how data should be structured and stored. The key to this type of database is in understanding the relationships within data, then structuring the information base to reflect those relationships. In this way, an information base would be built that could stand the test of time. The goal in a relational database is to build a database in which only the data changes, not the structure itself. The old way of doing things is called the *traditional approach*. To illustrate the difference between these two approaches, we start by taking a look at the traditional customer master file compared to its relational database counterpart. We will then look at characteristics of both approaches, and how changes are made using each. We will then examine the differences between the two models, and show why the relational approach is here to stay. In this and the next few sections, we use the terminology "approach" and "model" when discussing "traditional" and "relational." These terms can be used synonymously; they have the same meaning.

The Traditional Approach

Figure 1-1 illustrates a traditional customer master file. It contains all the normal fields you would expect to see: customer name, address, city, state, home phone, and work phone. There is a separate slot for each item of information; thus, the number of slots depends on the number of different types of data being recorded.

This traditional design was adequate until the use of fax machines became widespread. Incorporating a fax number into the old model required an additional phone field, which in turn required a complete restructuring of the database. Also necessary was a complete redesign of the application code (i.e., a rewrite of large portions if not all of the application) associated with the customer master file (not to mention the prohibitive cost of implementing the change). Using a traditional design, managers had to make the following decisions:

- If the application code was changed, there were high costs associated with adding new functionality to applications. Installations hoped their staff could facilitate the change rapidly; a mistake could cause an interruption in the ability to deal with customers and carry on business.

- If the application code was left as is, all the money associated with making the change was not spent. Money was saved, but there was a price to pay: you did business without access to fax machine phone numbers. Of course, if this continued to happen, your business was taking a great technological risk. In the long run, the competition (who made the change) might pass you by.

Customer master file
customer_name
address
city
state
home_phone
work_phone

FIGURE 1-1. *A traditional customer master file*

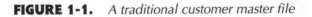

At this point, you might be sitting back and saying, "What's the big deal? Who cares if the application has to be changed every once in a while?" The reality is that we live in a changing world, and businesses that don't keep up risk dying. Fact: For over 100 years, the Swiss dominated the world's watch industry. When a new type of watch was invented using quartz movement, the Swiss didn't react. Today, the Swiss make a very small portion of the world's watches.

Using the traditional approach, had we altered the customer master file to include fax numbers, we would have had to reload the file (to populate the fax number field). On top of this, all the programs that used data in the customer master file would need modifying. At this point, we should also mention how data in traditional systems is stored. A traditional database might have the customer master file, the payroll master file, the health insurance master file, and so on. Each one of these master files is separate. This is a problem when an event affects more than one of the files.

To illustrate how cumbersome the traditional approach can get (not to mention how expensive), look at the following scenario. Traditional systems keep redundant information in multiple locations. The employee benefits application stores employee names in a benefits master file. The payroll people maintain employee names in a payroll master file. On top of this, the long distance system stores employee names in the telecommunications master file. Suppose a woman changes her last name after getting married and needs her paycheck written with her new last name. The name change gets done in the payroll master file but it may not get done elsewhere.

VIP
Synchronizing changes to the same data in multiple locations is the single most difficult thing to ensure in the traditional approach.

In the traditional database, it might take months to ensure the name is properly changed in every place it is stored, not to mention the time and effort it takes just to make the changes. Wouldn't Sally be upset if she got married and lost her health insurance benefits!

Traditional systems are *design-driven*; they require design changes when one needs to capture new kinds of data. Whenever a new business need is identified (i.e., the need to store fax numbers, cell phones, or car phones), a high-end systems analyst or database administrator (highly technical, not to mention highly priced) is required to review the existing application design and make the necessary design modifications. The bottom line: the design changes are expensive, and worse still, many installations don't make the changes for that very reason!

Now, let's examine how the relational approach handles this.

The Relational Approach

Using this approach, system designers isolate types of information that need capturing. They then identify the relationships between those information types, and implement a database structure similar to that shown in Figure 1-2. Using the relational model, what was previously referred to as master files are called tables. Notice how Figure 1-2 shows a customer table, a phone_number table, and a phone_number_types table. Each is a separate table within the database.

In Figure 1-2, the relationship between customer and phone_number is represented by the crow's feet, which shows that a customer may have one or more phone numbers. We also show a relationship between phone_number_types and phone_number. This single line represents the fact that a phone_number must be associated with one type of phone. Thus, we have some rules governing the relationships between our customer and phone number data:

■ Each customer may have one or more phone number(s).

■ Each phone number belongs to one and only one customer.

■ Each phone number must be one and only one type (e.g., a home voice number, a business number, a fax number, or a mobile phone).

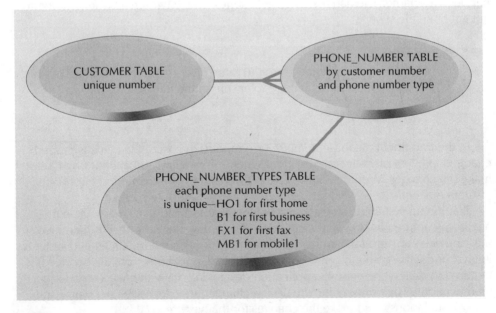

FIGURE 1-2. *Three tables (master files) using the relational model*

Now that we have designed the database to understand these relationships and to enforce our rules, all we have to do to add fax numbers is to add a row of data to the phone_number_types entity. There is no need to restructure the database; there is no need to do a complete redesign of the application programs; there is no need to program any new functionality. Using this approach, the work required to implement trapping of fax numbers is trivial.

Think back to poor Sally and her health insurance benefits. In the relational model (as illustrated in Figure 1-2), Sally's name is stored in one location. When the benefits application reads Sally's name, it gets it from the customer table. Likewise, when the payroll and telecommunications systems need Sally's name, they get it from the customer table as well.

Systems built using the relational model store information once. Changes and additions to that central repository are reflected immediately.

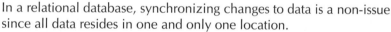

VIP
In a relational database, synchronizing changes to data is a non-issue since all data resides in one and only one location.

Relational systems are *data-driven*; you pay a highly technical person to come in and build a system so that the key relationships are identified and built into the system (e.g., a person may have one or more phone numbers). Then, when it becomes necessary to capture additional phone number types, it is not necessary to redesign the system. You don't need a high-priced analyst to affect changes—you add a new phone number type to the phone_number_types table.

In the relational database model, the relationship between customer and phone number stays the same. You merely need to register a new phone number type in the phone_number_types table.

Differences Between the Two Approaches

Table 1-1 summarizes how traditional and relational systems are built, and shows how they differ, using the fax number example.

In the Beginning: Summary of Points

To summarize the features of a relational database:

- A relational database is data-driven, not design-driven. It is designed once, and the data changes over time without affecting the applications.

- The data is self-describing. For example, the phone number type is identified as phone_number_type.

■ Data is stored in one place, read from one place, and modified in one place. Data is stored once, so maintaining consistency among all applications is easier.

■ Rules that control how the data will be stored are defined and enforced.

Oracle Today

Today, Oracle Systems Corporation, based in Redwood Shores, California, manufactures software products and delivers services for the electronic management of information. Oracle is a worldwide provider of computer software, with 1994 revenues in excess of $2 billion. Oracle does business in over 90

TASK	TRADITIONAL	RELATIONAL
Design applications	Figure what applications need what types of information, then set up a series of master files.	Define the types of data that will be collected, and define their relationships.
Implement applications	Load data into master files, placing one item of information into each slot in each master file.	Load types of data into their respective tables, ensuring each item ends up stored in one and only one location.
Modify applications (i.e., allow for capturing of more types of data)	Redesign the database, and modify all programs to reflect the change. Reload any master files affected by the change.	Isolate the table where the type of data affected is defined (i.e., the phone_number_types table). The data that exists in the tables remains unaffected.
Modify a subset of data	Read each master file from start to finish. If a row is part of the subset to be modified, process it, otherwise go on to the next record.	Isolate the set of rows that are part of the subset, and implement the change in one SQL statement.

TABLE 1-1.   *Differences Between Traditional and Relational Models*

countries around the world, and their software runs on upwards of 100 different computers. They are a major player on the information superhighway.

With the innovation of the Media Server and a number of cooperative agreements with worldwide communications giants, Oracle is actively participating in the race to bring video on demand to your living room. Oracle is part of the never-ending race to bring the biggest and the best to a computer screen or television set near you. Oracle manufactures a suite of products that revolve around its Oracle Server, as we discuss next.

Oracle Server

The Oracle Server is a state-of-the-art information management environment. It is a repository for very large amounts of data, and gives users rapid access to that data. The Oracle Server provides for the sharing of data between applications; the information is stored in one place and used by many systems. The Oracle Server runs on dozens of different computers, supporting the following configurations:

- **Host-based**—Users are connected directly to the same computer on which the database resides.

- **Client/server**—Users access the database from their personal computer (client) via a network, and the database sits on a separate computer (server).

- **Distributed processing**—Users access a database that resides on more than one computer. The database is spread across more than one machine, and the users are unaware of the physical location of the data they work with.

We believe the Oracle Server has helped position Oracle the company at the top of the list of successful database vendors.

Why Oracle Is Where It Is Today

There are many significant features that have catapulted Oracle to the top of the growing information management vendor community.

Security Mechanisms
Oracle's sophisticated security mechanisms control access to sensitive data by an assortment of privileges. Users are given rights to view, modify, and create data based on the name they use to connect to the database. Customers use these mechanisms to ensure specified users get to see sensitive data, while others are forbidden.

Backup and Recovery

Oracle provides sophisticated backup and recovery routines. Backup creates a secondary copy of Oracle data; recovery restores a copy of data from that backup. Oracle's backup and recovery strategy minimizes data loss and downtime when and if problems arise.

Space Management

Oracle offers flexible space management. You can allocate disk space for storage of data and control subsequent allocations by instructing Oracle how much space to set aside for future requirements.

Open Connectivity

Oracle provides for uninterrupted access to the database 24 hours a day. Oracle provides open connectivity to and from other vendors' software. Using add-ons to the Oracle database, you can work with information that resides in other data repositories, such as IBM's DB2, Sybase, or Microsoft Access. As well, you are permitted to store your data in Oracle's database and access it from other software, such as Microsoft Visual Basic, Powersoft's PowerBuilder, and Gupta's SQL*Windows.

Development Tools

The Oracle Server, commonly referred to as the database engine, supports a wide range of development tools, end-user query tools, off-the-shelf applications, and office-wide information management tools.

Components of the Oracle Server

Oracle sells its server technology with a number of add-on options that enhance the server capabilities. The base product provides all the functionality to support the requirements of most of Oracle's customers. When customers require the procedural, distributed, parallel query, or parallel server options to meet their business requirements, they purchase it in addition to the Server product. Let's look at these four options and what they do.

Procedural Option

With release 7.0, this option is purchased separately from the Server; with release 7.1, the option is part of the Server at no additional cost. The foundation of this option is Oracle's programming language, called PL/SQL. PL/SQL is discussed in Chapter 6. With this option, you can implement the following features.

Stored Procedures   Stored procedures are programs (or code segments) that are stored in the Oracle database and perform central functions for your installation. For example, in a cable television billing application, you may use a stored procedure to create a reminder letter to customers with delinquent accounts. The execution of that procedure is triggered by the creation of a customer's monthly statement when unpaid charges are due for over 60 days.

Database Triggers   These are code stored in the database triggered by events that occur in your applications. In a human resources application, for example, when a new employee is brought on board, the creation of a new set of personnel information could use a database trigger to create messages to be sent to other parts of the company. These messages, triggered by the new employee being added to the database, could alert the operators of the message center to the existence of the new individual.

Packages   Packages group procedures together and store the code as a single program unit in the database. For example, a central warehouse for a chain of bookstores could design a package that takes care of the routing of special orders to the appropriate retail location. There would be procedures within this package to initiate the transfer of goods, process notifications of short orders, process reorders, and so on.

Distributed Option

In many installations, portions of corporate data reside on different computers in different cities. Accounts receivable may be based in Dallas, procurement in Toronto, research and development in Jakarta, and head office in Lisbon. Each location has a segment of the corporate data, yet users need to access that information as if it all resided on the same central computer. The distributed option permits this scenario to become a reality. There is *location transparency,* such that a user in Yokohama working with the information stored in Toronto is unaware of the physical location of the data. The physical location of the procurement data is unknown to all users. Oracle's distributed option permits this to work.

Parallel Server Option

Some manufacturers make clustered computers: each machine in the cluster has its own memory, yet they have common disk storage devices. The parallel server option allows Oracle to operate with this configuration. Each machine is referred to as a *node* in the cluster, and the term *loosely coupled* is used to refer to the nodes. Figure 1-3 shows how this works.

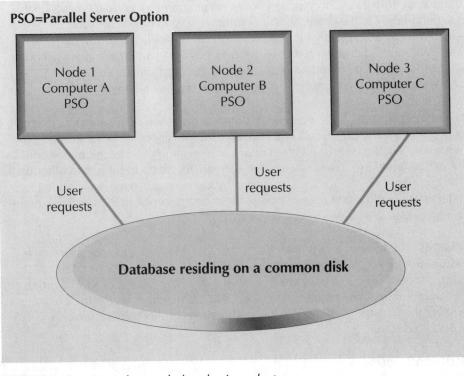

FIGURE 1-3. *Loosely coupled nodes in a cluster*

Parallel Query Option

Starting with the Oracle Server release 7.1, the parallel query option allows customers to take advantage of processing queries on computers with more than one central processing unit (commonly referred to as a CPU). On single CPU machines (or multi-CPU machines without the parallel query option), a single process accesses the database and displays the data that qualifies based on the selection criteria. The processing is handled as shown in Figure 1-4.

When using the parallel query option on multi-CPU machines, Oracle dispatches a number of query processes that work alongside one another. They partition the query processing and work simultaneously; the results are merged and presented to the user when ready. Figure 1-5 shows the basics of this option.

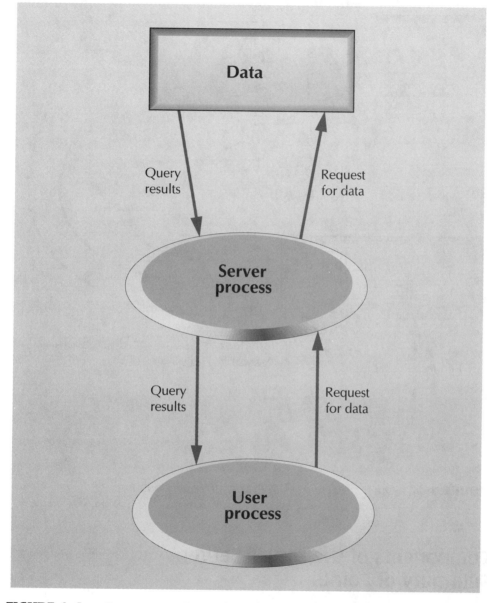

FIGURE 1-4.   *Query processing without the parallel query option*

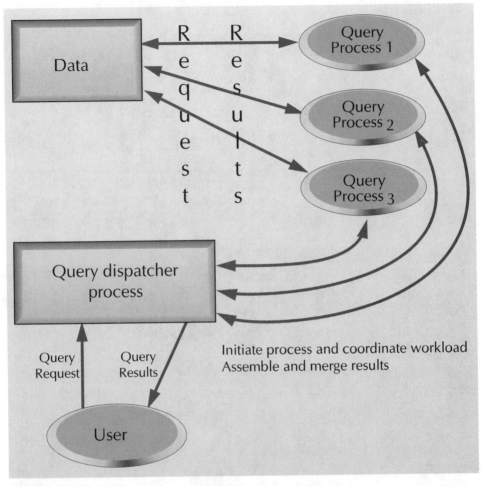

FIGURE 1-5. *Query processing with the parallel query option*

Components of the Oracle Server: Summary of Points

Let's summarize the main points from this section.

- Four options can be added to the Oracle Server base product. They provide added functionality, and additional features required by a portion of Oracle's customer base.

- The procedural option delivers PL/SQL, as well as stored procedures, database triggers, packages, and functions. These code segments reside in the database, and can be shared by applications.

- The distributed option allows users to work with data in a remote database as if it resided locally.

- The parallel server option enables a cluster of computers to share common disk space, yet have their own memory.

- The parallel query option caters to computers with multiple CPUs, and allows query processing to be split between multiple server processes.

SQL*Plus—The User-Friendly Interface

So far we have talked about the Oracle Server. Let's move on to SQL*Plus—the way you define and manipulate data in Oracle's relational database. SQL (Structured Query Language) is the industry standard adopted by all database vendors. (Some people pronounce SQL as "sequel," others pronounce each letter separately.) Oracle's SQL*Plus is a superset of standard SQL; it conforms to the standards of a SQL-compliant language, and it has some Oracle-specific add-ons, leading to its name (SQL and Plus). In the old days, SQL*Plus was called UFI, the user-friendly interface. Compared to writing in a typical programming language like FORTRAN, friendly it is.

The Oracle Server only understands statements worded using SQL—when tools such as Oracle Forms interact with the database, they pass nothing other than SQL statements for processing. Oracle's implementation of SQL through SQL*Plus is compliant with ANSI (American National Standards Institute) and ISO (International Standards Organization) standards. Almost all Oracle tools support identical SQL syntax.

SQL is tailored to harness the power of the relational model. Since all your data is stored via the relationship, it is possible to work with your data in sets, versus independent rows of data. With SQL*Plus, much of the work associated with retrieving data out of a traditional database goes away. For example, you no longer read a record. Instead, you write a program that deals with all the records associated with an entity. No one record is different than another. In SQL*Plus, whatever action you decide to take is done as a complete set. We demonstrate how this is done in Chapters 5 and 11.

VIP

All the vendors have gone the relational database route. The relational model is here to stay.

SQL*Plus: Summary of Points

Let's summarize what we have learned about Oracle's base programming language:

- SQL*Plus is Oracle's flavor of SQL. "Plus" refers to Oracle's addition to the SQL language.

- All work with a relational database is done with an SQL-based programming language.

- SQL*Plus is user friendly.

- When programming with SQL*Plus, you work on sets of data (i.e., information is not processed one record at a time).

- Using the "Plus" component of SQL*Plus, it is easy to write useful reports (Chapters 5 and 11 highlight report writing using SQL*Plus).

Oracle Forms—The Front End

With the foundation of a strong database and complemented by a strong language for reporting (SQL*Plus), it was only natural that Oracle would expand into a screen generator, since this is the primary way most users deal with the database. Oracle Forms is such a tool. It runs in a graphical user interface (GUI) environment, with the look and feel of Microsoft Windows.

Application developers design data entry and query screens with Oracle Forms; end users can then use these screens to manipulate data in the Oracle database. The interface with the user is event-driven or function key/keypad-driven. As summarized in Table 1-2, there are three types of modules one writes with Oracle Forms. Rolled together, they provide the developer and end user with a complete

PROGRAM TYPE	CONTENTS
forms	Allows update, creation, and deletion of data within Oracle objects.
menu	Defines an assortment of main menus and an optional subset of any number of submenus.
library	A repository for centralized PL/SQL code accessed by other types of Oracle Forms modules.

TABLE 1-2. *Oracle Forms Module Types*

forms-based corporate data entry solution. Combining an assortment of these three types of programs into a full-blown application is part of the art of working with Oracle Forms.

In Chapter 7, we discuss this tool in greater detail.

Oracle Reports–The Report Writer

With the foundation of a strong relational database and complemented by a robust suite of core development tools, Oracle continued to expand. While SQL*Plus is a great reporting tool, it was not designed with just reporting in mind. So Oracle developed various tools just for generating reports, including SQL*QMX, RPT, and Easy*SQL. Oracle Reports (and its predecessor SQL*Reportwriter) is the flagship report writer for Oracle. We discuss Oracle Reports in Chapter 8 and show you how to build a few simple reports.

Oracle Reports is a successor to SQL*Reportwriter that appeared with Oracle version 6. SQL*Reportwriter provides a reporting environment with which the developer designs reports and the end user executes them; it evolved into Oracle Reports as users insisted they wanted a Windows-based mouse-driven interface. With Oracle Reports, you can create graphical report representations of the data in your Oracle database.

Oracle Reports (starting with version 2.0) is a true multimedia reporting environment. You can include images, sound, and charts, and you can present reports in a variety of colors using an assortment of fonts. You can easily create popular report output styles with Oracle Reports. Using its powerful default features, developers can create the master/detail reports, matrix reports, and form letters with little programming.

Master/Detail Reports

When designing master/detail reports, the programmer defines a hierarchy of the data assembled for the report; you display all data for the first level, then the second level data it is related to. The following simple master/detail report uses automobile manufacturers as an example. The manufacturer is called the master; when a master is displayed, all of its associated detail information appears.

```
Manufacturer:   Ford
Model           Style        Price Class
Topaz           Wagon        D
Villager        Minivan      F
Fiesta          Sedan        B
```

```
Manufacturer:    GM
Model            Style        Price Class
Safari           Minivan      F
Impala           Sedan        E
TransAm          Sport        F
```

Matrix Reports

In matrix reports, you use the values of rows and columns as labels. For example, let's consider the following set of data:

```
Salesperson            Quarter           Commission
10                     1                 500
10                     2                 400
20                     1                 600
20                     2                 900
20                     3                 350
30                     2                 900
30                     3                 235
```

That data would be presented in the following way in a matrix report:

```
            1            2            3
10          500          400
20          600          900          350
30                       900          235
```

Notice how the quarter column values appear as column headers and the salesperson numbers appear as row headers.

Form Letters

With form letters, you take information from the database and include it in the body of a letter. Sometimes, one simply gets name and address information from the database. Other times, the text in the body of the letter is extracted from the database. In the next example, the text in italics has been printed based on address information stored in the database; the text in bold and italics forms part of the letter's body and comes from the database too.

```
...
Dear Ms. Stroud:
This is to inform you that ...... no later than the end of May, 1996.
...
Dear Mr. Flaherty:
This is to inform you that ...... no later than the middle of July, 1996.
...
```

VIP

Oracle Reports is a report writer. Unlike SQL*Plus, it is very
graphically based. Using the power of a computer and its mouse, you
are able to point and click to build very powerful reports.

Oracle Book

Oracle Book is an online document viewing facility for the sharing of text across
Oracle products. Since version 7.1 of the Oracle Server, Oracle has supplied a set
of online documentation you can read using Oracle Book. Oracle Book has three
components:

- *Designer* provides for the creation and maintenance of online documents.

- *Converter* takes older formats of Book documents and converts them to the
  latest release.

- *Runtime* provides viewing capabilities and is used to propagate Book
  documents to the user community.

The Runtime environment permits customization of user preferences, though
the documents' contents cannot be changed. Oracle now distributes the majority of
its products with electronic online documentation read using Oracle Book.
Developers use Oracle Book Designer to create and modify documents, and users
run Oracle Book to access them.

Oracle Loader and SQL*Connect

In the old days, Oracle had a special tool called ODL (Oracle Data Loader). Over
time, this has evolved into Oracle Loader, a tool that very quickly allows you to

load data into an Oracle database. Tools like this are very important to an Oracle database. In the real world, a great deal of customers' systems still use the traditional approach. Most agree that a relational database is a great tool, but migrating traditional systems to relational systems requires conversion of your existing systems' data. Well, that's what Oracle Loader is all about. It is a tool you use to move data into an Oracle database.

Like any good capitalistic company, Oracle grew its supply to meet the demand. A big demand exists in the industry for tools that enable you to move data from a traditional database to a relational database. There is also a great demand for tools that enable a relational database to talk to a traditional database. That is the thrust behind tools like SQL*Connect. This is a tool that enables an Oracle database to connect and talk to a traditional database, be it an IBM mainframe or a DEC VAX system.

It's clear that once the data is placed in an Oracle database, with the new tools it is easier to generate reports and screens to manipulate the contents. It is also the reality that this migration might take years to accomplish. Oracle has developed tools to move your data into Oracle, like Oracle Loader, or tools to talk to a traditional database, like SQL*Connect.

Oracle Using Its Own Tools—The Applications

As time went on, Oracle Corporation realized that there was a strong business opportunity available for off-the-shelf generic applications. So Oracle started to build financial applications. This had two major impacts on the rest of the Oracle environments (i.e., Oracle customers using the same products Oracle the company itself was using).

First, Oracle Corporation was actually using its own tools to build applications. The more they used the tools, the more the tools improved. The company started to live, eat, and breathe their own tools. The more Oracle used their own tools, the more they found ways to improve them. So, very quickly, we started to see major improvements in the quality and functionality of the tools.

Second, as soon as Oracle Corporation started to build applications based on the relational database model, companies started to use the Oracle software for mission-critical business functions (e.g., payroll). This accelerated the proliferation of Oracle's database software, and more and more companies started to reap the benefits of the new technology Oracle had developed.

Today, Oracle has a division that puts out applications in every major product area—from accounting to manufacturing to industry-specific solutions. Administrative support of today's application customer can be done using Oracle Office which we discuss next.

COMPONENT	DESCRIPTION
Office Mail	An integrated messaging environment, with the ability to manage your messages using folders, templates, and distribution lists.
Office Scheduler	Enables you to manage your time and schedule meetings with other personnel. Office Scheduler uses Office Mail messaging to distribute meeting requests to other users.
CoAuthor	A spelling and proofreader companion to all the other Oracle Office components. You can customize CoAuthor to fit your individual writing style, and you can train it to proof documents the same way every time.
Office Manager	The Oracle Office administration tool. Management of users, system defaults, and the office configuration are defined and modified using this component.
Office Directory	Places information about people, meeting rooms, and office equipment at your fingertips. This is the type of information you might require to set up meetings, schedule presentations, and carry on your company's marketing exercises. You can use Office Directory when addressing messages; recipient information is at your disposal.

TABLE 1-3.   *Oracle Office Components*

Oracle Office

Oracle Office is a suite of products designed to manage the administrative needs of any corporation. Table 1-3 lists the components that make up Oracle Office.

Competition is fierce today in the electronic office environment. Oracle Office allows companies to manage their office administration material in the same repository as their corporate legacy data.

Developer 2000 and Designer 2000

Developer 2000 (formerly called CDE2 or Cooperative Development Environment version 2) and Designer 2000 offer a complete solution when Oracle clients need to design, program, implement, and maintain systems. They provide for rapid application development in a client/server Windows environment. Their advanced functionality supports BPR (Business Process Reengineering) and mechanisms to take advantage of the server processing that can be done using Oracle's database engine; both are tightly integrated with the Oracle Server. Using stored procedures and triggers (as discussed in the "Components of the Oracle Server" section of this chapter), processing is split between the server and the client.

Developer 2000 bundles the following Oracle products together:

- Oracle Forms
- Oracle Reports
- Oracle Graphics
- Oracle Book
- Oracle Browser
- Oracle Procedure Builder
- Oracle Open Client Adapter for ODBC
- SQL*Plus
- SQL*Net

Common GUI functionality, as embedded in Oracle's latest generation of reporting and forms development tools, provides the interface between the analyst and Developer 2000/Designer 2000. Development can be done in small workgroups and applications easily deployed to hundreds of users. Developer 2000 offers automatic code generation as well as automated software distribution. PL/SQL, the language that Oracle has embedded in all its development products, offers Designer 2000 and Developer 2000 the same program development environment on client as well as server. Designer 2000 supports a wide range of business model functionality that enables companies to build systems ranging from the simplest to the most complex. Designer 2000 is the next generation of Oracle's suite of CASE products discussed in the next section.

NOTE
We have not yet had a look at Designer 2000. The next section on CASE will give you a flavor of what you can do with this product.

The bottom line of both products is rapid application development coupled with scalability, advanced application partitioning, and centralized code repository management features.

CASE

Oracle CASE (Computer Assisted Software Engineering) is a suite of products designed to help define business requirements, design systems, and generate data entry and reporting modules. There are four main components: CASE Dictionary, Oracle Forms Generator, Oracle Reports Generator, and CASE Designer.

CASE Dictionary allows you to collect and organize business information when designing new computer systems. Using Dictionary, you can define the following:

- Business rules
- Inputs to the application
- Modules used by the application
- Characteristics of the application data
- Functions the application will perform
- Processes the application performs
- Process flows
- Application outputs

CASE Dictionary is built using Oracle Forms screens, and most of the reports it produces are Oracle Reports. A CASE Dictionary administrator can control access in all of the CASE products to control what information users are permitted to change and what they can access as read-only.

Oracle Forms Generator takes the information in the Dictionary repository and creates Oracle Forms data entry and query screens. As the system evolves and changes, you go back and regenerate your screens. Changes made in the Dictionary appear in the Oracle Forms screens as they are re-created.

Oracle Reports Generator takes the information in the Dictionary repository and creates Oracle Reports. As the system evolves and changes, you go back and regenerate your reports. Changes made in the Dictionary ripple through the reports as they are regenerated.

CASE Designer is a graphic, mouse-driven tool with which you create a network of relationship diagrams that depict the makeup of your applications. The definition of work flows and objects in the Designer change the Dictionary data as if the data entry had been done there. CASE Designer is a system analyst and system engineer tool that is used throughout the cycle of system development.

Personal Oracle7

Since early 1995, Oracle has produced Oracle for personal computers in both DOS and Microsoft Windows environments. The following configuration is required for running Personal Oracle7:

- A 386 or stronger central processing unit (CPU), though a 486 or Pentium is preferred

- At least 60 megabytes (or 62,914,560 bytes) of available disk space

- A 40MHz or faster processor—speeds of 66 or better are preferable

- At least 8 megabytes of extended memory

- MS-DOS or PC-DOS versions 5 or 6, or Digital Research's DR-DOS version 6 or higher

- Microsoft Windows 3.1

Personal Oracle7 is a full-blown Oracle7 Server implementation; most of the topics we discuss in this book apply to the PC as well. Throughout this book, we include a section in most chapters that deals with Personal Oracle7 specifics. Most operations with Personal Oracle7 use the Windows point-and-click interface you may be familiar with already. You will not be able to run the Personal Oracle7 utilities and tools from your DOS command line—you will get the error you have probably seen all too many times: "This program requires Microsoft Windows."

The Services

The services wing of Oracle Corporation is a major component in what Oracle has to offer the marketplace. These services offer the following:

- **Education**—Skilled instructors teach about the wide range of the Oracle product set as well as some of the relational database modeling, design, and analysis theory.

- **Consulting**—Trained professionals are at your disposal to help facilitate corporate system solutions using Oracle's products and Oracle's partners' technology. There is a network of companies that develop and market their own products that work alongside Oracle's products; Oracle partners with these companies.

- **Industries**—Solutions to industry-specific business requirements, with special attention to addressing key issues with Oracle-based technology.

The services Oracle provides to the marketplace can be grouped into four components: Oracle worldwide customer support, Oracle Education, Oracle Industries, and Oracle Consulting.

Oracle worldwide customer support provides technical assistance to clients in the care and feeding of Oracle products. Support services are specifically geared to match customer needs, with a suite of support levels from around-the-clock personalized service (Oracle Gold) to online electronic support through the private support forum on CompuServe (Oracle SupportLink).

Oracle Education offers a wide range of courses on the full suite of products and applications. It can provide pre-classroom learning via the computer-based training (CBT) electronic medium. There are centers in over 50 countries that provide classroom and in-house training to end users, developers, analysts, and IT (information technology) managers.

Oracle Industries works with specific pockets of industry to identify key issues, using Oracle technology to create system solutions. It works alongside industry professionals to refine business system goals and to build systems that help companies stay one step ahead of the competition.

Oracle Consulting helps customers realize critical solutions by providing expert guidance and technology transfer. It assists with business process re-engineering exercises, the transformation to open systems, and application development, to name a few. Oracle Expert Services offers management (e.g., strategic planning), technical (e.g., performance tuning), development (e.g., custom systems), and Oracle applications implementation services.

An increasing portion of Oracle business is generated in the services area each year. Oracle services enable customers to implement dependable, state-of-the-art technology systems that deploy the Oracle Cooperative Server technology. Services are geared toward knowledge transfer and lasting success of system solutions realized in partnership with Oracle professionals.

Oracle User Groups—Events and Publications

There is a significant number of Oracle user groups and events around the world. Oracle Corporation, as well as the user group community, has aligned itself on a tricontinental basis: the Americas, Europe/Africa/Middle East, and Asia-Pacific. Contact information for all of these central user communities can be obtained through the headquarters of the International Oracle Users Group (IOUG)-Americas in Chicago at 1(312) 245-1579.

User groups around the world meet regularly to discuss technical issues related to using Oracle. There are presentations over a wide range of Oracle-related subjects from the user community, third-party vendors, and Oracle Corporation.

The three continental user groups' central contacts are in the U.S., Austria, and Australia. Each geographical area has one or more Oracle conferences in a year, the largest of which are the following:

- The Americas holds International Oracle User Week (IOUW), usually in September of each year in the U.S.

- The Asia-Pacific user forum is held in Australia or New Zealand, usually in November of each year.

- Europe/Middle East/Africa holds the European Oracle User Forum (EOUF), usually in March or April of each year.

A number of Oracle user groups around the world publish newsletters and magazines with articles on Oracle products and services. As examples: *Select* magazine is published quarterly by the IOUG-Americas, *Relate* magazine is published quarterly by the U.K. Oracle Users Group, and the Digital Special Interest Group in the U.S. publishes the *Lighthouse* newsletter periodically.

What's Next

Enough said! From reading this chapter, we trust you have a basic knowledge of what Oracle is and what they produce. You should have a clear understanding that Oracle Corporation's roots are based on the database. From this base, Oracle has branched out to a full-service vendor; a vendor that can supply a database that will run on a PC all the way up to an IBM 3090. Oracle also offers a core set of tools that will fully migrate up or down. In addition, Oracle is a full-service provider of turnkey applications, consulting, education, and new technologies, such as video on demand. Now it's time to get your feet wet. Read on!

CHAPTER 2

Architecture

After memorizing Chapter 1, you know about Oracle Corporation and some of the products it sells to its worldwide user community. We spent a great deal of time on the Oracle Server—it is the foundation of everything Oracle has out there. We feel the major reason Oracle is such a force in modern information technology is its staying power. Oracle has been down a number of times and bounced back up to bigger and better heights. This chapter delves further into Oracle database architecture. After reading this chapter, you will understand the following:

■ Components of an Oracle database

■ Tablespaces

■ Rollback segments

■ Online redo logs

■ Control files

■ Processes associated with an Oracle database

■ System global area (SGA)

■ An Oracle instance

Terminology

The following definitions will arm you with the technical jargon to make it through this chapter.

■ An *object* is a structure defined by the Oracle database and referenced in SQL statements within your applications. Most objects are tables, but SQL statements can refer to other kinds of objects.

■ An *instance* is a portion of computer memory and auxiliary processes required to access an Oracle database. These processes were discussed in Chapter 1 in the "Database Support Processes" section.

■ An *application* is a set of Oracle programs that solve a company's or person's business needs. In more day-to-day terms, the computer system that generates bills for a hydro-electric utility could be referred to as a *billing application*.

■ A *DBA* or database administrator is a technical wizard who manages the complete operation of the Oracle database. The DBA's job is highlighted in Chapters 13 and 17.

■ A *datafile* is a file on your disk that stores information. For example, when working with a word processor, you could call your document a datafile.

■ A *tablespace* is a collection of one or more datafiles. All database objects are stored in tablespaces. It is called a tablespace because it typically holds a database object called a table.

■ A *table* holds Oracle data. It contains space allocated to hold application-specific data in your database.

- *Rollback* is the activity Oracle performs to restore data to its prior state before a user started to change it. For example, you change the value for someone's location from "AL" to "MN" and then decide that you made a mistake—a rollback activity could change the location back to "AL."

- *Undo information* is the information the database needs to undo or rollback a user transaction due to a number of reasons. For example, when you change a customer's credit limit from $2,000 to $3,000, undo information is kept in case you decide not to save the change.

- A *dirty data block* is a portion of computer memory that contains Oracle data whose value has changed from what was originally read from the database. If a personnel application read the name "Julie Gelinas" into a data block in memory and the name was changed to "Julie Stojanov," the block in memory containing the new name is called a dirty data block. Think of dirty data blocks as data sitting in memory that has been changed but not yet written back to the database.

- A *hot data block* is a block whose data is changed frequently. In an inventory application, a popular part's quantity_on_hand would be in a hot data block since its value undergoes constant change.

- *LRU* (least recently used) is an algorithm Oracle uses when it needs to make room for more information in memory than will fit in the memory space allocated. Let's say Oracle has five slots in memory, holding information, and it needs to put some additional information into memory. Since the five slots are full, Oracle flushes the information that for the longest period of time has not been used.

Why Bother to Learn the Architecture?

We have found in our travels that many users do not see the need for understanding the internal architecture of the Oracle database. They just go out and code the application (the official term for this is *rapid prototyping*). The Oracle relational database and its tools make application building look easy—much the way a pro athlete makes a sport look easy. However, we all know from experience that what looks easy in theory might not be easy in practice.

Here's an analogy to illustrate why you should take the time to understand the Oracle database architecture. It all started a year ago, when I helped the plumber put a new heating system in our home. By helping the plumber, I was able to bring the installation cost way down; being a Yankee at heart, I found that money was a very strong motivator to do manual labor! The heating system installed was forced hot water: after the water is heated, electric pumps move it through the pipes.

During the installation process, I expended a great deal of effort bleeding the air pockets out of the heating system, as air prevents the heated water from circulating through the pipes. A few weeks later, the bedrooms were not getting enough heat. With some knowledge of the heating system, I was able to determine that an air pocket must be in the pipes. I took the time to bleed the air out, and shortly after, heat was restored.

A month later, a "Nor'easta" (in Boston, lobster is pronounced "lobsta" and chowder is pronounced "chowda") snowstorm hit Boston, and we lost our power. Within a few hours, without electricity to work the electric pumps, the house started to get very cold. With three small children at home, this was not a good situation. I kept thinking there must be a way to get the remaining hot water in the heating system to circulate through the pipes without electricity. Again, applying my limited knowledge of the architecture of a hot-water heating system, I came up with the solution: by opening up the return pipes, the cold water was replaced with the remaining hot water. Heat was then restored.

There is a point to the analogy: we are not plumbers. But a good understanding of how things were designed helped in ways we had never anticipated. With this in mind, you may want to take the time to read the rest of this chapter.

TIP
When starting to work with complex software such as Oracle, take the time to learn the architecture. Down the road, taking this time at the beginning will pay off.

What Is a Database?

We posed the question "What is a database?" to Scott Martin, one of the Oracle core developers who helped write the Oracle Parallel Server and who most recently engineered his own product called SQL*Trax. Scott replied: "It's a bunch of programs that manipulate datafiles." Scott's statement is absolutely correct. A *database* is a collection of datafiles and the software that manipulates it. So let's take a closer look at the Oracle database using Scott's definition as our starting point. We start at the datafile level.

Datafiles

Datafiles contain all the database data. The Oracle database is made up of one or more datafiles; datafiles are grouped together to form a tablespace. Especially important to note here is that the datafiles contain all of the data information stored

TYPE OF DATA	CONTAINS INFORMATION ABOUT
Customer Information	Last name, first name, phone number
Product Information	Product name, availability, price
Medical Information	Lab results, doctor's name, nurse's name
Inventory Information	Quantity in stock, quantity backordered
Financial Information	Stock price, interest rate

TABLE 2-1. *Common Types of User Data*

in the database. Think of disk drives on a PC. The files contained on those disk drives represent all the information currently available to that PC.

User Data and System Data

Two types of data or information are stored within the datafiles associated with a database: user data and system data.

User data is your application data, with all of the applications' relevant information. This is the information your organization stores in the database. Table 2-1 shows typical types of user data.

System data is the information the database needs to manage the user data and to manage itself. For example, with system data Oracle tells itself that the social security field in a table consists of all numbers and no letters and that it is a mandatory field. System data also tells Oracle the valid users of the database, their passwords, how many datafiles are part of the database, and where these datafiles are located. Table 2-2 shows typical system data.

TYPE OF DATA	CONTAINS INFORMATION ABOUT
Tables	The fields of the table and the type of information they hold
Space	Amount of physical space the database objects take
Users	Names, passwords, privileges
Datafiles	Number, location, time last used

TABLE 2-2. *Common Types of System Data*

What Is a Database? Summary of Points

To summarize what we have learned about databases:

- A database is a collection of programs that manipulate datafiles.

- Two types of information are stored in an Oracle database:

  1. User data is your particular application data (e.g., a customer invoice).

  2. System data is the data that the database needs to manage itself (e.g., the name and location of all the datafiles associated with a particular database).

Tablespaces–Oracle's Manila Folder

Since a database is a collection of datafiles, it's very important that you understand how an Oracle database groups these files together. It does this under the umbrella of a database object called a tablespace. Before you can insert data into an Oracle database, you must first create a tablespace, then a table within that tablespace to hold the data. When you create the table, you must include all the information about the type of data you want to hold. This is similar to the COBOL programmer defining a record layout. Look at the following code used to create the customer table; it illustrates how Oracle stores information about the type of data it will record. In the next listing, we give the table a name (i.e., customer), give a descriptive name to each element of information we wish to store (i.e., first_name or last_name), and tell Oracle the type of data we wish to capture (i.e., number and varchar2).

```
create table customer
   (first_name          varchar2(15),
    last_name           varchar2(15),
    phone_area_code     number,
    phone_number        number)
tablespace users;
```

Now that you understand why it is called a tablespace, let's try to understand why we need tablespaces to group datafiles together. The best analogy to explain a database, tablespace, datafile, table, and data is an image of a filing cabinet. Think of the database as the filing cabinet; the drawers within the cabinet are tablespaces; the folders in those drawers are datafiles; the pieces of paper in each folder are the tables; the information written on the paper in each folder is the data. Tablespaces are a way to group datafiles.

Keep this in mind: as with your own filing cabinet, you would not intentionally put your homeowner's insurance policy in a drawer called "school records." On the other hand, you might put your homeowner's policy in a drawer called "insurance." The same common sense rules should apply to the tablespaces within your database.

VIP
Do not mix application data in the same tablespace. When you create tablespaces for your applications, give them a descriptive name (e.g., your federal tax data may be held in the intern_rev_bound tablespace).

If you follow the previous recommendation, you will find out in no time how easy it is to manage your database—separate application means separate tablespace.

VIP
Keep in mind the limits placed on the length of filenames when working with Oracle on multiple platforms of which one may be DOS. The eight-character filename and three-character extension in DOS may impact on the names of the datafiles you select.

Tablespace Names and Contents

Let's take a look at a typical database and the tablespace names you might see. Since you have a lot of freedom in Oracle when naming tablespaces, notice how we use a descriptive name for each tablespace that describes the type of data it contains. The names we give you are merely an accepted convention; your site's DBA is not required to use them. Remember—the whole point of tablespaces is to help you organize your database.

System Tablespace
The system tablespace is a required part of every Oracle database. This is where Oracle stores all the information it needs to manage itself, such as names of tablespaces and what datafiles each tablespace contains.

Temp Tablespace
The temp tablespace is where Oracle stores all its temporary tables. This is the database's whiteboard or scratch paper. Just as you sometimes need a place to jot down some numbers so you can add them up, Oracle also has a need for some periodic disk space. In the case of a very active database, you might have more than one temp tablespace; for example, TEMP01, TEMP02, and TEMP03.

Tools Tablespace

The tools tablespace is where you store the database objects needed to support tools that you use with your database, such as Oracle Reports, with its own set of tables (Oracle Reports is discussed in Chapter 8). Like any Oracle application, Oracle Reports needs to store tables in the database. Most DBAs place the tables needed to support tools in this tablespace.

Users Tablespace

The users tablespace holds users' personal information. For example, when you are learning how to use Oracle, you might want to create some tables. This is where the DBA will typically let you place the tables.

Data and Index Tablespaces

From here, anything goes. In some installations, you see tablespace names such as DATA01, DATA02, DATA03, which represent different places to hold data. In other sites, you might see DATA01, INDEX01, etc. Think of a database index as the index in a book: to find a particular reference in the book, you look in the index for its location, rather than reading the whole book from page one. Indexes are a special database object that enable Oracle to quickly find data stored within a table. In Oracle, looking at every row in a database is called a *full table scan.* Using an index search is called an *index scan.* Many other shops name their tablespaces after the application data they hold. For example, in a hospital, the tablespace names might be lab_system or research.

Rollback Tablespace

All Oracle databases need a location to store undo information. This tablespace, which holds your rollback segments, is typically called rollback or rbs. One of the primary reasons you use a database management system such as Oracle is for its ability to recover from incomplete or aborted transactions as part of the core functionality. Recovery is discussed in more detail in the "Redo Logs—The Transaction Log" section of this chapter.

Back to Scott's original definition of a database: you start to realize that a database is certainly made up of lots of datafiles. Creating tablespaces and adding space to existing tablespaces are covered in Chapter 13 and Chapter 17.

Tablespaces: Summary of Points

To summarize what we have learned about tablespaces:

- A tablespace is a collection of one or more datafiles.

- The following tablespaces are either required or common to many databases:

  - The system tablespace contains the information Oracle needs to manage itself and your data. This tablespace name is mandatory.

  - The temp tablespace is Oracle's scratch area. On certain occasions, Oracle needs disk space to manage its own transaction or a transaction on your behalf.

  - The tools tablespace stores the objects needed by tools that run against an Oracle database.

  - The users tablespace keeps users' personal database objects.

  - The rollback tablespace is where the database object rollback segments are typically stored.

  - The data and index tablespaces store your application data.

- All the data you place within an Oracle database is called a table.

- An index is a special type of database object. Oracle uses indexes to speed up data retrieval. We discuss indexes and how they enhance Oracle's performance in Chapter 12.

- A full table scan means that Oracle reads every row of data within the database.

- Undo information is stored in a special database object called a rollback segment. A rollback segment is used to roll back the old value of a database object in case of a failure or aborted transaction.

Redo Logs–The Transaction Log

In addition to the datafiles associated with a tablespace, Oracle has other operating system files associated with it called online redo logs. Another common term for redo logs is transaction logs. These are special operating system files in which Oracle records all changes or transactions that happen to the database. As changes are made to the database, these changes occur in memory. Oracle handles these changes in memory for performance reasons. A disk I/O (input/output) is one thousand times slower than an action in memory. Since a copy of all transactions is always recorded to the online redo logs, Oracle can take its time recording back to the original datafile the changes to data that occurred in memory. Eventually the final copy of the change to the data is recorded back to the physical datafile. Since all the transactions are recorded in the online redo logs, the database is always able to recover itself from these transaction logs. It is a requirement that every Oracle database have at least two online redo logs.

How Redo Logs Work

Redo logs work in a circular fashion. Let's say you have a database with two online redo logs, logA and logB. As transactions create, delete, and modify the data in the database, they are recorded first in logA. When logA is filled up, a log switch occurs. All new transactions are then recorded in logB. When logB fills up, another log switch occurs. Now all transactions are recorded in logA again. This is shown in Figure 2-1.

VIP
Since redo logs are used in a cyclical fashion, when Oracle reuses logA, the transaction information sitting in logA is overwritten.

This point leads us into the discussion of how the Oracle database runs in either ARCHIVELOG or NOARCHIVELOG mode; these have a direct correlation to the online redo logs.

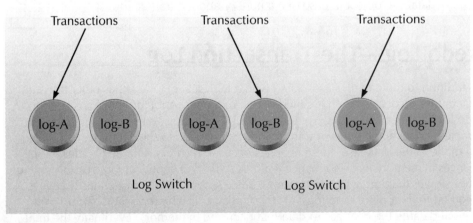

FIGURE 2-1. *How redo logs work*

ARCHIVELOG Mode: Full Recoverability

When a database is running in ARCHIVELOG mode, all transaction redo logs are kept. This means that you have a copy of every transaction that runs against the database, so even though the redo logs work in a circular fashion, a copy of the redo log is made before it is overwritten. In the event that the database needs to switch before the copy has been made, Oracle will freeze up until this action has completed. Oracle will not allow the old transaction log to be overwritten until it has a copy of it. By having a copy of all transactions, the database is now able to protect you against all types of failures, including user error or a disk crash. This is the safest mode to run your database in.

NOARCHIVELOG Mode

When a database is running in NOARCHIVELOG mode (the default), old redo logs are not kept. Because not all the transaction logs are kept, you are only protected from events such as a power failure (remember that a fill up of the log causes it to switch—when it circles around to the original, the previous information is lost).

Redo Logs: Summary of Points

To summarize what we have learned so far about redo logs:

- An Oracle database is made up of two types of files:
    - Datafiles grouped together into tablespaces.
    - Datafiles grouped under the family of redo logs.
- A database must have at least two redo logs.
- A redo log contains all the transactions that have occurred against the database.
- Another common name for the redo log is the transaction log.
- The transaction logs are necessary to protect your data against loss. Their sole purpose is for recovery against unexpected failures.
- An Oracle database runs in two modes:
    - ARCHIVELOG mode saves all transaction logs.
    - In NOARCHIVELOG mode, old redo logs are not kept.

Control Files

Every database must have at least one control file, though it is highly recommended that you have two or more.

VIP

It is good to have two or more control files in case one is damaged while the database operates. If you have a single control file, you will be in trouble without an additional control file to keep the database accessible to your users.

A *control file* is a very small file that contains key information about all the files associated with an Oracle database. Control files maintain the integrity of the database and help to identify which redo logs are needed in the recovery process.

The best analogy we can think of to illustrate this point is getting your yearly car inspection. Every year in the state of Massachusetts, residents must get their cars inspected to make sure they meet all safety and pollution guidelines.

Before the database is allowed to begin running, it goes to the control file to determine if the database is in acceptable shape. For example, if a datafile is missing or a particular file has been altered while the database was not using it, then the control file informs the database that it has failed inspection. If this happens, as in a car inspection, you will not be allowed to continue until the problem is corrected.

VIP

If Oracle reads the control file and, based on the information it contains, determines the database is NOT in acceptable shape, it will not permit the database to run.

Whenever a database checkpoint occurs or there is a change to the structure of the database, the control file is updated. If you do not have a valid control file, your database will not start.

VIP

Have at least two control files for your database and store them on different disks.

Control File: Summary of Points

- Every database must have at least one control file. You are strongly advised to have at least two control files, and they should be on separate disks.

- All major changes to the structure of the database are recorded in the control file.

Programs

We have defined a database as being "a bunch of programs that manipulate datafiles." It's now time to discuss the programs; we prefer to call them processes since every time a program starts against the database, it communicates with Oracle via a process. Later in this chapter we talk about support processes required to run the Oracle database (see the section "Database Support Processes"). There are two types of Oracle processes you should know about: user and server.

User (Client) Processes

User processes work on your behalf, requesting information from the server processes. Examples of user processes are Oracle Forms, Oracle Reports, and SQL*Plus. These are common tools any user of the data within the database uses to communicate with the database.

Server Processes

Server processes take requests from user processes and communicate with the database. Through this communication, user processes work with the data in the database.

The best analogy we have ever heard comes to us compliments of a company called J3 that makes training videos. A good way to think of the client/server process is to imagine yourself in a restaurant. You, the customer, communicate to the waiter who takes your order. That person then communicates the request to the kitchen. The kitchen staff's job is to prepare the food, let the waiter know when it is ready, and stock inventory. The waiter then delivers the meal back to you. In this analogy, the waiter represents the client process, and the kitchen staff represents the server processes.

Programs: Summary of Points

- There are two types of programs or processes:

  - One type is the user (client) process. Examples include SQL*Plus, Oracle Forms, and Oracle Reports—in other words, any tools you might use to access the database.

  - Server processes take requests from client processes and interact with the database to fill those requests.

Database Support Processes

As we stated before, server processes take requests from user (client) processes; they communicate with the database on behalf of user processes. Let's take a look at a special set of server processes that help the database operate.

Database Writer (DBWR)

The database writer is a mandatory process that writes changed data blocks back to the database files. It is one of the only two processes that are allowed to write to the datafiles that make up your Oracle database. On certain operating systems, Oracle allows you to have multiple database writers. This is done for performance reasons.

Checkpoint (CKPT)

Checkpoint is an optional process. When users are working with an Oracle database, they make requests to look at data. That data is read from the database files and put into an area of memory where users can look at it. Some of these users eventually make changes to the data that must be recorded back onto the original datafiles. Earlier in the chapter, we talked about redo logs and how they record all transactions. When the redo logs switch, a checkpoint occurs. When this switch happens, Oracle goes into memory and writes any dirty data blocks' information back to disk. In addition, it notifies the control file of the redo log switch.

These tasks are normally performed by the log writer (lgwr) discussed in the next section. For performance reasons, the DBA can make changes to the database to enable the checkpoint process. Its sole job is to take the checkpoint responsibility away from the log writer.

Log Writer (LGWR)

The log writer is a mandatory process that writes redo entries to the redo logs. Remember the redo logs are a copy of every transaction that occurs in the database. This is done so that Oracle is able to recover from various types of failure. In addition, since a copy of every transaction is written in the redo log, Oracle does not have to spend its resources constantly writing data changes back to the datafiles immediately. This results in improved performance. The log writer is the only process that writes to the redo logs. It is also the only process in an Oracle database that reads the redo logs.

System Monitor (SMON)

System monitor is a mandatory process that performs any recovery that is needed at startup. In the parallel server mode (Oracle databases on different computers sharing the same disk farm—see Figure 2-2), it can also perform recovery for a failed database on another computer. Remember, the two databases share the same datafiles.

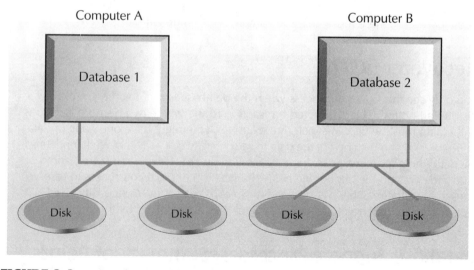

FIGURE 2-2.   *Oracle in parallel server mode*

Process Monitor (PMON)

Process monitor is a mandatory process that performs recovery for a failed user of the database. It assumes the identity of the failed user, releasing all the database resources that user was holding, and it rolls back the aborted transaction.

Archiver (ARCH)

Archiver is an optional process. As we discussed earlier in the "Redo Logs" section, the redo (transaction) logs are written to in a sequential manner. When a log fills up, there is a log switch to the next available redo log. When you are running the database in ARCHIVELOG mode, the database goes out and makes a copy of the redo log. This is done so that when the database switches back to this redo log, there is a copy of the contents of this file for recovery purposes. This is the job of the archiver process. Similar to a copy machine, it makes a copy of the file.

Lock (LCKn)

Lock is an optional process. When you are running the Oracle database in the parallel server mode, you will see multiple lck processes. In parallel server mode (see Figure 2-2), these locks help the databases communicate.

Recoverer (RECO)

You only see this optional process when the database is running the Oracle distributed option. The distributed transaction is one where two or more locations of the data must be kept in synch. For example, you might have one copy of data in Boston and another copy of the data in Mexico City. Let's say that while updating the data, the phone line goes down to Mexico due to a severe rainstorm, and a mud slide washes the phone line away. It is the job of the reco process to resolve transactions that may have completed in Boston, but not in Mexico City. These transactions are referred to as *in-doubt* until they are resolved by this reco process.

Database Support Processes: Summary of Points

There are a number of support processes that help communication between the user processes and the database server. These support processes are responsible for:

■   Writing data back to the datafiles when a checkpoint occurs (dbwr).

- Ensuring dirty data blocks are written back to disk when a checkpoint occurs (ckpt).

- Reading from and writing to the redo logs (lgwr).

- Running any database recovery that may be required at startup (smon).

- Releasing resources that a user acquired if that user's session ends abnormally (pmon).

- Archiving a copy of a redo log when a log switch occurs when running ARCHIVELOG mode (arch).

- Managing locking in a parallel server configuration (lck).

- Recovering in-doubt transactions when using the Oracle distributed option (reco).

Memory Structure–The Phone Line

Up to this point, we have talked about the datafiles and the programs. We have also talked about server processes and client processes. Now we will talk about how the client and server processes communicate to each other and themselves through memory structures. Just as the name implies, this is an area of memory set aside where processes can talk to themselves or to other processes.

Oracle uses two types of memory structures: the system global area, or SGA (think of it as an old-fashioned telephone party line or the conference calling option on your phone), and program global area, or PGA (think of this as an intercom system).

System Global Area (SGA)

SGA is a place in memory where the Oracle database stores pertinent information about itself. It does this in memory, since memory is the quickest and most efficient way to allow processes to communicate. This memory structure is then accessible to all the user processes and server processes. Figure 2-3 shows how the SGA is in the center of all communication.

Since the SGA is the mechanism by which the various client and server processes communicate, it is important that you understand its various components. The Oracle Server SGA is broken into the following key components.

Data Buffer Cache
The data buffer cache is where Oracle stores the most recently used blocks of database data. In other words, this is your data cache. When you put information

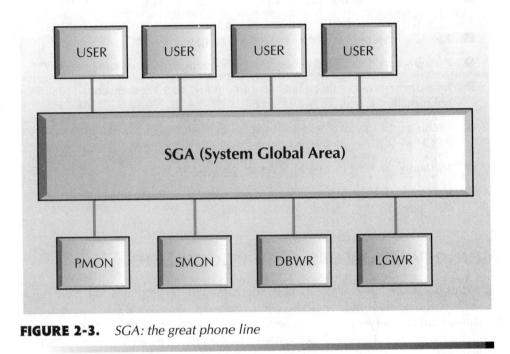

FIGURE 2-3. *SGA: the great phone line*

into the database, it is stored in data blocks. The data buffer cache is an area of memory in which Oracle places these data blocks so that a user process can look at them. Before any user process can look at a piece of data, the data must first reside in the data buffer cache. There is a physical limit on the size of the data buffer cache. Thus, as Oracle fills it up, it leaves the hottest blocks in the cache and moves out the cold blocks. It does this via the least recently used (LRU) algorithm.

An important point to clarify: if a client process needs information that is not in the cache, it goes out to the physical disk drive, reads the needed data blocks, then places them in the data buffer cache. It does this so that all other client and server processes get the benefit of the physical disk read.

Dictionary Cache (Row Cache)
A dictionary cache contains rows out of the data dictionary. The data dictionary contains all the information Oracle needs to manage itself, such as what users have access to the Oracle database, what database objects they own, and where those objects are located.

Redo Log Buffer

Remember that another common name for the online redo logs is the transaction log. So before any transaction can be recorded into the redo log (the online redo logs are needed for recovery purposes), it must first reside in the redo log buffer. This is an area of memory set aside for this event. Then, the database periodically flushes this buffer to the online redo logs.

Shared SQL Pool

Think of the shared SQL pool as your program cache. This is where all your programs are stored. Programs within an Oracle database are based on a standard language called SQL (pronounced "sequel"). This cache contains all the parsed SQL statements that are ready to run.

To summarize, the SGA is the great communicator. It is the place in memory where information is placed so that client and server processes can access it. It is broken up into major areas: the data cache, the redo log cache, the dictionary cache, and the shared SQL cache. Figure 2-4 shows the caches Oracle maintains in the SGA—we call the SQL cache the sqlarea; these two terms can be used synonymously.

Program Global Area (PGA)

PGA is an area of memory that is used by a single Oracle process. The program global area is not shared; it contains data and control information for a single process. It contains information such as process session variables and internal arrays. Like an intercom system in your home, the various parts of the process can communicate to each other but not to the outside world.

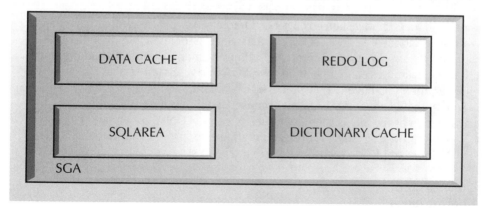

FIGURE 2-4. *SGA—a closer look*

Memory Structure: Summary of Points

- There are two types of memory areas:
    - System global area (SGA).
    - Program global area (PGA).
- The SGA is shared by all server and client processes.
- The SGA has four major components:
    - The data buffer cache is your data cache.
    - The dictionary cache (rows cache) is the information Oracle needs to manage itself.
    - The redo log buffer is the transaction cache.
    - The shared SQL pool is your program cache.
- Before a user process can look at information out of the database, it must first reside in the SGA.
- The SGA is the great communicator by which all processes can share information.
- The PGA is not shared between processes.
- The PGA contains data and process control information.

What Is an Oracle Instance?

Simply put, an Oracle instance is a set of Oracle server processes that have their own system global area and a set of database files associated with them. For example, let's say you have a computer with two databases on it, called prd and tst. If these databases each have their own SGA and a separate set of Oracle server processes, then you have two instances of the database. This is shown in Figure 2-5.

So that the database does not get confused, each instance is identified by what's known as the SID (system identifier). On most UNIX computers, it is set by the variable "ORACLE_SID." Then, each of the server processes is named to match the SID. For example, on the tst database, the processes would be named

```
ora_tst_dbwr
ora_tst_pmon
ora_tst_smon
ora_tst_lgwr
```

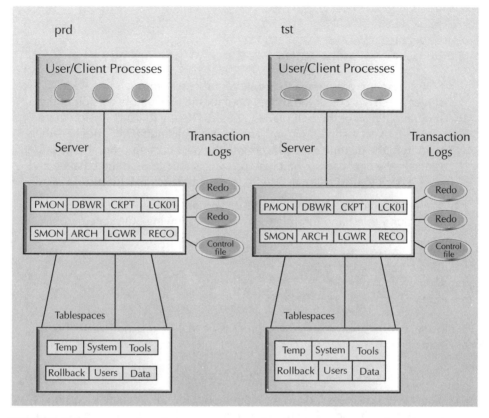

FIGURE 2-5. *Two Oracle instances*

Let's Put It All Together

Now that we understand the Oracle architecture, we'll follow a transaction. Let's say we are strolling through Freeport and we approach a bank machine to see if we have enough money for a bottle of wine. Let's go through the transaction:

1. We ask for an account balance. The machine is running a program called SQL*Plus as the client process. It takes our question and formulates it into the following SQL statement:

```
select account_balance
   from bank_table
 where account_number = '1112222333'
   and account_type = 'SAVINGS';
```

SQL statements are passed to the server processes through the SGA. The server processes check the shared pool for the executable version of the program. If it's not there, it places a parsed "Ready to Run" version there and then executes the program. The account balance "Data Block" is then read from the datafiles and placed into the data cache portion of the SGA. Once in the data cache, the client process is able to read the balance and pass it back to the customer. We're told the balance is $325.00.

2. We see the balance and request a $25 withdrawal. The client process takes our request and formulates it into the following SQL statement:

```
update bank_table
   set account_balance = 300
 where account_number = '1112222333'
   and account_type = 'SAVINGS';
```

In closing, here is a summary of the processing that Oracle does with this update statement:

1. The client process passes the statement to the server process through the SGA.

2. The server processes look in the shared pool for an executable version of the program. If one is found, proceed to step #4; if not, proceed to step #3.

3. Process this SQL statement and move its executable version into the pool.

4. Execute the SQL statement.

5. Is the data this statement manipulates in the data cache? If it is, proceed to step #7; if it is not, proceed to step #6.

6. Read the data from the database file into the data cache.

7. Record the old value of the data in a rollback segment (the rollback segment holds the old balance of $325).

8. Create a copy of the transaction in the redo logs.

9. Change the data in the data cache to reflect the new balance of $300.

10. The bank machine signals through the SGA that all is complete.

11. Record the completion of the transaction in the redo log.

12. Free up the undo information in the rollback segment.

13. Deliver money to customer.

14. Buy a great bottle of wine for half the price we would pay in Boston!

VIP
In step #7 of this process, if the user cancels the transaction OR the system comes down during the transaction, the information held in the rollback segment is used to restore the original balance.

VIP
As with every transaction, eventually the database writer writes the data cache copy of the data block back to the original datafile.

As you can see, a lot goes on for your client process to be able to access the database. After you work with Oracle for a while, its value becomes clear.

What's Next

We leave this chapter with two suggestions:

■ Ingest the information we have discussed here and look at your database configuration and try to recognize all the components we have highlighted. Walk through the chapter again, and as you cross into a new section, ensure you can identify them as they appear in your database. For example, where we discuss database support processes, stop and run a program status command on your machine and identify every process by name.

NOTE
In UNIX this would be done using the command **ps -ef\grep oracleprd** for a database with an ORACLE_SID of prd. In VMS the command is **sho system/out=temp.lis** followed by **search temp.lis ora_**.

■ Keep running back to parts of this chapter as you read the rest of the book. It is remarkable how much you will understand about Oracle having this chapter as a foundation.

In the next chapter, we discuss the assortment of objects stored in the Oracle database and the jobs some special objects perform as your database operates.

CHAPTER 3

Database Objects

This chapter deals with all the major database objects you will encounter while working with Oracle. Each of these objects has a specific purpose or job to do. In this chapter, we will explain what each object is used for and give you an example of how to use it. We will provide details on tables, views, indexes, and synonyms. In Chapter 1 we discussed how Oracle stores information in one place. If a payroll application needs personnel information for a firm's employees, rather than capture the required information itself, the payroll system reads data from the personnel system. Since data is stored in one place and read by all, we will also introduce object privileges in this chapter, and show you how privileges are used to control who can do what with data.

Terminology

The following definitions will arm you with the technical jargon to make it through this chapter.

- A *table* is a database object that holds your data. Information about every table is stored in the data dictionary; with this information, Oracle allows you to maintain data residing in your table.

- A *view* allows you to see a customized selection of one or more tables, and it uses a SQL query that is stored in the database. When using views, the SQL statement that defines the view is executed as if you had coded the defining statement yourself.

- An *index* is a mini copy of a table. Index entries for a table allow Oracle rapid access to the data in your tables.

- A *synonym* is an alternate name for an object in the database. Think of a synonym as a nickname for an object—somewhat like calling a woman named Margaret by the name Maggie instead.

- *Grants* are privileges given out by owners of objects, allowing other users to work with their data.

- The *data dictionary* is maintained by Oracle containing information relevant to the tables that reside in the database. For example, in a telecommunications system, the data dictionary records the fact that a North American area code is three digits long.

- A *role* is a group of privileges that are collected together and granted to users. Once privileges are granted to a role, a user inherits the role's privileges by becoming a member of that role. This way, instead of updating every user's account on an individual basis, you can just manage the role.

Tables—Where Oracle Stores Your Data

A table is the database object that holds your data. The data dictionary holds information about every table; Oracle uses its data dictionary to ensure the correct type of data (e.g., number or character) is placed in Oracle tables. The best analogy is to think of a table as a spreadsheet. The cells of the spreadsheet equate to the columns of the table. Just like the cells of a spreadsheet, the columns of a table have a data type associated with them. If the number data type is associated with a spreadsheet cell, then you would not be allowed to store letters in the spreadsheet cell. The same applies to a table's column. Table columns that are of a number data type cannot accept letters. Data types are covered in detail in Chapter 5.

The way you create tables in Oracle is through the **create table** command. Let's take a closer look at an example of this command in its simplest form.

```
create table customer
  (last_name  varchar2(30),
   state_cd   char(2),
   sales      number);
Table created.
```

In this example, we create a table called customer. The columns associated with the table are last_name, state_cd, and sales. Each of these columns has a data type associated with it.

The column last_name has a data type of varchar2. Its maximum length is 30, which means the column cannot hold a name larger than 30 characters. The data type varchar2 tells the database that this column can accept letters, numbers, and special characters. In addition, varchar2 tells the database to store the information internally in a variable-length format. For example, the last name Lane takes less room to store than the last name Ellison. In other words, Oracle only uses the amount of space it needs to hold the name.

The column state_cd has a data type of char. The 2 tells us it has a length of two characters. The data type of char tells the database that this column can accept letters, numbers, and special characters. In addition, char tells the database to store the information internally in a fixed-length format. No matter how big the state_cd is, it can take up no more and no less space than it takes to hold two characters.

The column sales has a data type of number. This data type tells the database it can only accept numbers. In addition, since they are numbers, you can add, subtract, multiply, and divide the contents. In fact, Oracle has an extensive set of mathematical functions you can apply to columns of data type number.

VIP

A table is a database object that holds your data. It is made up of many columns. Each of those columns has a data type associated with it. This data type is the roadmap that Oracle follows so it knows how to correctly manipulate the contents.

Views—A Special Look at Your Data

A view is a database object that allows you to create a customized slice of a table or a collection of tables. Unlike a table, a view contains no data, just a SQL query. The data that is retrieved from this query is presented like a table. In fact, if you did not create the view, you would think you were dealing with a table. Like a table, you may **insert**, **update**, **delete**, and **select** data from a view.

VIP
You can always **select** data from a view, but, in some situations, there are restrictions on other ways data in a view can be manipulated.

Why Use Views?

It is important to know how to use views, since you will probably require views for one or all of the following reasons:

- Views can provide an additional level of security. For example, you might have an employee table within your company, and you might want to create a view that allows managers to see information on only their employees.

- Views allow you to hide data complexity. An Oracle database is made up of many tables. You can retrieve information from two or more tables by performing a join, and these joins can get very confusing for a typical end user and even your seasoned veteran. Many times, you will create a view that is the combination of many tables. For example, you might have a view that is a combination of the customer table and order table. Thus, the user of the database would only have to make a simple select off of the view called cust_ord. They would never know that this might actually be based on two tables.

- Views help you maintain naming sanity. Often, when we create column names for an Oracle database, we forget that people actually have to type them when wording SQL statements. For example, we might have a column named middle_initial_of_person. In the view, we could rename the column "mi."

Creating Views

You create a view using the command **create view** while connected to Oracle. This is usually done via SQL*Plus. Let's try creating a simple view:

```
create view cust as
  select last_name lname, state_cd
    from customer
  order by last_name
```

If users want to access the last_name and state_cd information stored in the customer table using the cust view, they could issue the command **select * from cust;** rather than **select last_name,state_cd from customer;**. When the command is issued, Oracle runs the SQL statement associated with the view. This query then brings back the data in a predetermined sorted order (note the view has an **order by** when it is created). The **order by** command is covered in Chapter 5.

Since this view did not include the column sales, you can allow people access to the customer data without giving them access to the sensitive data stored within the sales column. Like a table, you have complete control over who has access to the view.

VIP

A view is just a SQL query that is stored in the database. The results of that query are returned in the form of a table.

Indexes—A Quick Way to Speed Access to Your Data

Just like an index in a book, which helps you find information faster, an index placed on a table helps you retrieve your data faster. If your application is running slow, a well-placed index will make it run quicker.

VIP

A well-placed index on a table will help the database retrieve your data faster.

It has been our experience that if you think of indexes as minitables, you will be able to understand how they work. Let's imagine we have the following table (the four dots in the listing represent the definition of column d through column z, giving the table 26 columns):

```
create table sample_3
(a     char(30),
 b     char(30),
 c     char(30)
....
```

Every time you want to read the information stored in column c, Oracle must also bring back the information stored in columns a, b, and d through z. Like every resource in a computer, there is a limit to how much it can physically do at any point in time.

To understand the point we are making, let's say that when Oracle issues a request for data from the sample_3 table, it can only retrieve the equivalent of four records' worth of information. Since each of the 26 columns in the table is defined as data type char, Oracle reserves 30 spaces for each column in the table. Thus, when reading the equivalent of four records at a time, the buffer holds 3,120 characters (26 columns * 30 characters * 4 records) of information. So, even though you may only wish to see the information stored in column c, the database is forced to wade through all the information stored in the table. Well, you have a solution to this problem, called an index.

Let's say you create an index on column c with the SQL statement **create index colc_ind on sample_3(colc);**. Oracle creates the index object. Think of this as a minitable that holds only the column c information from the table named sample_3. In addition, it will retrieve the information needed to point back to the actual row within the table called sample_3 where the particular column c information came from. Like Siamese twins, these two objects are now linked together. Whatever happens to one happens to the other. If you delete a column c item from the main table, you will also delete the corresponding index entry.

Now, say you want to retrieve just the information stored in column c of the table called sample_3. Oracle knows it can resolve that request from the index, so rather than wading through the table, it just looks at the index. Oracle performs that same physical read, which was limited to four records' worth of information (or 3,120 characters at a time). By using the index just created, Oracle now only has to hold column c information. So instead of four records' worth of information, you can now get 104 records each read, since column c is 30 characters, and the buffer can hold 3,120 characters.

VIP
Index entries contain information only about the columns that are
part of the index, not all the columns in a table.

That same read can bring back much more focused information. It's limited to
looking at what you need and not required to wade through all the other columns
in the table. Before moving on, let's look at some features of and uses for indexes,
since indexes are so important.

Indexes Have a Sorted Order

By design, the data stored in a relational database has no particular order. The
record you insert into a table goes into the next available slot. So, when you issue a
SQL query looking for a particular date or range of dates (e.g., **select * from state
where state_cd = 'MA';**), Oracle is required to look at every row of data in the
table.

An index, on the other hand, is in a sorted order. If you have a date data type
column in a table, you could create an index on that column. The index created by
Oracle would contain all the dates in sorted order. It is typically much quicker for
Oracle to go to the index, find all the records for a desired date, then bring back
the information to you.

Indexes Can Guarantee Uniqueness

There are two types of index you can create. You can create a unique index and a
nonunique index. A unique index does not allow duplicates; a nonunique index
allows duplicates. As we stated earlier, an index is like a Siamese twin to the table.
If you create a unique index on column c in a table, then every time you try to
insert a row into the actual table, the index will check to make sure that column c
is still unique. The SQL statement **create index colc_ind on sample_3 (colc);** is
used to create a nonunique index, and the statement **create unique index colc_ind
on sample_3 table (colc);** creates a unique index.

Two Columns Are Better Than One

Oracle allows you to create concatenated indexes. These indexes are made up of
more than one column. Many times, you realize when looking at your tables that
you would never look at column a without looking at column b. So it makes sense

to index both together using a concatenated index. Let's build a concatenated index using the SQL statement **create index colabc_ind on sample_3 table (cola, colb, colc);**. Once this concatenated index is built, Oracle manages the index just as it does with those built on single columns.

The where Clause and Your Indexes

Oracle determines which index it will use to satisfy a query based on how the **where** clause is worded (i.e., the columns referenced in the **where** and **and** part of a SQL statement). Oracle examines the available indexes, and selects the index that will provide the quickest results.

VIP

Oracle determines which indexes it will use by looking at the **where** clause of the SQL query.

As your experience with formulating queries increases, you will find yourself becoming quite adept at wording SQL to allow Oracle to process queries using the available indexes.

Synonyms–A New Identity

Just as many actors change their names to make themselves easier to remember, and more recognizable, you can do the same for an Oracle table. When we created the table sample_3, the complete identity it received was the name of the owner of the table (e.g., ops$coreymj) and the table name. Then, if you are connected to Oracle as ops$coreymj, when you issue a SQL query, Oracle is smart enough to realize you are connected as the user who owns the table. So, behind the scenes, Oracle places the owner's name in front of the table name. Let's say you want to retrieve a column from the table and you issue the SQL query **select cola from sample_3;** which Oracle translates into the following:

```
select colA from ops$coreymj.sample_3;
```

A synonym is a database object that allows you to create alternate names for Oracle tables and views. Using our sample_3 table as an example, suppose a user who did not own the table issued the command **select cola from sample_3;**. Oracle would not know what to do. However, if the user had a synonym for the table, Oracle could successfully execute the SQL statement using the synonym.

This simple SQL statement illustrates how synonyms are used. When users who do not own a table wish to reference a table in a SQL statement, they must always use a synonym to refer to the table.

You may decide to set up synonyms for any Oracle table for a variety of reasons:

- You want to hide the true owner or name of a table.

- You want or need to hide the true location of a table. Some installations have one table in Boston and another table in Ottawa.

- You want to provide users with a table name less complicated than the real table name (e.g., s3 instead of sample_3).

With this in mind, let's create a synonym using the SQL statement **create synonym toast for ops$coreymj. sample_3;**. Now, the following statements will bring back the same rows from the same table:

```
select cola from ops$coreymj.sample_3;
select cola from toast;
```

Private Synonyms and Public Synonyms

As you can see, you can use synonyms to give a table an alternate identity. This can greatly simplify SQL statement syntax. The synonym we created in the previous section is called a private synonym: only ops$coreymj can use the synonym toast to point to the table ops$coreymj.sample_3. Another type of synonym is a public synonym, which all Oracle users are able to use. You can create a public synonym with the SQL statement **create public synonym tonic for ops$coreymj.sample_3;**. Any Oracle user can now refer to the table using the public synonym tonic. Now users can issue the statement **select cola from tonic;** and Oracle would know they really mean **select cola from ops$coreymj.sample_3;**.

Grants–May I Please Have Access?

Up to now in this chapter, we may have given the impression that every database user has access to every other database users' objects and their contents. This is not true in the real world. Oracle gives you extensive control over what a user can see, modify, delete, or change. It is one of the real strengths of the Oracle Server. Combine this with views, and you can even control what data a user can look at.

VIP
Grants are used to give one user privileges to work with another user's data. Once privileges have been granted, recipients of the grant have the ability to work with someone else's objects.

We will now discuss some types of privileges, and show how they are granted to other users.

Granting Privileges to Users

Granting of object privileges allows users to work with database objects and their contents.

VIP
When users are granted privileges on other users' tables, before they can reference those tables in SQL statements, there must be a public or private synonym through which Oracle can identify the table.

Say user jrstocks owns a table called sample_b, and gives all database users access to the table. Along comes user coreyam, and runs a statement against the sample_b table, and receives the following error message:

```
select * from sample_b;
                *
ERROR at line 1:
ORA-00942: table or view does not exist
```

Regardless of which privilege is being granted, there are three parts to each **grant** statement:

1. The keyword/privilege part is made up of the word **grant** followed by one or more privileges. When multiple privileges are placed in the same **grant** statement, they are separated by a comma.

2. The table name part starts with the keyword **on** and lists the table on which privileges are being given.

3. The recipient part lists one or more users who receive the privileges being given out.

Let's look at how four object privileges are given to users.

select

The **select** privilege allows other users to look at the contents of tables they do not own. The statement **grant select on sample_3 to public;** would allow all users to view the sample_3 table. The statement **grant select on sample_3 to ops$stojanzs,ops$abbeyms;** would allow the two users mentioned to look at sample_3. Notice when more than one user receives a grant, how the usernames are separated in the list by a comma.

> ### VIP
> When **public** is the target of any grant, all users of the database receive the privileges specified. If your database had 15,000 users, granting a privilege to public would be the same as issuing 15,000 grants separately (one to each user!).

insert

The **insert** privilege allows one to create rows in other users' tables. The statement **grant insert on sample_a to public;** allows all users to create new rows in sample_a. Oracle allows stacking of privileges in a single **grant** statement—the SQL statement **grant insert, select on sample_a to public;** is the same as the two statements **grant select on sample_a to public;** followed by **grant insert on sample_a to public;**.

update

The **update** privilege allows other users to modify or change data in tables they do not own. The statement **grant update on sample_a to teplownd;** would permit user teplownd to modify information in sample_a.

delete

The **delete** privilege permits users to delete rows of information from specified tables. We recommend using caution giving out this privilege since it is very powerful. Picture the following that actually happened to one of our acquaintances. A programmer was connected to the production database while she thought she was logged into a test database. She issued the command **delete from people_master;** and Oracle responded with

```
12003 rows deleted.
```

After exiting SQL*Plus, the next program that accessed people_master looking for a personnel record for Rick Bower was told the record did not exist!

The command **grant delete,update,select on sample_a to public;** gives the specified privilege to all database users. The command **grant**

select,update,insert,delete on sample_a to teplownd,greerw; allows users teplownd and greerw to do the listed activities on the sample_a table.

Recipients of Grants

Throughout this section, we have showed a number of **grant** statements where the recipients were either public, or an assortment of database users (e.g., teplownd). Imagine an installation where there are two distinct classes of users for a financial management system. One class of user is allowed to approve travel claims , cancel requisitions, and adjust quantities and unit prices on purchase orders. The other class is your everyday run-of-the-mill user who can only create requisitions. Say there was a list of 18 users in the first category, and over 900 in the second. Oracle uses roles to help manage grants to multiple users; we discuss roles in the next section.

Roles—A Way to Group Users Together

You can create a database object called a role, then grant privileges to that role, then grant that role to individual users. Sounds complicated, but it's very simple. For example, let's create a role called nurse by issuing the SQL statement **create role nurse;** and give the role some privileges by running the six commands:

```
grant insert on tableA to nurse;
grant insert on tableB to nurse;
grant insert,delete on tableC to nurse;
grant update on tableD to nurse;
grant delete on tableE to nurse;
grant select on tableF to nurse;
```

Now, let's give some users the nurse role by running the following three commands.

```
grant nurse to ops$abbey;
grant nurse to ops$teplow
grant nurse to ops$lane
```

When we want to effect a change to these three users, we just have to change the role nurse, and the users will automatically receive the change. If we want all three users to be able to delete from tablef, for example, we would issue the SQL statement **grant delete on tableF to nurse;**. All database users who have the role nurse would be affected by the new change.

What's Next

We have given you an introduction to the most common database objects and their use. This list is not complete, but we have highlighted what is by far the most common. Every day that we work with the Oracle Server, we learn something new. As our experience has taught us, you will continually learn about Oracle's vast capabilities while you travel down its path. Just when you think you have learned it all, you will either discover a new product or something new you want to learn to do with an existing one.

The next chapter discusses how to install Oracle. Many of you may have Oracle and some of its products already installed on your personal computers. Nevertheless, Chapter 4 will teach you how to do it yourself next time. Part of the chapter discusses installing Oracle on large multiuser machines referred to as minicomputers. Installation is where it all starts . . . carry on.

CHAPTER 4

Installation

So far, we have discussed Oracle the company, introduced you to Oracle architecture, and talked about the assortment of database objects. In this chapter, we will cover some installation issues and concepts, and we will provide you with some guidance about decisions you will have to make before, during, and after installation. There are four sections to this chapter. First, we will show you how to install Oracle using UNIX as a sample operating system. Second, we will show you how to install Oracle products in UNIX. The third part covers how to install Personal Oracle7 using Windows 3.1 for DOS as an example. The fourth part shows you how to install Oracle products in Windows. The UNIX install is an example of the installation session done by a DBA; the Personal Oracle7 install can be done by anyone wishing to put Personal Oracle7 on a personal computer. By the end of this chapter, you will know how to perform the following:

■ Install the Oracle Server in a nondesktop environment

■ Install Oracle products in a nondesktop environment

■ Install Personal Oracle7 for the first time in a desktop environment

■ Install Oracle products in a desktop environment

When reading this chapter and looking at the UNIX example, keep in mind that UNIX is case-sensitive; thus, the commands **START.SH** and **start.sh** are not the same. As well, some of the commands are prefixed with a period followed by a slash (./), which is a required part of the command.

Terminology

The following definitions will arm you with the technical jargon to make it through this chapter.

■ *ORACLE_HOME* is a directory name in UNIX underneath which all the Oracle software is installed. Think of it as the home of the Oracle database.

■ A *staging area* is used by Oracle when installing from CD-ROM. You do not read the CD-ROM directly. Oracle builds this staging area before you perform any installation.

■ A *database administrator* or DBA is a technical wizard who manages the complete operation of the Oracle database.

■ A *system administrator* is the person who manages computer resources and, alongside the DBA, manages hardware and computer peripherals.

■ A *local database* is one that resides on the same computer as the user. Accessing Personal Oracle7 from Windows on the same machine is an example of a local database configuration.

■ A *remote database* is one that resides on a different computer than the one the user or developer is using. The remote database is accessed using a vendor's (e.g., Novell) network software and Oracle's network product called SQL*Net.

■ *Desktop* is the environment found on personal computers that accesses local or remote databases. The Apple Macintosh and Microsoft Windows are examples of desktop computing.

■ A *patch* is a fix applied to a program. Patches do not change the overall functionality of a program; they simply fix or enhance an existing product.

Installing Oracle–Nondesktop

We have chosen a UNIX operating system install example, since such a large portion of Oracle installations are running one form or another of UNIX. If you are installing Oracle on another type of hardware using another operating system, the process might be somewhat different. Substitute that machine's equivalent command where we show UNIX commands. Hewlett-Packard (HP), Sun, Pyramid, Sequent, DEC Alpha, SCO, and Xenix are examples of popular UNIX systems. We will show you how to build a staging area, install the Oracle Server, then install an Oracle product other than the Server. We use a CD-ROM throughout all our discussions in this section; CD-ROM allows for the quickest and most flexible installations.

VIP
If you are not using CD-ROM and it is available on your hardware configuration, invest in a CD-ROM unit immediately.

Building the Staging Area

There are two kinds of staging areas: temporary and permanent. We recommend using the permanent staging area approach. It uses little disk space and speeds up subsequent installation or upgrades. In situations where you cannot (or do not want) to dedicate ongoing disk space for a permanent staging area, use a temporary staging area instead. Once this permanent staging area is built, you can skip the step that builds it each time.

VIP
As of release 7.1.4, a permanent staging area consumes roughly 5MB (5,227,520 bytes).

To build a permanent staging area in a directory called /oracle/oracle_link:

1. Ask your system administrator (the person who is the keeper of your hardware) to mount the CD-ROM device and make it accessible. The following steps will show /cdrom, since this is where we have mounted the CD-ROM. The name you use depends on how the CD-ROM is mounted on your system.

2. Log onto your machine using the UNIX account of the owner of the Oracle software. This account name is usually (but does not have to be) "oracle."

3. Create the staging area directory by entering the command **cd /oracle** followed by **mkdir oracle_link**.

4. Proceed to the installation directory on the CD-ROM by entering the command **cd /cdrom/ORAINST**.

5. Enter the command **./START.SH**.

6. When Oracle asks for the name of the link directory, enter the name **/oracle/oracle_link**.

Oracle then builds the staging area. The work takes between 5 and 20 minutes, depending on the size of the computer you are using. Once this completes, the staging area is ready, and you can install the Server or any other products.

VIP
The staging area does not contain a copy of the software being installed. All Oracle installs and upgrades require the CD-ROM to be placed in the CD-ROM drive beforehand.

Starting the Installer

The Oracle installer is referred to as "orainst" across all computer types. In UNIX, the installer is started by changing to the installer directory by entering the command **cd $ORACLE_HOME/orainst** then typing the command **./orainst**. The sections "Installer Environment" and "Other Information" will guide you through answering some of the questions with which you will be presented. First a word about the look and feel of orainst.

It's a Friendly Little Thing

We find orainst is remarkably friendly and easy to work with. Let's look at the screen in Figure 4-1 and the four buttons on it: OK, Help, Back, and Cancel. You move between the buttons with TAB and select a button using ENTER. The OK button accepts whatever Oracle has displayed on the screen. The Help button accesses orainst online help. The Back button backs up one step in the installer process, letting you revisit the screen in which you previously selected OK. It is remarkable

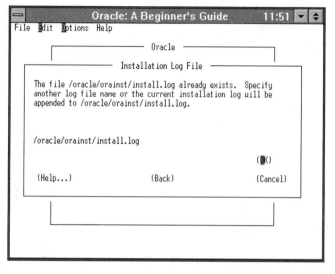

FIGURE 4-1. *Typical orainst screen*

how useful the Back button can be when you have answered a question, then wondered to yourself if this was what you actually wanted. The Cancel button terminates your orainst session and allows you to quit the installer any time.

Using the Products screen as an example (the one that lists Available and Installed Products in two windows side by side), pressing the MENU key (normally mapped to the 0 on your numeric keypad) sends the cursor to the menu at the top of the orainst screen. Pressing ENTER opens the very useful File menu, as shown in Figure 4-2. Selecting Restart from that menu begins orainst as if you had just entered the **orainst** command. Selecting OS Prompt positions you back at your operating system. If you use this option, you enter the command **exit** at the prompt to return to the installer.

After suggesting that the installer is friendly, you may find yourself presented with some questions you have never had to answer before. We now look at the issues orainst wants to settle through its series of questions and answers.

Installer Environment

When orainst starts, it asks you to provide details about the installation. In most cases, it suggests a response; however, if this is the very first time you are runnning the installer on your computer, you may have to enter each answer. Figure 4-3, the very first screen you see when you run orainst, is an example of an information screen. You move around the screen using the TAB key, and press ENTER to select a response.

```
┌─────────────────────────────────────────────────────────────┐
│  ─        Oracle: A Beginner's Guide        23:29  ▼ ◆      │
│ ▌ile  Edit  Options  Help                                    │
│ ┌─────────────────────┐ ┌─Products──────┐ ┌Products────────┐ │
│ │▌nstall From...      │ │               │ │ed on /oracle   │ │
│ │─────────────────────│ │/ernie/oracle_link│                │ │
│ │Restart              │ │               │ │                │ │
│ │─────────────────────│ │               │ │                │ │
│ │OS Prompt    Ctrl+O  │ │               │ │ad Files 1.0.0.0.1│ │
│ │Exit         Ctrl+X  │8.1             │ │8.0             │ │
│ └─────────────────────┘ │2.8.1          │ │2.8.0           │ │
│      CASE*Generator 2.0.8.2.0           │ │0.1             │ │
│      DECNet Protocol Adapter (V2) 2.1.4.1.0 │ │0.0         │ │
│      LU62 Protocol Adapter (V2) 2.1.4.1.0 │ │               │ │
│                        └───────────────┘ └────────────────┘ │
│                                                              │
│   (Install...)              (From...)          (To...)      │
│ ──────────────────────────────────────────────────────────  │
│ Selects product distribution disk. [I]-Install From... [R]-Restart [O]- │
│ OS Prompt [x]-Exit [Return]-Invoke [PF4]-Cancel [K3]-NextWindow │
└─────────────────────────────────────────────────────────────┘
```

FIGURE 4-2.   *File menu*

```
┌─────────────────────────────────────────────────────────────┐
│  ─        Oracle: A Beginner's Guide        23:25  ▼ ◆      │
│ File  ▌dit  ▌ptions  Help                                    │
│         ┌────────────── Oracle ──────────────┐               │
│         │         ┌── ORACLE_HOME ──┐        │               │
│      ┌──┴─────────┴──────────────────┴───────┴──┐            │
│      │ Enter the pathname for your ORACLE_HOME directory:    │
│      │                                          │            │
│      │                                          │            │
│      │                                          │            │
│      │ /oracle                                  │            │
│      │                                    (▌K)  │            │
│      │ (Help...)       (Back)          (Cancel) │            │
│      └──┬──────────────────────────────────┬──┘             │
│         └──────────────────────────────────┘                │
└─────────────────────────────────────────────────────────────┘
```

FIGURE 4-3.   *An orainst screen asking for the Oracle home directory*

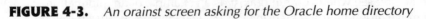

Let's delve into some of the specifics; the next four sections discuss question and answer boxes in the order they are presented by orainst.

ORACLE_HOME

As shown in Figure 4-3, orainst needs to establish the location of the Oracle software home directory. In most cases, it will be located in /oracle, but it depends on how the Oracle UNIX account has been configured. On our computer when Figure 4-3 appeared, the text /oracle was already there. You may have to check with your system administrator to ensure the value orainst presents is correct and, if it isn't, what the correct value should be.

Installation Log File

Orainst writes a log of every session to the file install.log. The installation log file name dialog box appears at the start of all orainst sessions. If there is a copy of that file around from a previous session, Oracle will ask you to specify another log filename or ask your permission to append to the existing file. We recommend browsing the installation log using your favorite text editor (e.g., vi in UNIX, or edt in VMS). If there are no errors listed in the log that require further intervention by you or Oracle Worldwide Customer Support, erase the log.

Online Documentation Location

Since version 7.1, Oracle has provided online documentation that orainst will load for you, if you desire. The program orainst uses the name ORACLE_DOC for the directory that holds this documentation. The program orainst wants a value for ORACLE_DOC; you must enter one whether or not you plan on loading online documentation. When this box appears, orainst suggests the name of the directory you are using for the permanent staging area. Since we used the directory /oracle/oracle_link when we built our staging area, orainst presented /oracle/oracle_link in this box during our session.

Owner of the Oracle Software

Lastly, orainst wants the name of the UNIX account that owns all the Oracle software. Normally, you are already logged onto your UNIX machine as the owner of the software, so just press ENTER to accept the value placed there by orainst.

Installer Activity

Having answered preliminary orainst questions in the previous sections, it is now time to specify what you wish to accomplish. Table 4-1 outlines the various activities that the Installer Action screen presents. The action "Product installation on a cluster" refers to the Oracle Parallel Server; this is discussed in Chapter 1.

Other Information

Based on the installer activity chosen in the previous section, there is an assortment of other information Oracle may want to know. These requests for information do

INSTALL ACTION	MEANING
Complete software/database fresh install	Used for a fresh install. This action creates a new Oracle database.
Build staging area only from tape	Reads software from tape and places it in the staging area.
Install/upgrade/patch software only	Installs, upgrades, or patches the software without doing anything to the existing database.
Create new database objects	Creates a new database when the Oracle Server is selected for installation or upgrade.
Upgrade existing database objects	Upgrades existing database objects to the new version of the Oracle Server being upgraded.
Software/database maintenance	Performs maintenance to Oracle products.
V6 to Oracle7 Migrate	Runs Oracle's migration utility to upgrade the software from version 6 to 7 and migrates the version 6 data to version 7 format.
Product installation on a cluster	Copies products onto other nodes in a cluster when running Oracle Parallel Server.

TABLE 4-1.   *Installer Action Choices*

not necessarily come up in the order we show them in the next few sections. Look at the headings of each of the following sections to find the right section to help answer questions you may encounter while running orainst.

Online Help Load

Oracle delivers online help support for most of its products. Specify that you want this loaded for all products, products of your choice, or no products. If you think you may use the online help, select products of your choice. The disk space consumed by online help is minimal. Unless you are very tight for disk space, do not worry about the space online help will consume.

TIP

In a production database, ask for online help for no products. In a development database, ask for products of your choice. We find SQL*Plus online help useful, for example.

Install Source

Even though we are installing from CD-ROM, for some reason Oracle asks what the source is for this session. With CD-ROM, you choose from the permanent staging area. We showed how this is built in the "Building the Staging Area" section earlier in this chapter.

Staging Area

Oracle asks for the path name for the staging area. In the example we use in this chapter, the staging area is /oracle/oracle_link. Usually, orainst knows the name of the staging area directory, displays it, and allows you to press ENTER to accept the directory shown.

NLS

NLS stands for National Language Support (yes, there are languages spoken other than yours!). Readers outside of North America know this. For example, one of us lives in Canada and is exposed to a multilingual society every day. This is where you specify the language for the installation, or you can accept ALL LANGUAGES for the default.

Relink All Executables?

Linking is a process whereby Oracle takes a series of computer programs, libraries, and object code (e.g., Oracle has already taken a C program called oracle.c and compiled it into object code oracle.o) and creates what's called an executable. If you are installing a patch, orainst relinks products automatically. As well, if installing or upgrading the Oracle Server, linking is automatic. It's your choice; if you want orainst to link products answer Yes.

TIP
We recommend relinking all products. We like that "warm and cozy" feeling knowing that the executables were created on our machine.

Root Install Script File

Most UNIX machines have a superuser account called root. This account is used by the systems administrator to perform secure operations such as making disk drives accessible, or performing hardware upgrades. After most orainst sessions, you are asked to get the system manager with access to the root account to run a script to complete the installation or upgrade. Answering Yes to the question presented will append anything to an existing root script; answering No will rename any existing script and write the current root-related requirements to a new script. If you choose to save the old root script file under another name, Oracle asks you to confirm a suggested directory and filename.

Information

This box simply confirms previous answers you have given orainst. Read the information, then TAB to OK and press ENTER to carry on.

Port-Specific Documentation

Similar to online documentation, which was discussed in this chapter's "Online Documentation Location" section, orainst wants to know if it should load documentation specific to your computer type and operating system. The amount of space taken up, if you choose Yes, is minimal.

Product Documentation Library CD-ROM Install

Since Oracle released version 7.1 of the Server, there has been a documentation library CD-ROM that contains just about every piece of documentation we ever refer to. This same library can be installed on your UNIX machine.

TIP
Get a hold of the product documentation library for desktop (e.g., Windows 3.1 or NT) and use it rather than placing it on the UNIX machine.

Maintenance Mode

If you chose Software/Database Maintenance as your desired installer action, this screen wants to know whether you wish to do Product Administration (work with existing products), Relink Product Executables, or Create/Upgrade Product Database Objects.

Available Products

After what seems an eternity, Oracle finally presents an Available Products screen. This is where you decide what to install. Scroll through the list of products, selecting ones to install by pressing the SPACEBAR. When you are happy with your choice and ready to proceed, TAB to the Install button and press ENTER to start. From time to time, we have scrolled through a list of products and not found the ones we were looking for. As it turned out, we had the wrong CD-ROM in the CD-ROM drive. On the Available Products screen, if you need to read a different CD-ROM, follow these instructions:

1. TAB to the From button and press ENTER.

2. Orainst displays an Open File dialog box. At this point, you can enter a filename in the Open File text box, or move through a list of directories in the Directory box. If you want, you can move around the directory tree displayed to find the CD-ROM drive. This directory tree window is shown in Figure 4-4.

VIP
Orainst reads files named "unix.prd". Regardless of where you look for files in this Open File box, you must select one by that name.

3. When you find the correct directory, TAB to the Open File area and enter the filename **unix.prd**.

4. TAB to the Open button, then press ENTER. Oracle will reread the CD-ROM.

As you use the installer more, you will find yourself breezing through its screens, knowing the answers orainst is going to display. Since the installer interface has been standardized across hardware and operating system type, the skills you gain from your very first session will be used in subsequent sessions. We now move on to the section of this chapter in which we will discuss product installation in a nondesktop environment.

Installing Oracle Products—Nondesktop

This activity is similar to installing products in desktop, but the interface uses the TAB and ENTER keys instead of the mouse. Product installation is selected from the Installer Actions screen by choosing the "Install/Upgrade/Patch software only" option. After answering the series of questions asked by orainst, and after you have

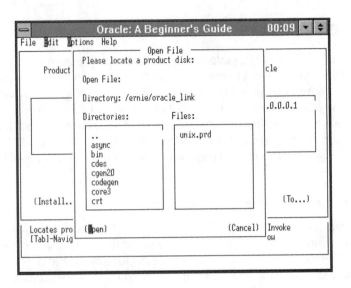

FIGURE 4-4.   *Directory tree list*

chosen one or more products to install from the Available Products screen, you begin the installation by selecting Install. Once product installation begins, after selecting Install, orainst looks at the version number of the installed product and the version of the product on the CD-ROM. You are informed of the results of the product version comparison, and you are asked whether you wish to continue. This confirmation screen is shown in Figure 4-5.

Orainst may inform you, for example, that the installed version of SQL*Plus is 3.1.3.5.1, and you have chosen a CD-ROM containing the same version. The choice to continue is yours. If you decide to install a product carry on by selecting Yes. After the product is installed, you are informed of the completed installation and returned to the Available Products screen. You are also informed if there were any problems with the install, and you should then refer to the installation log file whose name you may have chosen on the Installation Log File screen discussed in an earlier section.

When your requested product installation completes, orainst displays the Install Completed information box. Read the advice in that box, then select OK to return to the Available Products window. Leave the installer by pressing CTRL-X, or press the MENU key, and when the File menu appears, press X to quit orainst. Our experience dictates that most product installations proceed without a glitch; we have found orainst in the nondesktop environment stable and relatively easy to use.

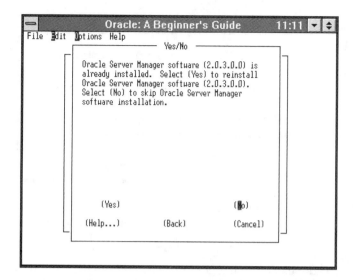

FIGURE 4-5.   *Confirmation to continue during product installation*

Installing Personal Oracle7–Desktop

Again, we will be using CD-ROM for this install. On the machine we use, the CD-ROM is called drive d. Substitute the drive letter from your machine where appropriate. Oracle has moved to CD-ROM as the standard distribution medium; if you don't have one, it's that time. The following configuration is required to run Personal Oracle7 in Windows:

- A 486 or stronger processor
- 60 megabytes (62,730,240 bytes) of disk space
- 8 megabytes of memory (though 16 is recommended)

Preinstallation Activity

Prior to installing Personal Oracle7, you must install the Microsoft product called Win32s. The version number must be at least 1.20. Some of you may already have this on your system; if so, you may skip this part. If you are unsure, proceed with the Win32s installation, and you will be told if it is already present, as shown in Figure 4-6.

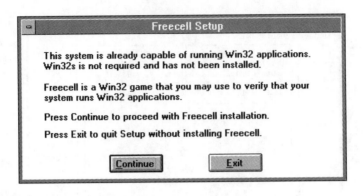

FIGURE 4-6.   *Win32s already installed*

To install Win32s, select Run under the File menu from the Windows Program Manager, proceed to the \win32s\disk1 directory on your CD-ROM, and run the program setup.exe.

Installing Personal Oracle7

Now, let's do the install:

1. Select Run then Browse under the File menu from the Windows Program Manager and proceed to the \po7_win\install directory on your CD-ROM, as shown in Figure 4-7.

2. Select orainst.exe and click on OK in the Browse dialog box, then OK in the Run dialog box to start installation.

3. When Oracle brings up the Installation Settings dialog box, as shown in Figure 4-8, enter your name and the Oracle home directory, then click OK to proceed.

4. When the next Installation Options dialog box appears as shown in Figure 4-9, notice the Complete Install is selected by default. Click OK to continue.

5. When Oracle finishes its work, it will show you two windows: Installation Notes, as shown in Figure 4-10, and Information as shown in Figure 4-11. Click OK after reading each to return to the Windows Program Manager.

The installation of the Personal Oracle7 database is now complete and you are looking at the Windows Program Manager.

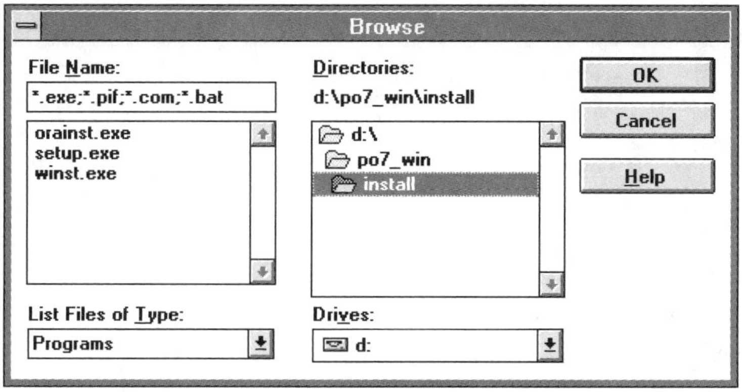

FIGURE 4-7. *Selecting the installer program*

Installing Oracle Products–Desktop

All installation work in desktop is done with the mouse and an assortment of dialog boxes, lists, and buttons. To install an Oracle tool follow these instructions:

1. Double-click on the Oracle Installer icon in the Windows Program Manager. You will be presented with the Oracle Installer screen, as shown in Figure 4-12. There are two parts to this screen. One shows a list of Available Products, the other a list of Installed Products.

2. When installing from CD-ROM, most of the time Available Products is empty. To select the CD-ROM, click on From. When the Open dialog box appears, select your CD-ROM drive from the Drives drop-down list.

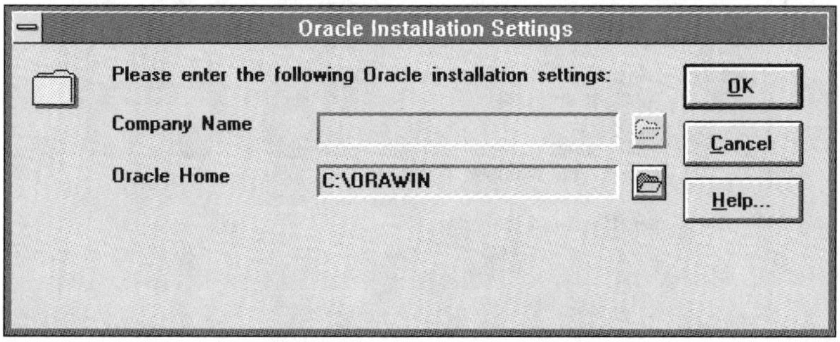

FIGURE 4-8. *Oracle Installation Settings dialog box*

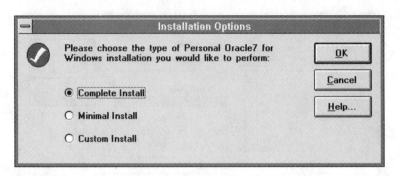

FIGURE 4-9. *Installation Options dialog box*

3. Double-click on the Install directory in the Directories area. Highlight the windows.prd filename in the File area of the Open dialog box.

NOTE
When the initial directory list is displayed, you may have to traverse the directory tree displayed to find the desired Install directory.

4. Click on OK. The installer populates the Available Products area of the Oracle Installer screen.

5. Find the tool you wish to install in the list of available products. Double-click on the tool, then click on Install to begin the installation process.

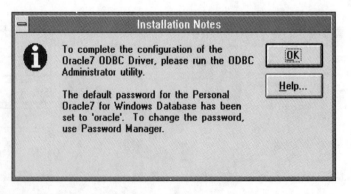

FIGURE 4-10. *Installation Notes dialog box*

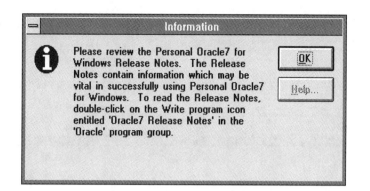

FIGURE 4-11. *Information dialog box*

From here on, the dialog boxes and information boxes Oracle displays depend on the tool you chose to install. When the available products are displayed, notice how some products have a plus (+) sign beside them. This means the product has a number of components. To expand the component list, double-click on the product name in the Available Products list. For example, in Figure 4-13 we have double-clicked on Oracle Forms to show its three components. Click on each component if you wish to install them separately.

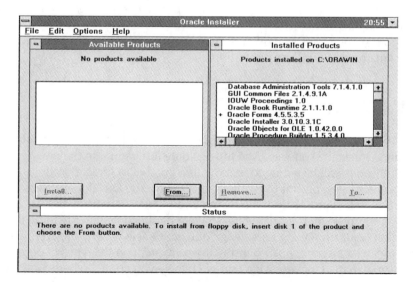

FIGURE 4-12. *Oracle Installer screen*

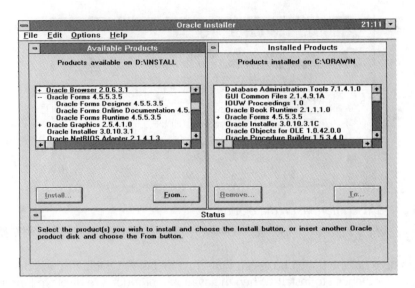

FIGURE 4-13. *Double-clicking on Oracle Forms in the Available Products list displays its three components*

When the component list is expanded, collapse the expanded list by clicking on the product name. This is the same process you follow in desktop regardless of the product being installed.

When orainst completes its work, return to the Windows program manager by double-clicking on the installer's control box.

What's Next

This completes the "Startup" section of this book. You now know about Oracle the company and Oracle the software. The fun has only just begun. In the next section, we will guide you through starting to work with a number of Oracle products, and we'll offer some suggestions for using them effectively. The Developer Basics section starts with an introduction to the Structured Query Language (SQL); knowledge of this product is fundamental to what has become (after reading this Startup section) your expanding knowledge of what Oracle is, why the company is where it is today (at the top), how to install the software, and the types of objects in every Oracle database. Get yourself a cup of coffee—you could be here for a while.

PART 2

Developer Basics

CHAPTER 5

SQL 101

In this chapter, we teach you the basics of SQL. This could be the most important chapter of this book, since, if you understand SQL, you understand a relational database. Back when we started working with Oracle, this was the tool of choice for writing all the reports. Then came along another tool called RPT. If you have ever used RPT, you will understand why some people thought it had limited use.

Today, you have lots of excellent choices for report writers. But if you just need to punch it, crunch it, and get it out the door, use SQL*Plus. With Oracle's enhancements to the core SQL language, you have a great reporting tool. We have found that many of the reports we generate every day could be accomplished with SQL*Plus alone.

VIP

SQL (Structured Query Language) is used by Oracle for all interaction with the database. SQL*Plus (one of many Oracle tools) is based on SQL, but it has some Oracle-specific features that can be used for writing reports and controlling the way screen and paper output is formatted.

Some people don't use SQL*Plus for many of these tasks, for the same reason that some people find it easier to add up numbers with pencil and paper instead of a calculator. We are of the "keep it simple" camp—make it happen quick. So SQL*Plus is our first choice for all reports. Only when our needs exceed the ability of SQL*Plus do we look for a better tool.

With this in mind, let's see what SQL*Plus can do. In this chapter, we will not try to teach you every nuance or detail about SQL*Plus; we will teach you what it takes to get at the information you need quickly. We will also teach you how to present this information in the best possible light. We will do this using a step-by-step process. First, we will teach you the two basic types of SQL statements. Next, we will create tables and populate those tables with data. Then, we will write some reports against those tables. This chapter will cover the following topics:

- DDL and DML: What they are and some practical examples of using them
- How to log into SQL*Plus
- The most common setup parameters
- How to retrieve data from the database
- How to format data using SQL*Plus
- How to update and delete data stored in the database
- How to create a table and insert data into a table
- How to alter a table

Terminology

The following definitions will arm you with the technical jargon to make it through this chapter.

- *DDL,* or Data Definition Language, is the SQL construct used to define data in the database. When you define that data, entries are made in Oracle's data dictionary. Common DDL keywords are **create**, **revoke**, **grant**, and **alter**.

- *DML,* or Data Manipulation Language, is the SQL construct used to manipulate the data in the database (rather than the definition of the data, done by DDL). Common DML keywords are **select**, **insert**, **update**, and **delete**.

- With Oracle, we use the word *commit* to indicate that data has been saved back to the database. Think of your favorite word processor. Each time you save your work, Oracle would refer to that action as committing your work.

- If you try to get information out of an Oracle database using a program such as SQL*Plus, then this action is called a *query*.

- *Functions* are operations performed on data that alter the data's characteristics. For example, forcing the text "Abbeflantro" to uppercase using the SQL keyword **upper** is an example of performing a function on the text.

Two Types of SQL Statements

SQL statements fall into two major categories: DDL (Data Definition Language) and DML (Data Manipulation Language). Let's take a closer look at their differences and similarities.

DDL

Data Definition Language allows you to perform the following tasks:

- Create a database object
- Drop a database object
- Alter a database object
- Grant privileges on a database object
- Revoke privileges on a database object

It's important to understand that when you issue a DDL SQL statement, Oracle commits the current transaction before and after every DDL statement. So if you were inserting records into the database and you issued a DDL statement like **create table**, then the data from the **insert** command would be committed to the database. Table 5-1 is a partial list of DDL statements.

In summary, SQL commands that **alter**, **drop**, **create**, and **grant** are the most frequently used examples of the Data Definition Language. Just as the name implies, DDL is the SQL statements that help define and create tables and privileges.

VIP
Data Definition Language is the set of SQL commands that create and define objects in the database, storing their definitions in the data dictionary.

DML

Data Manipulation Language allows you to **insert**, **update**, **delete**, and **select** data in the database. Just as the name implies, DML allows you to work with the contents of your database. Table 5-2 is a partial list of DML statements.

In summary, DML statements are SQL commands that allow you to manipulate the data in the database. The most common SQL statements are **insert**, **update**, **delete** and **select**.

SQL COMMAND	PURPOSE
alter procedure	Recompiles a stored procedure
alter table	Adds a column, *redefines* a column, *changes* storage allocation
analyze	Gathers performance statistics for database objects to be fed to the cost-based optimizer
create table	Creates a table
create index	Creates an index
drop index	Drops an index
drop table	Drops a table from the database
grant	Grants privileges or roles to a user or another role
truncate	Deletes all the rows from a table
revoke	Removes privileges from a user or database role

TABLE 5-1.   *Partial List of DDL Statements*

SQL COMMAND	PURPOSE
insert	Add rows of data to a table
delete	Delete rows of data from a table
update	Change data in a table
select	Retrieve rows of data from a table/view
commit work	Make changes permanent (write to disk) for the current transaction(s)
rollback	Undo all changes since the last commit

TABLE 5-2.   *Partial List of DML Statements*

VIP
Data Manipulation Language is the set of statements that allow you to manipulate the data in the database.

Now that we understand the two major types of SQL statements, let's get our feet wet. We will start by logging into SQL*Plus. From there, we will try some of the more common DDL and DML statements.

SQL*Plus: Getting In

The easiest way to learn about SQL is by using SQL*Plus. So let's begin by logging into SQL*Plus. For these examples, picture an Oracle username of *polly* whose password is *gone.* Enter SQL*Plus in one of four basic ways.

- ■ Log into SQL*Plus passing username and password on the command line, using the command **sqlplus polly/gone**.

- ■ Log into SQL*Plus passing just the username, as in **sqlplus polly**, and you are prompted for the account password.

- ■ Log into SQL*Plus passing no parameters, as in **sqlplus**, and you are prompted for the account and password.

- ■ In a Windows environment, double-click on the SQL*Plus icon. You are prompted for a username and password in a Connect dialog box.

After entering SQL*Plus, you should see the SQL*Plus prompt: SQL>.

create Statement

The first phase of any database always starts with DDL statements, since it is through DDL that you create your database objects. First, we will create four tables: customer, state, X, and Y:

```
SQL> create table customer(
  2>      last_name   varchar2(30) not null,
  3>      state_cd    varchar(2),
  4>      sales       number)
  5>  tablespace custspace
  6>  storage(initial 25k next 25k minextents 1);
Table created.
SQL> create table state (
  2>      state_cd    varchar(2) not null,
  3>      state_name  varchar2(30));
Table created.
SQL> create table x (
  2>      col         varchar2(30));
Table created.
SQL> create table y (
  2>      col         varchar2(30));
Table created.
```

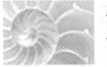

NOTE
In listings, numbers followed by > should not be entered by you. When you press ENTER to go to the next line, SQL*Plus puts those numbers there. The column definitions are bounded by a set of parentheses.

Data Types

By examining the **create table** scripts above, a few items become obvious. Not only do you have to give each table a name (e.g., customer), you must also list all the columns or fields (e.g., last_name, state_cd, and sales) associated with the table. You also have to tell the database what type of information that table will hold. For example, the column sales hold numeric information. An Oracle database can hold many different types of data. Table 5-3 is a partial list of the most common data types.

DATA TYPE	DESCRIPTION
char(size)	Stores fixed-length character data, with a maximum size of 255
varchar2(size)	Stores variable-length character data, with a maximum size of 2,000
varchar	Currently the same as char
number(l,d)	Stores numeric data, where "l" stands for length and "d" for the number of decimal digits
date	Stores dates from January 1,4712 B.C. to December 31,4712 A.D.
long	Stores variable-length character data up to 2Gb (gigabytes) in size

TABLE 5-3.   *Partial List of Data Types*

VIP
When defining numeric columns with a length and number of decimal digits, the length defines the total number of digits, including integer and decimal. For example, the largest number that can be stored in number(4,2) is 99.99.

Remember that an Oracle database is made up of tables and that those tables are defined by the columns or fields within the table. Those columns or fields have an attribute that tells what kind of data they can hold. The type of data they hold tells the database what it can do to the contents—this is especially relevant in the sections in this chapter entitled "Using Functions with the Number Data Type," "Using Functions with the Character Data Type," and "Using Functions with the Date Data Type." For example, the number type tells Oracle it can add, subtract, multiply, or divide the contents.

What Is Null and Not Null?

If you look closely at the customer table, you will see the qualifier "not null" next to the last_name column. This means the database will not accept a row of data for that customer table unless the columns so defined have data in them. In other words, not null columns are mandatory fields. In the customer table, this means the last_name and state_cd fields must contain a value in order to insert a row of data into the table.

VIP
Another way of thinking of not null is to use the word "mandatory." A not null column means data for that column can never be empty.

What's a Null Value?   A common question people ask is "What is a null value?" Null is a column that contains no data. Think of it as a character string with a length of 0. Many times, people will load null into a column value if it is unknown. The most common mistake people make is to load null into a numeric column. The problem is 1+null is null. So if you accidentally load null values into a numeric field, you can very quickly cause your reports to add up incorrectly.

VIP
Never use null to represent a value of zero in a numeric field. If you might perform arithmetic on a numeric column, give it a value of zero instead.

On the customer table **create** statement, notice the **storage** clause used to size the table. As well, we have used the **tablespace** clause to place the table in a certain tablespace in the database. The storage clause is mentioned in more detail in *Tuning Oracle* by Corey, Abbey, and Dechichio (Osborne McGraw-Hill/Oracle Press, 1995).

At the end of each line, you see a semicolon (;). This tells Oracle that you have finished entering the SQL statement and to begin execution.

describe

One of the nicest enhancements that Oracle has added to its implementation of SQL is the **describe** command. This command give you a quick summary of the table and all its columns. For example, the command **describe customer** yields the following output:

```
Name                             Null?     Type
-------------------------------- --------  ----
last_name                        not null  varchar2(50)
state_cd                         not null  char(2)
sales                                      number
```

NOTE
The **describe** command can be shortened to **desc** in SQL*Plus.

insert

Now that we have created some tables, let's use DML. We will start with the customer table. The statements **insert into customer values ('Teplow','MA',**

23445.67); and **insert into customer values ('Abbey','CA',6969.96);** create two rows in the customer table. Oracle responds with the following message for each set of column information created by the **insert** command:

```
1 row created.
```

The row created message is returned once for each successful **insert**; the message informs you of the number of rows created. If there are many **insert** statements in a program, the output would resemble the following:

```
SQL> insert into customer values ('Porter','CA', 6989.99);
1 row created.
SQL> insert into customer values ('Martin','CA',2345.45);
1 row created.
SQL> insert into customer values ('Laursen','CA',34.34);
1 row created.
SQL> insert into customer values ('Bambi','CA',1234.55);
1 row created.
SQL> insert into customer values ('McGraw','NJ', 123.45);
1 row created.
```

insert with Columns Specified

Next, we insert data into the state table, using a slight variation on the **insert** command: we will specify the column names into which the data is inserted. This is very useful on a very large table, for which you might not have all the data for every column in the table on the **insert**. A good example of not having all the data up front is a budget system where you won't have the actual dollars spent data until the end of the month. Let's take a look at a program with this variation of the **insert** command that allows you to selectively load columns in a table:

```
SQL> insert into state (state_name, state_cd)
   2> values ('Massachusetts','MA');
1 row created.
SQL> insert into state (state_name, state_cd)
   2> values ('California','CA');
1 row created.
SQL> insert into state (state_name, state_cd)
   2> values ('NewJersey','NJ',);
1 row created.
```

Let's finish up our inserts by loading data into tableX and tableY.

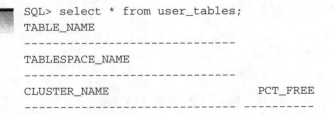

```
SQL> insert into X values ('1');
1 row created.
SQL> insert into X values ('2');
1 row created.
SQL> insert into X values ('3');
1 row created.
SQL> insert into Y values ('3');
1 row created.
SQL> insert into Y values ('4');
1 row created.
SQL> insert into Y values ('5');
1 row created.
```

select

The **select** command is how you retrieve data from an Oracle database. Simply put, you are telling the database which information you have selected to retrieve. This is the most common SQL statement you will see. The **select** command has four basic parts:

- The word **select** followed by what you want to see (i.e., the names of the columns in the tables mentioned in the next part). This is mandatory.

- The word **from** followed by where you get it from (i.e., the names of one or more tables where the data resided). This is mandatory.

- The word **where** followed by any selection criteria (i.e., conditions that restrict the data that the statement retrieves). This is optional.

- The word **order by** followed by the sort criteria (i.e., a list of column names from part one that control how the data is presented). This is optional.

Let's issue our first **select** statement against a data dictionary view called user_tables:

```
SQL> select * from user_tables;
TABLE_NAME
------------------------------

TABLESPACE_NAME
------------------------------

CLUSTER_NAME                              PCT_FREE
------------------------------  ----------
```

```
PCT_USED   INI_TRANS   MAX_TRANS INITIAL_EXTENT
---------- ----------- ---------- --------------
NEXT_EXTENT MIN_EXTENTS MAX_EXTENTS PCT_INCREASE B
----------- ----------- ----------- ------------ -
  NUM_ROWS      BLOCKS EMPTY_BLOCKS   AVG_SPACE
---------- ----------- ------------ ----------
 CHAIN_CNT AVG_ROW_LEN DEGREE       INSTANCES   CACHE
---------- ----------- ---------- ---------- ----
PERSON
USER_DATA
                                    10
        40           1         255         10240
     10240              1         121          50 N
                         0           0
         0           0           1           1    N
```

Let's discuss what has just happened. Based on our criteria, the text **select ***
tells Oracle to retrieve all the columns in the view. This is a special and very
popular form of the **select** command.

VIP
To see all the columns from a table, use the asterisk (*) with the
select statement.

In this chapter (and you may have noticed this elsewhere), we refer to the
Oracle feature called a view. Think of a view as a subset of one or more tables. A
view is a special database object that can be created to restrict access to certain
columns or rows of data in a table. A view acts like a table in all other aspects (i.e.,
in most cases, you can **update** or **insert** data using a view rather than a table). A
good example of why you might use a view is to allow managers to see only their
own employees' payroll records.

VIP
A view is a special database object that can be created to restrict
access to certain columns or rows of data within a table.

select with Columns Specified
Rather than using the asterisk as we did in the previous section, we can specify one
or more columns after the **select** keyword. The asterisk instructs Oracle to display

all the columns from a table. Let's now issue this same **select** statement but specify a column we want to see.

```
SQL> select table_name from user_tables;

TABLE_NAME
------------------------------
CUSTOMER
STATE
X
Y
4 rows selected.
```

where

Up to now, you have seen how the **select** command can be used to bring back all the columns (**select ***) or a subset of the columns (**select column1, column3**). What if you want to see only certain rows of your data? You do this with a **where** clause. For example, if you want to see all the customers with a state_cd of MA, you would issue the command **select state_cd, last_name, sales from customer where state_cd = 'MA';**. The output would resemble the following:

```
LAST_NAME                                          ST     SALES
-------------------------------------------------- --  ----------
Teplow                                             MA   23445.67
```

where Clause with and/or

A **where** clause instructs Oracle to search the data in a table and return only those rows that meet your criteria. In the example above, we asked Oracle to bring back only those rows that have state_cd equal to MA. This was accomplished by **where state_cd = 'MA'**.

Sometimes you want to bring back rows that meet multiple criteria. For example, you might be interested in the rows with a state_cd of CA and sales greater than 6,000. The statement **select * from customer where state_cd = 'CA' and sales > 6000;** produces the following output:

```
LAST_NAME                        ST     SALES
------------------------------   --  ----------
Porter                           CA    6989.99
Abbey                            CA    6969.96
```

In the above example, we wanted back rows that met all the criteria. What if you wanted to retrieve rows that met either criteria? Let's look at the statement **select * from customer where state_cd = 'CA' or sales > 6000;**. This produces the following output:

```
LAST_NAME                      ST     SALES
------------------------------ -- ----------
Porter                         CA    6989.99
Martin                         CA    2345.45
Bambi                          CA    1234.55
Teplow                         MA   23445.67
Abbey                          CA    6969.96
```

Notice how Teplow is displayed since his sales are greater than 6000, even though he is not from the state_cd CA. The **and** and **or** are known as logical operators. They are used to tell the query how the **where** conditions affect each other. The concept of logic as it applies to how Oracle evaluates multiple conditions could be a book in itself. Let's take the time to delve into some of the evaluation techniques. Table 5-4 explains how Oracle deals with **and** and **or** when they appear together in the same **where** clause.

The logic involved with multiple **and** and **or** words (referred to as compound conditions) can become confusing, unless you look at each statement separately and walk slowly through its logic. For example, let's examine the statement **select last_name from customer where state_cd = 'MA' and state_cd = 'CA';**. With the two conditions connected by the **and** keyword, both conditions must be true for the compound condition to be true.

VIP
Compound conditions connected by the **and** keyword must all evaluate to TRUE for the whole statement to be true.

OPERATOR	REASON
or	Returns TRUE when either one of the conditions is true
and	Returns TRUE only when both conditions are true

TABLE 5-4.   *Logical Operators and/or*

Using the statement **select last_name from customer where state_cd = 'MA' and state_cd = 'CA';**, let's look at a row whose state_cd value is MA. The first condition evaluates to TRUE (since MA equals MA), and the second condition evaluates to FALSE (since CA is not equal to MA). The logic of the statement says that only rows whose state_cd is MA and CA at the same time can be displayed. Of course this is impossible, and thus the condition fails, since TRUE+FALSE=FALSE. We deliberately created this **select** statement to show how complicated your **where** clauses can become in relatively no time.

where Clause with NOT

Oracle also supports the ability to search for negative criteria. For example, you might want to see all the customers who are not in state_cd MA. The statement **select * from customer where state_cd != 'MA';** (the characters **!=** mean "not equal" to SQL*Plus) would yield the output

LAST_NAME	ST	SALES
Porter	CA	6989.99
McGraw	NJ	123.45
Martin	CA	2345.45
Laursen	CA	34.34
Bambi	CA	1234.55
Abbey	CA	6969.96

where Clause with a Range Search

Oracle also supports range searches. For example, you might want to see all the customers with sales between 1 and 10,000. This would be done using the statement **select * from customer where sales between 1 and 10000;**, and the output would resemble the following:

LAST_NAME	ST	SALES
Porter	CA	6989.99
McGraw	NJ	123.45
Martin	CA	2345.45
Bambi	CA	1234.55
Laursen	CA	34.34
Abbey	CA	6969.96

where Clause with a Search List

Oracle also supports the concept of searching for items within a list. For example, you might want to see all the customers with a state code of NJ or CA. The statement **select * from customer where state_cd in ('NJ','CA');**

```
LAST_NAME                                          ST      SALES
-------------------------------------------------- --  ----------
Porter                                             CA     6989.99
McGraw                                             NJ      123.45
Martin                                             CA     2345.45
Laursen                                            CA       34.34
Bambi                                              CA     1234.55
Abbey                                              CA     6969.96
```

where Clause with a Pattern Search

Oracle also supports pattern searching through the **like** command. For example, you could tell Oracle to retrieve all the last names that begin with the letter M by issuing the statement **select * from customer where last_name like 'M%';**. The output would resemble the following:

```
LAST_NAME                                          ST      SALES
-------------------------------------------------- --  ----------
McGraw                                             NJ      123.45
Martin                                             CA     2345.45
```

You could also tell Oracle to look for all the last names that contain the characters "tin" by entering the command **select * from customer where last_name like '%tin%';**. It would return the following data:

```
LAST_NAME                                          ST      SALES
-------------------------------------------------- --  ----------
Martin                                             CA     2345.45
```

where Clause: Common Operators

As you can see from these many examples, Oracle has a very powerful set when it comes to restricting the rows retrieved. Table 5-5 is a partial list of operators you can use in the **where** clause.

OPERATOR	PURPOSE	EXAMPLE
=	Test for equality	select * from state where state_cd = 'MA';
!=	Test for inequality	select * from state where state_cd != 'MA';
^=	Same as !=	select * from state where state_cd ^= 'MA'
<>	Same as !=	select * from state where state_cd <> 'MA'
<	Less than	select * from customer where sales < 100;
>	Greater than	select * from customer where sales > 100;
<=	Less than or equal to	select * from customer where sales <= 10000;
>=	Greater than or equal to	select * from customer where sales >= 10000;
in	Equal to any member in parentheses	select * from customer where state_cd in ('MA','NJ');
not in	Not equal to any member in parentheses	select * from customer where state_cd not in ('MA','NJ');
between A and B	Greater than or equal to A and less than or equal to B	select * from customer where sales between 1 and 50;
not between A and B	Not greater than or equal to A and not less than or equal to B	select * from customer where sales not between 1 and 50;
like '%tin%'	Contains given text (e.g., 'tin')	select * from customer where last_name like '%tin%';

TABLE 5-5.   *Common Comparison Operators*

order by

Let's take another look at the contents of the customer table. This time, we will request the list sorted by last_name in descending alphabetical order. The command **select * from customer order by last_name desc;** gives the following results:

```
LAST_NAME                                           ST      SALES
-------------------------------------------------- --  ----------
Teplow                                              MA   23445.67
Porter                                              CA    6989.99
McGraw                                              NJ     123.45
Martin                                              CA    2345.45
Laursen                                             CA      34.34
Bambi                                               CA    1234.55
Abbey                                               CA    6969.96
7 rows selected.
```

As you can see, Oracle brought the list back in descending sorted order. We could have easily sorted the list in ascending order by issuing the command **select * from customer order by last_name;**. We could have also done a multilevel sort by issuing the command **select * from customer order by state_cd desc, last_name;**. This command would list customers sorted by state descending (i.e., Vermont before Mississippi) and ascending by last_name.

VIP
When no order (i.e., descending or ascending) is specified in an **order by**, Oracle sorts ascending.

Number Data Type

These fields contain only numeric data. Let's see what you can do to the columns of this type in a **select** statement. Table 5-6 highlights the most popular arithmetic operations and how they are worded in SQL*Plus.

OPERATOR	OPERATION PERFORMED	EXAMPLE
+	Addition	select ytd_sales + current_sales from customer;
–	Subtraction	select ytd_sales - current_sales from customer where state_cd = 'NJ';
*	Multiplication	select ytd_sales * commission from customer;
/	Division	select ytd_sales / 12 from customer;

TABLE 5-6. *Arithmetic Operators*

As you can see in Table 5-6, you can certainly perform all the standard arithmetic operations: add, subtract, multiply, and divide. With Oracle, your ability to manipulate the contents goes far beyond the standard list. In addition to the operators mentioned is an extensive list of functions. Before we present that list, let's talk about what a function is.

Using Functions with the Number Data Type

A *function* manipulates the contents of a column in a SQL statement. When using a function in a SQL statement, the column value upon which the function is performed is changed as the column value is displayed. Displaying a number column's absolute value is a good example of a function; a column that contains the number -321 has an absolute value of 321. In SQL*Plus, absolute value is indicated by placing parentheses around the column name, and the word "abs" in front, e.g., **abs(ytd_sales)**. Thus, a SQL statement worded **select abs(ytd_sales) from customer;** would display the value 321 when a ytd_sales column contained the value -321 or +321.

Table 5-7 shows some popular functions performed on number data type columns, how they are worded in SQL*Plus, and the value they display. Notice that the **select** statements in Table 5-7 use a table called dual. This table is owned by SYS and is used in situations where correct SQL syntax (i.e., must contain a **from** portion) must be used and there is no other table in the database used in the statement.

Table 5-7 presents an extensive list of functions that can be performed on number data. This is only a partial list; a full list with examples and explanations can be found by entering the command **help functions** while using SQL*Plus.

If you try to perform a numeric function on nonnumeric data, you will receive an Oracle error. For example, the statement **select floor('ABC') from dual;** will cause the following error since the data **ABC** is not numeric:

```
ERROR:
ORA-01722: invalid number
```

There is a whole different set of functions you perform with character data. Let's take a look at what Oracle can do with a character string.

Character Data Type

These are fields that are entered as char, varchar, or varchar2 in the **create table** statement. The character data type can be used to represent all the letters, numbers,

FUNCTION	RETURNS	EXAMPLE	DISPLAYS
ceil(n)	Nearest whole integer greater than or equal to number.	select ceil(10.6) from dual;	11
floor(n)	Largest integer equal to or less than n.	select floor(10.6) from dual;	10
mod(m,n)	Remainder of m divided by n. If n=0, then m is returned.	select mod(7,5) from dual;	2
power(m,n)	Number m raised to the power of n.	select power(3,2) from dual;	9
round(n,m)	Result rounded to m places to the right of the decimal point.	select round(1234.5678,2) from dual;	1234.57
sign(n)	If n = 0, returns 0; if n > 0, returns 1; If n < 0, returns -1.	select sign(12) from dual;	1
sqrt(n)	Square root of n.	select sqrt(25) from dual;	5

TABLE 5-7. *Common Functions on Number Data*

and special characters on your keyboard. There is a whole complete set of functions you can use with the character data type.

Using Functions with the Character Data Type

Table 5-8 lists the most common functions you will perform with the character data type.

The concatenation operator deserves special attention before moving onto the discussion of the date data type. This is quite useful when you want to join two character fields together. It is called an operator, though we include it in this section on functions. Two vertical bars (¦ ¦) indicate concatenation. The statement **select 'ABC' ¦ ¦ 'DEF' from dual;** returns the text ABCDEF. Think of a form letter. The statement **select 'Dear ' ¦ ¦ last_name ¦ ¦ ':' from customer;** would return the text "Dear John:" for the row whose last_name was John.

FUNCTION	RETURN	EXAMPLE	DISPLAYS
initcap(char)	Changes the first character of each character string to uppercase.	select initcap('mr. teplow') from dual;	Mr. Teplow
lower(char)	Makes the entire string lowercase.	select lower('Mr. Donald Briffett') from dual;	mr. donald briffet
replace(char, str1, str2)	Character string with every occurrence of str1 being replaced with str2.	select replace('Scott', 'S', 'Boy') from dual;	Boycott
soundex(char)	Phonetic representation of char. Commonly used to do fuzzy name searches. You can compare words that are spelled differently but sound alike.	select last_name from employee where soundex(last_name) = soundex('SMYTHE');	SMITH
substr(char,m,n)	Picks off part of the character string char starting in position m for n characters.	select substr('ABCDEF',2,1) from dual;	B
length(char)	Length of char.	select length ('Anderson') from dual;	8

TABLE 5-8. *Common Functions on Character Data*

Date Data Type

Date is the third most common type of data you find in an Oracle database. When we created the customer table, we could have easily included an additional column called sale_date, as in the following:

```
SQL> create table customer
  2> (last_name    varchar2(30) not null,
  3>  state_cd     varchar2(2),
  3>  sales        number,
  4>  sale_date    date);
Table created.
```

In Oracle, the date data type really contains two values: the date and the time. This is critical to remember when comparing two dates, since Oracle always stores a time with the date. The default date format in Oracle is DD-MON-YY. DD is the day, MON is the month, and YY is the two-digit year.

Using Functions with the Date Data Type

Oracle has provided you a list of extensive functions to help you manipulate the date data type. For example, suppose you want to send out a reminder to a customer on the last day of the month for an unpaid invoice. If you want to print the letter and send it when appropriate, you would perform the function **last_day** to place the correct date in the reminder's header. Table 5-9 shows the most common date functions.

FUNCTION	RETURN	EXAMPLE	DISPLAYS
sysdate	Current date and time	select sysdate from dual;	30-FEB-97 on February 30, 1997
last_day	Last day of the month	select last_day(sysdate) from dual;	31-MAR-97 on March 12, 1997
add_months(d,n)	Adds or subtracts n months from data d	select add_months(sysdate,2) from dual;	18-MAY-98 on March 18, 1998
months_between(f,s)	Difference in months between date f and date s	select months_between(sysdate, '12-MAR-97') from dual;	13 in April 1998
next_day(d,day)	Date that is the specified day of the week after d	select next_day (sysdate,'Monday') from dual;	04-SEP-95 on August 31, 1995

TABLE 5-9.   *Common Functions on Date Data*

Special Formats with the Date Data Type

You can use a number of formats with dates. These formats are used to change the display format of a date. Table 5-10 shows some date formats and their output:

FORMAT	RETURN	EXAMPLE	DISPLAYS
Y or YY or YYY	Last one, two, or three digits of year	select to_char(sysdate,'YYY') from dual;	996 for all dates in 1996
SYEAR or YEAR	Year spelled out; using the S places a minus sign before B.C. dates	select to_char(sysdate,'SYEAR') from dual;	-1112 in the year 1112 B.C.
Q	Quarter of year (Jan through March = 1)	select to_char(sysdate,'Q') from dual;	2 for all dates in June
MM	Month (01-12; Dec = 12)	select to_char(sysdate,'MM') from dual;	12 for all dates in December
RM	Roman numeral month	select to_char(sysdate,'RM') from dual;	IV for all dates in April
Month	Name of month as a nine character name	select to_char(sysdate,'Month') from dual;	May followed by 6 spaces for all dates in May
WW	Week of year	select to_char(sysdate,'WW') from dual;	24 on June 13, 1998
W	Week of the month	select to_char(sysdate,'W') from dual;	1 on October 1, 1995
DDD	Day of the year: January 1 is 001, February 1 is 032, etc.	select to_char(sysdate,'DDD') from dual;	227 on October 1,1995

TABLE 5-10. *Common Formats using Date Data*

FORMAT	RETURN	EXAMPLE	DISPLAYS
DD	Day of the month	select to_char(sysdate,'DD') from dual;	04 on October 4 in any year
D	Day of the week (1-7)	select to_char(sysdate,'D') from dual;	1 on October 1, 1995
DY	Abbreviated name of day	select to_char(sysdate,'DY') from dual;	FRI on December 8, 1995
HH or HH12	Hour of day (1-12)	select to_char(sysdate,'HH') from dual;	02 when it is 2 hours, and 8 minutes past midnight
HH24	Hour of day using 24-hour clock	select to_char(sysdate,'HH24') from dual;	14 when it is 2 hours and 8 minutes past noon
MI	Minutes (0-59)	select to_char(sysdate,'MI') from dual;	17 when it is 4:17 in the afternoon
SS	Seconds (0-59)	select to_char(sysdate,'SS') from dual;	22 when the time is 11:03:22

TABLE 5-10. *Common Formats using Date Data* (continued)

VIP
Be careful about using the format MM for minutes (you should use MI for minutes). MM is used for month; it will work if you try to use it for minutes, but the results will be wrong. This is a common pitfall.

Date Arithmetic

Just as soon as you start working with the date data type, you will ask the question "How many days ago did we change the oil in the car?" Date arithmetic allows you to find this answer. When you add two to a date column, Oracle knows that you mean two days. Say the column sale_date contains 03-MAR-97; in this case, the SQL statement **select sale_date+3 from customer;** would return 06-MAR-97. Let's look at two more examples with date arithmetic.

VIP

Date arithmetic can be one of the most frustrating operations in SQL*Plus. Oracle is very stringent with the rules on date formats upon which arithmetic can be performed.

The statement **select last_name, sale_date+10 from customer;** tells Oracle to add ten days to the value in the sale_date column. A sale_date containing 17-MAR-96 would display as 27-MAR-96. Oracle takes care of arithmetic that spans month or year boundaries. For example, the statement **select to_char(sysdate+14) from dual;** will return 06-JAN-96 on 23-DEC-95.

Converting from One Column Type to Another

Many times, you may want to convert a data column from one data type to another (e.g., number to date, character to number). Oracle has three main conversion functions.

- **to_char** converts any data type to character data type. The statement **select to_char(8897) from dual;** returns a character data type answer containing the characters 8897.

- **to_number** converts a valid set of numeric character data (e.g., character data 8897) to number data type. The statement **select to_number('8897') from dual;** returns a number data type answer containing the number 8897.

- **to_date** converts character data of the proper format to date data type. This is the conversion that provides the most problems. The statement **select to_date('12-DEC-97') from dual;** succeeds, since 12-DEC-97 is a valid date format. However, problems arise if you pass the statement **select to_date('bad date') from dual;** to Oracle.

VIP

Using the **to_date** conversion mechanism can generate a wide assortment of Oracle errors when it receives bad date format data.

■ Update, Delete, and Alter

You will probably use these three SQL commands the most after **select**. Many SQL programs you write will have a mixture of these statements coupled with queries starting with **select**.

update

Sometimes it is necessary to update data stored within a table. You do this via the **update** command. The command has three parts:

- The word **update** followed by the table you want to change. This is mandatory.

- The word **set** followed by one or more columns you want to change. This is mandatory.

- The word **where** followed by selection criteria. This is optional.

For example, say you want to change all the sales figures to zero in the customer table. You would issue the SQL statement **update customer set sales = 0;** and Oracle would respond with the number of rows updated. If you want to change only those customers from state_cd of MA to zero, you could use the SQL statement **update customer set sales = 0 where state_cd = 'MA';**. As you can see, the update command is a very powerful tool at your disposal.

delete

The **delete** command is used when you want to remove one or more rows of data from a table. The command has two parts:

- The words **delete from** followed by the table name you want to remove data from. This is mandatory.

- The word **where** followed by the criteria for the **delete**. This is optional.

Let's take a closer look at the **delete** command. If you want to remove all the customer records, you could issue the SQL statement **delete from customer;**. If you just want to delete records with customers from state_cd CA, you would use the SQL statement **delete from customer where state_cd = 'CA';**.

alter

After a table is created, you sometimes realize you need to add an additional column. You do this with the **alter table** command. For example, the statement **alter table customer add (sale_date date);** would successfully add the sale_date column to the customer table if it did not exist. Most of the time, you will use **alter** to add a column to a table. The statement **alter table x modify (col1 date);** is used to change the data type for a column that already exists in a table.

You are allowed to stack the columns in the **alter table** statement. The command **alter table x modify (col1 date, col5 number(3,1));** is just as valid as two separate alter statements.

> *VIP*
> There are some strict rules governing what types of **alter table** statements are valid under what conditions. If you enter an invalid **alter table** statement, Oracle informs you and tells you why it is not valid.

Joining Two Tables Together

In the real world, much of the data you need is in more than one table. Many times, you need to go to multiple tables. For example, let's say that in the customer table you only store the state code; then, if you want the state name, you would need to join the customer table to the state table. You do this by joining the tables together. By definition, relational databases such as Oracle allow you to relate (or join) two or more tables based on common fields. Most often, these fields are what we refer to as key fields.

There are two types of keys: primary and foreign. A primary key is what makes a row of data unique within a table. In the state table, state_cd is the primary key. The customer table also contains state_cd, which in this case is a foreign key. One table's foreign key is used to get information out of another (foreign) table. With this in mind, let's take a look at two tables, X and Y first mentioned in the "create Statement" section of this chapter. The SQL statement **select * from x;** returns these rows:

```
col
---
1
2
3
```

The statement **select * from y;** returns these rows:

```
col
----
3
4
5
```

Let's see what happens when you join the two tables together. Oracle allows you to give tables an alternate name, called an *alias*. In this case, we are going to give tableX the alias right and tableY the alias left. Then, we can use the alternate names with the columns to keep things clear. The statement **select right.col, left.col from x right, y left where right.col = left.col;** yields the following output:

```
right.col left.col
--------- --------
3               3
```

Notice the col column values in both tables were compared, and the SQL statement required both tables to match on their respective col column values. The only column value that matches both tableX and tableY is the row with the number 3 in the col column value. Hence, only one row is selected as the tables are joined.

Formatting the Output

Up to now, we have learned how to **create** and **alter** tables, **insert** data into the tables, **update** and **delete** from the tables, and convert from one data type to another. Now we'll learn how to put it all together and write a great report. In SQL*Plus, you can set many parameters to control how SQL*Plus output is displayed. You can see all the current settings by issuing the SQL*Plus command **show all**. The output from this command resembles the following:

```
feedback ON for 6 or more rows
heading ON
linesize 80
numwidth 10
spool ON
user is "SYSTEM"
space 1
worksize DEFAULT
lines will be wrapped
```

```
pagesize 14
showmode OFF
pause is OFF
ttitle OFF and is the 1st few ...
btitle OFF and is the 1st few ...
define "&" (hex 26)
escape OFF
concat "." (hex 2e)
sqlprompt "SQL> "
underline "-" (hex 2d)
null ""
verify ON
message ON
sqlcode 0
tab ON
scan ON
dclsep OFF
termout ON
echo OFF
sqlcase MIXED
headsep "¦" (hex 7c)
maxdata 32767
time OFF
cmdsep OFF
xisql OFF
sqlterminator ";" (hex 3b)
sqlprefix "#" (hex 23)
release 39512
sqlnumber ON
autocommit OFF
newpage 1
long 80
document ON
trimout ON
timing OFF
qbidebug OFF
numformat ""
synonym OFF
suffix "SQL"
flush ON
sqlcontinue "SQL>"
pno 1
lno 15
```

```
buffer SQL
embedded OFF
arraysize 15
crt ""
copycommit 0
compatibility version NATIVE
recsep WRAP
recsepchar " " (hex 20)
blockterminator "." (hex 2e)
copytypecheck is ON
longchunksize 80
serveroutput OFF
flagger OFF
```

As you can see, there are many parameters you can set to alter your environment. We are going to change the major ones.

Page and Line Size

The **set linesize** command tells Oracle how wide the page is. The most common settings are 80 and 132. To set the line size to 80, enter the command **set linesize 80**. The **set pagesize** command tells Oracle how long the page is. The most common settings are 55 and 60. To make it easier to see the page breaks, you can set this parameter to 30 using the command **set pagesize 30**.

Page Titles

You can also tell Oracle how you want the page title to show up. The **ttitle** command includes many options. We usually stick with the default settings: the text shown in the title is centered on the line, and the date and page number are printed on every page. To place the title on two lines, use the vertical bar character (¦) to get SQL*Plus to issue two lines. The command **ttitle 'Database Technologies¦Customer Report'** tells SQL*Plus to center the text "Database Technologies" on the first title line, then to skip to line two and center the text "Customer Report."

Page Footers

The **btitle** command is used to place something on the bottom of every page. We recommend putting the program name there. Then, when users want you to change a report, all they need to tell you is the name on the bottom. This can help avoid a lot of confusion. The command **btitle '--- sample.sql ---'** tells SQL*Plus to center the text "--- sample.sql ---" at the bottom of every page. You can use the words **left** or **right** to place the text in **btitle** elsewhere than the center of the page; if no placement word is included in **btitle**, Oracle places the text in the center.

Writing SQL*Plus Output to a File

The **spool** command tells Oracle to save SQL*Plus output to a datafile. To use the **spool** command, you include the name of the output file. On a PC, for example, this can be done by entering the command **spool c:\report\out.lis**. Most operating systems append the text .lst to the end of the name you specify. For example, the command **spool report** will produce a file called report.lst.

VIP
SQL*Plus adds an extension to the filename mentioned in the **spool** command. This extension can differ among operating systems.

Say we have issued the commands **set linesize 35**, **set pagesize 23** and formatted the sales column using the command **col sales format 99999999**. We want to save the output of the SQL statement **select * from customer;** to a file. The output from that command is shown in Figure 5-1; this output would be captured

```
                          Oracle SQL*Plus              18:15
 File  Edit  Search  Options  Help
Sat Mar 18                                          page    1
                    Database Technologies
                      Customer Report

LAST_NAME                 ST           SALES
---------------------     --    ----------------
Teplow                    MA           23446
Abbey                     CA            6970
Porter                    CA            6990
Martin                    CA            2345
Laursen                   CA              34
Bambi                     CA            1235
McGraw                    NJ             123




                    --- sample.sql ---

7 rows selected.
```

FIGURE 5-1. *Sample formatted output*

in the filename specified with the **spool** statement. Notice that there are no decimal digits in the sales since the column was formatted using **99999999**.

To stop spooling, issue the command **spool off** or **spool out**. The latter closes the output file and prints it as well.

Formatting Columns in the Output

Most times, you need to format the actual column data. You do this through the **column** command. Let's issue two additional formatting commands, then reissue the query on the customer table.

The command **column last_name format a8 wrap heading 'Last¦Name'** tells SQL*Plus that there should be only eight characters displayed in the last_name column. The **8** places a length on the display width of last_name, and the **a** tells SQL*Plus that it will be only character data. The **wrap** portion tells SQL*Plus that if a last_name shows up that is longer than eight characters, the extra characters should spill onto the next line. The **heading** portion tells SQL*Plus to print the heading "Last Name" on the report, split over two lines.

The command **column state_cd format a8 heading 'State¦Code'** tells SQL*Plus to reserve eight positions for display of the state_cd and put the two-line heading "State Code" at the top of the state code column.

Now the identical SQL statement **select * from customer;** will produce the output shown in Figure 5-2.

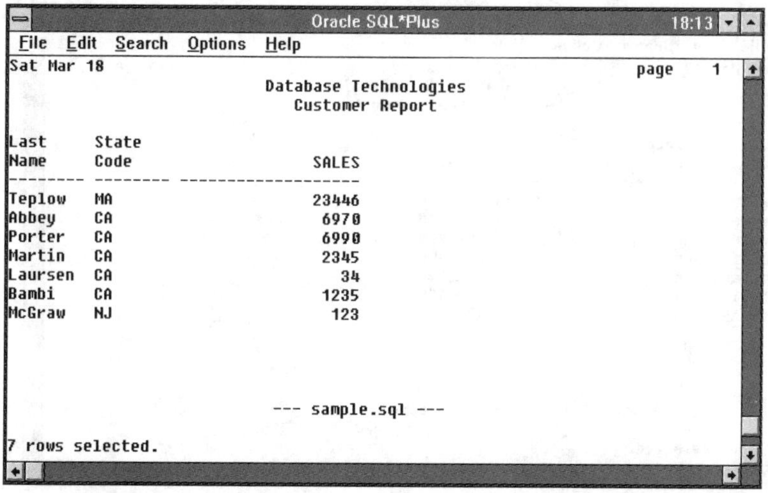

FIGURE 5-2.   *Output with two-column formatting commands*

Hey—pretty slick! Now let's format the number field. The **format** clause indicates the number of places to use to display each number and where to insert the commas. The statement **column sales format 999,999,999,999.999 heading 'Sales'** tells SQL*Plus to print up to 12 integer digits and three decimal digits, using the commas to separate the thousands. The enhanced report output is shown in Figure 5-3.

Break Logic

Now let's add some break logic. Refer to the "Sample Report #2" section of Chapter 8 where we explain control break logic. One of the things SQL*Plus makes easy is dealing with breaking. As soon as you issue the **break** command, SQL*Plus is smart enough to manage all break logic for you.

Let's look at the SQL query **select state_cd, last_name, sales from customer order by state_cd, last_name;**, with the column format command **col sales format 999999.99**. Without using break logic, the output from this query is shown in Figure 5-4.

Let's issue the command **break on state_cd**, and the same query output changes to what is shown in Figure 5-5.

Notice how the state_cd CA prints in line 1, is suppressed in lines 2 through 5 (since the state_cd has not changed from line 1), then prints again in lines 6 and 7 with different values.

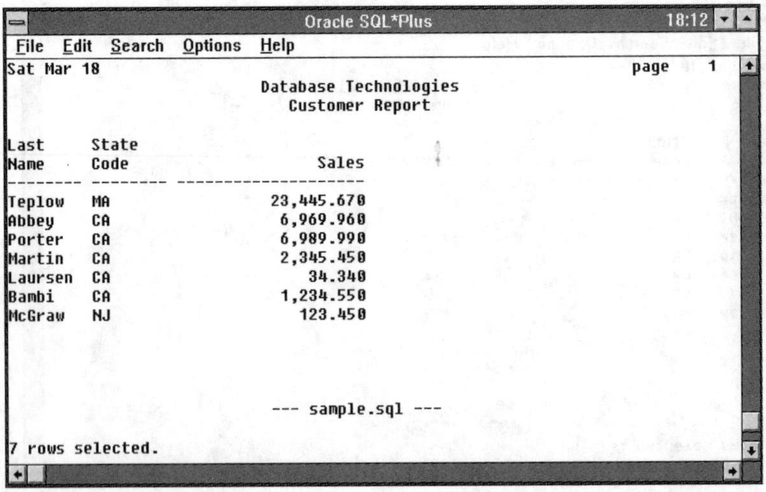

FIGURE 5-3. *Output with all columns formatted*

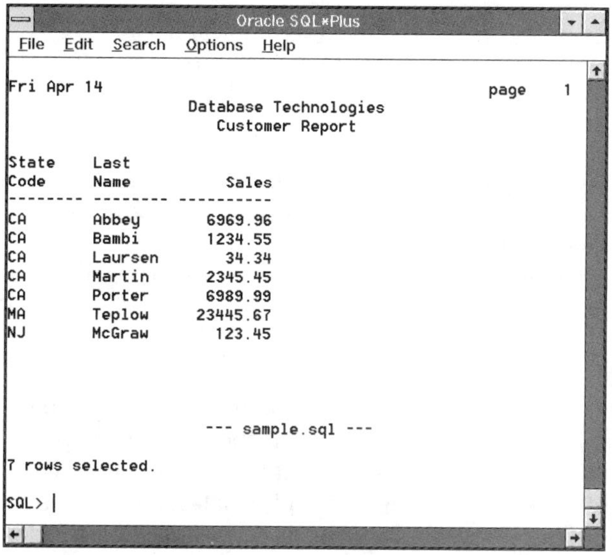

```
─                      Oracle SQL*Plus                 ▼ ▲
 File   Edit   Search   Options   Help
                                                            ↑
Fri Apr 14                                  page    1
                    Database Technologies
                      Customer Report

State     Last
Code      Name          Sales
--------  --------  ----------
CA        Abbey        6969.96
CA        Bambi        1234.55
CA        Laursen        34.34
CA        Martin       2345.45
CA        Porter       6989.99
MA        Teplow      23445.67
NJ        McGraw        123.45



                    --- sample.sql ---

7 rows selected.

SQL> |                                                     ↓
←  □                                                   →
```

FIGURE 5-4.   *Output after altering format of sales*

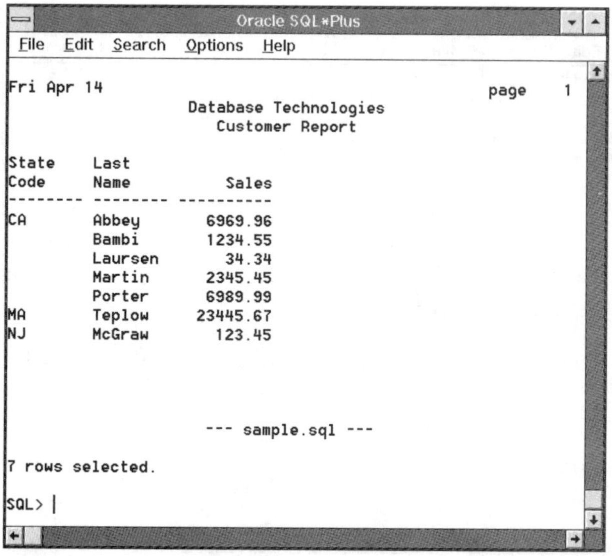

```
─                      Oracle SQL*Plus                 ▼ ▲
 File   Edit   Search   Options   Help
                                                            ↑
Fri Apr 14                                  page    1
                    Database Technologies
                      Customer Report

State     Last
Code      Name          Sales
--------  --------  ----------
CA        Abbey        6969.96
          Bambi        1234.55
          Laursen        34.34
          Martin       2345.45
          Porter       6989.99
MA        Teplow      23445.67
NJ        McGraw        123.45



                    --- sample.sql ---

7 rows selected.

SQL> |                                                     ↓
←  □                                                   →
```

FIGURE 5-5.   *Break report output*

VIP
To implement break logic in SQL*Plus, you must order the query by the same column on which the break command is issued.

To illustrate this point, the command **break on state_cd** followed by the query **select state_cd,name,sales from customer order by last_name;** would produce the output shown in Figure 5-6.

Notice how ordering the query results by last_name has interfered with the desired output.

Break and Skip

Let's take this one step further. Often, when implementing break logic, we want to leave one or more blank lines before displaying the new break column value. This is done with the **skip** command. Let's reformat the sales column with the command **col sales format $999,999,999.99 heading 'YTD¦Sales'** and reissue the break with **break on state_cd skip 1**. Now the statement **select state_cd,last_name,sales from customer order by state_cd,last_name;** produces the output shown in Figure 5-7.

Notice how Oracle suppresses printing of the state_cd every time. You could have easily told Oracle to compute total sales at each break. We discuss this in the next section.

```
─                        Oracle SQL*Plus                        ▼ ▲
 File  Edit  Search  Options  Help
Fri Apr 14                                          page      1      ↑
                      Database Technologies
                         Customer Report

State     Last            YTD
Code      Name           Sales
--------  --------  ----------
CA        Abbey       6969.96
          Bambi       1234.55
          Laursen       34.34
          Martin      2345.45
NJ        McGraw       123.45
CA        Porter      6989.99
MA        Teplow     23445.67




                --- sample.sql ---

7 rows selected.

SQL>                                                                ↓
 ←                                                                →
```

FIGURE 5-6. *Output with break on state_cd and ordered by last_name*

```
┌─────────────────────────────────────────────────────────┐
│ ═                    Oracle SQL*Plus             ▼ ▲     │
│  File  Edit  Search  Options  Help                       │
│ ┌───────────────────────────────────────────────────┐ ▲ │
│ │Fri Apr 14                                  page   1│   │
│ │                  Database Technologies             │   │
│ │                   Customer Report                  │   │
│ │                                                    │   │
│ │State   Last              YTD                       │   │
│ │Code    Name             Sales                      │   │
│ │-------- -------- ------------------                 │   │
│ │CA      Abbey         $6,969.96                      │   │
│ │        Bambi         $1,234.55                      │   │
│ │        Laursen          $34.34                      │   │
│ │        Martin        $2,345.45                      │   │
│ │        Porter        $6,989.99                      │   │
│ │                                                    │   │
│ │MA      Teplow       $23,445.67                      │   │
│ │                                                    │   │
│ │NJ      McGraw          $123.45                      │   │
│ │                                                    │   │
│ │                                                    │   │
│ │                                                    │   │
│ │                  --- sample.sql ---                │   │
│ │                                                    │   │
│ │7 rows selected.                                    │   │
│ │                                                    │   │
│ │SQL>                                                │ ▼ │
│ │←■                                                → │   │
│ └───────────────────────────────────────────────────┘   │
└─────────────────────────────────────────────────────────┘
```

FIGURE 5-7.   *Break report output with one line after break*

Computing Column Values at Break

You just need to tell SQL*Plus what you want added up, using the **compute sum** command. Let's now issue the commands necessary to complete the formatting of the break and to compute the YTD totals.

The command **compute sum of sales on report** forces a report total at the end of the output. The word **report** is used here to trigger the sum of a number field to be displayed at the end of a report. The command **compute sum of sales on state_cd** forces totals to be printed for a state when a new state code is printed.

To print the report total, we need to reset the break conditions with the command **break on report skip 1 on state_cd skip 1**. We change the SQL statement to sort the data by state_cd. Ordering the data by the same column mentioned in the **break** statement is necessary for break reporting.

NOTE

You may have to increase the page size to get the output from this section to print on one page. Do so by entering the command **set pagesize 28**.

The SQL statement is now **select state_cd, last_name, sales from customer order by state_cd, last_name;**. Figure 5-8 shows the break output after reformatting the sales column with the statement **col sales format $999,999,999.999 heading 'YTD¦Sales'**.

```
Oracle SQL*Plus
File   Edit   Search   Options   Help

Fri Apr 14                                          page    1

                   Database Technologies
                     Customer Report

State    Last                         YTD
Code     Name                        Sales
-------- --------        ------------------
CA       Abbey                  $6,969.960
         Bambi                  $1,234.550
         Laursen                   $34.340
         Martin                 $2,345.450
         Porter                 $6,989.990
xxxxxxxx                 ------------------
sum                            $17,574.290

MA       Teplow                $23,445.670
xxxxxxxx                 ------------------
sum                            $23,445.670

NJ       McGraw                   $123.450
xxxxxxxx                 ------------------
sum                               $123.450

                         ------------------
sum                            $41,143.410

                       --- sample.sql ---
```

FIGURE 5-8.   *Break report output with totals by state_cd and at end of report*

Break Logic and Compute Sum Using Two Tables

Finally, let's utilize what we've learned in this chapter to show a final report. Recall the earlier "Joining Two Tables Together" section where we discussed joins: you select data from more than one table and match column values from one against the other. Now, rather than printing the state_cd, let's print the state name instead.

We need the state_name column from the state table, and we can join the state table to the customer table via state_cd. The select statement becomes **select state_name, last_name, sales from state a,customer b where a.state_cd = b.state_cd order by state_name, last_name;**. And since we are using the state_name column, we have to restate the break conditions to SQL*Plus using **break on report skip 1 on state_name skip 1**. We also need to define the **compute sum** statements for state_name and the report with **compute sum of sales on state_name** and **compute sum of sales on report**. We are now ready to issue the query joining the two tables, and the output produced is shown in Figure 5-9.

What's Next

Now, that was a chapter! You've come a long way! You are well on your way to becoming familiar with the power of SQL and Oracle's SQL*Plus. Not a bad report writer, you say. No argument here. We have been using SQL*Plus since day one.

```
┌─────────────────────────────────────────────────────────────┐
│  ─                      Oracle SQL*Plus              ▼  ▲    │
│  File  Edit  Search  Options  Help                          │
│ ┌─────────────────────────────────────────────────────┐ ▲  │
│ │Fri Apr 14                              page    1      │ ▲  │
│ │                 Database Technologies                │    │
│ │                   Customer Report                    │    │
│ │                                                      │    │
│ │                         Last              YTD        │    │
│ │STATE_NAME               Name            Sales        │    │
│ │---------------------------   --------  ------------- │    │
│ │California               Abbey      $6,969.960        │    │
│ │                         Bambi      $1,234.550        │    │
│ │                         Laursen       $34.340        │    │
│ │                         Martin     $2,345.450        │    │
│ │                         Porter     $6,989.990        │    │
│ │xxxxxxxxxxxxxxxxxxxxxxxxxxxxxx       ------------- │    │
│ │sum                                 $17,574.290        │    │
│ │                                                      │    │
│ │Massachusetts            Teplow    $23,445.670        │    │
│ │xxxxxxxxxxxxxxxxxxxxxxxxxxxxxx       ------------- │    │
│ │sum                                 $23,445.670        │    │
│ │                                                      │    │
│ │New Jersey               McGraw       $123.450        │    │
│ │xxxxxxxxxxxxxxxxxxxxxxxxxxxxxx       ------------- │    │
│ │sum                                    $123.450        │    │
│ │                                                      │    │
│ │                                    ------------- │    │
│ │sum                                 $41,143.410        │    │
│ │                                                      │    │
│ │                 --- sample.sql ---                   │ ▼  │
│ │◄ ■                                                 ►│    │
│ └─────────────────────────────────────────────────────┘    │
└─────────────────────────────────────────────────────────────┘
```

FIGURE 5-9.   *Final report output*

It's a workhorse and always will be. As you experiment with its features, you will be amazed at how much you can do with it.

As the first chapter of the Developer Basics section of this book, you have a solid groundwork with SQL. Follow the next few chapters as we discuss more tools you need to be familiar with as you jump into Oracle at the deep end. We'll be back . . . .

CHAPTER 6

PL/SQL

Programmers need to be able to assemble a set of data and process the results of a query one row at a time. Imagine arriving at the supermarket checkout counter with a cartload of groceries and insisting the checkout person pass everything over the bar code scanner at once. That person would have absolutely no control over what is being processed—it's all or nothing. Without the ability to manipulate data row by row, the programmer, depending on the application's requirements, could be likened to that poor checkout person; you could be that checkout person. With version 6, Oracle implemented a procedural processing language referred to as PL/SQL (pronounced "pea ell sequel") that will make your job a great deal easier. PL/SQL has programming constructs that resemble most programming languages.

There are two versions of PL/SQL: one is part of the database engine, the other is a separate engine embedded in a number of Oracle tools. We call them database PL/SQL and tool PL/SQL. They are very similar; they use the same programming constructs, syntax, and logic mechanisms. Tool PL/SQL has additional syntax designed to support the requirements of the tools. For example, to place a push button on a form to navigate to the bottom of the screen, the movement would be coded using PL/SQL in an Oracle Forms system. This chapter will deal with database PL/SQL. The extra constructs and some of the extra syntax used in tool PL/SQL in Oracle Forms is covered in Chapter 7.

In this chapter, you will learn about the following:

- Where Oracle uses PL/SQL
- PL/SQL character set
- Variables and PL/SQL reserved words
- Common data types
- Components of PL/SQL
- Cursors
- Coding conventions
- The look and feel of PL/SQL
- Dealing with compilation errors

In the middle of some PL/SQL code examples in this chapter, we will use three dots (...) to indicate omissions. These dots are not part of the code; they indicate portions of code unnecessary to the point at hand.

Terminology

The following definitions will arm you with the technical jargon to make it through this chapter.

- An *executable* is the name of a program written using one of the assortment of computer programming languages. When you type the name of an executable, the program runs. For example, when you use SQL*Plus, you enter the command **sqlplus**.

■ A *character set* describes the range of characters that a computer language supports and displays in reports. Most programming languages, including PL/SQL, can display as text just about any character set.

■ *Arithmetic operators* are symbols used to define mathematical operations with data. Common operators are +, -, *, and / .

■ *Relational operators* define states of comparison or choice, such as comparing two dates to see their relationship to one another. Common operators are >, <, and <> .

■ *Variables* are programmer-defined names to hold items of information.

■ *Reserved words* have special meaning to PL/SQL. They are reserved for use by Oracle and cannot be used as variable names. For example, the word "declare" means something special to PL/SQL and cannot be used as a variable name.

■ A *data type* defines the class of a piece of information (data). In everyday terminology, we are used to classifying information as numeric or character. The character data type contains all representable characters from a specific alphabet. The numeric data type contains the decimal digits 0 through 9.

■ A *loop* is a construct in a computer program where a segment of code is executed repeatedly.

■ An *exit condition* is the part of a loop where a test is performed on data and, if the test evaluates to TRUE, the loop terminates.

■ *Control structures* influence the flow of processing in a computer program. If there were two different ways to process data, the mechanism used to decide which processing route to follow is a control structure.

Why Do I Need to Know PL/SQL?

When we first started using PL/SQL, we looked around on the disk for an executable called plsql. We did not find one, so then we tried writing PL/SQL blocks in SQL*Plus. Lo and behold—there it was! If you have access to Oracle Forms or its predecessor SQL*Forms version 3, then that is the best way to learn PL/SQL and hone your skills. When using Oracle stored procedures, database triggers, packages, and functions, all the coding is done using PL/SQL. You will not get very far with Oracle without knowing PL/SQL. It is the basis of all the programming you may end up doing in the following Oracle tools:

- Oracle Forms
- Oracle Reports
- SQL*Module
- Oracle Graphics
- Oracle Glue

If you want to become fluent with the Oracle product set, PL/SQL must become part of your skill set. If you have any programming experience with ADA, PL/SQL will seem very familiar. We will cover some introductory concepts and programming constructs in this chapter. As you become more familiar with PL/SQL, you will be able to take advantage of its rich features.

PL/SQL Character Set

As with all other programming languages, there is a set of characters you use in PL/SQL. Just about any character you can enter from the keyboard is a PL/SQL character, yet there are rules about using some characters in some situations. In this section, you will learn details on:

- Characters you may use when programming in PL/SQL
- Arithmetic operators
- Relational operators
- Miscellaneous symbols

Characters Supported

When programming in PL/SQL, you are limited to the following characters:

- All uppercase and lowercase letters
- Digits 0 through 9
- Symbols ( ) + - * / < > = ! ~ ; : . ' @ % , " # $ ^ & _ ¦ { } ? [ ]

Some of these characters are for code; others serve as arithmetic operators (division, addition, exponents, etc.) and relational operators (equal and not equal).

For example, in a communications application, the developer may use a variable named "area_code" to store a client's calling area. The choice "area_code" of the characters **a r e a _ c o d e** conform to the rules outlined in the Variables section of this chapter.

Arithmetic Operators

The following table shows the common arithmetic operators used in PL/SQL. If you are familiar with other high-level programming languages, this will not be new to you.

OPERATOR	MEANING	OPERATOR	MEANING
+	addition	-	subtraction
*	multiplication	/	division
**	exponentiation		

Relational Operators

The next table shows the PL/SQL relational operators. If you have experience with any other programming languages, then you have seen these symbols before.

OPERATOR	MEANING	OPERATOR	MEANING
<>	not equal	!=	not equal
^=	not equal	<	less than
>	greater than	=	equal

Miscellaneous Symbols

To support programming in PL/SQL, the following symbols are used. This table shows a partial list of symbols; they are the most commonly used symbols and the ones you must know to start using PL/SQL.

SYMBOL	MEANING	EXAMPLE
()	list separators	and NAME in ('JONES','ROY','ABRAMSON')
;	end-of-statement	procedure_name (arg1,arg2);

SYMBOL	MEANING	EXAMPLE
.	item separator (in the example, it separates an account name from a table name)	select '' from account.table_name;
'	character string enclosure	if var1 = 'SANDRA' ...
:=	assignment	rec_read := rec_read + 1;
¦¦	concatenation	full_name := 'LAUREL' ¦¦ ' ' ¦¦ 'LOWRY';
--	comment delimiter	-- This is a comment
/* and */	comment delimiters	/* This too is a comment */

Variables

Variables are names used in PL/SQL to process items of data. The programmer selects names to use for these variables based on the following rules.

- Variables must start with a letter (A-Z).
- Variables can be optionally followed by one or more letters, numbers (0-9), or the special characters $, #, or _.
- Variables must be no longer than 30 characters.
- There can be no spaces imbedded in the variable name.

With these three rules in hand, let's look at some examples. Table 6-1 shows sample variable names and determines their validity.

Reserved Words

Think of a reserved word as being copyrighted by PL/SQL. When choosing names for variables, you cannot use these reserved words. For example, the word "loop" means something to PL/SQL, and the following segment of code would be invalid.

```
declare
  employee varchar2(30);
  loop number;
```

You are not permitted to use a reserved word as a variable name. We do not recommend it, but if you want to, you may join two reserved words together (e.g.,

VARIABLE NAME	VALID?	REASON
23_skidoo	No	Must start with a letter
nature_trail	Yes	
nature-trail	No	Only special characters are $ # or _
love boat	No	Cannot contain any white space
a_very_insignificant_variable_name	No	Longer than 30 characters
me_____and$$$$$you	Yes	
lots_of_$$$$$$	Yes	
23	No	Must start with a letter

TABLE 6-1. *Valid and Invalid Variable Names*

loop_varchar2) to build a variable name. A complete list of PL/SQL reserved words can be found by entering the command **help command** while logged into SQL*Plus. SQL*Plus is discussed in Chapters 5 and 11 of this book.

NOTE
You or your database administrator must have installed SQL*Plus online help for this command to succeed. If Oracle responds with "HELP not accessible", help is not set up.

Common Data Types

So far, we have discussed the characters that can be used when programming in PL/SQL, naming variables, and reserved words. Now we move on to the data itself. A PL/SQL program is written to manipulate and display many different types of data. Oracle, like all computer software, has data types (e.g., character) divided into a number of sub-types. For example, some of the sub-types of the number datatype are integer (i.e., no decimal digits allowed) and decimal (i.e., number with one or more decimal digits). PL/SQL supports a wide range of data types. This section gives an overview of what you will run across most often and find most useful in your code.

In this section, you will learn details on the following data types:

 varchar2

 number

date

■ Boolean

varchar2

This is a variable-length, alphanumeric data type. In PL/SQL, it can have a length of up to 32,767 bytes. The definition in the **declare** section is terminated by the semicolon (;), and all varchar2 definitions are done to resemble

```
variable_name varchar2(max_length);
```

where the length in parentheses must be a positive integer, as in

```
vc_field varchar2(10);
```

It may be initialized (i.e., set to its initial value) at the same time by using the syntax

```
vc_field varchar2(10) := 'STARTVALUE';
```

number

This data type can be used to represent all numeric data. The format of the declaration is

```
num_field number(precision,scale)
```

where precision can be from 1 to 38 characters, and scale represents the number of positions specified by precision that are for decimal digits. Keep in mind that the declaration

```
num_field (12,2)
```

describes a variable that can have up to ten integer digits (precision[12] - scale [2]) and up to two decimal digits.

date

This data type is used to store fixed-length date values. The declaration takes no qualifiers and is done as

```
date_field date;
```

Oracle displays dates in the format *DD-MON-YY*; thus September 26, 1984 is displayed as 26-SEP-84. When programming with dates in PL/SQL, you must use this format.

boolean

This data type is a switch that holds the status TRUE or FALSE. When you use this data type, you test its status and then can do one thing if it is true, something else if false. For example, say you were trying to see if a corporation had distributed a 10K form for its 1996 fiscal year. Using a boolean variable, it would be set to TRUE if the form had been filed.

PL/SQL Components

We now move on to a discussion of how PL/SQL is put together. Using the knowledge from the previous few sections, we can start to formulate some living and breathing code examples. PL/SQL offers the standard set of procedural techniques that developers have been using since the dawn of computers: logic, looping, and error handling mechanisms.

In this section, you will learn details on the following topics:

- Exceptions
- Control structures, including program control, **if** logic structures, and looping structures
- "Do nothing" construct
- **declare** section

Exceptions

This is the PL/SQL method of dealing with error conditions. In a real-world application, you may not find the information you are looking for when you attempt to retrieve data. Oracle carries on processing until it completes successfully or encounters an error condition. Table 6-2 lists common PL/SQL exceptions; by testing for these exceptions, you can detect errors that your PL/SQL programs raise.

Control Structures

Control structures are the heart of any programming language. Since most systems are written to handle a number of different situations, the way different conditions

EXCEPTION	EXPLANATION
no_data_found	If a **select** statement attempts to retrieve data based on its conditions, this exception is raised when no rows satisfy the select criteria.
too_many_rows	Since each implicit cursor is capable of retrieving only one row, this exception detects existence of more than one row. (See the "Implicit Cursors" section later in this chapter, where we define and discuss implicit cursors.)
dup_val_on_index	This exception detects an attempt to create an entry in an index whose key column values already exist. For example, suppose a billing application is keyed on the invoice number. If a program tries to create a duplicate invoice number, this exception would be raised.
value_error	This exception indicates that there has been an assignment operation where the target field is not long enough to hold the value being placed in it. For example, if the text ABCDEFGH is assigned to a variable defined as "varchar2(6)", then this exception is raised.

TABLE 6-2.   *Most Common Exceptions Used in PL/SQL*

are detected and dealt with is the biggest part of program control. This section provides you with details on the following topics:

- Program control
- Three types of the **if** logic structure
- Four types of looping structures

Program Control

Program control is governed by the status of the variables it uses and the data it reads and writes from the database. As an example, picture yourself going to the DMV (license bureau) to renew your car registration. When you enter the building, you are presented with the instructions "Sticker renewals in Room 12-G." Once you find 12-G, you receive these instructions: "Cash/certified check ONLY in lines 1 and 2. All payment types accepted in lines 3 to 15." Your decision making begins with the question "Why am I here?" The program control for this decision making example is shown in Table 6-3.

PROCESS OR DECISION TO MAKE	NEXT STEP	
1. Here for driver's license transactions	YES=5	NO=2
2. Here for car registration renewals	YES=7	NO=3
3. Here for driving test	YES=11	NO=4
4. Oh oh, in the wrong building!	13	
5. Go to room 12-A and carry on desired transaction	13	
6. Go to room 12-B and carry on desired transaction	13	
7. Go to room 12-G	8	
8. Paying by cash or certified check	YES=10	NO=9
9. Paying by check or credit card	YES=11	NO=12
10. Do cash or certified check transaction	13	
11. Do check or credit card transaction	13	
12. They don't take play money!	13	
13. Leave building		

TABLE 6-3.   *Program Control Decision Making*

if Logic Structures

When writing computer programs, situations present themselves in which you must test a condition; when it evaluates to TRUE you do one thing, when it evaluates to FALSE you do something different. PL/SQL has three **if** logic structures that allow you to test true/false conditions. In most computer programs, many lines of code will test the value of a variable and, based on its value, do one or more operations. In everyday life, we are continually bombarded with decision making; this is how you code decision making with PL/SQL.

if-then   This construct tests a simple condition. If the condition evaluates to TRUE, one or more lines of code are executed. If the condition evaluates to FALSE, program control is passed to the next statement after the test. The following code illustrates implementing this logic in PL/SQL.

```
if var1 > 10 then
   var2 := var1 + 20;
end if;
```

The test (in this case, >) is a relational operator we spoke about in the "PL/SQL Character Set" section of this chapter. The statement could have been coded using the following instead, with the same results.

```
if not(var1 <= 10) then
    var2 := var1 + 20;
end if;
```

You may code nested **if-then** statements as shown in the following.

```
if var1 > 10 then
    if var2 < var 1 then
      var2 := var1 + 20;
    end if;
end if;
```

Notice the two **end if** parts in the previous code—one for each **if**. This leads us into two rules about implementing **if** logic in PL/SQL.

GUIDELINE 1
Each **if** statement is followed by its own **then**. There is no semicolon (;) terminator on the line that starts with "if."

GUIDELINE 2
Each **if** statement block is terminated by a matching **end if**.

if-then-else   This construct is similar to **if** except that when the condition evaluates to FALSE, one or more statements following the **else** are executed. The following code illustrates implementing this logic in PL/SQL.

```
if var1 > 10 then
    var2 := var1 + 20;
else
    var2 := var1 * var1;
end if;
```

Note that the same logic can be expressed the other way—adding 20 to var1 with the **else** and squaring var1 with the **if** branch of the statement.

```
if var1 <= 10 then
    var2 := var1 * var1;
else
    var2 := var1 + 20;
end if;
```

The statements can be nested, as shown in the following listing.

```
if var1 > 10 then
   var2 := var1 + 20;
else
   if var1 between 7 and 8 then
      var2 = 2* var1;
   else
      var2 := var1 * var1;
   end if;
end if;
```

This leads us to two more rules about implementing **if** logic in PL/SQL.

GUIDELINE 3
There can be one and only one **else** with every **if** statement.

GUIDELINE 4
There is no semicolon (;) terminator on the line starting with **else**.

if-then-elsif   This format is an alternative to using the nested **if-then-else** construct. The code in the previous listing could be reworded to read

```
if var1 > 10 then
   var2 := var1 + 20;
elsif var1 between 7 and 8 then
   var2 = 2* var1;
else
   var2 := var1 * var1;
end if;
```

This leads us into one final rule about implementing **if** logic in PL/SQL.

GUIDELINE 5
There is no matching **end if** with each **elsif**.

In this code segment, the **end if** appears to go with its preceding **elsif**:

```
if var1 > 10 then
    var2 := var1 + 20;
elsif var1 between 7 and 8 then
    var2 = 2* var1;
end if;
```

In fact, the **end if** belongs to the **if** that starts the whole block rather than the **elsif** keyword. Notice how the previous listings indent portions of the PL/SQL code to indicate to which conditions they belong.

NOTE

We recommend you use the indentation convention—it is easier to follow and understand the flow of logic and control.

Examine the following two listings, which illustrate nonindentation and indentation.

```
/* Code segment 1 - hard to follow. */
if var1 < 5 then var2 := 'Y'; elsif
var1 = 5 then
var2 := 'N';
else var2 := null; end if;
/*                                    */
/* Code segment 2 - easier to follow. */
if var1 < 5 then
    var2 :=  'Y';    --Statement is controlled by
                     --first test on var1 being true
elsif var1 = 5 then
    var2 := 'N';    --Statement is controlled by
                     --second test on var1 being true
else
    var2 := null;    -- Statement is controlled by second
                     --test on var1 being false
end if;
```

Using the license bureau (DMV) example from above, let's word the logic using PL/SQL

```
create or replace procedure licence_transaction
                (the_act in varchar2) as
```

```
begin
  if the_act = 'DLT' then
     room_12a
  elsif the_act = 'DT' then
     room_12g
  else
     room_12b
  end if;
end;
/
```

Looping

Looping provides the ability to execute a process over and over again until complete. In a real-life situation, think of looping when you unload your groceries from your car—there are two loops in this activity. The first is the repetitive action of picking up one or more grocery bags and walking in your front door. The second is the repetitive whine that comes from your lethargic 16-year-old: "Why is it always me who has to help?" In general, looping is based on the logic shown in Table 6-4.

One of the problems with coding loops is making sure there is code to allow it to terminate when an exit condition has been satisfied. Unfortunately, all too many times, developers write endless loops (we have never done that, of course, but we know many who have). The best way to sum up looping and the major problems programmers may have with it is to quote from an online technology dictionary we once saw:

Definition of LOOP: See "Definition of LOOP."

Implementing loops in PL/SQL is discussed in the next few sections.

PROCESS OR DECISION TO MAKE	NEXT STEP	
1. Set condition to enter loop (i.e., done_loop=N)	2	
2. End loop condition is true (i.e., done_loop=Y)	YES=6	NO=3
3. Process data	5	
4. There is more data to process	YES=2	NO=5
5. Set exit condition (i.e., done_loop=Y)	2	
6. Done processing		

TABLE 6-4. *Looping Logic*

Loop-exit-end loop   This construct contains three parts. Study the commented code below to see how this is used.

```
cnt := 1;                  --Initialize the loop counter before
                           --          loop starts
loop                       --Part 1: Loop keyword starts the loop
   cnt := cnt + 1;         --Part 2: Incrementing the loop counter
   if cnt > 100 then       --        Testing cnt for exit
                           --        condition
      exit;                --        End loop condition met,
                           --        so get out
   end if;                 --        "end-if" to match previous "if"
   ...
   ...
end loop;                  --Part 3: End loop keywords to end the
   ...                     --        loop
   ...
   ...
```

Loop-exit when-end loop   This is similar to the previous example, except the exit condition is detected differently.

```
cnt := 1;                  --Initialize the loop counter before
                           --     loop starts
loop                       --Part 1: Loop keyword starts the loop
   cnt := cnt + 1;         --Part 2: Incrementing the loop counter
   exit when cnt > 100     --        Test for exit condition by
   ...                     --        examining "cnt"
   ...
   ...
end loop;                  --Part 3: End loop keywords to end
   ...                     --        the loop
   ...
```

While-loop-end loop   With this construct, the exit condition is manually set somewhere inside the loop. The test for exit condition is accomplished by the comparison in the **while** part of the loop.

```
cnt := 1;                  --Initialize the loop counter before
                           --loop starts
while cnt <= 100 loop      --Part 1: The "while" checks exit
   ...                     --condition every time before executing
```

```
   ...                      --loop
   ...                      --Part 2: Code executed inside the loop
   ...
   cnt := cnt + 1;          --          Incrementing counter to arrive
   ...                      --          at exit condition
end loop;                   --Part 3: End loop keywords to end the loop
   ...
```

For-in-loop-end loop   The final construct we examine allows repetitive execution of a loop a predefined number of times. There are three parts to the loop:

- The **for in** portion, in which the variable to track the looping is defined

- The one or more statements within the loop that are executed until the variable controlling the loop reaches the exit condition value

- The **end loop** portion that terminates the loop

The following shows an example of how this loop mechanism can be used:

```
for cnt in 1 .. 3 loop
   insert into tab1 values ('Still in loop',cnt);
end loop;
```

"Do Nothing" or "Null" Construct

Sometimes, especially when using **if** logic, you end up testing a condition; when that condition is TRUE, you do nothing; when otherwise, you perform some operation. This is handled in PL/SQL in the following way:

```
if cnt >= 90 then
   null;
else
   insert into tab1 values (cnt,'Still less than 90');
end if;
```

The **null** keyword denotes performing no operation.

The declare Section

This part of PL/SQL blocks is where you define your variables. If you are familiar with COBOL, this is similar to working storage. You will see the common data types we discussed previously, plus the cursor variable type, which we cover in the next section. The following code is an example of a procedure's **declare** section.

```
create or replace procedure samp (parm1 in varchar2,
                                   parm2 in varchar2) as
begin
  declare
    accum1 number;
    accum2 number;
    h_date date := sysdate;   --Notice variables can be
                              --initialized here too.
    status_flag varchar2(1);
    mess_text varchar2(80);
    temp_buffer varchar2(1);
    cursor my_cursor is
      select ' '
        from person
       where last_name = parm1
         and sal_stat = parm2;
  begin
    ...
    ...
  end;
/
```

Cursors

PL/SQL uses cursors for management of SQL **select** statements. Cursors are chunks of memory allocated to process these statements. Sometimes you define the cursor manually, and other times you let PL/SQL define the cursor. A cursor is defined like any other PL/SQL variable and must conform to the same naming conventions. In this section, you will learn about both explicit and implicit PL/SQL cursors. Using explicit cursors, you must **declare** the cursor, **open** it before using it, and **close** it when it is no longer needed. Using implicit cursors, you do none of these; you simply code your **select** statement and let PL/SQL handle the cursor on its behalf.

Explicit Cursors

This technique defines a cursor as part of the **declare** section. The SQL statement defined must contain only **select** statements—there can be no **insert**, **update**, or **delete** keywords used. In this section, you will learn how to do the following:

- Name your explicit cursors
- Prepare (or open) an explicit cursor for use
- Fetch data using an explicit cursor
- Release the cursor's memory when done with it

The listing at the end of the previous section shows explicit cursor definition. When using explicit cursors, you always code four components:

- The cursor is defined in the **declare** section of your PL/SQL block.
- The cursor is opened after the initial **begin** in the PL/SQL block.
- The cursor is fetched into one or more variables. There must be the same number of receiving variables in the **fetch** as there are columns in the cursor's **select** list. For example, look at the following cursor definition:

```
declare cursor mycur is
  select first_name, last_name, ssn
    from person
  where pin = passed_pin;
```

- The cursor is closed after you are done using it.

The following listing puts these four parts together.

```
...
...
declare
  fname           varchar2(10),
  lname           varchar2(30),
  ssec_num        varchar2(8),
  cursor mycur is
    select first_name, last_name, ssn
      from person
      where pin = pin_in;
begin;
  open mycur;
  fetch mycur into fname, lname, ssec_num;
  if mycur%found then
     null;
  else
     insert into e_tab values (pin_in,sysdate);
```

```
    end if;
end;
...
...
/
```

Note the following points about explicit cursors:

■ The success or failure of the cursor (we call it "mycur" here) is determined by testing either "%found" or "%notfound." The cursor returns success if it retrieves a row from the database based on its selection criteria. This test must be done before the cursor is closed.

```
if mycur%found then
    ...
end if;
if mycur%notfound then
    ...
    ...
end if;
...
...
fetch mycur into temp_buffer;
close mycur;
--This will not work since the cursor has been closed.
if mycur%found then
    ...
    ...
end if;
```

■ If a cursor is repeatedly fetched in a loop construct, a running total of the number of rows retrieved so far can be found in the "%rowcount" system variable.

```
while counter < 100 loop
    fetch mycur into temp_buffer;
    if mycur%rowcount <= 50 then
        ...
    else
        ...
    end if;
counter := counter+1;
end loop;
```

■ All cursors must be fetched into one or more variables (depending on the number of columns in the cursor's **select** list). The following is not legal:

```
open mycur;
fetch mycur;
if mycur%found then
    ...
```

■ The target variable(s) of the cursor must match the columns in the table being selected in data type:

```
-- This is correct
--
declare
  cursor mycur is
    select pin,          /* pin is numeric        */
           last_name     /* last_name is character */
      from person
     where pin = pin_in;
  field1 varchar2(10);
  field2 number;
begin
  open mycur;
  fetch mycur into field2, field1;
  ...
-- This is incorrect
--
declare
  cursor mycur is
    select pin,          /* pin is numeric, last_name   */
           last_name     /* last_name is character data */
      from person
     where pin = pin_in;
  field1 varchar2(10);
  field2 number;
begin
  open mycur;
  fetch mycur into field1, field2;
  ...
```

In our example, the variable "temp_buffer" is used to receive the space selected, even though the ' ' (i.e., single space) is not a column in the person table.

A literal (e.g., the space or the characters ABC enclosed in single quotes) can be selected from any table.

You will receive an error if you try to open a cursor that is already open or close a cursor that has already been closed. You can check the status of a cursor using "%isopen", which evaluates to either TRUE or FALSE.

```
...
...
if mycur%isopen = 'TRUE' then
   null;
else
   open mycur;
end if;
```

If a PL/SQL block uses more than one cursor, each cursor must have a unique name.

Implicit Cursors

The following code segment uses implicit cursors. You place your **select** statement inline and PL/SQL handles cursor definition implicitly. There is no declaration of implicit cursors in the **declare** section.

```
...
begin
  if counter >= 20 then
     select last_name
        into lname from person
      where pin = pin_in;
     ...
  else
     ...
  end if;
end;
/
```

Note the following points that pertain to using implicit cursors:

■ There must be an **into** with each implicit cursor.

```
--This is incorrect
if this_value > 0 then
```

```
    select count(*) from person;
end if;
--This is OK
if this_value > 0 then
    select count(*) into cnter from person;
end if;
```

- As with explicit cursors, the variables that receive data with the **into** keyword must be the same data type as the column(s) in the table.

- Implicit cursors expect *only one row* to be returned. You must examine some of the exceptions, as discussed in Table 6-2. The most common ones to look out for are "no_data_found" and "too_many_rows."

```
...
if counter >= 10 then
    begin
      select age into person where pin = pin_value;
      exception
        when too_many_rows then
              insert into tabA values (pin_value, sysdate);
        when no_data_found then
              rollback;
    end;
end if;
...
...
/
```

Which Approach to Use

We find using explicit cursors more efficient and recommend you use them for the following reasons:

- The success or failure is found by examining the PL/SQL system variable "%found" or "%notfound". Code segments that use explicit cursors simply test one of these variables to detect success or failure of a **select** statement using an explicit cursor.

- Since the explicit cursor is manually defined in the **declare** section, the PL/SQL block can be more structured (the definitions are done in one place, and the code that uses the cursor is in another).

- The best programmers use them!

The Look of PL/SQL

PL/SQL is a mixture of SQL*Plus and procedural code. Comment text is delimited by the slash-asterisk combination (/* *comment* */) or two dashes (--), as in the following:

```
begin
  declare tfield varchar2(20);
  begin
    select desc
      into tfield
      from prod               /*  PROD is a central lookup */
     where pnum = 'FR4512';    /*  table owned by PLANNING   */
  end;
end;
/
```

or

```
begin
  declare tfield varchar2(20);
  begin
    select desc
      into tfield
      from prod               -- PROD is a central lookup
     where pnum = 'FR4512';    -- table owned by PLANNING
  end;
end;
/
```

Inspect the following PL/SQL code segment and study the comments. They will illustrate how the pieces of PL/SQL go together.

```
create or replace procedure do_trav
              (class_in in varchar2) as
  begin                       --This is the start of a PL/SQL block
    declare                   --Local variables and explicit
      cursor mycur is         --cursors are defined here
        select count(*)
          from person
         where class_code = class_in;
      cnt number;
      begin                   --This inner "begin" is start of the
```

```
    open mycur;              --code executed when the PL/SQL is
    fetch mycur into cnt; --invoked.
    if cnt > 100 then       --"If" procedural logic
       insert into trav_audit (class_in,cnt)
          values (classin,cnt);  --An implicit cursor
    else
       update trav_audit        --Inline update statement
       set cnt = cnt+1 where classin = class_in;
    end if;                  --"If" statement ends with "end-if"
  end;                       --Each "begin" terminated by
end;                         --matching "end" keyword
/                            --"/" terminates the PL/SQL block
```

Compilation Errors

When a PL/SQL block is passed to Oracle for compilation, you may be informed of some errors. As we indicate in the previous listing, the slash (/) terminates the PL/SQL block and passes the code to Oracle. Inspect the following error-ridden compilation. Note that the errors raised by a PL/SQL compilation are not displayed until you code the statement **sho errors**.

```
create or replace procedure temp (count in number) as
  begin
    declare cursor mycur is
      select count(*) from emp;
    begin;
      open mycur;
      fetch mycur;
    end;
 end;
/
Warning: Procedure created with compilation errors.
SQL> sho errors
Errors for PROCEDURE TEMP:
LINE/COL ERROR
-------- -------------------------------------------------
1/17     PLS-00103: Encountered the symbol "COUNT" when
         expecting one of the following:
         <an identifier> <a double-quoted string>
         Replacing "COUNT" with "<an identifier>".
5/8      PLS-00103: Encountered the symbol ";" when
```

```
expecting one of the following:
begin declare exit for goto if loop mod null
pragma raise
return select update while <an identifier> etc.
exit was inserted before ";" to continue.
```
7/16   PLS-00103: Encountered the symbol ";" when
```
expecting one of the following:
. into
Resuming parse at line 7, column 16.
```

As your experience with PL/SQL increases, you will become quite adept at debugging your code based on the output of this **sho errors** command.

Code Examples

We will now present three simple requirements and show how to do them using PL/SQL. The comments imbedded in these examples illustrate some of the points we have made throughout this chapter

Example #1

Let's see how to learn a person's date of birth by knowing his or her social security number. The code is commented to illustrate how PL/SQL works. We are using explicit PL/SQL cursors.

```
create or replace procedure get_ssc(ss_num in varchar2,
                                    bdate in date,
                                    sorf in out varchar2) as
begin                  --Begin of the outer block of code
  declare              --Starts list of variables and cursors
    sysd date;         --Local date field to hold system date
    cursor mycur is    --Name must conform to naming rules
      select dob,sysdate   --This table column from person
        from person        --Notice "ss_num" is
      where soc_sec_num = ss_num;
                           --passed into procedure and is
                           --not in the declare section
  begin                    --Inner block needs own "begin"
    open mycur;            --Must be manually opened to use
    fetch mycur into dob,sysd; --"into" mandatory using cursor
    if mycur%found then    --See if the select was successful
```

```
      null;                    --Don't do anything
    else
      sorf = 'F';              --Set SORF to "F" to tell calling
    end if;                    --procedure date of birth not
    close mycur;               --found since person doesn't exist
  end;                         --Termination of inner block
end;                           --Termination of outer block
/                              --"/" ends complete PL/SQL block
```

Let's study a few concepts based on the code in this listing.

- The line that defines the procedure has three variables enclosed in parentheses. The first contains the value of the social security number of the person whose date of birth we require. The second will receive the date. The third is a flag to tell the code that invoked this procedure whether the person information we are looking for is valid.

- Notice the semicolon (;) terminators are missing on the **declare**, the **cursor mycur is** and the **if-then** lines of code. These three lines never have a semicolon.

- The success or failure of a cursor is determined using the "%found" and "%notfound" words.

- The cursor is closed after it is used. You must examine the success or failure of a cursor before closing it.

Example #2

This example shows how to accomplish exactly the same result as above, but using implicit cursors. The code is similar, but the processing and dealing with errors is handled differently.

```
create or replace procedure get_ssc
                (ss_num in varchar2,
                 bdate in date,
                 sorf in out varchar2) as
begin                    --Start of outer block
  declare                --Starts list of variables and cursors
    birthd date;         --Local date field to hold birth date
  begin                  --"begin" for the inner block
    select dob
      into bdate         --"into" mandatory for all cursors
      from person
```

```
      where soc_sec_num = ss_num;
   exception            --Error raised when statement fails
     when no_data_found
       sorf := 'F';
     when others        --handles all other error situations
       exit;
   end;                 --Termination of inner block
end;                    --Termination of outer block
/                       --"/" terminates PL/SQL block
```

Let's study a few concepts based on the code in this listing.

- Since we are using an implicit cursor, we do not define it in the **declare** section of the procedure.

- The error situation "no_data_found" is the implicit cursor method of doing what "%found" or "%notfound" did with explicit cursors.

- The "when_others" error check is a bucket that traps all other types of errors and returns control to the code that invoked the procedure.

Example #3

Suppose an inventory application needs to check the available stock before placing an order; if a commodity's critical quantity is reached, then the application creates a warning in the office administration system to alert the order department.

```
create or replace procedure critical_check
        (id_num in varchar2, qnty in number) as
begin
  declare
    cursor mycur is
      select q_on_hand, q_critical
        from inv_mast
        where part_id = id_num;
    qhand number;       --These two are local variables used
    qcrit number;       --throughout the procedure
  begin
    open mycur;
    fetch mycur into qhand,qcrit;
    if mycur%found then             --Examine success/failure
       if qhand - qnty < qcrit then --before cursor closed
          --Create a row using two local variables and
```

```
          --the system date
          insert into reord_mast values (id_num, qcrit, sysdate);
        end if;
    end if;
    close mycur;
  end;
end;
/
```

Let's study some concepts based on the code in this listing.

- There are two receiving fields (**qhand** and **qcrit**) for the columns fetched in the cursor. Remember, the number of columns fetched and the number of fields in the **into** must be the same.

- After testing the relationship between **qhand - qnty** and **qcrit**, there is a row created in the record_mast table. As rows are created in your PL/SQL blocks, you can use a combination of local variables (**qcrit**), system variables (**sysdate**), and variables passed into the PL/SQL block (**id_num**).

What's Next

Starting with version 6, Oracle made a commitment to PL/SQL, and it has evolved into the standard programming language in all Oracle tools. We have discussed the basics of PL/SQL and shown you some bottom-line functionality and features to get you started. Work with PL/SQL, and in little or no time, you will find yourself comfortable with a remarkably powerful programming language.

As you read on and look at Oracle Forms and Oracle Reports, you will see how tool PL/SQL is used.

CHAPTER **7**

Oracle Forms 101

In this chapter, we will further round out your knowledge of Developer Basics. Using Oracle Forms, programmers create data entry and query screens with a mouse-driven user interface. There is a gamut of GUI (graphical user interface) products on the market; Oracle Forms, part of the Developer 2000 suite of products, is Oracle's offering. When you are done reading this chapter, you will know about the following topics:

- What Oracle Forms is and what it can do for you
- Hardware required to run Oracle Forms
- How to install Oracle Forms
- How to prepare your PC for running Oracle Forms
- Setting preferences in Oracle Forms
- How to build a few basic Oracle Forms screens
- Screen formatting in Oracle Forms
- How to use Oracle Forms Runtime

TIP
Learn the procedures and concepts presented in each sample
exercise in this chapter, one at a time. Before moving on to the next
exercise, practice what you have learned. While the forms we build
are simple, they illustrate fundamental Oracle Forms concepts.

Terminology

The following definitions will arm you with the technical jargon to make it through
this chapter.

- *ODBC,* or Open Database Connectivity, software allows communication
  between one vendor's data source (e.g., Oracle Server) and another
  vendor's tools (e.g., Powersoft's PowerBuilder). Using ODBC, you can use
  an Oracle Forms-based data entry screen to manipulate data stored in a
  non-Oracle database.

- *OLE2,* or Object Linking and Embedding version 2, allows dynamic
  sharing of objects between two OLE2-compliant software programs. Using
  Microsoft Word 6 for Windows (OLE2-compliant), you can embed a
  Microsoft Excel (OLE2-compliant) spreadsheet in a document; when the
  contents of the spreadsheet change, the OLE2 link gives Word immediate
  access to the changes.

- *Inheritance* allows the creation of objects in Oracle Forms that take on the
  look and feel and processing associated with other objects. Using

inheritance, changes made to the referenced object affect the objects that have inherited its properties.

- *WYSIWYG* stands for "what you see is what you get." In all GUI products, the look of your information on the screen is exactly the way printed output will look. For example, if you bold text in a WYSIWYG word processor, the text is bolded on the screen.

- A *block* is a container for items in Oracle Forms. Blocks can be related to tables in the database.

- *Interface items* are objects in Oracle Forms with which the operator interacts. Enterable fields, push buttons, check boxes, and radio buttons are all interface items.

- Oracle Forms uses *locking* to preserve the integrity of data. Locking ensures that more than one user is not allowed to modify the same item of information at the same time.

- When working with Microsoft Windows, the *control box* is in the upper left-hand corner of the screen. Double-clicking on a control box closes the window to which it belongs.

What Is Oracle Forms?

Oracle Forms version 4.5 is part of Developer 2000, an integrated software development and runtime environment with a Microsoft Windows look and feel. All Developer 2000 tools are integrated with one another, and all run primarily against an Oracle7 database.

Oracle Forms is a feature-rich application building tool that produces production-quality screens utilizing data stored in a database. You can embed graphics, sound, video, word processing documents, and spreadsheets through the use of OLE2. You can embed objects from Excel or 1-2-3 for Windows in your Oracle Forms screens. Oracle Forms can also share data with other Developer 2000 tools through a special module. Its predecessor, SQL*Forms 3.0, bundled with version 6 of Oracle, was a character-based screen environment. Oracle has emphasized programmer productivity with Developer 2000; the designer is a fully mouse-driven interface, with the ability to do most of the development without a great deal of coding. In this chapter, we will discuss the two main components of Oracle Forms: Oracle Forms Designer and Oracle Forms Runtime.

Hardware Requirements to Run Oracle Forms

The following minimum configuration is required to use Oracle Forms. The list is exactly the same as the one presented in Chapter 8, where we discuss Oracle Reports.

- A 386 or stronger central processing unit (CPU), though a 486 or Pentium is preferred

- At least 60 megabytes (or 61,440,000 bytes) of available disk space

- A 40MHz or faster processor—speeds of 66 or better are preferable

- At least 8MB (megabytes) of extended memory for Oracle Forms Runtime and 16MB for Oracle Forms Designer

- MS-DOS or PC-DOS versions 5 or 6, or DR-DOS version 6 or higher

- MS Windows 3.1 (and eventually Windows 95)

We recommend putting a CD-ROM drive on your machine. Oracle is moving towards this as the default distribution medium; as well, what easily fits on a fraction of a CD-ROM (each holds 600MB, or 638,976,000 bytes) could easily take up a very large number of 3.5-inch diskettes. When Personal Oracle7 was beta, one of our clients had over 86MB of Oracle and Oracle-support software on a 486 PC. Had they installed from diskette, that could have easily been over 60 diskettes!

How to Install Oracle Forms

As with the rest of the Oracle products for Windows, installation is done from the Oracle installer (referred to as *orainst* in Chapter 4). To begin installation, click on the Oracle Installer icon in the Oracle group of the Windows Program Manager. You will be presented with the Oracle Installer startup screen, shown in Figure 7-1.
Notice the two boxes on the screen in Figure 7-1, called Available Products and Installed Products. If Oracle Forms is not one of the available products, scroll through the list until it appears. Once in view, there may be a plus (+) sign beside the Oracle Forms name. This indicates that there are components that can be installed together or separately. Click on the plus (+) sign to expand the component list, as shown in Figure 7-2. While that component list is displayed, you may install each Oracle Forms component separately.
When you are ready to start installing, click on Install. During the installation process that follows, you will be asked to designate a directory for the product. Oracle suggests placing it in \orawin\forms45. Unless you are already using that

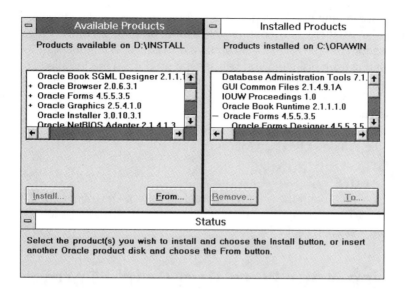

FIGURE 7-1.   *Oracle Installer startup screen*

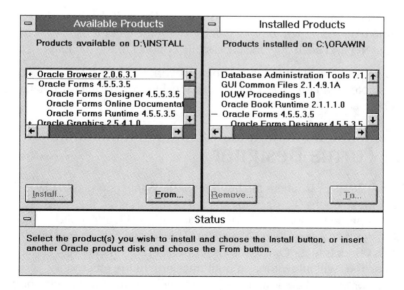

FIGURE 7-2.   *Oracle Forms components list expansion*

directory for something else, accept it as is. After selecting the directory for the installation, the installer goes about its work setting up Oracle Forms. When the installation terminates (be patient—it can take upwards of 20 minutes, or longer if you are installing from diskette), you will see the product in the Installed Products list on the right of the installer screen. You are now ready to use Oracle Forms. The installer will also create a CDE2 Demos program group. Many of the forms Oracle provides as demos contain code that illustrate how to use many new features of Oracle Forms 4.5. When orainst finishes, double-click on the installer's control box to return to the Windows Program Manager.

NOTE
Even though the products are called part of Developer 2000, the program groups created when they are installed are called CDE2 Tools and CDE2 Demos.

Preparing Your PC to Run Oracle Forms

The following must be done before running Oracle Forms.

- The DOS program share.exe or the Windows device vshare.386 must be loaded to permit Oracle Forms to share files and perform its locking.

- You must have access to a local or remote Oracle7 database. To access a remote database, you or your database administrator must have installed SQL*Net and been able to successfully connect to the database.

- You must have already loaded your network software if you are accessing a remote database. If you are using a local Personal Oracle7 database, this is not necessary.

Oracle Forms Designer

Oracle Forms Designer is where the building of the application takes place. Four components make up the interface to Oracle Forms Designer: the Object Navigator, the property sheet, the layout editor, and the PL/SQL editor. The most important of the four is the Object Navigator. This navigator is shared by all of the Developer 2000 tools (e.g., Oracle Reports, discussed in Chapter 8). Learning to utilize its functions will allow for a smooth transition to the other tools.

The single property sheet is a new idea in Oracle Forms 4.5 (Oracle Forms 4.0 had a separate sheet for each object type). Object attributes can be added, modified, or removed using the Oracle Forms 4.5 property sheet. The layout editor is now fully WYSIWYG. This is where you place all of the objects for the particular screen that is being developed. The PL/SQL editor is where all PL/SQL code can be added, modified, removed, and compiled. All work is done in the PL/SQL editor regardless of the type of PL/SQL object you are working with (i.e., a trigger, a stored procedure, or a library).

Before we dive into Oracle Forms, let's look at the assortment of buttons and tools you will be using in this chapter. Oracle Forms calls the collection of buttons along the top of its screen the *toolbar* and the collection of tools down the side of its screen the *tool palette*. Figure 7-3 shows the various buttons that we will be using throughout this chapter. There are many more buttons and tools you can use with Oracle Forms Designer than we discuss in this chapter. We only touch on the ones we will be using.

Object Navigator

The Object Navigator is used primarily to quickly move between the other three interfaces. Its other purpose is for drag-and-drop application development. Utilizing the Object Navigator, you can access objects and libraries both on disk and in the database. By dragging these objects into your Oracle Forms Designer workspace, you have added their functionality to your form.

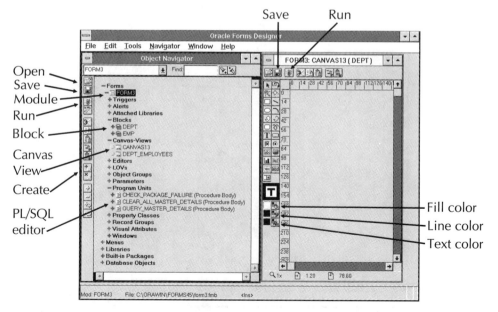

FIGURE 7-3.   *Oracle Forms buttons*

Canvas-view

Canvas-views are where you design the look and feel of your screens; this is what the client or user is going to have to interact with. If the layout of a canvas (screen) is pleasing to the eye, you are halfway there. While working with canvas-views, you can control the application's color, size, font, data access, and style. Think of a canvas-view as a layout editor where you paint your application's objects. The entire screen is your canvas. Figure 7-4 shows a canvas-view.

You create a new canvas-view in the Object Navigator by highlighting Canvas-Views and clicking the Create tool on the Object Navigator tool palette. You control what type of canvas it will be in the canvas-view property sheet. The property sheet can be reached in the Object Navigator by highlighting Canvas-Views and then choosing Tools from the main menu and then Properties.

Property Sheet

The property sheet is where you set object attributes. There are a lot of different looks that you can achieve, and most of them are determined by individual tastes. It is very important to carefully plan out what the screens are going to look like at the beginning of a project, especially when several developers are involved. Figure

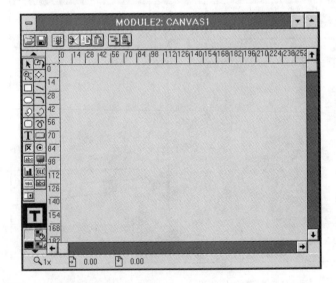

FIGURE 7-4. *A typical canvas-view*

7-5 shows a property sheet for the module MODULE1. Here you define characteristics of modules, for example the module's title and whether buttons used in the module should have a raised 3-dimensional visual effect. The nature of the characteristics you define using a property sheet depends on what type of object is being designed (i.e., property sheet for a module, a canvas-view, or a block).

As you move through the entries on most property sheets, you will find three ways to change properties:

■ Some properties are set by typing information into the text entry box that is highlighted when the property is selected. The Name property shown in Figure 7-5 is set this way.

■ Some properties are set by clicking on the DOWN ARROW that appears when the property is highlighted. A drop-down menu appears from which the property characteristics are chosen. The Class property shown in Figure 7-5 is set this way.

■ Some properties are set by clicking on a More button that appears when the property is highlighted. A dialog box appears within which the property characteristics are set. The Coordinate property shown in Figure 7-5 is set this way.

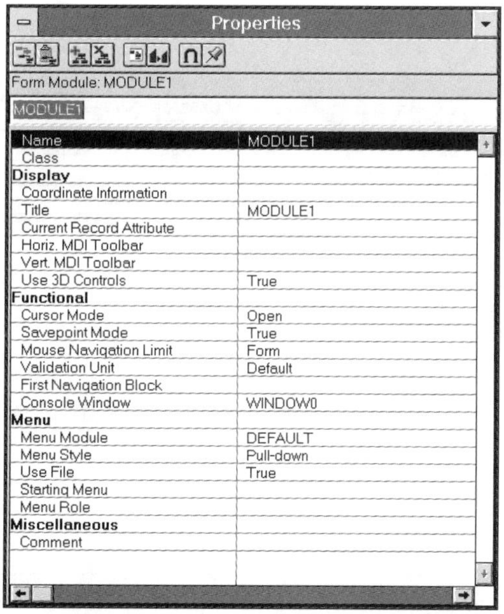

FIGURE 7-5. *Property sheet*

VIP
When you type in an entry for a property (e.g., the name of a canvas-view), press ENTER to update the value beside the property in the property sheet. Leave the property sheet by double-clicking its control box.

PL/SQL Editor

The PL/SQL editor is where the application will take on its specialized functionality. You can control exactly what the program can and cannot do based on the work you do in this editor. This is where all of the form's triggers and procedures are edited and compiled. It is also where database procedures can be accessed, modified, and compiled. The PL/SQL editor is accessed by double-clicking on the PL/SQL Editor button on the Object Navigator. A PL/SQL editor screen is shown in Figure 7-6.

NOTE
If there is a plus (+) sign beside Program Units on the Object Navigator, double-click on it to display any defined program units and their PL/SQL editor buttons.

```
┌─────────────────────────────────────────────────────┐
│  ─           PL/SQL Editor              ▼ ▲ │
├─────────────────────────────────────────────────────┤
│  Compile    New...    Delete    Close              │
│  Type: Program Unit ↓  Object            ↓        ↓ │
│  Name: CHECK_PACKAGE_FAILURE (Procedure Body)    ↓ │
├─────────────────────────────────────────────────────┤
│ Procedure Check_Package_Failure IS               ↑│
│ BEGIN                                             │
│   IF NOT ( Form_Success ) THEN                    │
│     RAISE Form_Trigger_Failure;                   │
│   END IF;                                         │
│ END;                                              │
│                                                   │
│                                                   │
│                                                   │
│                                                   │
│                                                   │
│                                                   ↓│
├─────────────────────────────────────────────────────┤
│ Not Modified                    Successfully Compiled│
└─────────────────────────────────────────────────────┘
```

FIGURE 7-6. PL/SQL editor screen

Now that we have had a look at the tools we will be using in this chapter's exercises, as well as the Object Navigator, canvas-views, property sheet, and PL /SQL, let's discuss setting options in Oracle Forms. You customize your preferred look and feel of Oracle Forms by setting options.

Setting Options

The first area to look at is setting options. This is where you set aspects of Oracle Reports Designer to suit your individual tastes. The menu at the top of the Designer screen is where you start:

1. Click on Tools on the menu at the top of the screen. This menu is available anywhere from any Oracle Forms screen.

2. Click on Options to open the dialog box shown in Figure 7-7. There are two folders in this box, one to set Designer options, the other to set Runtime. Figure 7-7 shows the default settings for Designer Options when the dialog box appears for the first time. Figure 7-8 shows the Runtime options folder. In Figure 7-7, notice how Generate Before Run, Run Module Asynchronously, and File are selected. These offer the most flexibility in Oracle Forms, and are usually left as is.

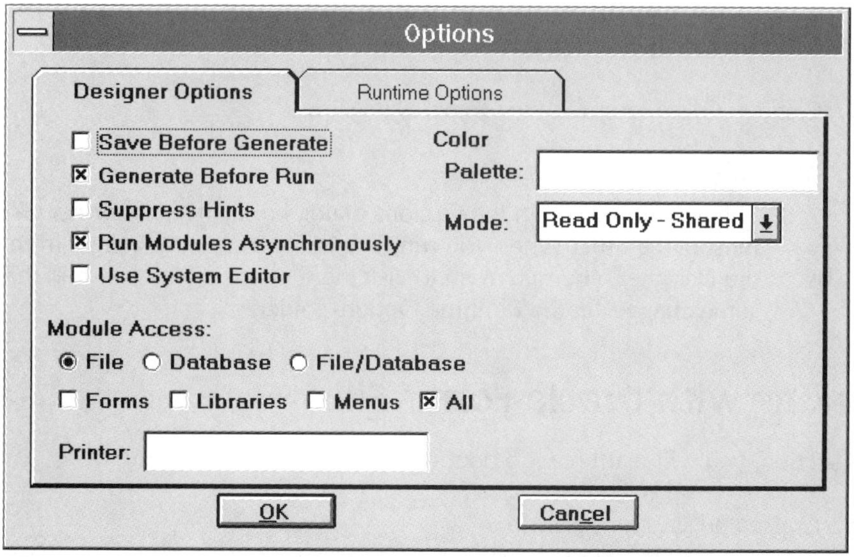

Options
Designer Options Runtime Options

☐ Save Before Generate
☒ Generate Before Run
☐ Suppress Hints
☒ Run Modules Asynchronously
☐ Use System Editor

Color Palette: _____
Mode: Read Only - Shared ↓

Module Access:
⦿ File ○ Database ○ File/Database
☐ Forms ☐ Libraries ☐ Menus ☒ All

Printer: _____

[OK]   [Cancel]

FIGURE 7-7. *Designer options folder*

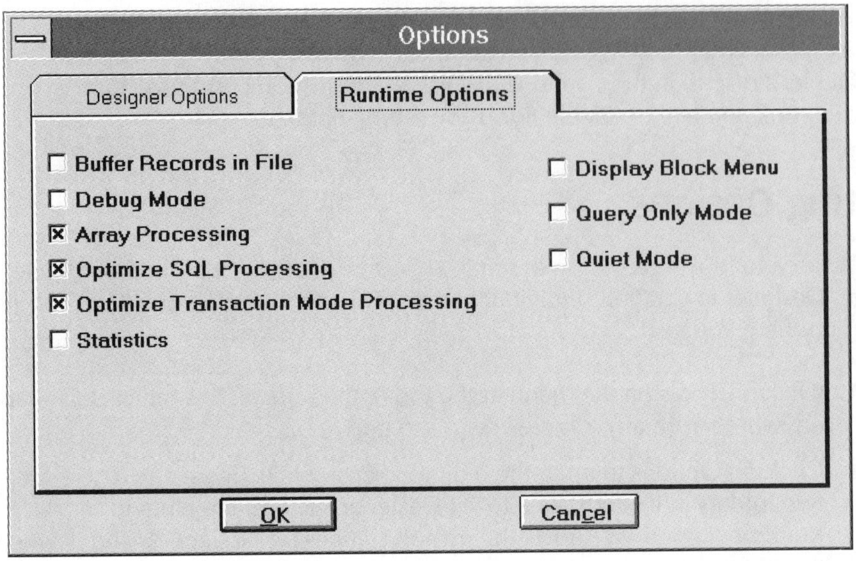

FIGURE 7-8. *Runtime options folder*

NOTE
We recommend using the Designer and Runtime option defaults. They reflect the most common preferences, and can be changed anytime by visiting this dialog box.

3. Click on OK to return to the Object Navigator.

NOTE
The default settings in the Options dialog box will suit your needs most of the time. When you run Oracle Forms programs right from the Designer, you may wish to visit the Options dialog box and make some changes in the Runtime Options folder.

Working with Oracle Forms Files

In this section, you will learn how to do the following:

■ Create and save a new form

■ Open an existing form

■ Change the name of a form

After double-clicking on the Oracle Forms Designer icon in the Windows Program Manager, Oracle Forms Designer will appear. The form name MODULE1 will be highlighted in the Object Navigator. At this point, you can open an existing form or begin working on a new one.

Creating a New Form

After loading Oracle Forms Designer, you are ready to begin creating an application. By default, Designer starts with a new form ready to go (with the name MODULE1). If you have done some work on a form in the Designer, and wish to start a new form, select New on the File menu at the top of the screen. Alternatively, you can highlight the text Forms at the top of the Object Navigator, and double-click on the Create tool on the Object Navigator tool palette.

TIP

After loading Oracle Forms, if you immediately open an existing form, the MODULE1 form created by default is removed automatically.

Opening an Existing Form

To open a form that already exists, select Open on the File menu at the top of the screen. The Open dialog box appears, as shown in Figure 7-9. Alternatively, you may click on the Open tool on the Object Navigator tool palette. Double-click on

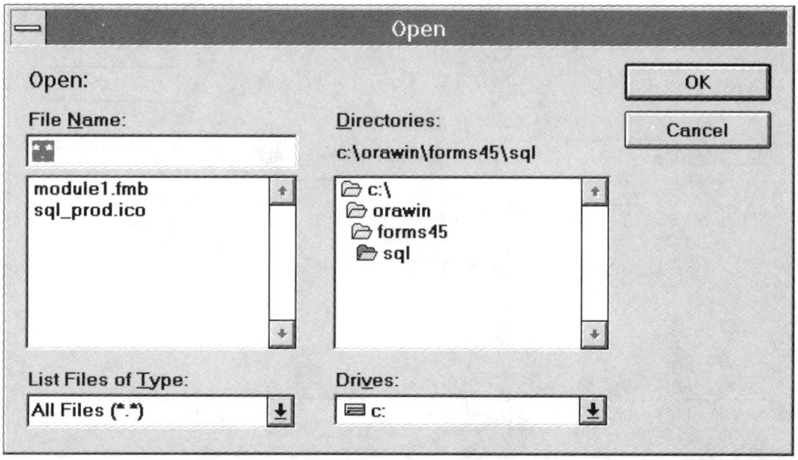

FIGURE 7-9. *Open dialog box*

a filename, or click on a filename to highlight it, then click OK to open the report. The title of the form in the Object Navigator will change to show the name of the form you have opened.

TIP
The quickest way to open a form is to use the shortcut key CTRL-O. This brings up the same dialog box shown in Figure 7-9.

Saving a Form

To save a form you have been working with, select Save on the File menu at the top of the screen, or click on the Save tool on the Object Navigator tool palette. If this is the first time you are saving a form, Oracle Forms displays the Save As dialog box shown in Figure 7-10. Enter a filename for the report, then click on the OK button to complete the save. The name of the file you enter must conform to DOS file naming conventions. If Oracle Forms knows the name of the form you are working with (i.e., you have saved it previously in the same session), it saves the form without opening the Save As dialog box.

TIP
The quickest way to save a form is to use the shortcut key CTRL-S. If Oracle does not know the name of the report you are saving, it will open up the dialog box shown in Figure 7-10.

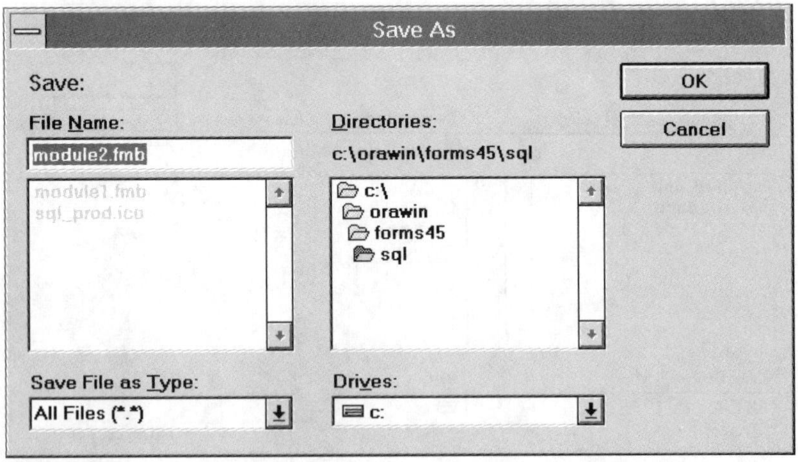

FIGURE 7-10. *Save As dialog box*

Changing the Name of a Form

If you wish to change the name of a form, select Save As on the File menu at the top of the screen. Oracle Forms brings up the dialog box shown in Figure 7-10. Enter a new filename, then click on the OK button to complete the save using the new name.

The Right Mouse Button

The right mouse button has special meaning to Oracle Forms. It allows quick access to the layout editor (also referred to as canvas-view), PL/SQL editor, and property sheets. For example, when you click the right button while the mouse cursor is on the Object Navigator, a menu appears as shown in Figure 7-11.

As well, clicking the right button while the mouse cursor is on a canvas-view shows the menu in Figure 7-12. Notice how the available options in these menus are context-sensitive: the Cut, Copy, and Layout Editor options are inactive.

NOTE
If you have your mouse defined with the right button as the primary one, you would use the left button to accomplish what we discuss in this section. Most mouse software allows redefining of the two mouse buttons.

Let's now move on to discuss the quickest way to start building forms with Oracle Forms Designer.

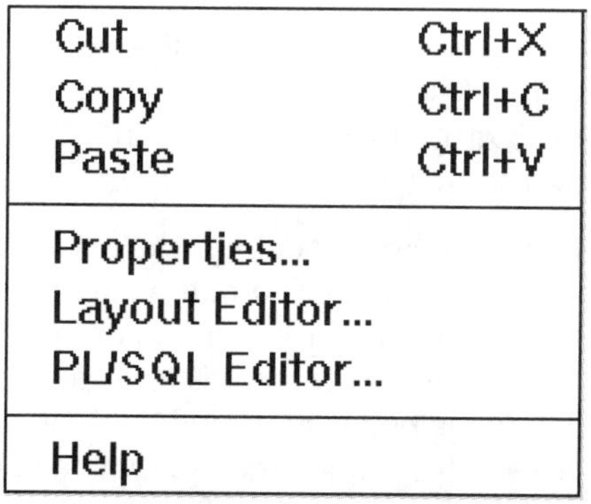

Cut	Ctrl+X
Copy	Ctrl+C
Paste	Ctrl+V
Properties...	
Layout Editor...	
PL/SQL Editor...	
Help	

FIGURE 7-11. *Right mouse button menu on Object Navigator*

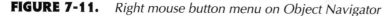

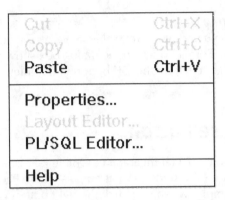

FIGURE 7-12. *Right mouse button menu on canvas-view*

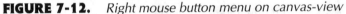

Default Block Facility

When starting with Oracle Forms, there are some quick ways to get your hands dirty (i.e., define a form and do some programming). Within the New Block function, there is the ability to create a default block. All items used in Oracle Forms, whether they come from a table in the database or not, must be in a block. To define a new block, select New Block from the Tools menu at the top of the screen. A dialog box is brought up as shown in Figure 7-13. There are four areas of control in this dialog box:

- **General folder**—Here is where you specify a name for the block, a table (if any) the block references, and a canvas-view the block belongs to.

- **Items folder**—Here is where fields can be selected and their basic attributes can be defined, such as Label, Width, and Object Type. The Type is chosen from a drop-down list shown in Figure 7-14. The list contains Windows-specific types, such as Radio Group and Check Box.

- **Layout folder**—Here is where you define whether the fields should be Tabular (for multi-record blocks) or Form (for single-record blocks). You also set the orientation of the records (vertical or horizontal), the space left between fields, and the number of records to display. This is where you set some of the familiar dialog box features in Windows, such as whether the block should have a scroll bar and whether Oracle Forms should create an additional block with VCR-style buttons for executing standard navigation and query functions.

■ **Master/Detail folder**—Here is where you define relationships between blocks (we will go into detail about these relationships in Exercises #2 and #3 in this chapter).

Hands-On Experience

Enough said! Let's build a few simple forms from scratch to illustrate how to develop screens with Oracle Forms. For these forms, we are accessing a Personal Oracle7 database using some of the tables delivered with the software, belonging to the Oracle user *scott* whose password is *tiger*.

Exercise #1

In this exercise, we will start from the beginning and work through some important steps in creating a new form. We will show you how to do the following:

■ Create a window

■ Create a content canvas-view

■ Create a default block, then customize some of the item attributes

■ Save and run the form

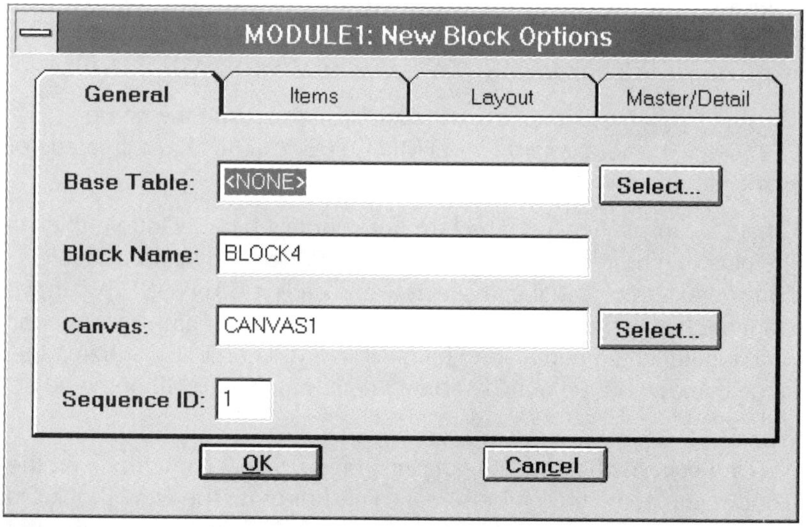

FIGURE 7-13. *New Block Options dialog box*

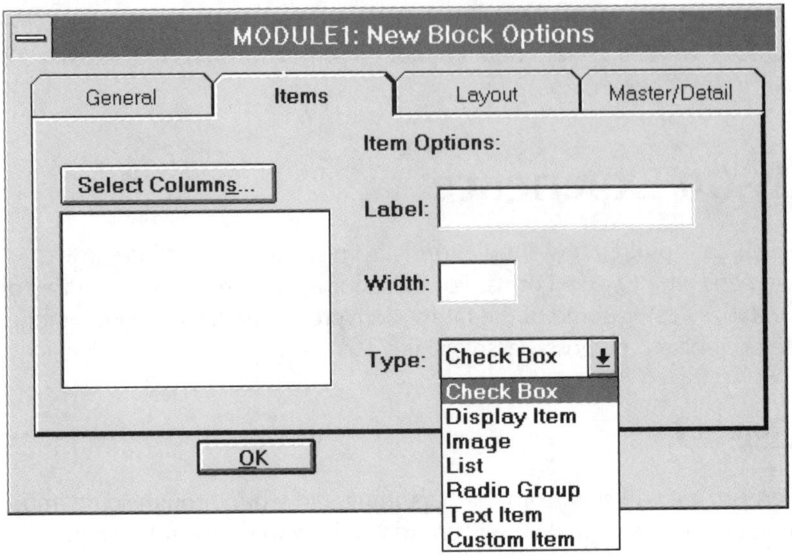

FIGURE 7-14. *Object Type drop-down list*

When Oracle Forms starts up, it automatically creates a new form and window to start working with. Let's get started by performing the following steps:

1. Click on Windows in the Object Navigator. The plus (+) sign in front of the Windows branch indicates that there are lower levels that can be expanded. Click on the plus sign to expose WINDOW0.

2. Change the name of the new window by highlighting the name WINDOW0, and changing it to EMPLOYEE. You have just created your first window (fun, eh?).

3. Create a canvas-view on which to put your first block. Double-click on the plus sign beside Canvas-Views on the Object Navigator. Oracle Forms creates the initial canvas-view and calls it CANVAS1. Again, you want to change this name to something more meaningful, so click once on the highlighted name and change it to EMPLOYEE. By utilizing these same names, you are quickly able to determine where all of the objects are located.

4. You are now ready to create your first block. Select New Block on the Tools menu at the top of the screen. This brings up the New Block Options dialog box we first saw in Figure 7-13.

TIP
The New Block Options dialog box can also be brought up by clicking on Blocks in the Object Navigator, then clicking on the Create tool on the Object Navigator's tool palette.

5. Click on the General tab, then enter **emp** in the Base Table text box. TAB to the Block Name text box, and **emp** should appear in the Block Name text box. Since there is only one canvas-view defined, Oracle Forms places the text EMPLOYEE in the Canvas text box.

6. Click on the Items tab, then click on the Select Columns button. You will be asked to connect to the Personal Oracle7 database. Enter the username **scott** and the password **tiger**.

7. When connected, Oracle Forms will bring up all the columns in the emp table with a plus sign in front of each. To deselect a column (i.e., not use it in the block) in the Items folder, double-click in its name or, while the column is highlighted, click on the Include check box to make the "x" disappear. Set the width for the hiredate column to **40** and change its Label to **Hired**. Set the width for the sal column to **40**, and change its Label to **Salary**.

8. Click on the Layout tab. Click on the arrow beside Style, and choose Form from the drop-down list that appears.

9. Accept the block you have just defined by clicking the OK button. Your canvas-view looks like the screen in Figure 7-15.

VIP
Sometimes your canvas-view does not appear when you close the New Block dialog box. If this happens, double-click on the Canvas-View button on the Object Navigator to bring up the screen shown in Figure 7-15.

10. Save the form by pressing CTRL-S to open the Save As dialog box. Enter the name **form1**, then click OK.

NOTE
When we discussed Designer Options earlier in the "Setting Options" section, we accepted a Designer default by telling Oracle Forms to Generate Before Run. This is why we do not have to generate here.

11. Press CTRL-R to run the form. When the form appears, select Execute from the Query menu, then select Execute on the menu at the top of the screen

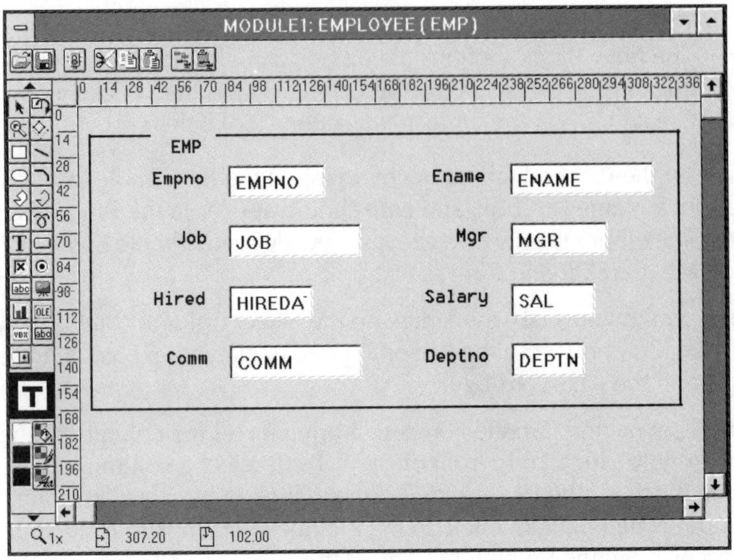

FIGURE 7-15. *Completed employee canvas-view*

to bring up data as shown in Figure 7-16. Click on the control box in the Oracle Forms 4.5 (Runform) window to return to the Designer.

Pretty nice form, if you don't say so yourself! Before moving on, let's look at two items. The first is a display problem you may have noticed in Figure 7-16. See how the entire date in the hiredate column is not showing. To fix this, follow these steps:

1. Position yourself on the canvas-view EMPLOYEE, then click on the display area for hiredate.

2. Click on the handle (six handles surround the field when it is selected) on the right side of the field, and stretch it a bit to the right. When you release the mouse button, the field will be resized to accommodate all of the data in hiredate.

3. Save the form by pressing CTRL-S, then look at the changes by pressing CTRL-R. Click on the control box in the Oracle Runform window to return to the Designer.

Let's also look at a quick way to customize item attributes on a canvas-view.

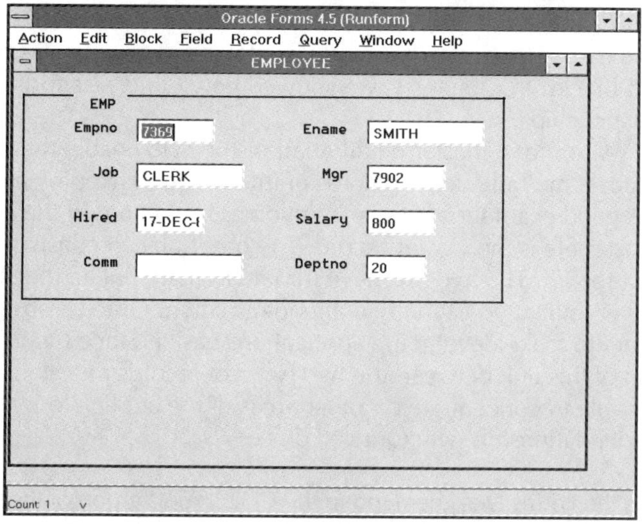

FIGURE 7-16. *Emp table record displayed in employee window*

1. Navigate to the EMPLOYEE canvas-view by clicking in its window if it is still visible, or double-clicking on its button in the Object Navigator.

2. Hold down CTRL and click on each field on the canvas. Each field shows six handles after all fields are selected.

3. Place the cursor on the canvas-view, and press the right mouse button. Choose Properties from the menu that appears.

4. Select Background Color property, and change it to Green.

5. Close the property sheet by double-clicking in its control box.

6. Save the form by pressing CTRL-S.

The next time you run the form, its background color will be green. This completes our first exercise.

Exercise #2

In this exercise, you will learn what a master-detail relationship is, when to use it, and how to create it. A master-detail relationship is an association between two base table blocks; the parent is called a master block, and there is a detail block whose records are associated with the parent's. The master-detail relationship in Oracle Forms ensures that the detail block displays only those records that are associated with the current record in the master block and coordinates querying between the two blocks. In Chapter 1, we showed how Oracle Reports handles this master/detail relationship.

The primary reason for a master-detail relationship is to enable the users of your application to access multiple detail records of information linked by a common master record. A good example of this is an invoice. The record of the customer in the customer master file is the master record. The order placed consists of many items—the detail record. The two pieces of information are linked together to give the users greater visibility and usability of the information. Oracle Forms provides this unique feature to make developing applications easier. Since Oracle Forms allows definition of this link between the two types of records as a standard feature, the developer is able to concentrate on other areas of the application. Now we will create this type of relationship with Oracle Forms:

1. Click on the Forms Designer icon in the CDE2 Tools group of the Windows Program Manager. When the Designer is done loading, follow steps 1 through 10 from the previous section ("Exercise #1") to create your first block.

NOTE
Alternately, you can open the previous form, click on File then Save As to change its name, and save it under the name **form2** (or whatever name you choose).

2. Let's now create the second block. Position yourself on the Object Navigator by selecting Object Navigator from the Window menu at the top of the screen, then click on Block. With the Block text highlighted, click on the Create tool on the Object Navigator tool palette to open the New Block Options dialog box.

3. Enter **dept** in the Base Table text box in the New Block Options General folder, then TAB to the block name (notice Oracle Forms puts the table name as the block name). Click on the Items tab, then click on Select Columns. When Oracle displays all the columns in the dept table, they all have the plus (+) sign beside them.

4. Click on the Master/Detail tab, then enter the block name **emp** in the Master Block text box.

5. Enter the text **emp.deptno = dept.deptno** in the Join Condition text box. The dialog box now looks like Figure 7-17.

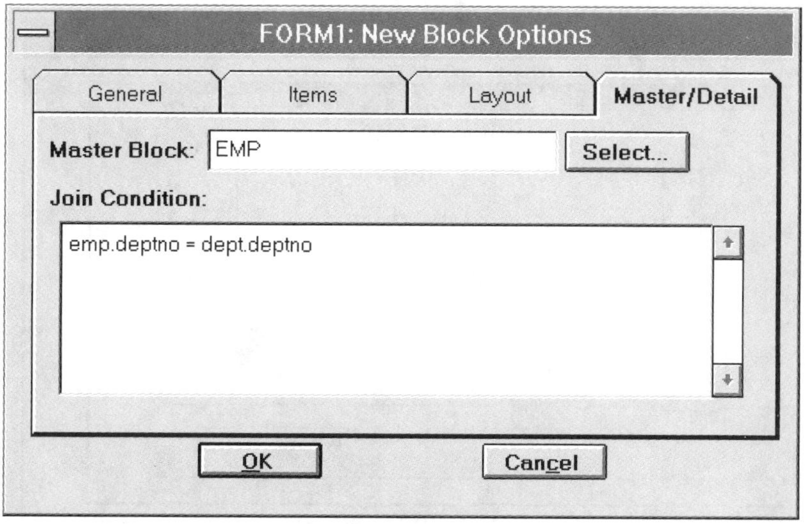

FIGURE 7-17.   *Master/Detail folder showing link between master and detail block columns*

6. Click on OK to accept the setup for the new dept block. Save the form by pressing CTRL-S.

7. Press CTRL-R to run the form. When the form appears, select Execute from the Query menu at the top of the screen. Figure 7-18 shows the screen after the query executes.

8. Select Next from the Record menu at the top of the screen. Notice that when the data scrolls to the next record in the top block, the bottom block scrolls as well. Figure 7-19 shows the second row from the emp and dept tables.

9. Double-click on the Oracle Forms 4.5 (Runform) control box to return to the Designer. Press CTRL-W to close the form.

You are then positioned at the Object Navigator once again. Double-click on the Oracle Forms Designer control box to return to the Windows Program Manager. We have now built a master/detail form, something you will do time and time again with Oracle Forms.

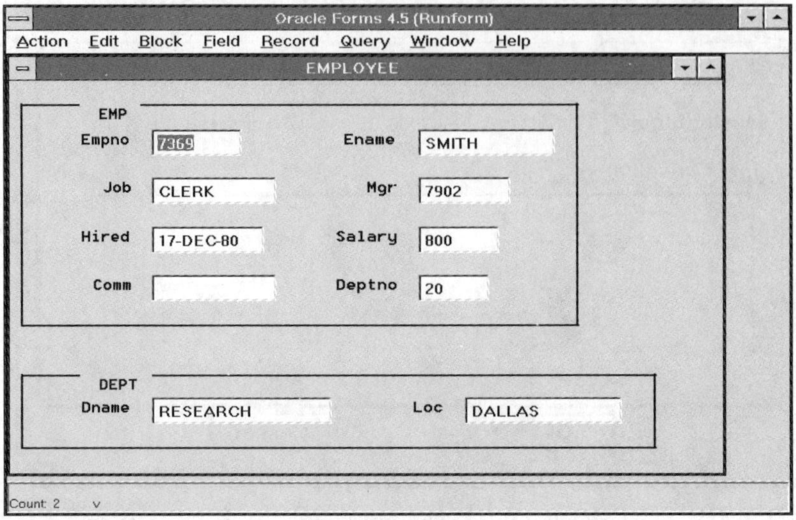

FIGURE 7-18. *Master/detail form, first record*

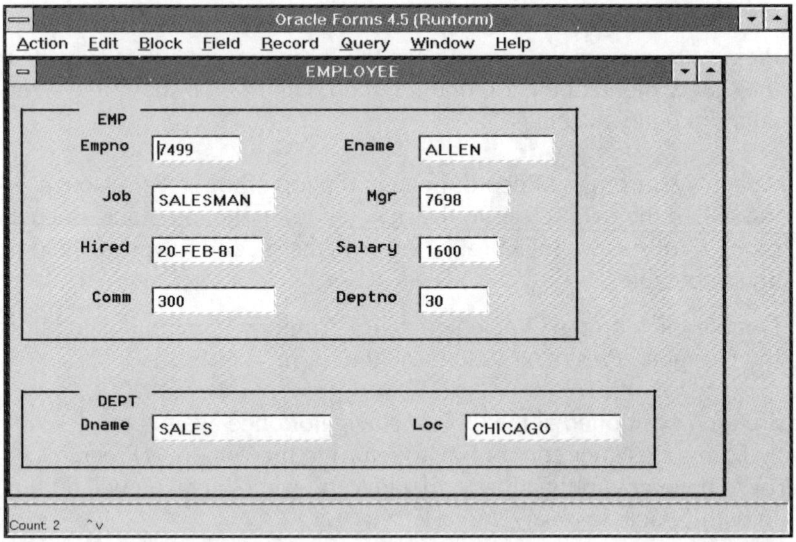

FIGURE 7-19. *Master/detail form, second record*

Exercise #3

In this exercise, we will create another master/detail form, using the dept table as the master and emp as the detail. We will use a different layout, so that multiple rows from the detail table are displayed at one time. In this exercise, we will show you how to format the detail block using a nondefault layout. We will also place a scroll bar in the detail block. Let's get started:

1. Double-click on the Forms Designer icon in the Windows Program Manager to start the Designer. Select New from the File menu at the top of the screen, then Form on the menu that opens up to the right.

2. Click on Block on the Object Navigator, then click on the Create tool on the Object Navigator tool palette to bring up the New Block Options dialog box. Enter **dept** for the Base Table and **dept** for the Block Name in the General folder.

3. Click on the Items tab, then click on Select Columns. When Oracle Forms retrieves the column names from dept, click on OK. You are now done creating the master block.

4. Click on the Layout tab, then select Form from the drop-down list beside Style.

5. If you aren't already, return to the Object Navigator. Click on Block, then click on the Create tool on the Object Navigator tool palette to start the detail block.

6. Enter **emp** for the Base Table and **emp** for the Block Name in the General folder.

7. Click on the Items tab, then click on Select Columns. Oracle Forms retrieves the column names from dept.

8. Click on the Layout tab. The Style should be set to Tabular, and the Orientation to Vertical. If either of these values is incorrect, change them using each one's drop-down list. Change the Records to **6** and Spacing to **8**.

9. Click on Integrity Constraints and Scrollbar in the Layout folder, and Oracle Forms fills their boxes with an "x."

10. Click on the Master/Detail tab, then the Select button to bring up the dialog box shown in Figure 7-20. Select the single constraint displayed by clicking OK. This returns you to the Master/Detail folder. Click on OK to complete defining the new block.

11. Save the report by clicking on the Save tool on the Object Navigator's tool palette. Enter the name **form3** then click OK in the Save dialog box.

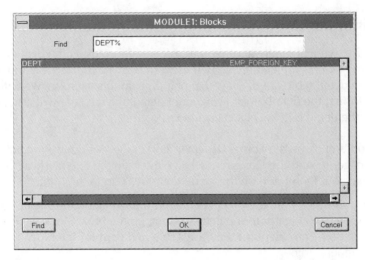

FIGURE 7-20. *Blocks dialog box where link between blocks is chosen*

12. Run the form by clicking on the Run tool on the tool palette (you will find this tool on most tool palettes and toolbars, not just on the Object Navigator). When the screen appears, notice that there is more than one emp record for the displayed dept information. This is shown in Figure 7-21.

13. Select Next from the Record menu at the top of the screen to get to the next record, and the contents of both blocks change together. The new record is shown in Figure 7-22.

14. Double-click on the Oracle Forms 4.5 (Runform) control box to return to the Designer.

This completes our hands-on exercises. We have built three forms, saved, run, modified them, and modified them again. Let's move on to screen formatting. Since Oracle Forms runs on PCs, the assortment of colors, fonts, graphics, and fill you have to become familiar with can be used here as well.

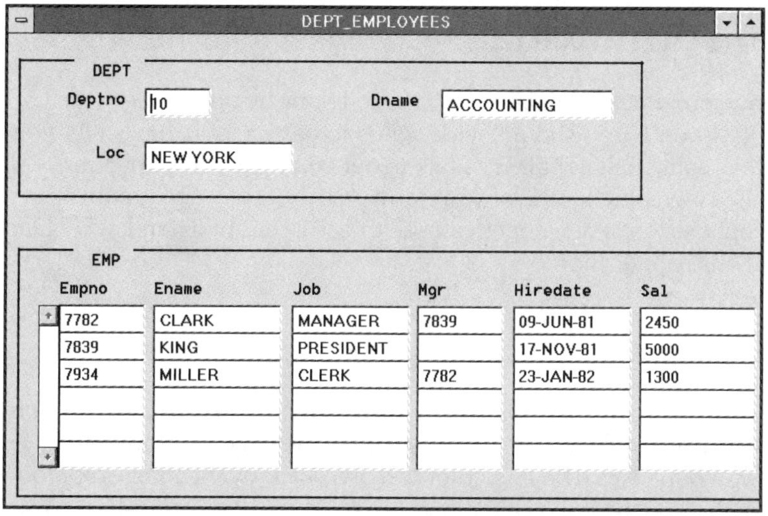

FIGURE 7-21. *Master/detail with multiple detail rows displayed together*

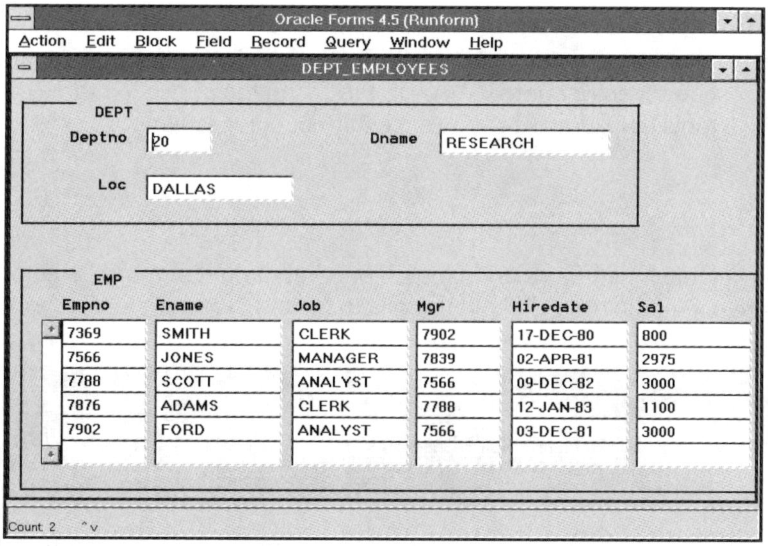

FIGURE 7-22. *Second row in multiple detail row window*

Screen Formatting

We will now round out the chapter on Oracle Forms by discussing screen presentation issues. Forms should be designed to have a look that is pleasing to the eye as well as being functional. Let's talk about color and fonts, then move on to how to embed a graphic in one of your forms. Color, fonts, and graphics are just a few of the options that a developer can use to ensure usability and acceptance of an Oracle Forms application.

Color

There are three areas of color that can be controlled: fill, line, and text. Fill is the color of the background, and it is represented by the Fill Color tool on the canvas-view tool palette. The line color is represented by the Line Color tool on the tool palette; this sets the color of the outer edge of any geometric shape. Text is the color of the alphanumeric characters, and it is represented by the Text Color tool on the tool palette. To set the color for one of these items, click on its tool on the tool palette, then move around the color selection palette, as shown in Figure 7-23.

> **NOTE**
> The boxes beside the three tools for choosing colors indicate the current color choice. As well, the "T" button above the three color tools in Figure 7-24 shows the current color scheme.

Fonts

Fonts are available for all fields and labels. Fonts vary from computer to computer, and they are one of the most difficult options to control. The best fonts to use are

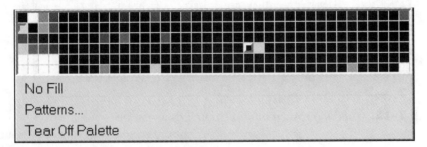

No Fill
Patterns...
Tear Off Palette

FIGURE 7-23. *Color selection palette*

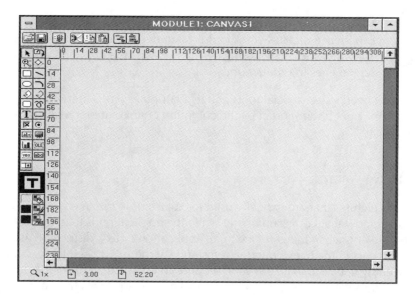

FIGURE 7-24. *The "T" button showing the current color scheme*

the standard Windows fonts, or, if the application will span multiple platforms, one of the more common ones, such as MS Sans Serif. When the selected font is not available on a particular system, the system defaults to a different font, which may not be that similar. For instance, on all Windows computers, the TTF font Times New Roman is very popular. If this book were read into a Motif environment, it might default to MS Sans Serif.

It is important to realize that proportional fonts are much more pleasing to the eye than fixed fonts, such as Courier. With proportional fonts, thin letters such as "I" take less space than wider letters such as "G". The text in this paragraph uses proportional fonts. Using fixed fonts, all letters regardless of their width take up the same amount of horizontal space. To change the font of an item:

1. Select the item to change by clicking on it.

2. Select Font from the Format menu at the top of the screen.

3. Scroll through the Font dialog box, select the desired font, and select any desired attributes, such as bold and italic.

4. Click on OK to choose the selection you have made. When you return to the canvas-view, the font for the selected item changes.

VIP
Experience dictates you should use underline and bold sparingly. They may look nice during design but can be a nuisance when a screen goes to production.

When you need to use special fonts and text attributes, keep in mind that all attributes may not be supported by the computer configuration on all your clients' machines.

Graphics

Graphics are pictures that are typically used for splash or logo screens. A splash screen is a window that comes up briefly while the application is loading. They can be used to announce the entrance to an application or as a distraction as processing occurs in the background. For instance, if there is a need to do extra setup or security checks that take several seconds to complete, a developer may want to include a splash screen to let end users know that processing is occurring or to distract them from the time it takes to complete that processing. Another use of graphics is the inclusion of the company logo. To use a graphic in your form, follow these steps:

1. Position yourself on a canvas-view by double-clicking on the Canvas-View button on the Object Navigator.

2. Select Import from the Edit menu at the top of the screen. When the Import (for Drawings) or Import Image (for Images) dialog box appears, enter the filename of the image or drawing to import, or use the browser to select the file to import.

3. Click on OK to import the image or drawing.

VIP
When you select Import from the Edit menu, if the Image and Drawing choices are not active, click anywhere in the Canvas-Views editor, and repeat the operation. The active options on this menu depend on the active object when Edit is selected.

We now move on to Oracle Forms Runtime, leaving you with one last point that, unfortunately, should restrict just how fancy you may get with screen design. As with all fun things in life, enjoy these options (colors, fonts, and graphics) in moderation. Too much of any of the available screen formatting techniques will cause unpleasant side effects. Remember, you are not the only one who will have to stare at your application for long periods of time. It may be a good idea to get a second opinion on the aesthetics of your screen design.

Oracle Forms Runtime

This part of Oracle Forms is used to run menus and screens. It is invoked by clicking on the Forms Runtime icon in the CDE2 Tools program group. When you are presented with the Runtime welcome screen, do the following to run a report:

1. Press CTRL-R to bring up the Open dialog box. Enter the name of the form to run, or browse and then select the one you want.

2. Once you have selected a report (e.g., form1), click on OK.

3. Enter the username and password when asked to connect to the Personal Oracle7 database.

4. Go about whatever you need to do with the form, then exit Oracle Forms 4.5 (Runtime) by double-clicking on its control box.

After developers code Oracle Forms programs, the source code is compiled and becomes part of the set of application code delivered to the end user. The end user invokes Forms Runtime within an application to work with the network of system screens and menus.

What's Next

Oracle Forms 4.5 has reinforced Oracle's position as one of the major players in the GUI data entry environment. We have shown you some basics and have hopefully tickled your fancy, and now you can't wait to try bigger and better things. Our next chapter discusses another component of Oracle's Developer 2000 suite of products: Oracle Reports. A lot of the techniques you have picked up in this chapter can be applied to Oracle Reports, since, as you will soon see, it has the same look and feel and operator interface as Oracle Forms.

CHAPTER 8

Oracle Reports

In this chapter, we will discuss the Developer 2000 tool called Oracle Reports. Programmers familiar with some ad hoc query tools on the market will find the look and feel of Oracle Reports very familiar. Version 2.0 of this tool was a major rewrite from its predecessor called SQL*Reportwriter. The version we feature in this chapter, version 2.5, has a sophisticated programmer interface and has been significantly enhanced for ease of use. When you are done reading this chapter, you will know about the following:

- Oracle Reports and what it can do for you

- Hardware required to run Oracle Reports

- How to install Oracle Reports

- How to prepare your PC to run Oracle Reports (Oracle Reports runs on computers other than PCs, but we will concentrate on PCs in this chapter)

- How Oracle Reports processes queries

- Where to set preferences in Oracle Reports

- How to work with Oracle Reports files

- How to build a two-query report

- How to create and display a computed field

- Basic output formatting using Oracle Reports

- How to build a single-query matrix report

- How to use Oracle Reports Runtime

NOTE
Learn the procedures and concepts presented in each sample report in this chapter one at a time. Before moving on to the next exercise, practice what you have learned so far. While the reports we build are simple, they illustrate fundamental Oracle Reports concepts.

Sample Data

You can run the following SQL program to create and populate the tables used in the exercises in this chapter. The username and password you enter when requested are the same ones through which you connect to the database to run the following program:

```
rem *  -----------------------------------------------------------
rem *  Script to set up tables used in Chapter 8 from
rem *  Oracle: A Beginner's Guide ISBN 0-07-882122-3
rem *  -----------------------------------------------------------
set echo on
drop table person;
drop table clssn;
drop table bonus;
drop table factory;
```

```
drop table commission;
create table person (
    pin             number(6),
    last_name       varchar2(20),
    first_name      varchar2(20),
    hire_date       date,
    salary          number(8,2),
    clssn           varchar2(5));
create table clssn (
    clssn           varchar2(5),
    descr           varchar2(20));
create table bonus (
    emp_id          number(4),
    emp_class       varchar2(2),
    fac_id          varchar2(3),
    bonus_amt       number);
create table factory (
    fac_id          varchar2(3),
    descr           varchar2(20),
    prov            varchar2(2));
create table commission (
    sales_id        number(3),
    qtr             varchar2(1),
    comm_amt        number(8,2));
insert into person values
(100110,'SAUNDERS','HELEN','12-DEC-87',77000,'1');
insert into person values
(100120,'FONG','LYDIA','11-MAY-88',55000,'3');
insert into person values
(100130,'WILLIAMS','FRANK','09-DEC-82',43000,'4');
insert into person values
(100140,'COHEN','NANCY','14-AUG-93',44000,'4');
insert into person values
(100150,'STEWART','BORIS','11-NOV-91',48000,'4');
insert into person values
(100160,'REDMOND','KENNETH','01-FEB-92',32000,'5');
insert into person values
(100170,'SMYTHE','ROLLY','11-JUL-83',33000,'5');
insert into person values
(100180,'FRANKS','HENRY','31-JUL-83',55000,'3');
insert into person values
(100190,'GREENBERG','JOE','30-MAR-86',21000,'6');
```

```
insert into person values
(100200,'LEVIS','SANDRA','06-DEC-89',18000,'7');
insert into person values
(100210,'APPOLLO','BILL','12-APR-89',44000,'4');
insert into person values
(100210,'JENKINS','SALLY','12-DEC-87',44000,'4');
insert into clssn values ('1','Manager');
insert into clssn values ('2','Chief');
insert into clssn values ('3','Leader');
insert into clssn values ('4','Analyst');
insert into clssn values ('5','Clerk');
insert into clssn values ('6','Trainee');
insert into clssn values ('7','Part time');
insert into bonus values (123,null,'AE',2000);
insert into bonus values (124,null,'AF',2200);
insert into bonus values (125,null,'AH',1200);
insert into bonus values (126,null,'AH',1200);
insert into bonus values (127,null,'AF',1200);
insert into bonus values (128,null,'AT',1500);
insert into bonus values (129,null,'AT',1100);
insert into bonus values (130,null,'AU',1400);
insert into bonus values (131,null,'AE',200);
insert into bonus values (132,null,'AF',220);
insert into bonus values (133,null,'AG',120);
insert into bonus values (134,null,'AG',200);
insert into bonus values (135,null,'AG',200);
insert into bonus values (136,null,'AU',1400);
insert into bonus values (137,null,'AH',100);
insert into bonus values (138,null,'AU',1400);
insert into factory values ('AE','Northeast','ON');
insert into factory values ('AF','Northwest','MN');
insert into factory values ('AH','Southeast','ON');
insert into factory values ('AT','Central','MN');
insert into factory values ('AU','South','CA');
insert into commission values (10,1,140);
insert into commission values (10,2,10);
insert into commission values (10,3,null);
insert into commission values (10,4,810);
insert into commission values (20,1,1200);
insert into commission values (20,2,200);
insert into commission values (20,3,500);
insert into commission values (20,4,100);
```

```
insert into commission values (30,1,40);
insert into commission values (30,2,19);
insert into commission values (30,3,340);
insert into commission values (30,4,null);
```

Terminology

The following definitions will arm you with the technical jargon to make it through this chapter.

- *Comma insertion* is used to format numeric data for display purposes. It places commas in large numbers to make them more readable to the user (e.g., the number 83892029 is displayed as 83,892,029).

- *Zero suppression* replaces leading zeros with spaces in numeric data for display purposes. Using zero suppression, the number 00003487 would be displayed as 3487 (i.e., with four blanks in front of the number where the zeros used to be).

- Asking Oracle to convert PL/SQL code into executable format is referred to as *compiling* PL/SQL. While coding PL/SQL in Oracle Reports, you'll come across many dialog boxes with which you can ask Oracle to compile your PL/SQL before dissolving the box.

- *Binary* is a format used by computers to store executable programs. In the DOS world, the programs winword.exe (used to invoke Word 6 for Windows) or control.exe (used to run the Windows main program group control panel option) are examples of binary files.

- Asking Oracle to convert your report definition to binary format is called *generating* a report.

- You may wish to have a suggested layout for the report output, based on the report type and number of fields being displayed. This is referred to as using Oracle Reports' *default layout* feature.

What Is Oracle Reports?

Oracle Reports is a feature-rich reporting tool that produces production quality output using data sources such as the Oracle database. Developers are able to embed graphics, sound, video, and a wide assortment of visual aids in screen and hard-copy (printed) output. Its predecessor, SQL*Reportwriter, which was bundled with version 6 of Oracle, was a character-based reporting environment. In Oracle Reports, the designer interface is mouse-driven.

In this chapter, we will discuss the two most frequently used components of Oracle Reports: Oracle Reports Designer and Oracle Reports Runtime. Because all Developer 2000 tools are integrated with one another and run against an Oracle database, Oracle Reports can share data with other Developer 2000 tools. They all have a Microsoft Windows look and feel.

Hardware Requirements to Run Oracle Reports

The following minimum configuration is required to use Oracle Reports.

- A 386 or stronger central processing unit (CPU), though a 486 or Pentium is preferred

- At least 60 megabytes (or 61,440,000 bytes) of available disk space

- A 40MHz or faster processor—speeds of 66 or better are preferable

- At least 8MB (megabytes) of extended memory

- MS-DOS or PC-DOS versions 5 or 6, or DR-DOS version 6 or higher

- Microsoft Windows 3.1 (and eventually Windows 95)

We recommend putting a CD-ROM drive on your machine. Oracle is moving towards this as the default distribution medium; as well, what easily fits on a fraction of a CD-ROM (each holds 600MB, or 638,976,000 bytes) could easily take up a very large number of 3.5-inch diskettes. When Personal Oracle7 was beta, one of our clients had over 86MB of Oracle and Oracle-support software on a 486 PC. Had they installed from diskette, that could have easily been over 60 diskettes!

Installing Oracle Reports

As with the rest of the Oracle products for Windows, installation is done from the Oracle installer (referred to as *orainst* in Chapter 4). To begin installation, click on the Oracle Installer icon in the Oracle group of Program Manager. You will be presented with the Oracle Installer startup screen shown in Figure 8-1. Notice that there are two boxes side-by-side on the screen: Available Products and Installed Products. If Oracle Reports is not one of the available products, scroll through the list until it appears. Once in view, there may be a plus (+) sign beside the product

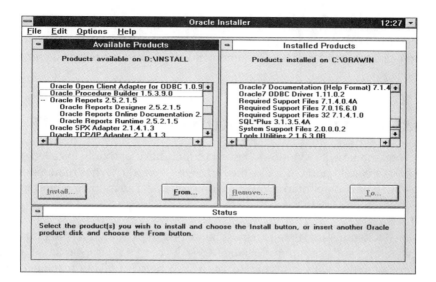

FIGURE 8-1. *Oracle Installer startup screen, showing the Oracle Reports component list in the Available Products box*

name. This indicates that components of the product can be installed together or separately. Double-click on the product name to expand the component list, as shown in Figure 8-1. While that component list is displayed, each one may be installed separately. We recommend you install all three components of Oracle Reports. If the component list is expanded, select all three by holding down CTRL and clicking on Designer, Runtime, and Online Documentation. If the component list is not expanded, simply click on Oracle Reports.

NOTE
To expand a product list, double-click on the product name. To collapse a list when product components have been expanded, click on the product name with the "-" sign beside it. When a product can be expanded, there is a "+" sign beside its name.

During the installation process, you will be asked to designate a directory for the product. Oracle suggests placing it in \orawin\reports25. Unless you are already using that directory for something else, accept it as is. When the installation terminates (be patient—it can take upwards of 30 minutes), you will see the product in the Installed Products box on the right side of the Oracle Installer screen. To leave the installer, double-click on the control button. You are now ready to use Oracle Reports. When you return to the Program Manager, you will see the Oracle

Reports-specific icons in the CDE2 Tools program group as shown in Figure 8-2. (This is the suite of tools currently referred to by Oracle as Developer 2000.) The installation also produces a CDE2 Documentation program group separate from CDE2 Tools.

Preparing Your PC to Run Oracle Reports

Those of you familiar with Windows-based products have probably installed one of them before. Oracle Reports, just like the rest of these products, has requirements for its operating environment to allow it to run properly. The following must be done before running Oracle Reports.

- The DOS program share.exe must be loaded to permit Oracle Reports to share files and perform its locking. Consult your DOS user's manual if you are unfamiliar with this program, or, if DOS help is on your machine, enter the command **help share** and you will be told

```
Installs file-sharing and locking capabilities
                          on your hard disk.
SHARE [/F:space] [/L:locks]
   /F:space   Allocates file space (in bytes) for
              file-sharing information.
   /L:locks   Sets the number of files that can be
              locked at one time.
```

- You must have access to a local or remote Oracle7 database. To access a remote database, you or your database administrator must have installed SQL*Net and been able to successfully connect to the database.

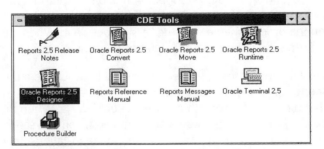

FIGURE 8-2. *Oracle Reports icons*

■ You must have already loaded your network software if you are accessing a remote database. If you are using a local Personal Oracle7 database, this is not necessary.

How Oracle Reports Processes Queries

Oracle Reports can be a very complex product, yet you can design useful and sophisticated output with little or no programming. A network of nested **select** statements can produce the desired results in a short time period. Nested **select** statements are a series of SQL statements in which column values from a high-level query (called the *parent query*) are passed down for further processing to a lower-level query (referred to as the *child query*). A query that is a child of a higher-level query can in turn be the parent of a query of a lower level. Table 8-1 shows an example of how Oracle Reports handles this processing. The information in the Type column indicates a parent (P) or child (C) query.

There is a significant difference in the way these queries are worded; usually when more than one table is referred to in a SQL statement, you place both table names in the **from** line of that statement. The parts of SQL statements are discussed in Chapter 5 and Chapter 11. Asking SQL to process a statement using more than one table is called a *join* operation. The column values in the tables are compared against one another using a *join condition*. Rows whose column values match one another appear as the results of the query. Most join conditions are done using equality as the relational operator, though conditions using other operators (such as

QUERY NAME	QUERY TEXT	TYPE	COLUMN VALUES
Q_1	select oname,location,province from offices	P	Passes oname to Q_2 Passes location to Q_3
Q_2	select oname, leader_name, leader_rank from leaders	C P	Receives oname from Q_1 Passes leader_rank to Q_4
Q_3	select location, desc_e, desc_f from locations	C	Receives location from Q_1
Q_4	select leader_rank, rank_weight, rank_desc from ranking	C	Receives leader_rank from Q_2

TABLE 8-1. *Parent/Child Query Example*

>, <, or <>) are possible. The following listing shows how a common join condition is worded.

```
select oname,location,province,
       desc_e,desc_f          /* The columns come from both tables. */
   from offices,locations     /* For a row to be fetched, its   */
 where offices.location =      /* location column values must be  */
       locations.location;    /* the same in both tables. */
```

In Table 8-1, notice how the SQL text in Q_2 mentions the column oname but does not equate it to the value passed from its parent query (Q_1). As well, Q_3 does not equate location to the value it receives from its parent (Q_1). Finally, Q_4 does not explicitly equate leader_rank to the value it receives from its parent (Q_2). Thus, when a row is selected from Q_1, it passes down its oname column value to Q_2 and its location column value to Q_3. As well, when a row is selected in Q_2, it passes its leader_rank column value to Q4.

Oracle Reports Designer

This component is where the developer defines new reports and enhances existing ones. It is invoked by double-clicking on the Reports Designer icon in the CDE2 Tools program group. Before we dive into Oracle Reports, let's take a look at the assortment of buttons and tools you will be using in this chapter.

Oracle Reports calls the buttons along the top of its screen the *toolbar* and the tools down the side of its screen the *tool palette*. Figure 8-3 shows the Data Model button in the Object Navigator. Figure 8-4 shows the various tools and buttons in the Data Model. Figure 8-5 shows the Run tool on the Layout toolbar. There are many more buttons and tools you can use with Oracle Reports Designer than we discuss in this chapter. We only touch on the ones we will be using.

The Object Navigator

The Object Navigator is shown in Figure 8-6. You access all objects used in your reports from this central navigator. Oracle Reports uses the term *object* to refer to a report's component parts. Some of these parts (shown in Figure 8-6) are discussed in sections of this chapter (specifically the Data Model).

Oracle Reports uses the "+" and "-" signs in the Object Navigator similar to the installer we talked about earlier. To expand an object in the Object Navigator, click on its "+" sign; when an object is expanded, click on its "-" sign to collapse the expanded list.

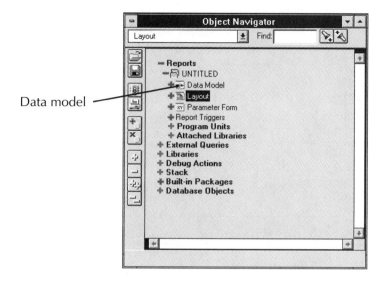

FIGURE 8-3. *Data Model button on the Object Navigator*

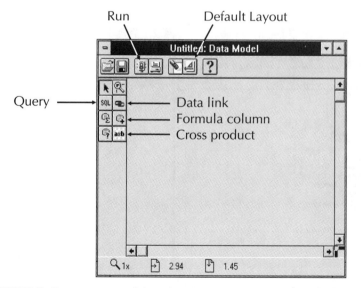

FIGURE 8-4. *Data Model tools*

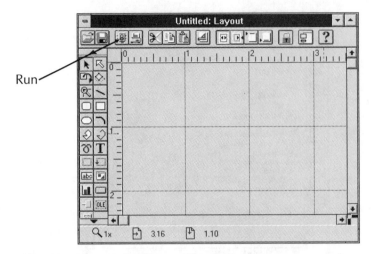

Run

FIGURE 8-5. *Run tool on the Layout toolbar*

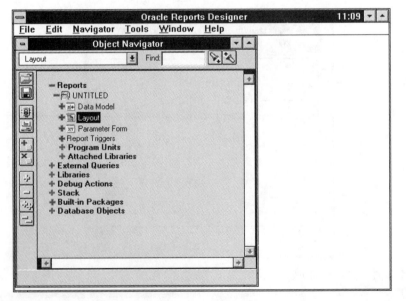

FIGURE 8-6. *Object Navigator*

Setting Preferences

By setting preferences, you can tell Oracle Reports about your work habits and how you would prefer Oracle Reports to behave. You can store Oracle Reports programs in the database or in DOS files on your PC; in Preferences, you tell Oracle Reports which you want to use during each session. Once preferences have been set, some of the dialog boxes will not appear, since you have specified the way you want Oracle Reports to behave. For example, to tell Oracle Reports to save all report programs to files, do the following:

1. Click on Tools on the menu at the top of the screen, then Tools Option to bring up the Tools Option dialog box. There are three folders in this box; if the Preferences folder is not showing, click on its tab to bring it to the front of the screen.

2. In the Object Access area, click on the Storage Type drop-down arrow. Click on File from the drop down menu that appears to return to the Preferences folder. If this is the first time you have set preferences, the options already selected (e.g., Suppress Define Property Sheets) are Oracle Reports defaults.

3. Click on Save Preferences, then click OK as shown in Figure 8-7 to complete the activity.

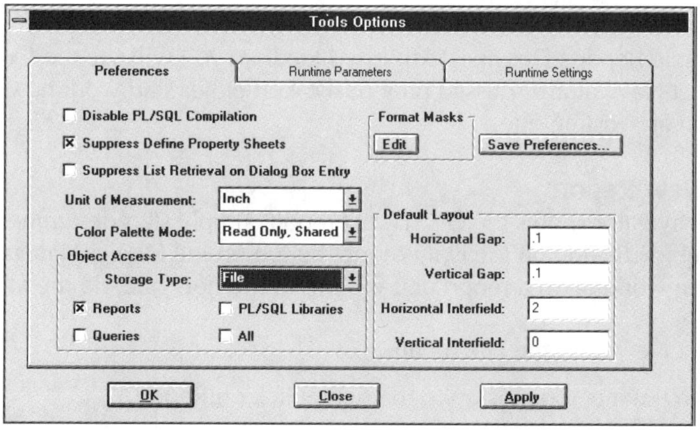

FIGURE 8-7. *Preferences object access selected*

You are then returned to the Object Navigator or where you were before setting the object access preference. Other preferences you can choose include the following:

■ You can format masks for numeric data, utilizing comma insertion and zero suppression. Using this feature, you can tell Oracle Reports to display the number 012730 as 12,730.

■ You can adjust the horizontal and vertical space between fields on a default layout. Some people find the amount of space left between fields too little; this space can be changed and saved for future reference.

■ You can instruct Oracle Reports about when you want PL/SQL to be compiled. You can choose to compile whenever you leave a dialog box in which you have written some PL/SQL code, or you can tell Oracle Reports to compile only when generating a report.

How to Work with Oracle Reports Files

Now that you have told Oracle Reports to save report files to your hard disk, let's cover working with these report definition files. In this section, you will learn how to do the following:

■ Create a new report

■ Save a new report

■ Open an existing report

Once Oracle Reports Designer is finished loading, you will see the Oracle Reports Object Navigator discussed previously. You either start working with a new report or open an existing one.

Creating a New Report
If the object navigator shows the UNTITLED report, simply start designing the new report by double-clicking on the Data Model button on the Object Navigator. If you have been working on a report and wish to start a new one, do the following.

1. Select New from the File menu.

2. When the menu opens up to the right, click on Report.

Oracle Reports creates the new report and calls it UNTITLED. The Object Navigator now shows both reports.

TIP
The quickest way to start a new report is to use the shortcut key
CTRL-E. If your work needs to be saved before the new report
definition begins, Oracle will prompt you to save before starting a
new report.

Opening an Existing Report
You can open an existing report by doing the following.

1. Select Open from the File menu.

2. When Oracle Reports brings up the Open Report dialog box, double-click
on the filename to open, or click once to highlight a name, then click on
the OK button to open the report.

After opening the report, Oracle Reports changes the Object Navigator to
display the report you have just opened.

TIP
The quickest way to open a report is to use the shortcut key CTRL-O.
This opens the Open Report dialog box.

Saving a Report
You can save a report by doing the following.

1. Select Save from the File menu.

2. When Oracle Reports brings up the Save Report dialog box, enter a
filename for the report.

3. Click on the OK button to complete the action. The name of the file you
enter must conform to DOS file-naming conventions.

TIP
The quickest way to save a report is to use the shortcut key CTRL-S. If
Oracle does not know the name of the report you are saving, it will
open up the Save Report dialog box and ask you for the name.

Changing the Name of a Report
If you wish to change the name of a report, do the following.

1. Select Save As from the File menu.

2. After Oracle Reports brings up Save As dialog box, enter a new filename for the report.

3. Click on the OK button to complete the action. The name of the file you enter must conform to DOS file-naming conventions.

Two Main Designer Components

You will spend most of your time in the Designer using either the Data Model screen or the Layout screen. Using the Data Model screen, you define the data you will use in the report and its relationships with other data in the report. It is shown in Figure 8-8. You invoke the Data Model screen by double-clicking on the Data Model button on the Object Navigator.

Access the Layout screen by double-clicking on the Layout button on the Object Navigator. The Layout screen, as shown in Figure 8-9, is where you define the look of your report. You cut and paste objects on this screen to fine-tune the placement of information on your report output.

Moving Between the Screens

When the Data Model screen is active, you move to the Layout screen by double-clicking on the Layout button on the Object Navigator. You move to the Data Model screen by double-clicking on the Data Model button on the Object Navigator.

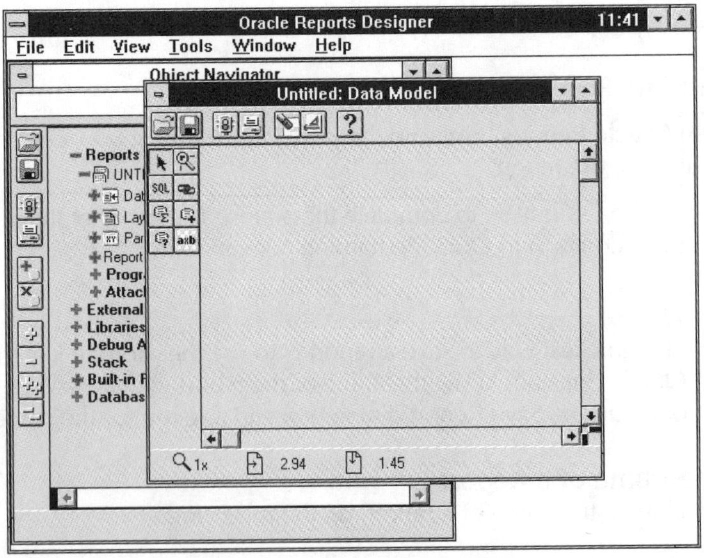

FIGURE 8-8. *Reports Data Model screen*

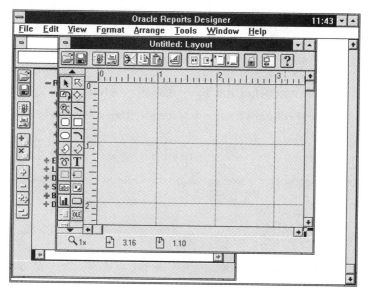

FIGURE 8-9. *Reports Layout screen*

TIP
You can tile or cascade the two screens by selecting Tile or Cascade from the Window menu. Then, you can move back and forth between the two simply by clicking somewhere in the one you wish to work with.

Sample Report #1

This first example illustrates the simplest form of Oracle Reports output: displaying a few columns in a table, nothing fancy. We use the person and clssn tables shown in Table 8-2. The information in the Matches column indicates if the clssn column in person relates to the clssn column in clssn. We will use these columns to create a *link condition.* This condition instructs Oracle Reports on how to link two queries together; once defined, Oracle Reports processes the queries using the parent/child technique, which we discussed earlier in the "How Oracle Reports Processes Queries" section.

Exercise #1
You are required to print a list showing everyone's pin and full name. The output will resemble the following:

```
Pin        Full name
101210     SALLY JENKINS
```

In this section we will show you how to:

- Create a query and define the query selection criteria
- Pick tables and columns for query selection from a Personal Oracle7 database
- Define a computed field and where it is displayed
- Customize headings on a report using the Default Layout dialog box
- Run a report

To program this report, do the following.

1. In the Object Navigator, double-click on the Data Model button to open the Data Model screen, if it isn't already open.

2. In the Data Model screen, click on the Query tool.

3. The cursor changes to a large plus (+) sign. Drag the cursor into the workspace. Click to create a query box, as shown in Figure 8-10.

4. Double-click on query Q_1 to bring up the Query dialog box shown in Figure 8-11. It is now time to define the query used for this report. The query dialog box has two folders. To define the query, if the General folder is obscured, click on its tab to bring it to the front of the box.

PERSON TABLE		**MATCHES**
pin	number(6)	
last_name	varchar2(20)	
first_name	varchar2(20)	
clssn	varchar2(5)	clssn in CLSSN

CLSSN TABLE		**MATCHES**
clssn	varchar2(5)	clssn in PERSON
descr	varchar2(20)	

TABLE 8-2.   *Tables Used in Sample Report #1*

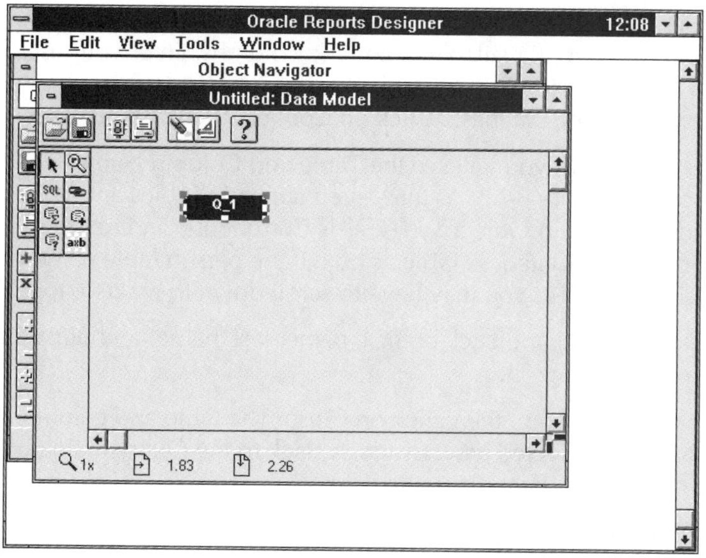

FIGURE 8-10. *Data model showing a first query*

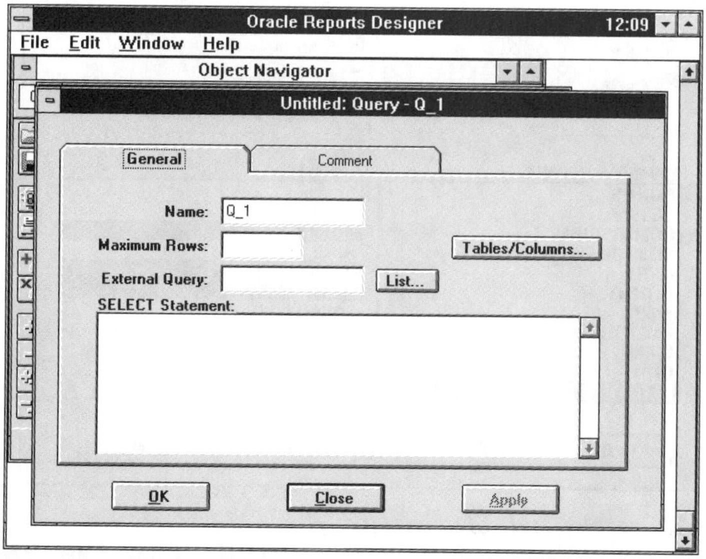

FIGURE 8-11. *Query dialog box*

5. Click on Tables/Columns. Oracle Reports asks you to connect to the database to bring up a list of available tables and columns. Enter your username and password. Leave the Database blank, since you are accessing a local Personal Oracle7 database. Click on Connect to log into the database.

6. Once connected, you will see the Table and Column Names dialog box, as shown in Figure 8-12. As the screen appears, Tables and Views are already selected in Object Types, as is Current user in User types. Click on PERSON in the Database Objects box. If the person table name is not in the table name list, you may have to scroll down to make it appear.

7. Hold down CTRL, and click on first_name, last_name, and pin, as shown in Figure 8-12.

8. Click on Select-from, then click on Close. The table and column names you have just selected are transferred back to the Query dialog box as if you had entered them manually.

9. Click on Apply, then click on Close to return to the data model shown in Figure 8-13.

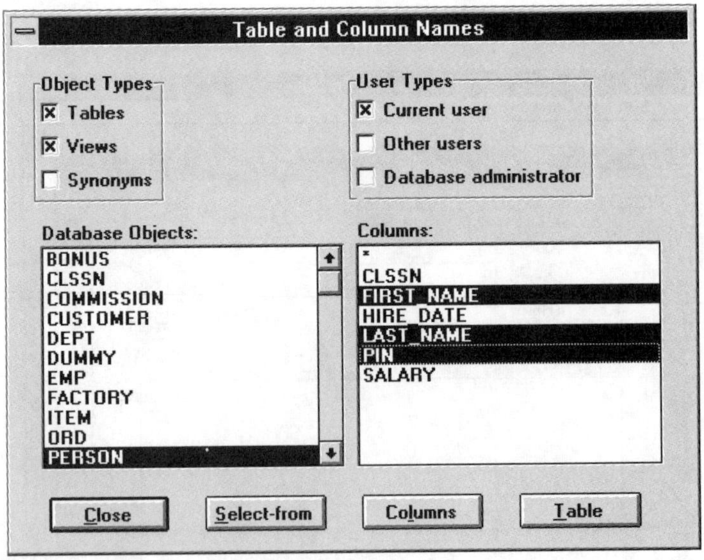

FIGURE 8-12. *Tables and columns selected*

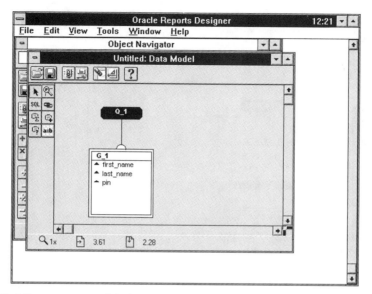

FIGURE 8-13. *Data model showing Q_1 and G_1*

NOTE
If you know the names of the table and columns you will be using in your query, you may proceed to the SELECT Statement text box in the Query dialog box and type in your query. After typing the query text, enter your username and password, then click on Connect to log into Personal Oracle7. After Oracle verifies your query text, click on Close to return to the Data Model screen.

10. Click on the Formula Column tool to define a formula field. The cursor changes to a large plus (+) sign. Drag the cursor into the workspace and click somewhere in the group G_1 box. A field called CF_1 appears when the button is released, as shown in Figure 8-14.

11. Double-click on the CF_1 field to bring up the Formula Column dialog box, as shown in Figure 8-15. The Formula Column dialog box has two folders. To define the formula, if the General folder is obscured, click on its tab to bring it to the front of the box.

12. Click on the Datatype drop-down arrow. Select Char.

13. In the Width box, enter **30**.

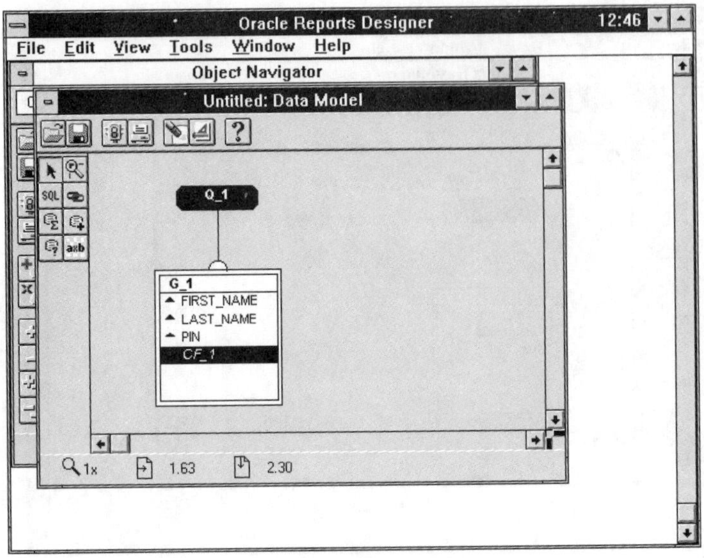

FIGURE 8-14. *Data model with a computed field*

14. Click on Edit to bring up the Program Unit definition box. Enter the formula
text **return (:first_name⌐'´'⌐:last_name);** as shown in Figure 8-16.

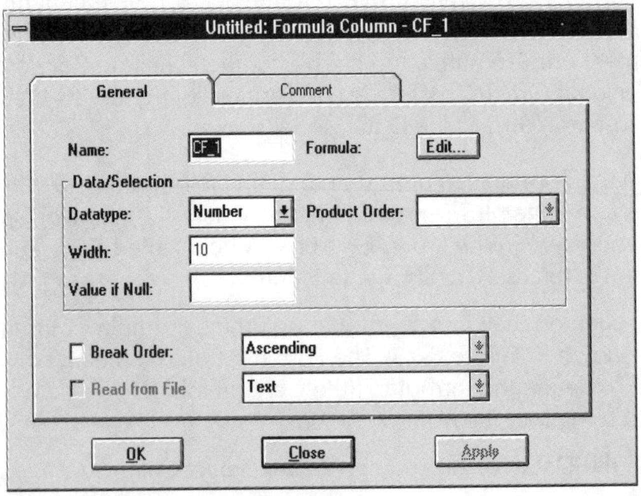

FIGURE 8-15. *Formula Column dialog box*

```
┌─────────────────────────────────────────────────────────────┐
│ ─        Oracle Reports Designer         14:44 ▼ ▲           │
│  File  Edit  Window  Help                                    │
│ ┌───────────────────────────────────────────────────┐  ↑    │
│ │ ─  Reports: UNTITLED: Program Unit - CF_1FORMULA ▼ ▲│      │
│ │ ┌────────┐ ┌──────┐ ┌──────┐ ┌──────┐ ┌──────┐ ┌──────┐    │
│ │ │Compile │ │ Apply│ │Revert│ │ New..│ │Delete│ │Close │    │
│ │ └────────┘ └──────┘ └──────┘ └──────┘ └──────┘ └──────┘    │
│ │ Type: │Object Level  ▼│ Object:│Column    ▼│ │CF_1    │ ▼  │
│ │ Name: │Formula                                         │ ▼ │
│ │ ┌───────────────────────────────────────────────┐ ▲       │
│ │ │function CF_1Formula return Char is            │         │
│ │ │begin                                          │         │
│ │ │  return (:first_name||' '||:last_name);       │         │
│ │ │end;                                           │         │
│ │ │                                               │         │
│ │ │                                               │         │
│ │ │                                               │         │
│ │ │                                               │ ▼       │
│ │ └───────────────────────────────────────────────┘         │
│ └───────────────────────────────────────────────────┘       │
└─────────────────────────────────────────────────────────────┘
```

FIGURE 8-16.   *Formula Program Unit dialog box*

NOTE
When the Program Unit definition box appears, you may have to shunt the windows around on the screen to make its data entry area appear.

15. Click on Compile, then click on Close to return to the Formula Column dialog box.

16. Click on Apply, then click on Close to return to the Data Model screen. The formula field you have just defined shows up as CF_1.

NOTE
You may find that when you compile the formula you have entered in the Program Unit definition box, Oracle Reports returns you to the Data Model screen. You must move to the Formula Column box and click on Apply then Close before continuing.

17. Click on the Default Layout tool. When presented with the six style options as shown in Figure 8-17, notice that the Tabular option is selected. If the Data/Selection folder is at the front of this box, click on the Style folder's tab to bring it to the front.

```
┌──────────────────────────────────────────────────────────────┐
│ ─                  Untitled: Default Layout                    │
├──────────────────────────────────────────────────────────────┤
│  ┌──────────────┐ ┌──────────────────┐                        │
│  │    Style     │ │  Data/Selection  │                        │
│  ├──────────────┴─┴──────────────────┴────────────────────┐   │
│  │  ◉ Tabular       ○ Master/Detail       ○ Form          │   │
│  │    [icon]          [icon]                [icon]         │   │
│  │                                                        │   │
│  │  ○ Form Letter   ○ Mailing Label       ○ Matrix        │   │
│  │    [icon]          [icon]                [icon]         │   │
│  │                                                        │   │
│  │  ┌─ Options ──────────────────────────────────────┐   │   │
│  │  │  ☐ Use Current Layout Settings                 │   │   │
│  │  └────────────────────────────────────────────────┘   │   │
│  │                                                        │   │
│  │        ┌────────┐              ┌────────┐              │   │
│  │        │   OK   │              │ Cancel │              │   │
│  │        └────────┘              └────────┘              │   │
│  └────────────────────────────────────────────────────────┘   │
└──────────────────────────────────────────────────────────────┘
```

FIGURE 8-17. *Default Layout style selection*

18. Click on the Data/Selection tab, then click on FIRST_NAME and LAST_NAME. The text changes from white on black to black on gray; this indicates the fields will not display on the report.

19. Highlight the value in the Label column for CF_1 and change it to the text **Full Name**.

20. Click on OK. You are presented with the Oracle Reports Layout screen. Since we have defined the layout using the Default Layout dialog box, there is no work to be done here.

21. Save the report by pressing CTRL-S.

VIP
We recommend you save your work every few minutes. Good habits you may have learned doing word processing should be practiced with Oracle Reports.

22. Enter the name **reports1** for the report, then click on OK to complete the save.

23. Click on the Run tool.

24. Click on Run Report in the Runtime Parameter Form to bring up the report output on the Previewer window, as shown in Figure 8-18.

25. Click on Close to close the Previewer window.

```
 ▭                      Oracle Reports Designer              16:54 ▾ ▲
 File   Edit   Window   Help
 ▭                      reports1: Previewer                     ▾ ▲ ▲
 Prev   Next   First   Last   Page:  1              Print  Close  New
                                                                  ▲ ▲

        Pin    Full Name
       100110  HELEN SAUNDERS
       100120  LYDIA FONG
       100130  FRANK WILLIAMS
       100140  NANCY COHEN
       100150  BORIS STEWART
       100160  KENNETH REDMOND
       100170  ROLLY SMYTHE
       100180  HENRY FRANKS
       100190  JOE GREENBERG
       100200  SANDRA LEVIS
       100210  BILL APPOLLO
       100210  SALLY JENKINS                                     ▼ ▼
 Q Q ◄                                                         ►
```

FIGURE 8-18.   *Report output on the Previewer window*

26. Press CTRL-W to close the report and return to an empty Object Navigator.

   Congratulations! You have just used Oracle Reports 2.5 to build a simple report, reading data from a Personal Oracle7 database.

Exercise #2
We need to modify the report output to capitalize the first name and surname of each person and sort the data by last name. The output will resemble the following:

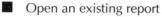

```
Pin        Full name
101210     Sally Jenkins
```

   In this section we will show you details on how to:

■   Open an existing report

■   Modify an existing query

■   Sort the rows returned from a query

■   Format data in a computed field

The following modifications to the initial report will accomplish this:

1. Press CTRL-O to open the Open Report dialog box. Double-click on reports1 to open the report.

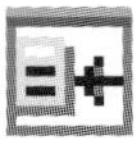

2. Double-click on the Data Model button to display the Data Model screen.

3. Double-click on query Q_1, and when the Query dialog box appears, add the text **order by last_name** at the end of the existing query.

4. Click on Apply, then click on Close to record the change to query Q_1.

5. Double-click on field CF_1. In the Formula Column dialog box, click on Edit.

6. In the Program Unit definition box, change the line starting with "return" to **return initcap((:first_name¦¦' '¦¦:last_name));** as shown in Figure 8-19.

7. Click on Compile, then click on Close to return to the Formula Column dialog box.

8. Click on Apply, then click on Close to return to the Data Model screen.

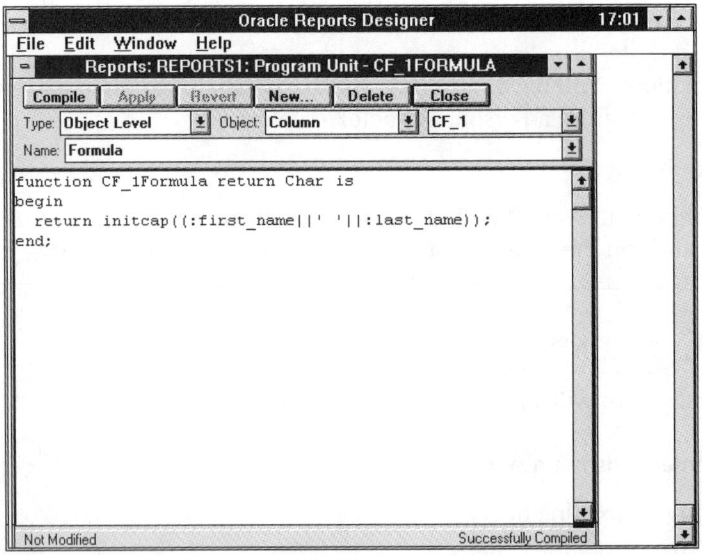

```
function CF_1Formula return Char is
begin
  return initcap((:first_name||' '||:last_name));
end;
```

FIGURE 8-19.   *Capitalizing the full name*

VIP
You may find that when you compile the formula you have entered in the Program Unit definition box, Oracle Reports returns you to the Data Model screen. You must move to the Formula Column box and click on Apply, then click on Close before continuing.

9. Save the report by pressing CTRL-S. Oracle Reports does not open a dialog box when you save the report, since it already knows the name (reports1).

10. Click on the Run tool.

11. Click on Run Report in the Runtime Parameter Form to bring up the report output on the Previewer window, as shown in Figure 8-20.

12. Click on Close to close the Previewer window.

Exercise #3
We need to further enhance the report output to list each person's classification. The output will resemble the following:

```
Pin              Full name                    Classification
101210           Sally Jenkins                Analyst
```

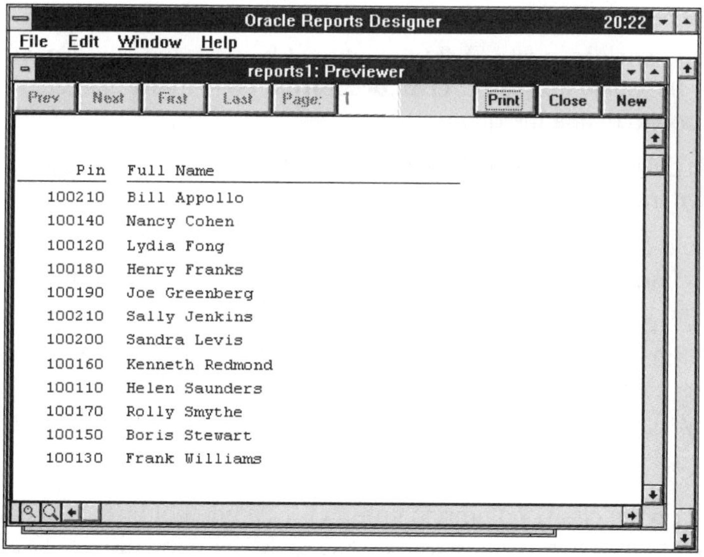

FIGURE 8-20. *Report output on the Previewer window*

In this section we will show you details on how to:

- Create a second query
- Add a column to an existing query
- Define the link condition between two queries
- Suppress double display of the linking column

NOTE
We assume you are working uninterrupted from the previous exercise. If, for some reason, you are not yet connected to the database, Personal Oracle7 will ask you to reconnect with the username and password during this exercise.

Program this by doing the following:

1. At this point, you should be looking at the Data Model screen. If you are not, double-click on Data Model button on the Object Navigator.

2. Click on the Query tool.

3. The cursor changes to a large plus (+) sign. Drag the cursor into the workspace. Click to create the query box called Q_2.

4. Double-click on query Q_2 to open the Query dialog box, General tab. Enter the query text **select clssn,descr from clssn** in the SELECT Statement text box to define the query.

5. Click on Apply, then click on Close to return to the Data Model screen shown in Figure 8-21.

6. Double-click on query Q_1 to return to the query dialog box, and add the text **,clssn** (be sure to enter the comma before **clssn**) to the query after the text **pin** in the SELECT Statement text box. It now looks like Figure 8-22.

7. Click on Apply, then click on Close to return to the Data Model screen. Oracle Reports uses the name clssn1 in group G_1 for the clssn column in query Q_1.

8. Click on the Data Link tool.

9. Click on the clssn1 column in group G_1. While holding CTRL, drag the cursor to the clssn column in group G_2. Release the mouse. Oracle Reports draws the link shown in Figure 8-23.

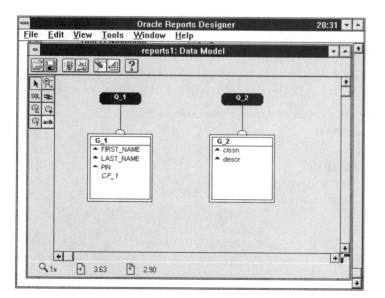

FIGURE 8-21. *Q_1 with new column added*

FIGURE 8-22. *Data model showing Q_1 and Q_2*

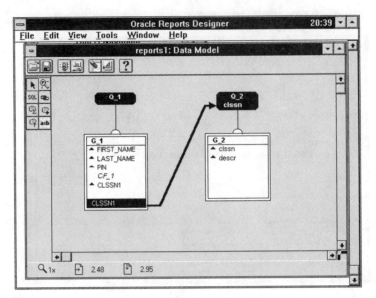

FIGURE 8-23. *Data model showing link condition*

10. Click on the Default Layout tool. When the Default Layout box appears, if the Data/Selection folder is obscured, click on its tab to bring it to the front of the screen.

11. Click on clssn and clssn1. The text changes from white on black to black on gray; this indicates the fields will not display on the report.

12. Highlight the value in the Label column for descr and change it to **Classification**.

> **NOTE**
> You may have to scroll down the list of columns to make the descr column appear.

13. Click on OK to accept the layout just entered. Oracle Reports may ask you if you want to replace the existing layout with the one you just entered. Click on OK to confirm this replacement, and you are presented with the Layout screen.

14. Save the report by pressing CTRL-S.

15. Click on the Run tool.

16. Click on Run Report in the Runtime Parameter Form to bring up the report output on the Previewer window, as shown in Figure 8-24.

17. Click on Close to close the Previewer window, then press CTRL-W to close the report.

Sample Report #2

In this example we will discuss:

■ Suppressing display of some column values

■ Changing field headings and display widths using the Default Layout dialog box

■ Splitting the makeup of an existing group

■ Creating and displaying running totals

This exercise uses the Bonus table, shown in Table 8-3.

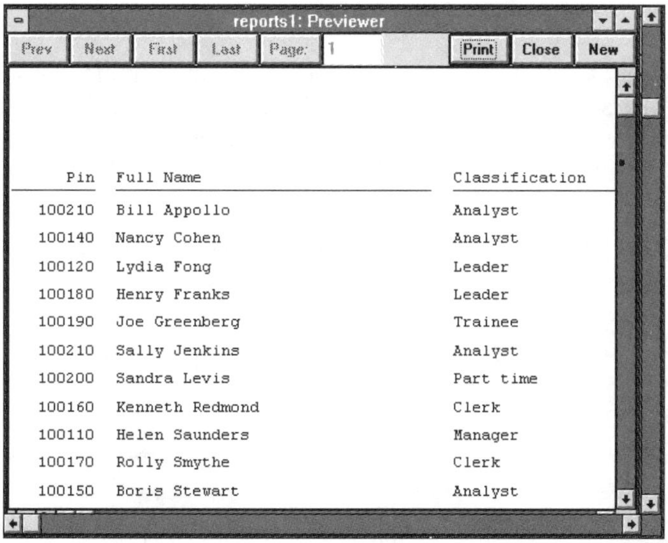

FIGURE 8-24.   *Report output on the Previewer window*

BONUS TABLE

emp_id	number(4)
emp_class	varchar2(2)
fac_id	varchar2(3)
bonus_amt	number

TABLE 8-3. *Table Used in Sample Report #2*

Exercise

We need to produce a listing of employees with bonuses sorted by factory. The output should resemble the following:

```
Factory  Emp ID   Bonus
  AE      123     2000
          131      200
  AF      124     2200
          127     1200
          132      220
  AG      133      120
          134      200
```

Notice how the factory is not repeated when successive employees are in the same factory. This is a concept called *control break*. Control breaking means that data is only printed on a report when there is a change in value. Control break works as illustrated in Table 8-4, using the factory values from the previous listing.

ROW #	CURRENT FACTORY	PREVIOUS FACTORY	PRINT CURRENT
1	AE	undefined	Y
2	AE	AE	N
3	AF	AE	Y
4	AF	AF	N
5	AF	AF	N
6	AG	AF	Y
7	AG	AG	N

TABLE 8-4. *Control Break Column Suppression*

In Table 8-4, the factory values should only be printed for rows 1, 3, and 6. By examining the previous listing, this appears to be the case.

If double bonuses were handed out to employee 124, the report would then resemble the following:

```
Factory                 Emp ID          Bonus
   AE                      123            4000
                           124            1000
                                           250
   AF                      126            4000
```

This can be accomplished by doing the following:

1. Position yourself back in the Object Navigator, then click on the text "Reports", then the Data Model button on the Object Navigator.

2. Click on the Query tool.

3. The cursor changes to a large plus (+) sign. Drag the cursor into the workspace. Click to create query box Q_1.

4. Double-click on query Q_1 to bring up the Query Definition dialog box.

5. Enter the query text **select fac_id,emp_id,bonus_amt from bonus order by fac_id** in the SELECT Statement text box.

6. Click on Apply. If you are not still connected to Personal Oracle7, enter the username and password when Oracle asks you to connect. Leave the Database area blank, since you are using a local database.

7. Click on Close to return to the Data Model screen as shown in Figure 8-25.

8. Click on the Default Layout tool. When the Default Layout dialog box appears, if the Data/Selection folder obscures the Style folder, click on the Style tab to bring the Style folder to the front. When presented with the six style options, notice that the Tabular option is selected.

9. Click on the Data/Selection tab. Change the headings for the columns to **Factory**, **Emp ID**, and **Bonus**, and the display widths for Factory to **7** and for Bonus to **12**. Click on OK to go to the Layout screen.

10. Click on the Run tool. Click on Run Report in the Runtime Parameter Form to bring up the report output on the Previewer window, as shown in Figure 8-26. Notice how the values for fac_id repeat even if the next factory is the same as the previous.

11. Define another group to allow for control break suppression of a repeating fac_id. After returning to the Data Model screen, click on fac_id in group

					Untitled: Previewer				
Prev	Next	First	Last	Page:	1		Print	Close	New

Factory	Employee	Bonus
AE	123	2000
AE	131	200
AF	124	2200
AF	132	220
AF	127	1200
AG	133	120
AG	134	200
AG	135	200
AH	125	1200
AH	126	1200
AH	137	100
AT	128	1500
AT	129	1100
AU	130	1400
AU	138	1400

FIGURE 8-25. *Report output on the Previewer window*

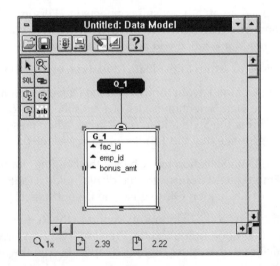

FIGURE 8-26. *Data model showing Q_1 and G_1*

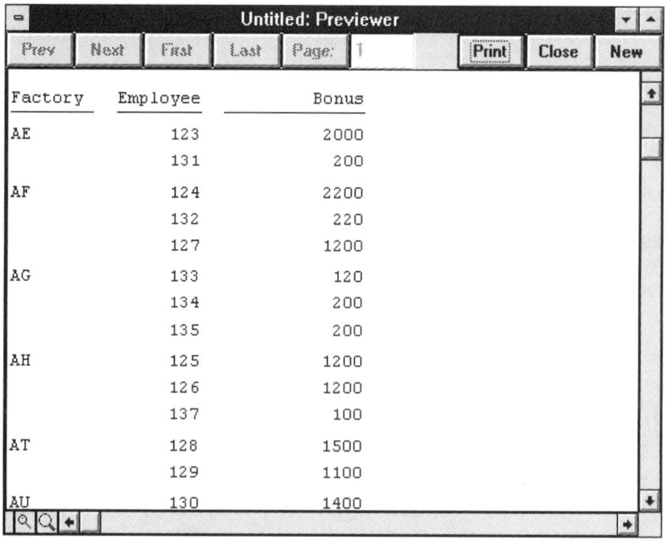

FIGURE 8-27. *Report output with fac_id control break suppression*

G_1 and drag it somewhere else on the data model. The act of moving fac_id out of group G_1 and placing it on its own in group G_2 is what causes it not to be repeated until its value changes. Notice how group G_2 is created when the mouse is released.

12. Click on the Default Layout tool, then click on OK to go to the Layout screen. You need to go to the Default Layout dialog box (even though you do nothing there), so Oracle Reports can react to the creation of group G_1 and suppress repeating fac_id values until it changes.

13. Click on the Run tool. When presented with the Runtime Parameter Form, click on Run Report to produce the output shown in Figure 8-27. Notice how the fac_id value only shows at the start of the report and when its value changes.

14. Click on Close to close the Previewer window.

15. Press CTRL-S to save the new report, and when prompted, enter the name **reports2**.

16. Press CTRL-W to close the data model and return to the Object Navigator.

Sample Report #3

In this example we will:

- Define and show examples of matrix reports
- Show you how to break up a report group to allow for matrix reporting
- Show you how to define the matrix report cross-product group
- Show you how to modify the matrix report default layout

This example illustrates a feature of Oracle Reports called matrix reports. A *matrix report* uses values from columns selected in the report query as column and row headings. Using the data described in Table 8-5, the output from this type of report looks like the following.

	1	2	3	4
10	200	300	400	70
20	150	40	600	
30		500	890	50

Notice how the sales_id column values are displayed down the page as row labels; the qtr column values display across the page as column headers; the actual comm_amt data populates the cells defined by the other two column values. The interesting thing about the matrix report is that if there is no data for the fourth quarter, the report display would change to this:

	1	2	3
10	200	300	400
20	150	40	600
30		500	890

COMM TABLE

qtr	number
sales_id	number
comm_amt	number(8,2)

TABLE 8-5. *Table Used for Sample Report #3*

Now, let's build this report.

1. Position yourself back at the Object Navigator, click on the text "Reports", then the Data Model button.

2. Click on the Query tool. The cursor changes to a large plus (+) sign. Drag the cursor into the workspace. Release the mouse, then double-click on query Q_1 to bring up the Query dialog box. Enter the query text **select qtr, sales_id, sum(comm_amt) from comm group by qtr, sales_id order by qtr, sales_id** in the SELECT Statement text box. Give the query a more descriptive name changing the Name from Q_1 to Q_matrix.

3. Click on Apply, then click on Close to return to the data model.

4. Create groups G_2 and G_3 from group G_1. Click on qtr in group G_1 and drag it elsewhere in the data model to create group G_2. Click on sales_id in group G_1 and drag it elsewhere in the data model to create group G_3. Having these separate groups is required for matrix reporting. The resulting data model is shown in Figure 8-28.

5. Create the cross-product group (the secret behind matrix reporting). Oracle Reports uses the term "cross-product" to define a special group for matrix reporting. Click on the Cross Product tool and lasso the work area around groups G_2 and G_3. This creates group G_4 and the data model changes to that shown in Figure 8-29.

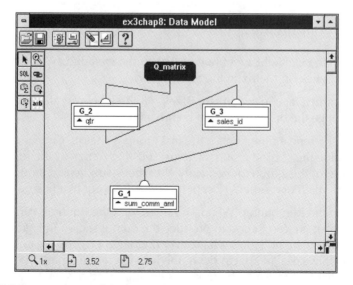

FIGURE 8-28. *Data model showing groups G_1, G_2, and G_3*

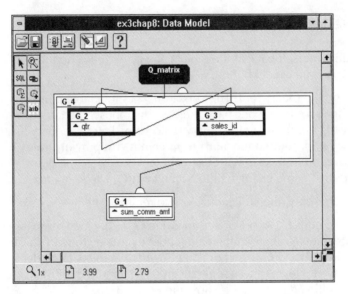

FIGURE 8-29. *Data model showing cross product group G4*

VIP
Before you lasso groups to create a cross-product group, you may have to move the groups around on the Data Model screen. The lasso you create cannot intersect any groups that are not in the cross-product group.

6. Click on the Default Layout button. When the Default Layout dialog box appears, click on Matrix in the Style folder.

7. Click on the Data/Selection tab. Blank out the labels for all three columns, and change the display width of comm_amt to **12**.

8. Notice the repeat direction for the first group is Matrix. Change the Repeat text beside the second group to Across. Having Across as the repeat function for this group immediately after the Matrix repeat group is another secret of matrix reporting. Accept this default layout by clicking on OK.

9. Click on the Run button. When presented with the Runtime Parameter Form, click on Run Report to produce the output shown in Figure 8-30. Notice there are no labels whatsoever on the report, and the column values from sales_id appear down the left side of the report. The qtr values appear across the top of the report as column headings.

10. Click on Close to close the Previewer window.

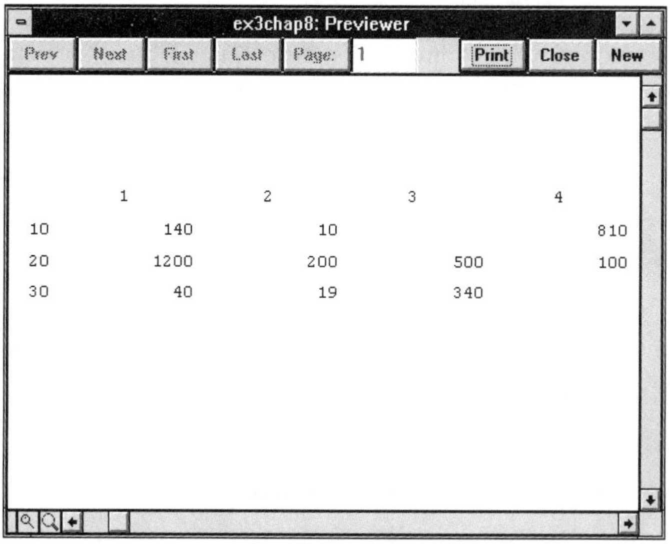

FIGURE 8-30. *Report output for matrix report*

11. Press CTRL-S to save the report, and when prompted, enter the name **reports3**.

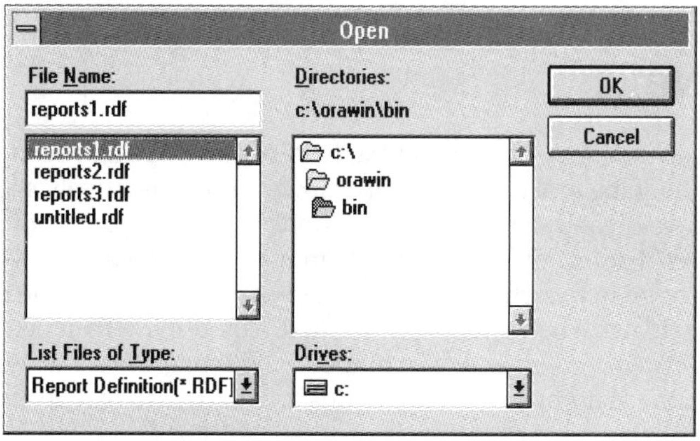

FIGURE 8-31. *Open report dialog box*

12. Press CTRL-W to close the report, then exit Oracle Reports by double-clicking on the control box, or selecting File then Close from the menu at the top of the Oracle Reports screen.

This finishes the hands-on exercises using Oracle Reports Designer.

Oracle Reports Runtime

This part of Oracle Reports is used to run reports. It is invoked by clicking on the Reports Runtime icon in the CDE2 Tools program group. When you are presented with the Runtime welcome screen, do the following to run a report:

1. Press CTRL-R to bring up the Open dialog box shown in Figure 8-31.

2. Once you have selected a report (e.g. **reports1**), click on OK.

3. Enter the username and password when asked to connect to the Personal Oracle7 database.

4. When presented with the Runtime Parameter Form, click on Run Report. The next thing you will see is your report output.

5. Click on Close when done browsing the output.

This will leave you positioned at the Reports Runtime startup screen. After developers code Oracle Reports programs, the source code is compiled and becomes part of the set of application code delivered to the end user. The end user invokes Reports Runtime within an application to browse and print report output.

What's Next

We have just touched the surface with Oracle Reports—you can spend hours learning more about the tool's functionality; however, in a relatively short period of time, you can develop and deploy Oracle Reports to take advantage of its advanced features. For example, using the Parameter Screen Painter (we have not discussed this feature in this chapter), you can format the design of the dialog box Oracle Reports initiates when a report is invoked. You use the Parameter form to tell Oracle Reports where you want the output to be sent (printer or screen). Experiment with the features of Oracle Reports and make use of a very flexible and powerful reporting tool.

Our next chapter is about Oracle Loader. It rounds out the "Developer Basics" section of the book. One of the nice things about Oracle Loader is that, after you learn how to use it, you can take all your favorite data from one of your existing systems, move it into Oracle, then write programs using the skills you have just acquired in this chapter and its predecessor ("Oracle Forms 101"). You've come a long way.

CHAPTER 9

Oracle Loader

This chapter introduces Oracle Loader, the tool used to move data from another data source into the Oracle database. In this chapter we'll also offer some advice on using this tool effectively. When existing systems are converted to Oracle, Loader ensures that all the data is moved from an old system's format into Oracle's format. By the end of this chapter, you will know details on the following topics:

■ How to run Oracle Loader and the parameters it requires

■ The parts of an Oracle Loader control file

■ The files written by Oracle Loader as it runs

■ How to run Oracle Loader using Personal Oracle7

Oracle Loader is pretty much the same regardless of the computer you are using. It behaves the same way whether running on a Macintosh or on an HP minicomputer.

Terminology

The following definitions will arm you with the technical jargon to make it through this chapter.

■ A *text file* contains data that is made up of the numerals 0-9, the uppercase and lowercase characters A-Z, and the special characters ~`!@#$%^&*()_−+=¦\?/>.<,"':;{[]}. You use text files to move data between different operating systems and computer types.

■ A *control file* provides information to a program in the format of keywords and values. For example, when using Oracle Loader, the keyword **bad=** tells where to place the data that for some reason is not loaded into the Oracle database.

■ A *record* is a row of information made up of all the data elements stored in an Oracle table. For example, in an inventory application, each occurrence of a part_id and part_description is called a record. The next table illustrates this concept:

RECORD #	PART ID	DESCRIPTION
1	ABW34E	Thingimajigg
2	ABW45W	Whatchamicallit
3	ABW77H	Gitgatgiddle
4	ABW99K	Framazan

■ A *unique key* is used to uniquely identify each record in an Oracle table. There can be one and only one row with each unique key value.

What Is Oracle Loader?

Oracle Loader reads text files and places the data in the Oracle database based on the instructions in a control file. The control file tells Oracle Loader where to place data, and it describes the kinds of data being loaded into Oracle. It can filter records (i.e., not load records that do not conform), load data into multiple tables at the same time, and generate a unique key or manipulate data before placing it in an Oracle table.

Moving data out of your existing system into Oracle is a two-step process. First, you create a text file copy of your existing data using your current software, then you load the data from that text file into Oracle using Oracle Loader.

Sometimes Oracle Loader is called SQL*Loader; we use the two product names synonymously. Over the past few years, Oracle has taken the "SQL*" prefix off most of its products and replaced it with the company name. Since you may use Oracle Loader to move data into one or more tables, throughout this chapter we will also use the words "table" and "tables" interchangeably.

Running Oracle Loader

By the end of this section, you will know how to invoke Oracle Loader and the parameters supplied when Oracle Loader is invoked.

To invoke Oracle Loader, enter the command **sqlldr** or **sqlload**. If you do not include any parameters, you are given online help—the output will resemble that shown in the following listing.

```
SQL*Loader: Release 7.1.4.1.0 - Production on Mon Mar  6 14:07:50 1995
Copyright (c) Oracle Corporation 1979, 1994.  All rights reserved.
Usage: SQLLOAD keyword=value [,keyword=value,...]
Valid Keywords:
    userid -- ORACLE username/password
   control -- Control file name
       log -- Log file name
       bad -- Bad file name
      data -- Data file name
   discard -- Discard file name
discardmax -- Number of discards to allow         (Default all)
      skip -- Number of logical records to skip   (Default 0)
      load -- Number of logical records to load   (Default all)
    errors -- Number of errors to allow           (Default 50)
```

```
     rows -- Number of rows in conventional path bind array or
             between direct path data saves
             (Default: Conventional path 64, Direct path all)
 bindsize -- Size of conventional path bind array in bytes
             (Default 65536)
   silent -- Suppress messages during run (header,feedback,
              errors,discards)
   direct -- use direct path                       (Default FALSE)
  parfile -- parameter file: name of file that contains
             parameter specifications
 parallel -- do parallel load                      (Default FALSE)
     file -- File to allocate extents from
PLEASE NOTE: Command-line parameters may be specified either by
position or by keywords.  An example of the former case is 'sqlload
scott/tiger foo'; an example of the latter is 'sqlload control=foo
userid=scott/tiger'.  One may specify parameters by position before
but not after parameters specified by keywords.  For example,
'sqlload scott/tiger control=foo logfile=log' is allowed, but
'sqlload scott/tiger control=foo log' is not, even though the
position of the parameter 'log' is correct.
```

There is a long list of parameters; however, most sessions will be started with commands similar to **sqlload username control=cfile.ctl**. In the following sections, we will discuss **userid** and **control** plus a few more keywords from the previous listing which, if used, influence how Oracle Loader runs. Afterwards, we present a few examples and show the command lines to accomplish the desired results.

NOTE
The keywords discussed in the next few sections have no specific order. If you provide keywords and values on the command line, they can be in any order.

Userid

Userid must be the username and password for an account that owns the table being loaded or that has access to someone else's table for loading. If you omit the password, Oracle will prompt you for it as the session begins. Along with the **control** parameter, this is one of the two required inputs to Oracle Loader.

TIP
Let Oracle Loader prompt you for the password to protect password confidentiality.

Normally, rather than include the keyword **userid** on the command line, you include an Oracle username and let Oracle Loader prompt for the password. Thus, the command **sqlload username** is the same as **sqlload userid=username**; in both cases, you are prompted for the control filename, then the account password.

Control

Control names a file that maps the format of the input datafile to the Oracle table. The format of the control file is discussed in the "Oracle Loader Control File" section later in this chapter. If you do not include the **control** keyword when calling Oracle Loader, you are prompted, as in

```
sqlload frieda
control = person
Password:
SQL*Loader: Release 7.1.4.1.0 - Production on Sat Mar 11 13:21:54 1995
Copyright (c) Oracle Corporation 1979, 1994.  All rights reserved.
```

TIP
Use the file extension .ctl for your Oracle Loader control files. It will be obvious that the control file is using this extension.

Parallel

Running Oracle Loader in parallel can speed up the time Oracle Loader takes to complete and, in situations where there are large amounts of input data, shrink runtimes dramatically. Invoking Oracle Loader with **parallel=true** runs multiple sessions loading data simultaneously into the same table. When using this option, the target tables must have no indexes. The parallel sessions' data is merged by Oracle in a number of temporary tables, then inserted as a single unit of data. This parameter defaults to **false**; a parallel session is started by coding **parallel=true** as Loader is invoked.

Direct

When using a direct load, data is assembled in memory in the same format as Oracle data blocks, and the data block is copied directly into data blocks in the target datafile. This parameter defaults to **false**; to run a direct load, code **direct=true**. The direct load runs faster than conventional loads, especially when accompanied by **parallel=true**.

VIP
If you choose **direct=true** for an Oracle Loader session, the target
table must have no indexes. If there are any indexes, the session will
terminate without loading any data.

Skip

This parameter defaults to **0**. If you code a positive integer value, Oracle Loader
skips over the specified number of rows and starts loading with the record
immediately after the specified number. This may prove useful in large loads. For
example, you might browse the log file for a load that was supposed to move
1,000,000 rows into Oracle and find that the table has run out of space and
received only 275,000 rows. Rather than redo the load from scratch, for the next
session you could include the parameter **skip=275000**.

Load

This parameter defaults to **all**. If you code a positive integer value, Oracle will load
that exact number of rows, then quit. You may want to use this if you want a subset
of a very large amount of data moved into a development or test database for a
system on its way to production.

Log and Bad

These two parameters are not normally mentioned on the command line. They
inherit their filenames from the name of the control file used for the session. The
command **sqlload/control=person.ctl** would log the session to **person.log** and
write records that contain bad data into the file **person.bad**.

Discard

Sometimes you place one or more conditions on the input data; records that do not
pass the condition(s) are discarded. If you include this parameter followed by a
filename, these discarded records are written to the specified file. See the "Discard
File" section later in this chapter, where we give an example of placing a condition
on a load session.

Example #1

Pretend you want to invoke an Oracle Loader session using the parameters and
parameter values from the following table. Say it's a large load, and you want to
run multiple load sessions at the same time.

COMPONENT	VALUE
Username	frieda
Password	shoemaker
Control file	bruce
Load	all records
Parallel	yes
Direct	no

The command to accomplish the load as described in the previous table would be **sqlload frieda/shoemaker control=bruce parallel=true**. Note that there is no filename extension on the file bruce, so Oracle Loader assumes the control filename is bruce.ctl. By excluding the parameters **load** and **direct**, they assume their defaults (i.e., **all** and **false**, respectively).

Example #2

This time we want lo load an additional 1,000 records into a table. Record numbers 1 to 499 were loaded in a previous session. To speed things, we wish to use the direct load path with parallel sessions.

COMPONENT	VALUE
Username	frieda
Password	shoemaker
Control file	bruce.crl
Skip	500
Direct	yes
Load	1000
Parallel	yes

The command to accomplish the load described in the previous table would be **sqlload frieda/shoemaker control=bruce.crl parallel=true direct=true skip=500 load=1000**. Note the filename extension on the file bruce since it is not the Oracle Loader .ctl default.

Example #3

For this example, suppose you wanted to load records number 501 to 520 using the direct path load mechanism. This also illustrates how Oracle Loader prompts for missing components of a parameter (i.e., Oracle Loader expects a username and password after the **userid** parameter, but we only supply the username).

COMPONENT	VALUE
Username	frieda
Skip	500
Direct	yes
Load	20

Notice in this example that we will not supply a password or the name of the control file when invoking Oracle Loader. The command would be **sqlload frieda direct=true load=20 skip=500**. Oracle will prompt for the missing parameters, as shown in the following listing:

```
control = bruce
Password:
SQL*Loader: Release 7.1.4.1.0 - Production on Thu Dec  29 18:08:43 1995
Copyright (c) Oracle Corporation 1979, 1994.  All rights reserved.
```

Notice that we enter **bruce** for the control filename, and Oracle Loader assumes its extension will be .ctl.

Oracle Loader Control File

We now move on to building the control file. The control file sets up the environment for a Loader session; it tells Loader where to find the input datafile, what Oracle table the data should be loaded into, what, if any, restrictions to place on what data is loaded, and how to match the input data to the columns in the target table. When getting started with Oracle Loader, the control file is the area that can cause the most problems. If the control file has errors, the Oracle Loader session stops immediately. Let's look at the four main parts of an Oracle Loader control file, as presented in Figure 9-1.

We will now discuss the four parts shown in Figure 9-1, discussing the format and the instructions each part gives to Oracle Loader.

```
- Notice this is how you embed
- comments in a control file.
load data                           - Part 1
infile 'person.dat'                 - Part 2
into table personnel                - Part 3
(first_name position (01:14) char,  - Start of part 4
 surname     position (15:28) char,
 clssn       position (29:36) char,
 hire_date  position (37:42) date 'YYMMDD')
```

FIGURE 9-1.   *Sample control file*

Part 1: Load Data

The keywords **load data** start most Oracle Loader control files, regardless of the contents of the rest of the control file. They serve as a starting point for the rest of the control file, and nothing else. Think of these two keywords as the title page of a book.

Part 2: Infile

This line names the input file. Notice in Figure 9-1 how the input filename is enclosed in single quotes. Though the quotes are not mandatory, in some situations they are required. For example, in UNIX, let's say the input file description line is **infile $HOME/person.dat**. The dollar sign causes the following error to be raised:

```
SQL*Loader: Release 7.1.4.1.0 - Production on Thu Dec  21 18:28:36 1995
Copyright (c) Oracle Corporation 1979, 1994.  All rights reserved.
SQL*Loader-350: Syntax error at line 2.
Illegal combination of non-alphanumeric characters
infile $HOME/person.dat
```

TIP
We recommend enclosing the input filename in single quotes. Get in the habit in case you find yourself working with Oracle Loader under circumstances where they are mandatory.

Part 3: Into Table

This line instructs Oracle Loader where to place the data as it is loaded into Oracle. There are four modifiers to the **into table** portion of the control file:

- **Insert** is the default and expects the table to be empty when the load begins.

- **Append** adds new rows to the table's existing contents.

- **Replace** deletes the rows in the table and loads the new rows.

- **Truncate** behaves the same as **delete**.

Normally, you will not code the **insert** qualifier with Oracle Loader, since it is the default. The most common error you may encounter is when you try to load data into a table that contains rows, and you have not included **append**, **replace**, or **truncate** on the **into table** line. If this happens, Oracle Loader returns the following error:

```
SQL*Loader: Release 7.1.4.1.0 - Production on Thu Dec 19 22:17:50 1995
Copyright (c) Oracle Corporation 1979, 1994.  All rights reserved.
SQL*Loader-601: For INSERT option, table must be empty.  Error on PERSON
```

Part 4: Column and Field Specifications

This section of the control file matches characters in the input file to the database columns of the target table. There are four parts to each line in this specification: the column name in the target table, the keyword **position**, the start and end character positions, and the data type of those characters in the input file. In Figure 9-1, the data in the input file starts in position 1 and goes to position 42, using every character in the input record. The **position** keyword followed by character number specifications become more meaningful when you wish to load parts of each line in the input file rather than the entire line. Picture the following column and field specifications in a control file:

```
(first_name position (01:14) char,
 surname    position (15:28) char,
 clssn      position (29:36) char,
 hire_date  position (40:46) date 'YYMMDD')
```

Whatever characters lie in positions 37 through 39 are ignored.

Loading date fields into Oracle deserves special mention. Oracle dates default to the format DD-MON-YY, where DD stands for the day, MON for the three-character month name, and YY for the two-digit year. If the data in the input file is not this format (and it usually isn't), you must tell Oracle how the dates appear in that file. Suppose the following four lines were fed into Oracle Loader:

```
BORIS        ABBEFLANTRO   AU2    830101
NANCY        BESDESMITH    MX     840926
FRANCIS      DEFWAYNO      DX     860422
NORMAN       NADROJIAN     CR5    860422
```

The column and position section of the control file would be

```
(first_name position (01:14) char,
 surname    position (15:28) char,
 clssn      position (29:36) char,
 hire_date  position (37:42) date 'YYMMDD')
```

VIP
The date format you specify in the control file is the format of the data in the input file, NOT the format you want Oracle to use for storage.

Since there are rules for dates (e.g., the month 13 is impossible, as is the day number 31 in the month of June), Oracle will reject data in the input file that violates these rules. Examine the errors returned while loading data into the created column in a table using the date format YYMMDD:

```
BORIS        ABBEFLANTRO   AU2    831501
NORMAN       NADROJIAN     MX     860422
NANCY        BESDESMITH    DX     840926
FRANCIS      DEFWAYNO      CR5    870229
Record 1: Rejected - Error on table STUFF, column CREATED.
ORA-01843: not a valid month
Record 4: Rejected - Error on table STUFF, column CREATED.
ORA-01847: day of month must be between 1 and last day of month
```

The first record is rejected because there is no month number 15 (831501). The fourth record is rejected because there is no day number 29 in February, 1987 (870229)—1987 was not a leap year.

Oracle Loader Outputs

As Oracle Loader runs, it writes a number of files that are used to figure out how successful the load was. By default, Oracle Loader writes a log file and, based on the success or failure of the load and the parameters used when it is invoked, may write a bad and a discard file. Unless specified otherwise, these two extra files have the same name as the control file with the extensions .bad and .dsc, respectively.

Log File—Complete Load

The output shown in the following listing was produced by a session using the command **sqlload/control=person**. Oracle Loader does not put the line numbers in the log file—we put them there for referencing in our discussion. The log file produced is called person.log.

```
 1  SQL*Loader: Release 7.1.4.1.0 - Production on Fri Mar 12 10:44:14 1996
 2  Copyright (c) Oracle Corporation 1979, 1994.  All rights reserved.
 3  Control File:   person.ctl
 4  Data File:      person.dat
 5  Bad File:      person.bad
 6   Discard File:  none specified
 7  (Allow all discards)
 8  Number to load: ALL
 9  Number to skip: 0
10  Errors allowed: 50
11  Bind array:     64 rows, maximum of 65536 bytes
12  Continuation:    none specified
13  Path used:      Conventional
14  Table PERSONNEL, loaded from every logical record.
15  Insert option in effect for this table: REPLACE
16  Column Name                      Position   Len   Term Encl Datatype
17  ------------------------------ ---------- ----- ---- ---- -------------
18  FIRST_NAME                           1:14   14             CHARACTER
19  SURNAME                             15:28   14             CHARACTER
20  CLSSN                               29:36    8             CHARACTER
21  HIRE_DATE                           37:42    6             DATE YYMMDD
22  Table PERSONNEL:
23  2609 Rows successfully loaded.
24  0 Rows not loaded due to data errors.
25  0 Rows not loaded because all WHEN clauses were failed.
26  0 Rows not loaded because all fields were null.
```

```
27   Space allocated for bind array:                    3584 bytes(64 rows)
28   Space allocated for memory besides bind array:    52603 bytes
29   Total logical records skipped:         0
30   Total logical records read:            2609
31   Total logical records rejected:        0
32   Total logical records discarded:       0
33   Run began on Fri Mar 12 10:44:14 1996
34   Run ended on Fri Mar 12 10:44:16 1996
35   Elapsed time was:      00:00:02.12
36   CPU time was:          00:00:00.54
```

Lines 1 and 2 are the Oracle Loader herald displayed at the top of all log files. Lines 3 to 15 report on the parameters that were in effect as the session ran. Lines 16 to 21 report the column and table information as specified in the control file. Lines 22 to 26 show the number of rows loaded successfully as well as the number rejected. Lines 27 through 36 show the size of some of the Oracle Loader memory structures, start and stop times of the session, and the CPU time accumulated.

NOTE
The length of your Oracle Loader control file depends on the outcome of the session and the amount of table and column information displayed.

Log File–Incomplete Load

When one or more rows are rejected because of invalid data, Oracle Loader writes the bad rows to its bad file. The log file from an incomplete load is similar to the output shown earlier produced by a complete load, but with additional information.

Rejected Row Explanations
As Oracle Loader writes rejected rows to its bad file, it makes an entry in the session log file similar to the following:

```
Record 222: Rejected - Error on table PERSONNEL.
ORA-00001: unique constraint (PERSON.U_FIRST_LAST) violated
```

The target table insists each first_name and surname combination must be unique; thus the data in record 222 is rejected, since it contains duplicate first_name and surname information. In the following listing, record 87 has no value in the first_name position in the input record, and the row is rejected:

```
Record 87: Rejected - Error on table PERSONNEL.
ORA-01400: mandatory (NOT NULL) column is missing or NULL during insert
```

Finally, record 1189 has been rejected, since the month number columns contain the number 14, which is not a valid month. The full date lies in columns 37 to 42 in the input data file; thus positions 39 and 40 are expected to contain a two-digit month number.

```
Record 1189: Rejected - Error on table PERSONNEL, column HIRE_DATE
ORA-01843: not a valid month
```

The log file displays the Oracle error number with some descriptive text to help you zero in on the reason.

Load Statistics
When one or more rows are rejected, the statistics change to reflect those numbers:

```
Table PERSONNEL:
  2903 Rows successfully loaded.
  3 Rows not loaded due to data errors.
  0 Rows not loaded because all WHEN clauses were failed.
  0 Rows not loaded because all fields were null.
```

VIP
You should verify that all the records in the input file were read by summing the numbers in the load statistics section of the log file. The result should equal the number of lines in the input file.

Bad File

This file is only written when one or more rows from the input file are rejected. In our example, we invoked Oracle Loader using the command **sqlload / control=person**. Thus, rejected rows, if any, are placed in a file called person.bad. The format of the rows in the bad file is the same as the input file. For example, record 1189 would be written to this bad file:

```
FWUFFEROO     DES          FE8     851429
```

There is no descriptive information in the bad file, so you must match the log file error messages with the bad file information.

VIP
If you use the same control file for successive Oracle Loader
sessions, deal with the rows in each run's bad file before running the
next session.

Here's a story of how not checking the bad file affected one of our clients. The
client ran three Oracle Loader sessions using the same control file. The input to the
three sessions were **accrec1.dat**, **accrec2.dat**, and **accrec3.dat**, each containing
11,000 records. The first run loaded 11,000 records successfully and created no
bad file. The second run loaded 10,811 rows successfully and wrote 189 rows to
the bad file. The client did not deal with the rows written to the bad file and
instead ran the third session, which wrote a bad file containing 42 rows. The 189
rows written to the bad file by the second session were lost and were never loaded
properly. When the client started to use the data on their application, they
wondered why information was missing!

Discard File

The control file shown in Figure 9-1 instructed Oracle Loader to attempt to load all
records in the input file. In the following listing, the control file uses the **when**
keyword to discard rows whose clssn column positions contain the text "CR4."

```
load data
infile 'person.dat'
into table personnel
when clssn <> 'CR4'
(first_name position (01:14) char,
 surname    position (15:28) char,
 clssn      position (29:36) char,
 hire_date  position (37:42) date 'YYMMDD')
```

The discard file is not created unless the **discard=** parameter is used when
invoking Oracle Loader.

Personal Oracle7

Oracle Loader runs the same as from Personal Oracle7, except you use the mouse
and an assortment of dialog boxes to specify what to do. We will show you how to
prepare for an Oracle Loader session and where to tweak some advanced options if

desired. Before running Oracle Loader from Personal Oracle7, you have to create the control file.

Getting Started

To start an Oracle Loader session, click on the SQL*Loader icon in the Personal Oracle7 group in the Windows Program Manager. You are presented with the screen shown in Figure 9-2.

   The Database text box is filled in with <local host> since the Personal Oracle7 database is on the same machine. Move through the dialog box, entering values for the Username, Password, and Control File text boxes. When you enter a control filename (either manually or using the Browse button to find one), the Log text box in the Optional Files area is filled in with the name of the control file you have entered.

VIP
Unless you specify otherwise, Oracle Loader expects the control file to be located in the directory \orawin\bin.

```
┌─────────────────────────────────────────────────────┐
│ ▬              SQL*Loader                            │
│                                                      │
│ U̲sername:  [                    ]      [ L̲oad    ]   │
│                                                      │
│ P̲assword:  [                    ]      [ Ad̲vanced...]│
│                                                      │
│ D̲atabase:  [<local host>        ]      [ C̲ancel  ]   │
│                                                      │
│ Co̲ntrol File: [                 ]  [B̲rowse...] [Help]│
│                                                      │
│ ┌─Optional Files──────────────────────────────────┐ │
│ │ D̲ata:  [                ]   [ Bro̲wse... ]        │ │
│ │ Lo̲g:   [                ]   [ Def̲aults ]         │ │
│ │ B̲ad:   [                ]                         │ │
│ │ Di̲scard: [              ]                         │ │
│ └──────────────────────────────────────────────────┘ │
└─────────────────────────────────────────────────────┘
```

FIGURE 9-2.   *SQL*Loader dialog box*

When you enter the control filename, the Browse and Defaults buttons in the Optional Files area are activated. Figure 9-3 shows the completed dialog box after you click on Defaults.

Advanced Options

Proceed to the Advanced Options dialog box to specify additional session parameters. In the SQL*Loader dialog box, click on Advanced to access the screen shown in Figure 9-4.

The values you enter in this dialog box will be passed to Oracle Loader, similar to the command line method discussed in the "Running Oracle Loader" section earlier in this chapter. Click on the Defaults button on this screen to reset all fields to the values shown in Figure 9-4. When done, click on OK to return to the SQL*Loader dialog box.

Running Oracle Loader

After filling in the required information, click on Load to start loading data. Oracle displays a SQL*Loader Status window while it runs, as shown in Figure 9-5. All

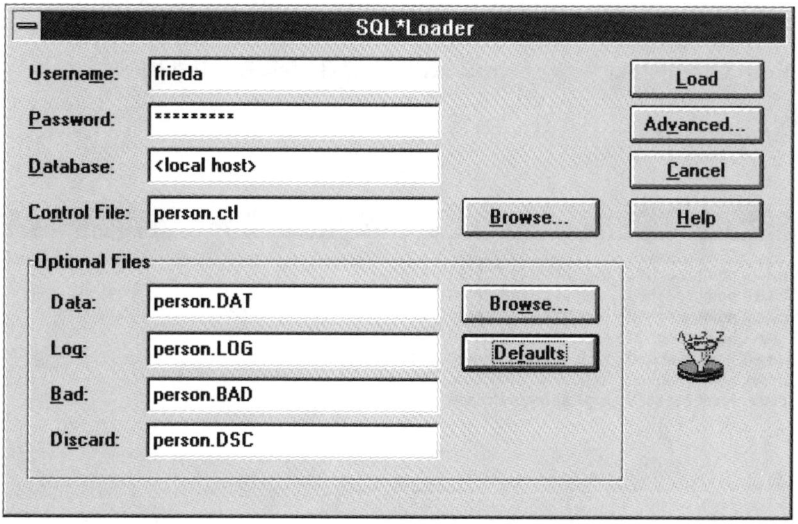

FIGURE 9-3. *SQL*Loader dialog box filled in*

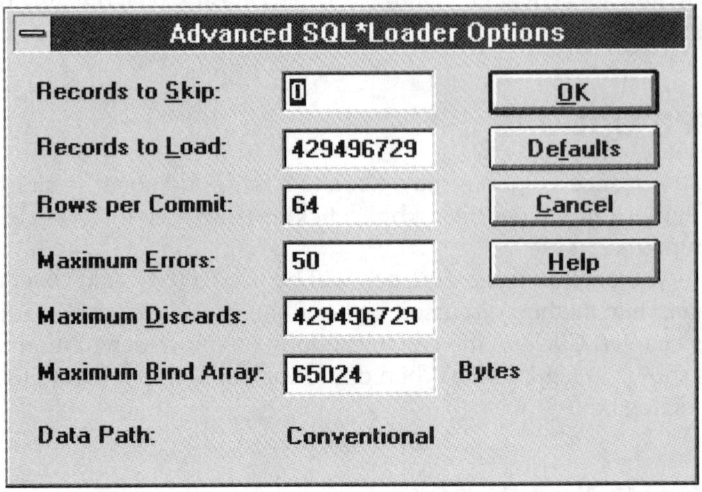

Advanced SQL*Loader Options

Records to Skip:	0	OK
Records to Load:	429496729	Defaults
Rows per Commit:	64	Cancel
Maximum Errors:	50	Help
Maximum Discards:	429496729	
Maximum Bind Array:	65024	Bytes
Data Path:	Conventional	

FIGURE 9-4. *Advanced SQL*Loader Options dialog box*

information and any errors are displayed in this window as Oracle Loader operates. When Oracle Loader finishes, click on Close to return to the screen shown in Figure 9-3, then Cancel to return to the Windows Program Manager. To view the outputs from Oracle Loader, use your favorite text viewer or editor.

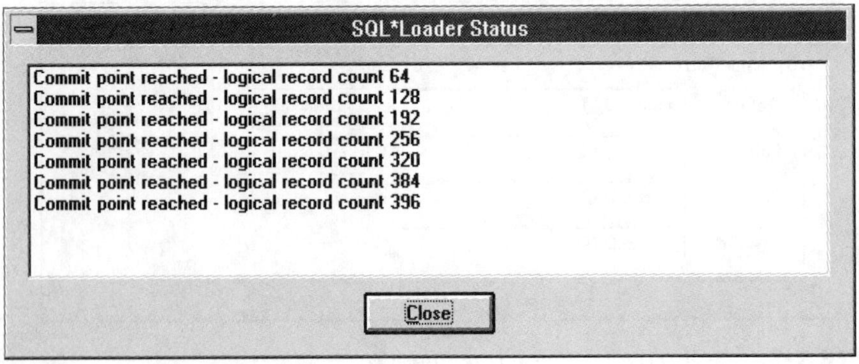

SQL*Loader Status

```
Commit point reached - logical record count 64
Commit point reached - logical record count 128
Commit point reached - logical record count 192
Commit point reached - logical record count 256
Commit point reached - logical record count 320
Commit point reached - logical record count 384
Commit point reached - logical record count 396
```

Close

FIGURE 9-5. *Oracle Loader Status window*

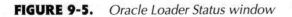

What's Next

We have introduced you to Oracle Loader and shown you how it is used to move data from text files into Oracle database tables. The material we covered here just skims the surface; but you have enough information to use Oracle Loader for most load session requirements. There is a wealth of additional functionality you can use for more sophisticated sessions. Experiment with Oracle Loader and investigate its power—you will use it from day one.

This chapter completes the Developer Basics section of this book, in which we have talked about SQL, PL/SQL, Oracle Forms, Oracle Reports, and Oracle Loader. Armed with the knowledge gained from this section, carry on. In the "Developer Bells and Whistles" section that comes next, there are three advanced chapters to tickle your fancy . . . enjoy!

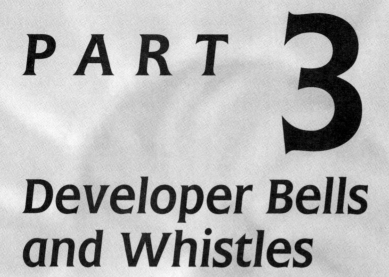

PART 3

Developer Bells and Whistles

CHAPTER 10

Application
Tuning 101

This chapter is the first of three in the "Developer Bells and Whistles" section of this book. In the "Developer Basics" section (Chapters 5 through 9), we provided you with a foundation. Now it's time to move on.

Most corporations and individuals purchase software to help them carry on their day-to-day activities. All of us expect systems written using this software to operate efficiently—we expect them to ingest gobs of information and do exactly what we want them to do quickly. Realistically, we can only expect them to do this if the applications are tuned. *Tuning* is a process whereby applications are optimized to run as quickly as possible and use as few computer resources as possible.

Oracle, like all other vendors, provides tools with which to write custom applications. In this book, we discuss some of the tools Oracle provides for this purpose: SQL*Plus (Chapters 5 and 11), Oracle Forms (Chapter 7), Oracle Reports (Chapter 8), and PL/SQL (Chapter 6). Developers (also called programmers) who write code with these Oracle products will want to write code that uses the Oracle Server efficiently. All too often, when a new computer system is installed, the users complain about how slow the system is and how long it takes to get responses to queries on its screens. By the end of this chapter, you will have some basics on the following:

- Why applications should be tuned
- The two main components in the tuning process
- How Oracle stores data
- How Oracle processes SQL statements
- The shared pool or shared SQL area
- Writing SQL statements to use the shared pool
- Using indexes to access data more efficiently

Why Tune Oracle Systems?

As new applications come onboard, we hear constant complaining about how poorly they perform. As applications are written, you should attend to their performance and make it as important a component as the programming itself. There are many short- and long-term benefits to tuning applications:

- Well-tuned applications require less attention down the road.
- Your end users will be happier with the system's performance and its ability to process more data in less time.
- Applications that have been tuned make more efficient use of resources on your computer.

There is only a finite amount of computing power on any computer. This is especially crucial in a multiuser system when more than one person is using the system simultaneously. The throughput of your systems will be better with tuned applications. *Throughput* is a measurement of the amount of data your systems are capable of processing in a given time period. The more time you spend tuning applications, the more information they will be able to ingest and send back to you as reports, graphs, and onscreen query results.

Tuning applications can be a time-consuming and frustrating exercise, but using the ideas and guidelines in this chapter, you will get the most bang for your buck. In Chapter 12, we discuss more technical details of the tuning process.

Terminology

The following definitions will arm you with the technical jargon to make it through this chapter.

- A *query* is a request for information from the database. For example, when you press the green key (commonly the one that tells the machine which account you wish to work with) on the automatic teller, you are requesting a balance from your checking account.

- *Query results* are the data that satisfies a query. The account balance displaying on the ATM screen is an example of query results.

- *Disk access* is the act of reading information from the database files on disk.

- A *view* is a subset of one or more tables' data assembled in memory to satisfy the results of a SQL statement. One example of a view is a list of all employees in the western region of a company; the table on which that view is built contains all the employees regardless of their location.

- A *synonym* is a name stored in the data dictionary used to refer to tables and views. Think of a synonym as a nickname for tables and views.

- A *public synonym* is created by the DBA (database administrator), pointing at an object somewhere in the database. Any user can refer to that object using the public synonym.

- A *data dictionary* is maintained by Oracle containing information relevant to the database. It is used by Oracle to find out who is allowed to log into the database, what datafiles are associated with the database, and other information required to permit your systems to operate.

■ An *object* is an umbrella definition encompassing all data source names stored in Oracle's data dictionary. Objects are usually tables, but they can also be views or synonyms.

■ A *cache* is a portion of memory that Oracle reserves to do a specific job as the database operates. The caches contain data that has been read from the database, information about the SQL statements that have been processed, and other information required to run the instance.

■ The *data dictionary* is where Oracle stores information about what the data in the database looks like. For example, Oracle's data dictionary defines the fact that a North American area code is three numbers (i.e., no letters or special characters) and that the states and provinces are two letters (no numbers or special characters).

■ An *execution plan* is the "map" that Oracle builds to get at the data that satisfies a user's query. The plan is built using statistics about the data that reside in the data dictionary. When Oracle builds an execution plan, it looks for the shortest and least costly route—somewhat like using the ABCFHI route rather than the ABDEGHI route, as shown in Figure 10-1.

■ A *block* is the smallest unit of storage that Oracle uses. The block size of the database is set when the database is created and can range from 2K

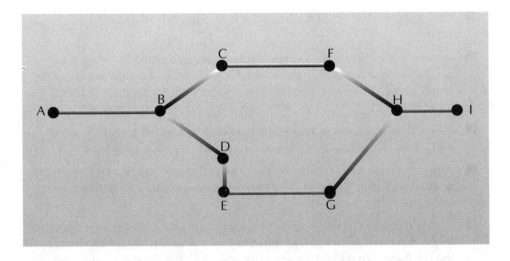

FIGURE 10-1. *Two paths to get from A to I*

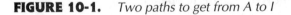

(2,048 bytes) up to 16K (16,384 bytes). Oracle maintains a list in memory of free data blocks and places new information in them created by your applications.

■ The operation that reads data from and writes data to disk is called *I/O* (input/output).

■ Oracle assigns a *rowid* to data as it places it in data blocks. The rowid uniquely identifies each row in the database.

■ An *index* is a structure separate from a table that contains one or more column values from a table plus the rowids of the rows with those values.

■ A *select list* is the group of columns mentioned in the SQL statement, following the **select** keyword up to the list of objects referenced in the **from** portion of the statement. In the following SQL statement, the boldfaced text is called the select list.

```
select last_name, first_name, date_of_birth
   from person
 where pin = 100720;
```

■ A *secure database* operation is an Oracle database operation usually restricted to DBA users. Creating a tablespace, creating new users, and managing rollback segments are examples of secure database operations.

■ A *system privilege* is given to users and allows them to perform secure database operations. For example, the system privilege *select any table* allows the recipient to select data in any object anywhere in the database.

Main Components in the Tuning Process

Tuning Oracle applications is much the same exercise regardless of the size of a computer on which Oracle is running. Tuning zeros in on a computer's main components, and ensures they are being used efficiently. All computers are made up of the following components:

■ The central processing unit (CPU) is responsible for all operations the computer will undertake. You often hear of a 386, 486, and Pentium in the microcomputer world, or DEC Alpha in the minicomputer environment. These are processor class names that have become part of computer lingo. The faster the processor, the faster the computer.

■ Secondary storage devices such as hard drives, floppy disk drives, and CD-ROM are used to save information applications create as they operate.

■ Computer memory is where programs operate and commonly requested data waits in anticipation of the next request for information.

■ The other peripherals that complete the requirements are a computer monitor and keyboard.

VIP
The two main components in the tuning process are reading information from memory and reducing I/O operations.

The next section of this chapter will discuss the role reading information from memory and reducing I/O operations play in the tuning process.

Memory

Since all computers contain a finite amount of memory, making optimal use of memory is a contributing factor to tuning. In this section we will discuss the basics on the following:

■ How all data is routed through memory

■ The communication lines from the database to the users

■ The shared SQL area

■ The key to efficient use of memory

As Oracle runs, it receives requests for data from users. The data sits in an assortment of datafiles on disk. The flow of information among users, memory, and the database is outlined in Figure 10-2.
Notice the four communication lines:

■ **User to memory (UM):** Requests for data initiated by applications are assembled in memory, where Oracle decides the most efficient way to get to the desired data.

■ **Memory to user (MU):** Results of queries are transferred from memory to the user session that made the request.

■ **Disk to memory (DM):** As requests are received, data that satisfies the request is transferred to memory.

■ **Memory to disk (MD):** Data that has been changed or created is written to disk.

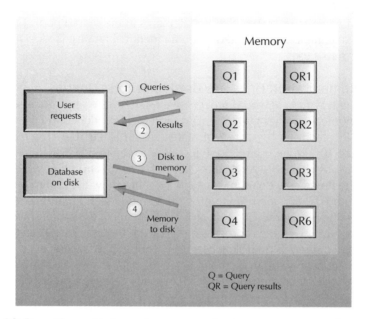

Q = Query
QR = Query results

FIGURE 10-2. *Flow of information among database, memory, and users*

There is no direct communication between the database and the users. All reads, writes, and changes to data pass through Oracle memory structures. This stresses the importance of using memory efficiently.

VIP
Oracle keeps the results of previously executed queries in memory until the space they occupy is required for results to more recent queries.

Oracle maintains a *shared SQL area* in memory, also referred to as the shared pool. All SQL statements are executed from this pool. When a SQL statement is passed to Oracle, before loading a SQL statement into this pool, Oracle searches this pool for an identical statement. If it finds a match, the new statement is discarded and the one already in the pool is executed in its place. We'll refer to the preparation for execution and placement in the shared pool as the *preparation phase*.

When a SQL statement is passed to Oracle for execution, it must first be placed in the shared pool. Oracle executes SQL statements after loading them into the shared pool.

VIP
Oracle keeps prepared SQL statements in the shared pool. These statements are executed when an identical request is received from a user.

How the Communication Lines Are Used to Process Queries

Let's look at the way Oracle would process five queries from user processes using the four communication lines UM, MU, DM, and MD introduced in Figure 10-2. The indicator PR stands for "prepare SQL statement" in Table 10-1. The memory shown in Figure 10-2 is the shared pool; it contains prepared SQL statements Q1, Q2, Q3, and Q4 as well as query results QR1, QR2, QR3, and QR6, which are still in memory. The Processing column values in the table show the communication lines from Figure 10-2 that are used to process each query and return its results.

The processing for queries Q1, Q2, and Q3 is the most desirable, since there is no disk access. Next desirable is processing Q6; even though the SQL statement has to be prepared, there is no disk access. Q4 requires disk access; even though the prepared statement is still in memory, its query results are not in memory. Oracle prepares the statement issued by Q5 and must retrieve its results from disk.

VIP
Access to data in memory is quicker than access to data on disk. It is desirable to get as much information as possible from memory.

VIP
If you can write SQL statements that match those sitting in the pool, the preparation phase can be skipped. Avoiding the preparation phase is the single most important area to attend to when tuning Oracle applications.

Disk Access

Reading information from disk is referred to as *disk access*. Minimizing disk access is important given the operations the computer performs when reading from disk. It takes time to position the reader above the exact spot on the disk where the data resides, and the time to transfer the data to memory can become quite significant. In this section, we will discuss the basics on the following:

- How Oracle stores data
- How Oracle accesses your data
- How to minimize disk access

QUERY	PROCESSING	REASON
Q1	UM MU	This can be satisfied in memory since the prepared SQL statement Q1 as well as its query results QR1 still reside there.
Q2	UM MU	This too can be satisfied in memory since the prepared SQL statement Q2 as well as its query results QR2 still reside there.
Q3	UM MU	This too can be satisfied in memory since the prepared SQL statement Q3 as well as its query results QR3 still reside there.
Q4	UM MD DM MU	The prepared SQL statement Q4 still resides in the shared pool. The results to that query the last time it was executed have been removed from memory. Hence, the new request must read data from disk, put it in memory, then pass it back to the user.
Q5	UM PR MD DM MU	There is no prepared SQL statement in memory. Hence, this request needs to prepare the SQL statement, read data from disk, put it in memory, then pass it back to the user. This is the least desirable of all processing situations since the SQL statements need to be prepared, then data must be read from disk.
Q6	UM PR MU	There is no matching prepared SQL statement though the query results QR6 are still in memory.

TABLE 10-1. *Query Processing Using Memory*

We mentioned in the previous section how all data is transferred from disk to memory before being made available to users. I/O is required to make this transfer. Oracle places data in blocks in the datafiles that make up the database. When a data block is too full to hold any more data, Oracle places its data in the other blocks in the datafile. Each row in a data block can be identified by its address or rowid. Oracle fetches data for your queries using one of the two methods discussed in the next few sections. We now discuss using indexes to help minimize disk access. When we show you how Oracle processes data with and without an index, you will begin to see their advantages when attending to application tuning.

Processing with an Index

If an index exists, and a SQL statement is worded in a way to take advantage of the index, the index is searched first. Oracle reads the index and processes according to the steps shown in Table 10-2.

VIP

The number of I/O operations to process a query using an index can be significantly lower than the number required to process a query without an index.

Think of an index as an address book: the rows of data are the names in that book, and the rowids are the street addresses. If you know that the Jacobs live at 234 Rideau, you can proceed directly to the location of their house. If you know the Jacobs live on Rideau but you don't have their address, you would have to go from house to house until you found them. Oracle goes through the same exercise when using indexes. Indexes provide rapid access to your data.

Figure 10-3 shows a very simple example. Suppose the column values shown for tableA are in the column named ID. IndexA contains ID column values plus the location of the first column with that ID value (i.e., the first row with ID=15 can be found in location 005).

PROCESS	NEXT STEP	
1. Are there more index entries to process?	YES=2	NO=7
2. Do all column values in the index match the selection criterion?	YES=4	NO=3
3. Read the next entry in the index.	1	
4. Are all the columns in the select list included in the index?	YES=6	NO=5
5. Get the rowid of the row the index points to.	6	
6. Mark the data for inclusion in the query results.	1	
7. Display query results.		

TABLE 10-2. *Processing Query Using an Index*

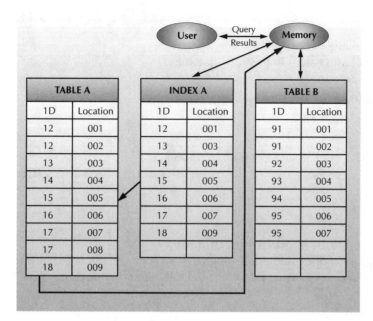

FIGURE 10-3.   *Tables with and without an index*

The user passes a SQL statement to Oracle on tableA looking for the data in the row with ID=15. Oracle reads entries in indexA to find where it should look in the table data to find the desired row. If Oracle read indexA from start to finish, it would encounter the address for ID=15 in the fourth entry in the index and proceed to get the data from the row at address 005. If indexA did not exist, Oracle would read tableA, and find the ID=15 in the fifth row in the table. This example shows how Oracle would need to perform one additional I/O if indexA did not exist.

Processing Without an Index

When no index exists that can be used to satisfy a query, Oracle does a full table scan. It reads every row in a table and evaluates column values against the selection criterion. It discards rows that do not qualify and includes rows that do. Oracle reads every row in the table, processing according to the steps in Table 10-3:

PROCESS	NEXT STEP	
1. Are there more rows in the table?	YES=2	NO=4
2. Do the column values in this row match the selection criterion?	YES=3	NO=1
3. Mark the data for inclusion in the query results.	1	
4. Display query results.		

TABLE 10-3.   *Processing Without an Index*

I/Os Required with and Without an Index

Now that we have discussed processing with and without an index, let's examine a real-life example. Let's say a table holds the following information:

```
book_number                  varchar2(20)
publisher                    varchar2(40)
year_printed                 varchar2(4)
```

and there are 80,000 rows in the table. Oracle has packed 40 book records into each data block. Thus, data blocks numbered 0001 to 2000 contain book information. Suppose Oracle has placed a book with ISBN 882122-3 in data block number 0807. If the table has an index, fetching that book's data would require two I/O operations— the first to read the index entry and get the rowid of where the 882122-3 row is stored, and the second to retrieve the book's publisher and year in print. If there is no index, Oracle would have to read the table's data starting with data block 0001 until it reached a data block with the desired ISBN (data block 0807). Thus, without an index, fetching the book's data would require 807 I/O operations!

Using Statements in the Shared Pool

As we stated near the start of this chapter, using memory efficiently is a large contributor to the application-tuning process. Coupled with using indexes (which results in minimizing disk access), you are well on your way to tuning applications. In this section, we will discuss some of the basics on the following:

- How Oracle processes SQL statements
- How to word SQL statements to reuse ones already in the pool
- How to implement coding conventions
- How to store code in the database

Steps in SQL Statement Processing

When Oracle receives a SQL statement, it runs an internal routine to compute the statement's value. To illustrate computing a value, let's run a very simple routine using the U.S. cities shown in Table 10-4.

Notice that each city/state combination has been assigned a six-digit ID. Let's pretend the ID is the same as the identifier that Oracle assigns to every table as it is created. Now we will look at some SQL statements that use these city names as table names, and we'll figure out the value of each statement. You can see how the statement

```
select col1, col2, col3, col4
  from PORTLAND              /* OR in this case */
 where col5 > col6;
```

is not the same as

```
select col1, col2, col3, col4
  from PORTLAND              /* ME in this case */
 where col5 > col6;
```

CITY	STATE	ID
Portland	ME	446721
Portland	OR	978219
Springfield	MA	893417
Springfield	MO	662198

TABLE 10-4. *U.S. Cities, States, and Identifiers*

The value of the city coded in the former statement is 978219, and the one in the latter is 446721. Similarly, in the next three statements, the first two statements are the same, but the second and third are not.

```
select col1, col2, col3, col4
   from SPRINGFIELD             /* MA in this case */
 where col5 > col6;
select col1, col2, col3, col4
   from SPRINGFIELD             /* MA in this case */
 where col5 > col6;
select col1, col2, col3, col4
   from SPRINGFIELD             /* MO in this case */
 where col5 > col6;
```

The value of the city coded in the first two statements is 893417, and the value in the third statement is 662198.

> **VIP**
> Using the same name for objects in a SQL statement is not enough; the names must evaluate to the same object in the database.

Table 10-5 gives a thumbnail sketch of how a statement is evaluated when sent for processing. The computing of a statement's value is shown as the first step.

PROCESS	NEXT STEP	
1. Compute the value of statement.	2	2
2. Is there a statement in the pool with the same value?	YES=3	NO=4
3. Is there a statement in the pool that matches character by character?	YES=8	NO=4
4. Prepare the SQL statement for execution.	5	
5. Make room for the new statement in the pool.	6	
6. Place the statement in the shared pool.	7	
7. Update the map of the pool showing statement values and location in the pool.	8	
8. Execute the prepared SQL statement.		

TABLE 10-5.   *Simplified Steps for Parsing a SQL Statement*

Ideally, statements should be processed using steps 1, 2, 3, and 8. Statements passed to Oracle that do not pass the tests in both steps 2 and 3 are processed using steps 1, 2, 3, 4, 5, 6, 7, and 8. Wording SQL statements in such a way to take the 1-2-3-8 path is more efficient than taking the 1-through-8 path.

Wording SQL Statements to Reuse Ones in the Pool

In this section, we will discuss adopting coding conventions and storing code in the database.

When SQL statements are passed to Oracle for processing, the secret is to reuse a statement already in the pool rather than forcing Oracle to prepare each new statement as it is received. We stated previously that Oracle reuses statements in the shared pool if it receives one identical to one already in the pool. In the next two sections, we discuss standardizing the format of the code you write and using centralized code stored in the Oracle data dictionary.

Coding Conventions

We will present one of many possible schemes for coding SQL statements. Adopt this method if you like the looks of it.

NOTE

Establishing and USING a coding convention is more important than the actual style you decide to use.

Once you have a convention in place, you can start coding SQL statements to take advantage of ones already in the shared pool. To get the most out of this discussion, you should have read Chapter 5 and/or Chapter 11.

The select statement in SQL is made up of five parts. Using the following code, let's review the components of a statement.

```
select col1, col2, sum(col3)    /* Part 1 */
   from fiscal_year             /* Part 2 */
  where col1 > col2             /* Part 3 */
    and col1 > 10               /* Part 3 */
  group by col1, col2           /* Part 4 */
  order by col1;                /* Part 5 */
```

These are the five component parts of a SQL statement:

- The **select** keyword that starts the statement followed by the list of columns being displayed in the query results
- One or more tables from which the data is obtained
- One or more conditions that determine which values are desired
- The **group by** keyword followed by one or more column names on which some summarizing is to be done as the data is fetched
- The **order by** keyword followed by a list of one or more columns that determine the sorting method for the desired rows

The guidelines we now present help ensure that SQL statements you code can find a match against one already prepared and sitting in the shared pool.

Formatting the Parts of the SQL Statement   Rather than letting the statement spill haphazardly onto the next line at column 80, do the following.

```
select col1, col2, sum(col3)
  from fiscal_year
 where col1 > col2
   and col1 > 10
 group by col1, col2
 order by col1;
```

NOTE
You could take a plastic ruler and line it up with the **select** keyword to ensure that all other lines' keywords align with the letter "t" from **select**. The ┆ (vertical line) in the next listing represents that ruler.

```
select┆col1, col2, sum(col3)
  from┆fiscal_year
 where┆col1 > col2
   and┆col1 > 10
 group┆by col1, col2
 order┆by col1;
```

GUIDELINE 1
Use a separate line for each part of the SQL statement. Align the first keyword in each line to end in the same column as the **select** keyword on the first line.

Uppercase or Lowercase?   Lowercase code is easier on the eyes than either mixed case or all uppercase. Some installations decide to use uppercase for all SQL special words and lowercase for all others. The problem is that developers forget which is which. You could easily end up with the following two statements:

```
SELECT col1, col2
  FROM fiscal_year;
```

and

```
select COL1, COL2
  from FISCAL_YEAR;
```

Both statements are written by developers trying to ensure they conform to the uppercase and lowercase convention. Using mixed case, it's just too easy to forget which is which.

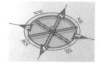

GUIDELINE 2
Use lowercase characters in all SQL statements.

Commas Embedded in the Statement   We find the code easier to read leaving a space after the comma. For example, we find the first code easier to read than the second in the following:

```
select col1, col2, sum(col3)
```

```
select col1,col2,sum(col3)
```

GUIDELINE 3
Put commas right beside the text they follow, and leave one space afterwards.

Commas as the Last Character on a Line   In come cases, developers like to place the trailing comma on one line as the first character in the next line:

```
select col1, col2
      ,col3
```

We prefer to see it the following way:

```
select col1, col2,
       col3
```

GUIDELINE 4
When a comma is the last character on a line, put it on that line rather than skipping to the next line then inserting the comma.

Formatting Continuation Lines   When the same part of a SQL statement continues onto the next line, line them up as in the following listing:

```
select col1, col2, sum(col3), col4, col5, sum(col6),
       col7, col8, col9, col10, col11, col 12, col13
```

GUIDELINE 5
Start lines in column 8 that belong to the same part as the previous line.

Formatting the Statement Qualifiers

When formatting the **where** and **and** part of the SQL statement (also referred to as the predicate), the placement of each **and** should resemble

```
where
   and
   and
   and
   and
```

GUIDELINE 6
When you have the **where** followed by one or more lines that start with **and**, start the former in column 2 and the latter in column 4.

Formatting Parentheses   Syntax requires the use of parentheses in many SQL statements. The most common spot is where a function (e.g., finding the largest value with **max** or taking the first three characters of a ten-character string with **substr**) is used is a column in a select list as in

```
select col1, col2, sum(col3)
```

GUIDELINE 7
Leave no spaces on either side of parentheses when they appear in SQL statements.

Statement Terminator   This statement terminator is the signal to Oracle that you are done coding your statement, and wish to begin processing. You may use the semi-colon (;) or the forward slash (/).

GUIDELINE 8
Use the semicolon (;) terminator for SQL*Plus statements. When your programs contain a mixture of SQL*Plus and PL/SQL, you must terminate a group of PL/SQL statements with a slash (/). Reserve using the slash for that purpose.

Formatting Operators   When you compare column values in your SQL statements, you most commonly use the equal sign (=). Other operators, such as <> for not equal or > for less than, are coded like the equal sign.

GUIDELINE 9
Leave a space on either side of operators used anywhere in SQL statements.

SQL statements are easier to read with spaces, as shown in the following example:

```
where x = y
   and d = c
   and j = p
```

rather than

```
where x=y
   and d=c
   and j=p
```

VIP
Design your coding conventions (or use the ones we've recommended) and stick to them. Passing statements for processing that are identical to ones already in the pool helps tune your applications.

Examples   Theory is all fine and dandy, plus a whole bunch of guidelines as we have outlined. Seeing them put into practice will crystallize the theory we speak about in the previous section. Let's look at two more complex examples; they are commented to highlight the implementation of the guidelines we have presented.

```
rem *************** Example #1 ******************

rem * The decode in the column list starts back in column 8 so the code
rem * in parentheses within the decode is not broken onto two lines.
rem * There is a single space left after each comma as well as
rem * no space before the opening parenthesis in the decode.
select fy_code, prd.prod_num, prd.sdesc_e, proj_num, prj.sdesc_e,
       comm_amt, comm_amt*1.10,
       decode(fiscal, 'Y', 'multi', 'single'), bud_class
  from prod prd, project prj, bud_mast bud, commitment
 where prd.prod_num = prj.prod_num
   and bud.rpt_cat = prd.rpt_cat
 order by fy_code, prd.prod_num;


rem *************** Example #2 ******************

select max('&1'), max('&2'), max(sysdate), max('DETAIL'), max(a.sr),
       b.sdesc_e,
       /*  Note how the parentheses have no spaces on either side  */
       /*  and there is one space after each comma but nothing     */
       /*  before.                                                 */
       nvl(round(sum(nvl(a.comm_amt, 0)), 0), 0),
       nvl(round(sum(nvl(a.precomm_amt, 0)), 0), 0),
       nvl(round(sum(nvl(a.budget_orig, 0)), 0), 0),
       nvl(round(sum(nvl(a.budget_rev,0)), 0), 0),
       nvl(round(sum(nvl(a.exp_accr, 0)), 0),0),
       nvl(round(sum(nvl(a.exp_accr_comm, 0)), 0), 0),
       nvl(round(sum(nvl(a.free_bal, 0)), 0), 0),
       nvl(round(sum(nvl(a.adj_bal, 0)), 0), 0)
  from fms_financials a, fms_control_obj b
 where b.cobj_type = 'SR'       /* The first word in each line ends in  */
   and b.cobj_code = a.sr       /* column 8.                            */
   and b.fy_code = '&2'
   and a.repname = '&1'         /* All the where and and lines line     */
   and a.fy_code = '&2'         /* up with one another.                 */
   and a.qualifier = 'SRDETAIL'
 group by a.sr,b.sdesc_e;
```

Storing Code in the Database

Oracle provides the ability to store segments of code in the database. As your applications operate, this code is read from the database and passed to the shared pool for processing like any other SQL statement.

VIP

Code read from the database will almost always match a code segment already prepared and resident in the shared pool.

Suppose you work at a library, and you want to be able to generate an electronic reminder to the front desk every morning that identifies the borrower, book title, and author of books more than seven days overdue. You may have a number of applications that can initiate these reminders by clicking on an Overdue Note button on a lending information screen. Each of those screens may have its own code behind the scenes handling overdue notice generation, or each screen may invoke a routine similar to the following.

```
create or replace procedure overdue_notice (book_ident char,
                                            borrower_ident char,
                                            book_auth char,
                                            book_title char,
                                            was_due date) as
begin
  declare
    temp_buffer varchar2(1);
    — See if there already is a notice for this book ID
    cursor mycur is
      select ' '
        from overdue_notes
       where book_id = book_ident
         and borrower_id = borrower_ident
         and due_date = was_due;
  begin
    open mycur;
    fetch mycur into temp_buffer;
    if mycur%found then  — Checking to see if notice exists yet
       null;             — Nothing more to do since notice already there
    else
       — Create an overdue notice
       insert into overdue_notes values (book_ident, book_auth, borrower_ident,
                                         book_title, was_due, sysdate, user);
    end if;
  end;
end;
```

The following SQL text places the PL/SQL in the database:

```
create or replace
```

VIP
Design your applications to take advantage of code stored in the database. Look at all your business processes and centralize common procedures.

VIP
Study existing applications and convert their centralized processing routines into code segments stored in the database.

Implementing Stored Procedures   In conjunction with the DBA you work with, there are some things to do before you can store procedures in the database and start using them. It is not simply a matter of deciding to use stored procedures. You must consult with your DBA or the implementation may not work for the reasons outlined below.

- Stored procedures occupy space in the system tablespace in your database. You may have to work with the DBA to ensure the space in this tablespace is sufficient. The DBA may have allocated space for this system tablespace before stored procedures were investigated.

- Before users can execute procedures owned by others, the DBA needs to give out a system privilege called *execute any procedure*.

- You must give other users privileges to execute your procedures, by issuing a command similar to **grant execute on overdue_notice to public.**

- The DBA must create a public synonym for your stored procedure, for example **create public synonym overdue_notice for polly.overdue_notice;**

Calling Stored Procedures   Stored procedures can be executed from a PL/SQL block (we discuss PL/SQL blocks in Chapter 6), as in

```
 -- other PL/SQL statements followed by
if sysdate - :due_back >= 6 then
    execute overdue_notice (book_id, borr_ident, bk_auth, bk_title, due_back);
end if;
```

Stored procedures can be executed from SQL*Plus (we discuss SQL*Plus in Chapter 5 and Chapter 11), as in

```
-- other SQL statements followed by
overdue_notice ('882122-3', 'A45R', 'ABBEY COREY',
                        'Oracle: A Beginner''s Guide', '06-JAN-96')
```

Triggers, Functions, and Packages

Besides stored procedures, Oracle provides for three other kinds of centralized code that is stored and read from the database: triggers, functions, and packages.

- *Triggers* are associated with tables and run transparently when predefined events happen to the data in the table. For example, you may use a database trigger to log the fact that an accounts receivable clerk has lowered the amount owing on an outstanding account.

- *Functions* accept a number of parameters and pass a single value back to the calling program. For example, the validation of a ZIP code could be done with a function. The routine would be invoked with a ZIP code, and the function could pass back true or false depending on whether the ZIP code is valid.

- *Packages* are single program units that contain procedures and functions. By grouping them together, the developer defines a set of routines that are commonly invoked together or one after another.

Refer to *Tuning Oracle* (Corey, Abbey, and Dechichio; Osborne McGraw-Hill/Oracle Press 1995), in particular Chapter 7 ("Application Tuning"), where writing generic code using procedures, triggers, functions, and packages is discussed in more detail.

What's Next

After reading this chapter, you've come a long way! Perhaps you (as we were one time) are just getting started on the road to application tuning. We have provided you with some bottom-line theory, and pointed you in the right direction to get started. Even though the points we make are the basics of application tuning, they are applicable to all developers regardless of how long they have been using Oracle.

In Chapter 11, we will cover some advanced SQL concepts, and we'll show you some more complex examples. The SQL language is a powerful programming environment; after reading Chapter 11, you will be well on your way to exploiting some of its remarkable functionality.

CHAPTER 11

Advanced SQL

T his chapter will teach you the finer points of SQL as a programming language. Our experience has shown that SQL is a very flexible programming tool once you master some of its more advanced features. One of our favorite tricks is using SQL to write SQL. We show you this feature, plus a number of others that will put you on the fast track to becoming a skilled SQL developer. Here is a list of the major items we will discuss:

- Grouping results from a SQL statement
- Using subqueries (query within a query)
- Using SQL*Plus to generate SQL and create datafiles for other programs
- Using **decode** and **new_value**
- Defining variables in SQL*Plus
- Passing values into SQL*Plus
- Advanced **ttitle** features
- Set theory in SQL*Plus
- Structured programming
- Using an editor in SQL*Plus

This chapter is intended to teach you more about Oracle and its SQL implementation; when you finish this chapter, you will be able to create very sophisticated reports. You will also be able to determine when it is appropriate to use SQL*Plus or when it makes more sense to use a different tool, like Oracle Reports.

Terminology

The following definitions will arm you with the technical jargon to make it through this chapter:

- A *command file* contains a series of commands that are read by a program such as SQL*Plus. The work accomplished by a command file is the same as if you had typed each command interactively one after the other.

- *Functions* perform operations on data that alter the display or data type of the data. For example, reformatting the date 11-DEC-97 to be displayed as December 11, 1997 is done by using a function.

Functions That Group Results

These functions allow you to group sets of data together for the purpose of getting summary information. When you group rows together, think of this as an operation that lumps similar types of information together as the information is retrieved from the database. Table 11-1 lists the most common group functions, using the customer table we introduced in Chapter 5.

After looking at the most common group functions, let's move on and look at how they can be applied. A large part of the queries you write in SQL*Plus perform group functions as the data is retrieved from the database. Mastering the use of functions is fundamental to your understanding of the power of SQL and SQL*Plus.

Using the group by Clause

We discussed in Chapter 1 how the relational database model works with sets of rows. These sets can also be thought of as a group. You may use the functions described in Table 11-1 with or without the **group by** clause. When you don't mention the **group by** clause in a query, such as **select max(sales) from customer;**, you are telling the database that you want to treat all the rows in the table as one group. For example, you might want to know the average sales of all your customers or the total sales for all customers. The query **select avg(sales) from customer;** gives you the average, and **select sum(sales) from customer;** gives you the total sales for all customers. This is useful, but many times you are really interested in looking at your data in predetermined classes or groups. For example, to know the average sales by state, we use the query **select state_cd, avg(sales) from customer group by state_cd;**. Most people understand the purpose of the **group by** statement at first but have trouble implementing it. You must ensure that the **group by** clause references the correct number of columns in each SQL statement.

FUNCTION	RETURNS	EXAMPLE
avg(column_name)	The average value of all the values in column_name	select avg(sales) from customer;
count(*)	The number of rows in a table	select count(*) from customer;
max(column_name)	The maximum value stored in column_name	select max(sales) from customer;
min(column_name)	The minimum value stored in column_name	select min(sales) from customer;
sum(column_name)	The sum of the values residing in column_name	select sum(sales) from customer;

TABLE 11-1. *Most Common Group by Functions*

VIP
When using **group by**, whatever columns are not mentioned in the **group by** portion of the query must have a group function on them.

Let's look at where omitting the function can cause problems. If we issue the statement **select last_name,state_cd,sum(sales) from customer group by last_name;**, the following error is returned:

```
ERROR at line 1:
ORA-00979: not a GROUP BY expression
```

Since the column state_cd is not included in the **group by** clause, it must have a group function on it. In other words, we must use a function such as max(), min(), sum(), count(), or avg(). If you can't find a group function you want to use on a particular column, then move that column to the **group by** clause.

Using the having Clause

Just as you have search conditions (e.g., **where state_cd = 'MA'**) for individual rows of a query, you can use the **having** clause to specify a search condition for a group of rows. For example, suppose you only wanted to see the states that have more than 300 customers. Using the **having** clause, the query would be **select state_cd, avg(sales) from customer group by state_cd having count(state_cd) > 300;**

VIP
The **having** clause allows you to specify a search condition for a group of rows. The traditional **where** search condition works with an individual row, not a group of rows.

Query Within a Query

Another powerful ability of SQL is having a query within a query; this is also called using a subquery. The format of using a subquery is

```
{main query text} where {condition}
        ({sub query text});
```

For example, in the following, the main query looks at the customer table, the subquery at state:

```
select last_name,sales
   from customer
 where state_cd =
          (select max(state_cd)
             from state);
```

Note the subquery is enclosed in parentheses. As well, the condition in the **where** clause is resolved based on the results of a query. In other words, your **where** clause contains a SQL statement itself.

Say you only want to see the sales of customers that exceed the average of all sales for the whole company. You would enter the query **select state_cd, sales from customer where sales > (select avg(sales) from customer);**. As you can see, this ability to have a query within a query is very powerful. You are able to build SQL statements that return data based on the information stored in the database. As your database changes, the query stays the same. Suppose you had determined beforehand that the average sales figure was $12,800 and you had worded the previous query **select state_cd, sales from customer where sales > 12800;**. You'd be in trouble if the average sales figure changed—you would have to change the query.

VIP

Using subqueries allows you to write SQL statements that can stay the same as your data changes (which it ALWAYS does!).

Creating Datafiles for Other Programs

One of the most common programs we see people write is one that will feed data from an Oracle database into a spreadsheet. Let's use SQL*Plus to do this. Most spreadsheets require data in which each item is separated by a comma. Character-type data needs to be enclosed in single or double quotes. If we need single quotes, the following code will do this for us:

```
rem * Make spreadsheet data program
set heading
set pagesize 0
set feedback off
set echo off
spool out.dat
/* Notice you need to select four single quotes to */
/* put a single quote in the output data file      */
select ''''||last_name||''''||','||''''||
       state_cd||''''||','||''''||sales
```

```
   from customer;
spool off
```

VIP
Since the single quote means something special to Oracle (i.e., it starts and ends a literal), you must **select** four of them together if you want the single quote character in your query results.

If we need double quotes, the following will work:

```
set heading
set pagesize 0
set feedback off
set echo off
spool out.dat
/* Notice how you place a double quote between two single */
/* to place a double quote in the output data file        */
select '"'||last_name||'"',"'||state_cd||'"','||sales
   from customer;
spool off
```

The output would be

```
'Teplow','MA',23445.67
'Abbey','CA',6969.96
'Porter','CA',6989.99
'Martin','CA',2345.45
'Laursen','CA',34.34
'Bambi','CA',1234.55
'McGraw','NJ',123.45
```

with single quotes, or

```
"Teplow","MA",23445.67
"Abbey","CA",6969.96
"Porter","CA",6989.99
"Martin","CA",2345.45
"Laursen","CA",34.34
"Bambi","CA",1234.55
"McGraw","NJ",123.45
```

with double quotes. Table 11-2 discusses the lines in the program to make the spreadsheet data.

COMPONENT	MEANING
set heading off	Since you are creating a datafile, you do not want headings.
set pagesize 0	You do not want page breaks, so you set this to zero for datafile output.
set linesize 80	You set this to the size of the longest line in your output datafile.
set feedback off	Suppresses SQL*Plus from telling you how many rows are retrieved to satisfy the query.
set echo off	Tells SQL*Plus not to echo the SQL statement as it is run.
spool out.dat	Tells Oracle to send the results of the query to a file named out.dat.
spool off	Tells Oracle to close the output datafile.

TABLE 11-2. *Discussion of lines of code from a spreadsheet data creation program*

As you can see from Table 11-2, SQL*Plus is a very flexible tool. It is also a very easy tool to create datafiles with. Getting data into and out of an Oracle database is typically very easy from the Oracle side.

SQL Creating SQL

There is no reason why you cannot get SQL to create SQL programs. In fact, this is a technique most DBAs find very useful. The following SQL code will generate a SQL file called out.sql that will contain SQL statements:

```
set heading off
set pagesize 0
set feedback off
set echo off
spool out.sql
select 'set pagesize 55' from dual;
select 'grant select to public on '||table_name||';'
        from user_tables;
spool off
```

As you can see, we have a program that creates another SQL program. The first **select** references the dual table. This is a table owned by Oracle user SYS that contains only one row. We use it in this case to load a setup command for the output file called out.sql; we then follow up with the **grant** statements. You have all the elements you need to generate numerous SQL programs from SQL programs. Say this code was run from an Oracle account that owned a customer and state table. The contents of out.sql would be

```
set pagesize 55
grant select on CUSTOMER to public;
grant select on STATE to public;
```

The decode Statement

The **decode** statement is how you implement if-then logic in SQL*Plus. (We discuss how this is done in PL/SQL in Chapter 6.) One of the most powerful functions within SQL*Plus is the **decode** statement. Most people shy away from it, due to its ugly syntax. As soon as you add other functions onto the columns, you can very quickly get what we call "ugly SQL." Like a small dog, its bark is far worse than its bite. With that in mind, let's take a look at the format for a **decode** statement:

> **decode (column_name,comparison,action,comparison, action,. . . else action)**

The **decode** statement compares the column contents to the comparison field. If they are equal, then **decode** does the action. If they are not equal, **decode** goes on to the next comparison. If none of the comparisons match, then the **else** action is performed.

Suppose we want to write a query that would categorize our customers by region, so that customers on the east side of the Mississippi come under the heading East and customers on the west side of the Mississippi come under the heading West. Let's take a look at how to do this with **decode**:

```
column region format a20 heading 'Region'
column sales  format 999,999,999,999,999.99
compute sum of sales on report
compute sum of sales on region
break on report on region
select decode(state_cd,     'MA', 'East',
                    'NJ', 'East',
                    'CA', 'West',
                    'Middle of River'),sales
from customer
order by 1;
```

The logic expressed by this listing is as follows:

```
if state_cd = 'MA' then
    display 'East'
elsif state_cd = 'NJ' then
    display 'East'
elsif state_cd = 'CA' then
    display 'West'
else
    display 'Middle of River')
```

This example demonstrates the power of using **decode**. Unlike a subquery (or a **select** within a **select**), which will abort if no rows are found, the **decode** statement has the **else** clause, which can handle exceptions. The bottom line is that the **decode** function is very powerful and can be used to implement logic in SQL*Plus.

Defining Variables in SQL*Plus

In SQL*Plus, it is possible to define variables that can then be used further on in the same program. Think of a variable as a table column with one row of data. Like a table column, a variable has a type (number or character), and, like a table column, it contains data. Think of a variable as a single row of data from a table with one column. The key thing to remember is that a command file can have one or more SQL queries within it. By using the SQL*Plus **define** statement, we are able to define a variable that can be referenced in all SQL statements in the command file. So let's see how you define variables, using the following code as an example:

```
define rpt_cd = "MA"
select sales from customer where state_cd = '&rpt_cd';
```

VIP

Though not mandatory, enclose the text assigned to variables in double quotes. This allows you to embed spaces in the value.

We have assigned the variable named "rpt_cd" the value MA. Thus, when issuing a query, we can prefix the variable name with an ampersand (&) and enclose it in single quotes. To view all variables that have been defined, enter the word **define** by itself. Say we have defined the three variables "rpt_cd," "sales_amt," and "cust_start." The command **define** would present the following output:

```
DEFINE RPT_CD           = "MA" (CHAR)
DEFINE SALES_AMT        = "18000" (CHAR)
DEFINE CUST_START       = "A" (CHAR)
```

To see the value of one variable, enter **define** followed by the name of the variable. If you entered **define sales_amt**, you would be told

```
DEFINE SALES_AMT        = "18000" (CHAR)
```

NOTE
All variables, regardless of the data type assigned, are character data.

If for some reason you wish to clear the value of a variable, enter the word **define** followed by the variable name. If you issue the command **undefine sales_amt**, then the command **define sales_amt**, you are informed the variable has been cleared by

```
symbol sales_amount is UNDEFINED
```

NOTE
The **define** and **undefine** words may be abbreviated to **def** and **undef**.

Substitution Variables in SQL*Plus

Many times when we are running a query, we do not know beforehand what value the user wants to use in the report. When the report is started, you want to type in a value to be used for the report. You do this by placing an ampersand (&) in front of the section of code you want replaced. For example, let's have Oracle prompt us for the value of "rpt_cd." The SQL statement would be **select sales from customer where state_cd = '&rpt_cd'**;. When this statement is executed, Oracle asks you to supply the value for "rpt_cd." Then the query runs based on the report code you supply. This way, you are able to build a report without knowing the user's specific needs.

Many times you want to avoid being prompted multiple times for a variable you use more than once. An easy way to do that is by using double ampersands. This tells Oracle to ask for the variable once and issue a **define** command on it. For example, the statement **select state_cd, avg(&&rptcol), max(&&rptcol) from customer group by state_cd;** will prompt for the value of "rptcol" only once (the three dots at the end of the old and new lines represent code not relevant to the listing):

```
Enter value for rptcol: sales
old   1: select state_cd, avg(&&rptcol), max(&&rptcol) . . .
new   1: select state_cd, avg(sales), max(sales) from . . .
ST AVG(SALES) MAX(SALES)
-- ---------- ----------
CA   3514.858    6989.99
MA  23445.67   23445.67
NJ    123.45     123.45
```

We all know that presentation is everything. The default prompt would not be acceptable for the typical end user we encounter. You use the **prompt** and **accept** command to give us a more descriptive prompt. Examine the following:

```
clear screen
prompt ******************************************
prompt Enter "ALL"  to see all your tables
prompt Or Enter a Partial table name
accept tname prompt "Enter ALL/Partial Tablename....:"
select table_name
  from user_tables
 where table_name like '%&tname%'
    or upper('&tname') = 'ALL';
```

When this is run, the following output is produced for the same user who owns a customer and a state table:

```
******************************************
Enter "ALL"  to see all your tables
Or Enter a Partial table name
Enter ALL/Partial Tablename....:ALL
old   3:   where table_name like '%&tname%'
new   3:   where table_name like '%ALL%'
old   4:          or upper('&tname') = 'ALL')
new   4:          or upper('ALL') = 'ALL')
TABLE_NAME
------------------------------
CUSTOMER
STATE
```

As you can see, Oracle generates the **prompt** statements and places the input you give it into a variable called "tname," then uses the value of "tname" in the **where** clause.

You should also pay special attention to the use of the word "ALL." It has a special meaning in this case. If you enter ALL at the prompt, then the condition **upper('&tname') = 'ALL'** becomes **'ALL' = 'ALL'** which is true. Thus every row is retrieved. If you do not enter ALL, then the database will only retrieve the table names that meet the entered criteria. This is a very powerful technique. Also notice the **clear screen** command that clears the screen before displaying the first prompt. This is used to make the prompt present better on the screen.

Sometimes you want to prompt the user for inputs and then pass those directly to SQL on the command line. This is also a very easy thing to do. If you name the variables in your program "&1," "&2," and so on, Oracle will take data passed into it on the command line and assign it to the variable "&1," "&2," and so on. For example, suppose we have a SQL program named test.sql containing the following:

```
select state_cd, sales from customer
 where sales > &1
    and state_cd = '&2';
```

If we wish to report on all data where the sales is greater than $1,000 and the state is CA, we could call the above program with the command

```
sqlplus username/password @test 1000 CA
```

and the output would be

```
old   1: select state_cd, sales from customer where sales > &1
new   1: select state_cd, sales from customer where sales > 1000
old   2: and state_cd = '&2'
new   2: and state_cd = 'CA'

ST     SALES
-- ----------
CA    6969.96
CA    6989.99
CA    2345.45
CA    1234.55
```

NOTE
Oracle displays old and new lines as it substitutes values for variables. This display can be suppressed with the SQL*Plus command **set verify off**, which can be abbreviated to **set ver off**.

If you are already in SQL*Plus, you use the **start** command to run a program, and pass variables after the name of the program. The **start** command tells Oracle to get the command file, load it, and then execute it (using any parameters you enter with the **start** command).

```
start test.sql 1000 CA
```

As you can see, SQL*Plus has quite a few capabilities when it comes to passing parameters. By passing values to SQL*Plus as you invoke a program, you can write one SQL query and have it satisfy a number of users' needs. In addition, you can very easily interface it with other programs.

NOTE
Most operating systems allow using the @ sign rather than the word "start." What's the difference between the two, you ask? Four keystrokes!

ttitle–The Whole Title and Nothing but the Title

Up to now, you have only seen examples where we use the default behavior of the **ttitle** command. As you know, the **ttitle** command is used to print a title at the top of each page. In Chapter 5, we showed you the default behavior, because from experience we have found this to be sufficient for the majority of your needs. There comes a time where you want more. Perhaps you need a clerk's name in the heading, or page numbers on the left. Regardless, there is much more you can do with the **ttitle** command. Table 11-3 takes a closer look at the **ttitle** command.

NOTE
The **bold** formatting command may not work on all operating systems.

The best way to understand these advanced formatting features is to use them. So let's do a more sophisticated **ttitle** command:

```
set linesize 62
ttitle left 'Michael Abbey Systems' skip center -
       'An Oracle Systems Consulting Company' -
       right 'Page: ' format 999 sql.pno -
       skip center bold 'Customer Report'
```

OPTION	MEANING
col n	Indents to position n of the current line.
skip n	Skips to the start of a new line; if you enter 0, then it goes to the beginning of the line.
left, right, center	Left align, right align, or center align.
bold	Displays data in boldface.
format char	Specifies the format model to be used (similar to the format command with col).
sql.lno	The current line number.
sql.pno	The current page number.
sql.user	The name of the user logged into SQL*Plus.

TABLE 11-3. *Advanced Formatting Command for ttitle*

The title would then show up on any report as

```
Michael Abbey Systems
                An Oracle Systems Consulting Company   Page:    1
                    Customer Report
```

The hyphen (**-**) in **ttitle** represents a line continuation, and the **skip** word instructs **ttitle** to skip the specified number of lines (or one line, if a number is omitted). As you can see, you can get pretty sophisticated with this command.

column–The Whole Column and Nothing but the Column

As you have seen from previous examples, the **column** command controls how your data is displayed. Just like the **ttitle** command, you have lots of options with **column**. We will now present a summary of the extra formatting commands for number and then character data.

NOTE
The **column** command can be abbreviated to **col** and the **format** command to **form**.

Formatting Number Data

The **format** command determines how the information from the database will be displayed. Table 11-4 highlights the most useful formats for number data.

FORMAT CHARACTER	EXAMPLE	DESCRIPTION
9	format 999999	Determines the display width based on the number of digits entered. When you have a number overflow, it will display "######'. You will not see any leading zeros.
0	09999	Displays leading zeros.
	99990	When value is zero, it displays a zero instead of a blank space.
$	$99999	Places a dollar sign in front of the number.
B	B99999	Displays a zero as a blank.
MI	99999MI	Displays a minus sign when the value is negative.
PR	99999PR	Places <> around a negative number.
,	9,99,999	Places a comma in the position specified.
.	999.999	Places a decimal point where specified and rounds appropriately.
EEEE	9.99EEEE	Prints in scientific notation. Must be four Es.

TABLE 11-4. *Common Number Formats Used with column Command*

The next listing shows some of these formats in action:

```
column sales    format 999,999,999.99
select sales from customer;
```

```
Michael Abbey Systems
        An Oracle Systems Consulting Company              Page:     1
                            Customer Report

            SALES
    ---------------
       23,445.67
        6,969.96
        6,989.99
        2,345.45
           34.34
        1,234.55
          123.45
7 rows selected.
```

```
SQL> column sales         format $099999
SQL> select sales from customer;
```

```
Michael Abbey Systems
        An Oracle Systems Consulting Company              Page:     1
                            Customer Report
SALES
--------
 $023446
 $006970
 $006990
 $002345
 $000034
 $001235
 $000123
7 rows selected.
```

Formatting Character Data

Character data can be harder to deal with. For example, say you want to print a report in which the number of characters across a page is 80. The report lists names and salaries. Some of the names (e.g., Alexandre Springhurst, at a length of 21 characters) are longer than others (e.g., Sue Ray, at a length of 7 characters). If you allocate the necessary space to accommodate short names, the long names could be broken over multiple lines and become hard to read.

Wrapping and Truncating Character Data

The following three words can be used to format character data and are useful when a report needs to display character data that is longer than the width of the column display you have set.

- **wrap:** This command tells SQL*Plus to display the specified number of characters, then go to the next line and continue. Using our long name example, if the full_name column were formatted using the column expression **column full_name format a18 wrap**, the name would appear as

```
Name                 City
------------------   ----------------
Alexandre Springhu   Winnipeg
rst
```

- **word_wrap:** This command tells SQL*Plus to display the specified number of characters, but move a word to the next line rather than split the word into pieces. Using the column expression **column full_name format a18 word_wrap**, the name would appear as

```
Name                 City
------------------   ----------------
Alexandre            Winnipeg
Springhurst
```

- **truncate:** This command tells SQL*Plus to display the specified number of characters, and ignore the rest. Using the column expression **column full_name format a18 truncate**, the name would appear as

```
Name                 City
------------------   ----------------
Alexandre Springhu   Winnipeg
```

Justify left, center, or right

This controls the centering of the column heading (not the data in the column). By default, a number column heading is right-justified, character is left-justified. The following listing illustrates how these affect a column heading display format using the statement **select state_name from state;**:

```
column state_name justify right
          STATE_NAME
--------------------
Massachusetts
California
NewJersey
col state_name justify center

      STATE_NAME
--------------------
Massachusetts
California
NewJersey
```

new_value

You can create a variable that will hold data from a column using **new_value**. Once a variable is defined, you can then place its value into a **ttitle** command. This is useful when you want to create a master/detail report with a value from the report appearing in the heading. To place a value in the heading, you must always reference a column from your query (in our example the column state_cd) in the **break** command, with the **skip page** option. For example, using the SQL statement **select state_cd, last_name, sales from customer order by 1;**, examine the following output:

```
column state_cd new_value rpt_cd
ttitle left 'STATE CD: ' rpt_cd skip 1
break on state_cd skip page

STATE CD: CA

ST LAST_NAM SALES
-- -------- ------------
CA Abbey          6,970
   Porter         6,990
   Martin         2,345
   Bambi          1,235
   Laursen           34

STATE CD: MA

ST LAST_NAM SALES
```

```
-- -------- ------------
MA Teplow        23,446

STATE CD: NJ

ST LAST_NAM SALES
-- -------- ------------
NJ McGraw            123

7 rows selected.
```

You could also use this technique to put today's date in the heading.

Examine the following code to see how today's date is put in a report title using **new_value**.

```
column today new_value today_date
select to_char(sysdate,'HH24:MM:SS DD-Mon-YYYY') today
  from dual;
ttitle center 'Michael Abbey Systems' skip left today_date -
       right 'Page: ' format 999 sql.pno skip
select sales from customer;
```

When this is run, the date appears on line two of the title (format resembling 18:12:13 26-Mar-96), with the page number on the left side of the same line.

```
                     Michael Abbey Systems
14:03:22 26-Mar-1996                                  Page:    1

      SALES
   ----------
    23445.67
     6969.96
     6989.99
     2345.45
       34.34
     1234.55
      123.45
```

SQL*Plus Set Theory

The nice thing about a relational database is that you write SQL queries that act upon sets of data versus a single row of data. Not having to issue a read makes it very, very powerful. SQL by design has a very strong relationship to math theory. There are a series of set functions that work very nicely with an Oracle database using SQL*Plus. We will discuss these set operators in the next few sections, using tables x and y (both have a single column of character data type). The next listing shows the contents of these tables.

```
select * from x;

COL
---
1
2
3
4
5
6

6 rows selected.

select * from y;

COL
---
5
6
7
3 rows selected.
```

union

Using this operator in SQL*Plus returns all the rows in both tables with no duplicates. In the previous listing, the tables both have columns with the value of 5 and 6. The query **select * from x union select * from y;** returns the following results as expected:

```
COL
---
1
2
3
4
5
```

```
6
7
7 rows selected.
```

intersect

Using this operator in SQL*Plus returns all the rows in one table that also reside in the other. Using tables x and y, the column values 5 and 6 are in both tables. The query **select * from x intersect select * from y;** returns the following results as expected:

```
COL
---
1
2
```

minus

Using this operator in SQL*Plus returns all the rows in the first table minus the rows in that table that are also in the second table. Using tables x and y, the column values 5 and 6 are in both tables. The query **select * from x minus select * from y;** returns the following results, as expected:

```
COL
---
1
2
3
4
```

VIP
When using these set operators with Oracle, the data types of the column(s) in both tables must be the same.

The following error occurs if the data types differ (using table z, whose single column is number data type):

```
select * from x union select * from z
       *
ERROR at line 1:
ORA-01790: expression must have same datatype as corresponding expression
```

Structured Code Techniques

SQL is a programming language like any other. To do it right requires care.
The first thing we recommend you do is have a SQL script with common
setup information and the most common column definitions. Look at the
following example:

```
rem ****************
rem * setup.sql
rem ****************
rem This script contains common set-up information and
rem formatting information I use for many sql scripts
rem Michael Corey    05/23/95   Created
rem Michael Abbey    10/23/97   Changed pagesize to 60,
REM                            to add additional
rem                            5 lines for new printer.
rem Standard set-up
set echo off
set pagesize 55
set linesize 80
rem *************************************
rem * common column format statements
rem *************************************
column bytes heading 'Bytes' format 999,999,999.99
column kbytes heading 'K Bytes' format 999,999,999.99
column less1 heading 'Under 1|Minute' format 999,990
column sales heading 'Sales|Ytd' format 999,999,999,999,999.99
state_cd heading 'St|Cd' format a2
state_name heading 'State|Name' format a20 truncate
column sum(sales) heading 'Sales|Ytd' format 999,999,999,999,999.99
column sum(bytes) heading 'Bytes'    format 999,999,999.99
column table_name heading 'Table|Name' format a20 wrap
rem *******************
rem * End of script
rem *******************
```

This command file holds the most common setup items (i.e., **pagesize** and
linesize) and the most common column format statements. The next step is to write

your SQL query and invoke the preceding program to format and set up the report. This is done in the following listing:

```
rem ****************************************
rem *    customer.sql
rem ****************************************
rem * This report gives a complete customer listing
rem * Mike Corey  10/23/94
rem * Call in standard setup residing in central repository
@/oracle/ora7/sql/setup.sql
rem * Set the report title and page footer
ttitle center 'Database Technologies' skip center 'Customer Report'
btitle center '*** customer.sql ***'
```

By using a standard setup file, you merely execute it first. This sets up the environment. Then your program (i.e., customer.sql) contains the query to get the data, any break logic (the **break** statement), any totals you want to display, and the **ttitle** and **btitle** commands the report uses (we discussed **btitle** in the "Page Footers" section of Chapter 5). You don't spend a lot of time formatting the data; you spend your efforts on the program logic needed to accomplish the task.

Notice how the **btitle** name is the name of the command file. That is so when an end user calls you up about a report, you can easily tell what the source code is. In real life, many SQL statements you use for your reports tend to be slight variations of each other. By putting the report title in the footer of the report, you can zero in on which report needs attention.

Command Line Editing

When working with SQL*Plus, it becomes apparent very quickly that Oracle holds the last command executed in a buffer. To access that buffer, you merely have to enter a slash (/) and hit the ENTER key. This action will cause the last SQL query entered to run again. If you have ever left two semicolons at the end of your command file, you learn very quickly that the query ran twice.

Many times when building these command files, if you are like most of us, you have fat-fingered the typing and need to make a minor change. We find in these cases that it's much easier to use the command line editor you get with SQL*Plus than retyping the whole line. Even though this editor is very crude, it has always served a very useful purpose. You can very quickly make changes to the SQL buffer and then execute a SQL statement once again. Table 11-5 takes a look at the core commands.

EDITOR COMMAND	PURPOSE
(a)ppend	Add text to the end of the current line
(c)hange /old/new/	Replace old text with new text in the current line
(c)hange /text/	Remove the text from the current line
del	Delete the current line
(i)nput text	Add a line after the current line
(l)ist	Show all the lines in the buffer
(l)ist n	Show line number n in the buffer

TABLE 11-5. *SQL*Plus Line Editing Commands*

The key to this editor is knowing what the current line is; it's the only line that you are able to change. With that in mind, let's try a few things. Let's look at our query by entering the command **list**:

```
1    select state_cd, last_name, sales
2    from customer
3*   order by 1
```

The asterisk tells us what the current line is. So let's change the current line to line one. From now on, we will use the abbreviated form of the command (presented in parentheses in Table 11-5). Type the command **l 1** (the letter "l" followed by the number one), and SQL*Plus lists line one:

```
1*   select state_cd, last_name, sales
```

Now the current line is set at line one. Let's change state_cd to customer.state_cd. You enter the command **c/state/customer.state_cd/** and SQL*Plus responds with

```
1*   select customer.state_cd, last_name, sales
```

Now let's list the entire query again using the command **l**:

```
1    select state_cd, last_name, sales
2    from customer
3*   order by 1
```

Let's remove the **order by** statement. Since we are pointing to line three, we just enter the delete command **d** and then list our query with the command **l**:

```
1    select state_cd, last_name, sales
2*   from customer
```

Notice how SQL*Plus leaves the current line as line two after doing the delete we requested. With the edited command in the SQL buffer, we can run it again using the command **r** or by typing the slash (/) character. Either produces the following query output:

```
ST LAST_NAME
-- -----------------------------
MA Teplow
CA Abbey
CA Porter
CA Martin
CA Laursen
CA Bambi
NJ McGraw
```

Your last SQL query is kept in the buffer until you exit SQL*Plus.

Arrrghh! We Need a Real Editor

As we said, this command line editor is great for simple tasks. But it only allows you to edit the SQL query itself. Many times, a lot of formatting and setup goes on to make a simple SQL query into a usable report. That job is best done with a full editor. There is a command in SQL*Plus that lets you define your favorite editor for use directly from SQL*Plus. The command is formatted as **define _editor="editor_name"** where **editor_name** is the name of the program that runs your favorite editor. In UNIX, that text may be **vi**, in VMS it may be **edt**.

You can set up any editor of your choice. To use the editor you define in this manner, type the command **edit** or abbreviate it to **ed**. Oracle will then issue the command you have used in the **define _editor** command.

What's Next

What we have given you in this chapter is all the pieces to be really productive with SQL and SQL*Plus. We did not intend this to be the complete guide to programming in SQL; it's a guide to the most useful techniques and commands. Armed with our introductory chapter on SQL, you now have an understanding of how to word queries and how to format SQL*Plus report output. Remember, SQL is the foundation of Oracle. The better you know it, the better you can use Oracle.

In the next chapter, we will discuss some advanced concepts about application tuning. You will be able to add some more SQL skills to your repertoire as we look at ways to write efficient SQL queries and take advantage of its truly remarkable features.

CHAPTER 12

Advanced Application Tuning

In Chapter 10, we discussed the two most important concepts in application tuning: writing SQL statements that match ones resident in the shared pool, and minimizing reads from disk by using indexes. In this chapter, we take it to the next step. Each component part in the application tuning exercise can seem rather insignificant on its own. Rolled together into a tuning methodology, each component in the tuning process is a worthwhile contributor.

Tuning applications should begin with the programmer and the very first line of code, and continue throughout the system life cycle. There are always many different ways to do something with a given requirement—the good way, and all the others. It is not enough just to know how to use Oracle. Tuning your applications will enable you to get the best performance out of Oracle. When your applications are tuned, they use fewer resources, which has a ripple affect. Efforts to tune the Oracle software could be wasted without your taking the time to tune applications. In this chapter, we will highlight the following issues that pertain to application tuning:

■ Rule-based approach to SQL statement optimization

■ Cost-based approach to SQL statement optimization

■ The three phases in SQL statement processing

■ Naming variables in Oracle tools

■ Data access path chosen by Oracle

■ Unique indexes

■ Looking at the contents of the shared pool

■ Explain plan

■ SQL trace and tkprof

We will discuss ways to maximize your available resources and focus on the areas of tuning your applications that will give you the most gain.

Terminology

The following definitions will arm you with the technical jargon to make it through this chapter.

■ An *access path* is the method Oracle determines to get at your data. It chooses this path based on a number of evaluation processes over which we have no control.

■ The *execution plan* is a roadmap to the data involved in every SQL statement, and it is built by Oracle based on a set of predefined optimization techniques.

■ *Locks* are internal mechanisms Oracle maintains to ensure the integrity of your data. For example, when a user starts to change the information in a personnel record, Oracle issues a lock to ensure that no one else can make changes until the first user is finished.

■ The *environment* is a section of memory allocated to each session on a computer. This memory contains session-specific information, such as the user's name, the system identifier of the user's database, and a list of directories to search for programs when the user issues a command.

■ *ORACLE_HOME* is the location on one of your disks (a directory) under which the Oracle software resides. It is defined at installation time, and it becomes part of the environment as Oracle operates.

■ When you inspect a series of characters (e.g., the text ahdjek9kk) for the occurrence of one or more characters (e.g., k9), the characters you are looking for are referred to as the *lookup string*.

■ The *optimizer* is a set of internal Oracle routines that decides the most efficient access path to your data. These routines are run when Oracle is trying to arrive at the most efficient way to access data to satisfy a SQL statement.

■ A *unique* or *primary* key refers to one or more column values in a table that can uniquely identify each row in a table. Picture a primary key as one's social insurance number, used by the Canadian government to identify each resident of Canada (even though a study once found over 700 people had the same social insurance number—guess the Department of Employment and Immigration was not using Oracle then!). For one or more columns to be a primary key, the values cannot be duplicated anywhere else in the table's data.

■ A *host* character is placed in a SQL*Plus program to drop back to the operating system to issue a command. Execution of the SQL script is suspended until the operating system command completes. You are then returned to SQL*Plus.

Optimization

Advanced application tuning requires an understanding of how Oracle optimizes SQL statements. Oracle uses one of two approaches to accomplish this. With the *rule-based* approach, Oracle ranks data access path efficiency based on a set of rules. With the *cost-based* approach, which is Oracle7's default, Oracle examines the data in one or more tables in the SQL statement and selects the access path that will cost the least (i.e., use the least resources and take the least amount of time). By the end of this section, you will understand the advantages of each approach and have a good feel for which one you should use.

Rule-Based Approach

Oracle ranks access paths on a weight of 1 to 15, then chooses the access path with the lowest rank. Think of ranking as going into a grocery store and inspecting the Granny Smith apples. As you pick them up, you turn them over, look for bruises, and examine the color of the skin. Ones you like the most are ranked with the number "1"; those you prefer the least are ranked with the number "15." Just like the rule-based approach to optimizing, the rank number affects whether the apple is chosen or discarded in favor of one with a better (or lower) rank.

When retrieving data, Oracle can find the location of a desired row fastest if it knows its rowid (each row can be uniquely identified by its rowid). The *rowid* provides immediate access to data; it identifies the exact location of the data. Picture the rowid as the address of each piece of data stored in the Oracle database.

Access path rankings are determined by the available indexes and how the SQL statement is worded. Let's look at the most common rule-based access path weights and their meaning. For the next few sections, we will refer to the part of the SQL statement using **where** and one or more **and** as the **where/and** part of the statement.

VIP
The lower the rank of the access path chosen to satisfy a query, the faster and more efficient the processing.

Rule-Based Access Path Rank 1
This path is available when the **where** keyword equates the rowid to a single value. For example, the statement

```
select *
  from fin_mast
 where rowid = '008A4.0002.009D';
```

would be ranked using this weight. In the SQL statements that you write for your applications, you never know rowids, so this path is not explicitly used very often. However, using Oracle tools such as Oracle Forms, when a row of information is retrieved onto a screen, its rowid is fetched as well. When you update the row and save the information back to the database, Oracle Forms passes a SQL statement to Oracle using this rowid construct. You may have seen this if you have ever received an Oracle error from Oracle Forms (yes, Oracle errors do happen):

```
Oracle error occurred while executing KEY-COMMIT trigger:
update tabA set name=:nam,address=:addr ........ where rowid=:rowid
```

Oracle knows the rowid of the record on the screen you are attempting to update, and uses this access path to perform the update.

Rule-Based Access Path Rank 4

This path is available when all columns in a unique or primary key are referenced by your SQL statement in equality conditions. Let's look at the following table:

COLUMN	PART OF PRIMARY KEY
street_name	Y
house_number	Y
city	N

The SQL statement

```
select *
  from street_master
 where street_name = 'ROBSON'
   and house_number = '2802';
```

could take advantage of this access path; all the columns in the primary key are mentioned in the **where/and** and they are compared using equality. The SQL statement

```
select *
  from street_master
 where street_name = 'ROBSON'
   and house_number >= '2802';
```

could not take advantage of this access path, since the comparison condition performed on the house_number column is not equality (there is a greater than or equal to comparison). Likewise, the statement

```
select *
  from street_master
 where street_name = 'ROBSON';
```

does not use all the primary key columns in the **where/and** and cannot be ranked with this weight.

Rule-Based Access Path Rank 8

If the statement's **where** clause mentions all the columns in a composite index and performs equality comparisons, this access path will be used. Remember, a composite index is one built on more than one column in a table.

Rule-Based Access Path Rank 9

This access path is used if the **where/and** portion of the SQL statement uses one or more single-column indexes. If more than one single-column index is used, the conditions must be connected with **and**. For example, consider the fin_mast table indexed on fin_id. The following SQL statement uses this access path:

```
select max_out
  from fin_mast
 where fin_id = '1234M';
```

If there is also an index on the fin_rel column of the same table, the following statement will not use this access path, since the conditions are connected using **or** not **and**.

```
select max_out
  from fin_mast
 where fin_id = '1234M'
    or fin_rel is not null;
```

Rule-Based Access Path Rank 15

The full table scan is used for any SQL statement that does not satisfy the criteria for other weighted access paths. Each record in the table is read sequentially; those that qualify for all selection criteria are chosen, those that do not are discarded.

The rule-based access path weights not discussed in this section are beyond the scope of this book.

Cost-Based Approach

When using the cost-based approach, Oracle optimizes a SQL statement to cost the least. This cost is a measurement of how long Oracle thinks it will take to process the SQL statement. It is based on factors such as the number of rows in each table and the number of distinct values in columns in the tables. For example, the cost-based approach estimates the I/Os that will be performed based on the selection of available access paths, and then tries to find the least expensive I/O path. As we mentioned earlier, I/O activities are amongst the slowest a system performs.

To use this approach, you must gather statistics to be examined by the cost-based optimizer when selecting a data access path during determination of the execution plan. You collect statistics manually using the SQL **analyze** keyword for tables, indexes, or clusters. Clusters offer an alternative way of storing Oracle data. *Tuning Oracle* by Corey, Abbey, and Dechichio (Osborne McGraw-Hill/Oracle Press, 1995) discusses clusters in more detail. Gather statistics using one of the following commands:

```
analyze table tabA estimate statistics;
analyze table tabA compute statistics;
analyze index indA estimate statistics;
analyze index indA compute statistics;
```

Compute calculates exact statistics but is more time-consuming; for the purposes of most applications, estimate will suffice. Keep in mind that if you want to use cost-based optimization and do not collect statistics manually, Oracle will estimate them during the parse phase of each new SQL statement. This is an undesirable situation—this on-the-fly collection can be time-consuming. The results of the analysis appear in the user_tables and user_indexes data dictionary views. Values in the following columns in those views prove most useful when Oracle uses the cost-based optimization approach.

```
user_tables:
num_rows                         number
blocks                           number
empty_blocks                     number
avg_space                        number
chain_cnt                        number
avg_row_len                      number

user_indexes:
blevel                           number
leaf_blocks                      number
distinct_keys                    number
avg_leaf_blocks_per_key          number
avg_data_blocks_per_key          number
clustering_factor                number
status                           varchar2(11)
```

Which Approach to Use

When Oracle7 first appeared in late 1992, the cost-based approach was touted to be a dream come true. Developers no longer had to expend much energy optimizing SQL statements. At run time, Oracle would decide an execution plan based on statistics in the data dictionary. Since the cost-based approach is able to optimize statements based on the current data volumes and distribution of indexed column values, execution plans are more dynamic. As the data changes, so may the selected optimal plan.

However, installations that moved to Oracle7 (circa early 1993) started to find a degradation in system performance with this approach. As it turns out, the theory of cost-based optimization is very sound, but its implementation is considerably more difficult. As late as Oracle version 7.1.4, we recommend that you stay with the rule-based approach as the default and experiment with the cost-based approach. When you are happy with its advantages and with the results (plus advice from Oracle itself and other informed sources), then use the cost-based approach as the default.

To help invest in the cost-based approach, Oracle has provided a technique called hints. Using *hints,* you can influence choices made by cost-based optimization and experiment with different access paths to your data. Oracle has done its homework. Users have been provided with a new optimization technique and can now influence Oracle choices by using these hints. The cost-based optimizer approach is maturing. As this book is being written, the cost-based technique is becoming increasingly more dependable. We offer the following guidelines to help you choose between the rule-based and cost-based optimization approaches:

- Applications that have migrated from earlier versions of Oracle (version 6 and earlier offer only rule-based optimization) should be left running rule-based.

- Experiment with the cost-based approach and familiarize yourself with using optimizer hints.

- New application development and tuning exercises should look at the cost-based approach.

- Do not use the cost-based approach as the default until the user community and Oracle jointly endorse it.

- Tune SQL statements using the tools we introduce in the next section of this chapter: SQL trace with tkprof and explain plan.

SQL Statement Processing

All SQL statements are processed in three phases—parse, execute, and fetch— regardless of the tool (e.g., Oracle Forms, Oracle Office) that passed it to Oracle for processing. Let's look briefly at these phases.

Parse

Parse is the most time-consuming of the three phases. This phase is the most costly. In the section of this chapter covering the shared pool, we will discuss ways to avoid parsing SQL statements prior to execution. During this phase, the optimizer does its job of selecting the most efficient access path and execution plan. Using the following SQL statement as an example, let's look at the tasks involved in this phase.

NOTE
This section offers an oversimplified explanation of the parse phase of SQL statement execution. It gives you a flavor of the amount of work involved. It is NOT the way Oracle directly processes your SQL statements.

```
select a.class_group, descr, sum(mon_amt + tue_amt + wed_amt + thu_amt +
                               fri_amt + sat_amt + sun_amt)
   from timesheets a, classes b
  where a.class_group like 'CS%'
    and a.class_group = b.class_group
  group by a.class_group, descr;
```

The next four sections illustrate some of the processing required to parse every SQL statement.

Word Meaning

Oracle examines the code from the bottom to the top. It finds different kinds of words in the statement: words it knows as part of its own lingo (e.g., **select** or **where**), words that refer to your tables and their columns (e.g., timesheets a or class_grp), and all other miscellaneous words and punctuation (e.g., commas and parentheses). Table 12-1 outlines the decisions Oracle has to make using the last four lines of the previous listing.

Once Oracle works through the statement, bottom to top, it can start to put the whole thing together. Based on what it found, it deduces the following:

- The objects in the SQL statement are timesheets and classes, using the aliases "a" and "b" respectively. Therefore, column names using one of those prefixes must reside in the appropriate object.

- The columns enclosed in parentheses all belong to the timesheets object. Since they are being summed in the statement, they all must be defined as numeric.

	COMPONENT	DECISION MADE	DECISION
1	a.descr	Not a reserved word	Store until the prefix "a." can be resolved
2	a.class_group	Not a reserved word	Store until the prefix "a." can be resolved
3	by	Reserved word	
4	group	Reserved word	
5	b.class_group	Not a reserved word	Store until the prefix "b." can be resolved
6	a.class_group	Not a reserved word	Store until the prefix "a." can be resolved
7	and	Reserved word	
8	'CS%'	Text enclosed in quotes	Nothing more to do
9	like	Reserved word	
10	a.class_grp	Not a reserved word	Store until the prefix "a." can be resolved
11	where	Reserved word	
12	classes b	Not a reserved word	Must be an object name and its alias
13	timesheets a	Not a reserved word	Must be an object name and its alias
14	from	Reserved word	

TABLE 12-1. *Parse Phase Decisions*

Resolve Object Names
After learning what it has, Oracle then tries to find out what objects and columns are in the statement. Table 12-2 shows the decisions that must be made. The numbers in the Item column are the component numbers from Table 12-1.

Syntax Checking
Oracle checks the following to ensure the statement is syntactically correct:

 Parentheses: Some portions require parentheses.

 Commas: Members of lists are usually separated from one another by commas.

■ Location of reserved words: Oracle checks the placement of these words and verifies they are in the proper order and do not appear more times than permitted.

SQL statement syntax is verified and the objects mentioned in the statement are resolved.

Determining of the Execution Plan and Data Access Path

The execution plan is determined after the optimizer evaluates the available access paths. The choices the optimizer makes are influenced by the tables accessed in the SQL statement, and the way the statements are worded. We discussed cost-based and rule-based optimization approaches earlier in this chapter. The execution plan selected by Oracle during the parse phase is influenced by the optimization approach in use.

VIP

Over 75 percent of application tuning can be realized by avoiding the parse phase altogether. By using ready-parsed statements already in the shared pool, you are more than three-quarters of the way there.

As we discussed in Chapter 1, the shared pool consumes a significant part of the memory allocated to running the Oracle database. To use ready-parsed statements in the shared pool, you may need to allocate more memory to the shared pool.

ITEM(S)	ASSUMPTIONS	ERROR IF NOT TRUE
13	The user must have access to an object called timesheets.	Table or view does not exist
12	The user must have access to an object called classes.	Table or view does not exist
5	The classes table must contain a class_group column.	Invalid column name
10, 6, and 2	The timesheets table must contain a class_group column.	Invalid column name
1	The timesheets table must contain a descr. column.	Invalid column name

TABLE 12-2.   *Resolving Object Names*

VIP
You may have to work closely with your database administrator (DBA) to ensure there is adequate space in the shared pool to accommodate an optimal number of ready-parsed SQL statements.

Let's spend a little time on the data access path. When the optimizer parses a SQL statement, it evaluates possible access paths in order to use the best access path. To some degree, users can help the optimizer choose an access path through deliberate wording of SQL statements.

Let's use the following scenario to illustrate the concepts of access path and optimizer. Suppose you need to get from Montreal to Boston. Your goals are to realize as little wear and tear on your vehicle as possible, spend as little money as possible, and avoid traffic in any large urban centers along the way. The assortment of possible routes is similar to the access path. Like your data, there is a fixed number of ways of getting from one end to the other (e.g., if a road has not been built, you cannot include it in your plans). In the midst of selecting the best route, you decide where the fewest bottlenecks are, and you avoid routes that pass through states with higher gasoline prices. You weigh the costs and benefits of each potential route and decide which is best.

With Oracle, this decision-making process is the job of the Oracle optimizer. In more detailed technical discussions of application tuning, we would highlight ways to influence Oracle while it chooses the most efficient access path to your data. For discussions on some of these issues, consult other publications, such as *Tuning Oracle* by Corey, Abbey, and Dechichio (Osborne McGraw Hill/Oracle Press, 1995).

VIP
Oracle chooses the access path that will yield the fastest results and consume the least amount of computer resources.

Execute

The reads and writes required to process the statement are performed during the execute phase. Oracle now knows how it will get at the data (based on the execution plan determined during the parse phase). It knows the optimal access path (as determined during the parse phase), and it is armed with all the information necessary to fetch the data that qualifies based on the selection criteria in the SQL statement. Locks are obtained, as required, if the SQL contains any update or delete operations.

Fetch

All rows that have qualified are retrieved during the fetch phase. If the query requires sorting, this is done now. The results are formatted and displayed according to the query's instructions.

VIP
The golden rule about processing SQL statements is: PARSE ONCE, EXECUTE MANY TIMES. By reusing parsed statements in the shared pool, you have made the biggest step towards application tuning.

Naming Variables

You need to standardize on a convention to use when naming variables in your programs. Using the same name across SQL statements coupled with the coding conventions discussed in Chapter 10 helps ensure SQL statements you pass to Oracle will match ones already in the shared pool. When using a tool such as Oracle Forms, the names of variables, especially block names, must be standardized. We discuss coding conventions in Chapter 10. The same theory holds when choosing names for variables in your SQL and PL/SQL programs.

When programming using Oracle Forms, a block groups a number of fields on the screen together, permitting creation, modification, and deletions to database data. Fields within blocks and the block name together form what is referred to as *bind variables*. Referencing a block name and a field name prefixed by a colon allows direct manipulation of values in fields on a form. By standardizing block names, SQL statements using these bind variables may match statements already in the shared pool. For example, the first pair of statements in the following listing match, whereas the second pair differ. The same bind variable is used in the first two statements; the latter two may be referring to the same data, but they use different bind variable names.

```
select count(*) into :people.class_count from classif where class_1 =
:people.classif;
select count(*) into :people.class_count from classif where class_1 =
:people.classif;
select last_name||' '||first_name into :person.full_name from person;
select last_name||' '||first_name into :person.fnam from person;
```

VIP
Even if two bind variables with different names (e.g., ":nam" and ":name)" hold the same data (e.g., the name Wilson), they are still treated as different variables.

TIP
We recommend using block names that match the table name they refer to. When the same table is referenced in more than one block in a program, call the blocks table_name_1 and table_name_2.

What Should Be Indexed?

Where to use indexes is a difficult decision. Using indexes properly contributes to the application tuning process. Towards the end of this chapter in "Tools of the Tuning Trade," we show you how to assess what indexes are used as your applications operate. Indexes are optional structures maintained by Oracle that provide rapid access to your data. When you create an index, you specify the table name and one or more columns to keep track of. Once an index is created, Oracle maintains it automatically as data is created, changed, and deleted from your tables. The following rules help you decide when to create indexes:

- You should index columns that are mentioned in the **where** or **and** sections (also referred to as the *predicate*) of a SQL statement. Suppose the first_name column in a personnel table is displayed as query results, but never as part of the predicate. The column, regardless of what values it contains, should not be indexed.

- You should index columns that have a range of distinct values. Here's the rule of thumb: if a given value in a table's column is present in 20 percent or less of the rows in the table, then the column is a candidate for an index. Suppose there are 36,000 rows in a table with an even distribution (about 12,000 each) of values through one column in the table. The column is not a good candidate for an index. However, if there are between 2,000 and 3,000 rows per column value in another column in that same table (between 5 percent and 8 percent of the rows), then that column is a candidate for an index.

■ If multiple columns are continually referenced together in SQL statement predicates, you should consider putting these columns together in an index. Oracle will maintain single column indexes (those built on one column) or composite indexes (those built on more than one column). Composite indexes are also referred to as concatenated indexes.

Unique Indexes

When building an index on a table, if all the column values in the index are distinct, then use the keyword **unique** to create the index. Finding ways to use unique indexes assists the application tuning process.

VIP
Data retrieval using a unique index is faster than using indexes that are not unique.

Suppose the following table has a unique index on its id column.

```
SQL> desc person
 Name                            Null?   Type
 ------------------------------- ------  ----
 ID                                      NUMBER
 LAST_NAME                               VARCHAR2(30)
 FIRST_NAME                              VARCHAR2(20)
 START_DATE                              DATE
 SALARY                                  NUMBER
SQL>
```

While processing the following SQL statement

```
select last_name,first_name,salary
  from person
 where id = 289;
```

Oracle would proceed directly to the index entry when looking for a certain id column value. If it did not find the right index entry, Oracle would know the row does not exist. The unique index offers the following two attractions:

■ Since the index is unique, Oracle knows there can only be one entry with the desired value. If the desired entry is found, the search terminates at once.

■ The sequential search of the index can be terminated as soon as an entry greater than the desired one is encountered; if a greater index entry (in this case, anything over 289) is encountered, then the desired entry cannot exist.

Tools of the Tuning Trade

We have discussed SQL statement processing, execution plans, access paths, optimization, and indexes. We now show you how to peek at the contents of the shared pool. Once you know how to inspect the SQL statements in the pool, you can start coding SQL to match the statements already there. Then with a brief introduction to tools supplied with Oracle, you will be armed with enough knowledge to start, or continue, tuning applications. In this section, you will learn details on the following:

■ Where to look to see what sits in the shared pool

■ How to issue the SQL statement to display the shared pool contents

■ How to display the contents of the shared pool using full-screen sqldba

■ Using explain plan to analyze the access path Oracle chooses to access your data

■ How to present output from explain plan in a readable tree-like fashion

■ How to use SQL trace and the tkprof utility to report on SQL statement processing and CPU utilization

Seeing What Is in the Shared Pool

So far we have talked (or is it nattered at you on and on!) about the shared pool. We will now take the time to show you how to look around the pool and see its contents. Seeing the current contents of the shared pool may help you make decisions about standardizing as outlined in this chapter as well as Chapter 10.

Viewing the Contents of the Shared Pool in SQL*Plus

A data dictionary view called v$sqlarea will serve our purpose. You are interested in a column called sql_text. The following code shows you what is in the shared pool:

```
rem *  The sql_text column is 1,000 characters wide so
rem *  set it to 80 for this display
col sql_text format a80
select sql_text from v$sqlarea where lower(sql_text)
        like lower('&text'||'%');
```

TIP

When comparing text against the values of the sql_text column in v$sqlarea, force your lookup string and the sql_text column to the same case (using one of the SQL functions lower and upper).

When this is run, you will see something similar to the following (the code you see will of course depend on what is happening in your database when the query is issued).

```
SQL>  select sql_text from v$sqlarea where lower(sql_text) like
  2>         lower('&text'||'%');
Enter value for text: select surname
```

```
old 2: select sql_text from v$sqlarea where lower(sql_text) like
lower('&text'||'%')
new 2: select sql_text from v$sqlarea where lower(sql_text) like
lower('last_name'||'%')
SQL_TEXT
-----------------------------------------------------------------
select surname||' '||first_name into :person.fname from person
select surname||' '||first_name into :person.fnam from person
SQL>
```

NOTE

The v$sqlarea view is owned by Oracle user SYS, and you must be granted access to the v$ views manually. There is a script called utlmontr.sql in the rdbms/admin directory under $ORACLE_HOME that can be run from the SYS account to grant access on most v$ views.

Viewing the Contents of the Shared Pool in Full-screen sqldba

To monitor the shared pool, start sqldba, then follow these steps:

1. Enter **connect internal**.

2. Enter the command **monitor sqlarea** and see the screen shown in Figure 12-1.

3. Move the cursor to the Start button.

4. Press ENTER to begin monitoring, as shown in Figure 12-2.

5. Tab over to the Quit button and press ENTER to return to sqldba.

NOTE
You may also invoke the full-screen sqldba monitor sqlarea screen with the sqldba menu at the top of the screen. Press your terminal's MENU key, then open the Monitor menu. Select the sqlarea option to access the screen shown in Figure 12-2.

You will not find a key labelled MENU on your keyboard. This is the name used by Oracle, and is usually mapped to the 0 key on the numeric keypad of your keyboard.

```
┌─┐ ───── Oracle: A Beginner's Guide ─── 22:40 ▼ ◆
│ File Edit Session Instance Storage Log Backup Security Monitor Help
│ ┌──────────────────── Output ────────────────────┐
│ │ ──── ORACLE Shared Memory SQL Area Monitor ──── │
│ │                                                 │
│ │ Statement Filter: %%                            │
│ │                                                 │
│ │                      Version Sharable --Per User Memory-- │
│ │ SQL Statement Text     Count  Memory  Persistent  Runtime │
│ │                                                 │
│ │                                                 │
│ │                                                 │
│ │                                                 │
│ │                                                 │
│ │                                                 │
│ │                                                 │
│ │                                                 │
│ │ ├─────────────────────────────────────────────┤ │
│ │   Mandatory              ( Start ) (Hide) (Quit) │
│ │                                                 │
│ └─────────────────────────────────────────────────┘
└─────────────────────────────────────────────────────┘
```

FIGURE 12-1.   *Monitoring the shared pool in sqldba*

```
┌──────────────────────────────────────────────────────────────┐
│  ─          Oracle: A Beginner's Guide       22:40  ▼  ▲│▼    │
│ File  Edit  Session  Instance  Storage  Log  Backup  Security  Monitor  Help │
│ ┌─ Output ──────────────────────────────────────────────────┐ │
│ │         ─── ORACLE Shared Memory SQL Area Monitor ───      │ │
│ │                                                            │ │
│ │Statement Filter: XX                                        │ │
│ │                                                            │ │
│ │                          Version Sharable --Per User Memory-- │ │
│ │SQL Statement Text         Count  Memory Persistent Runtime │ │
│ │                                                            │ │
│ │            select lang_pref       1    7825     552   1464 │ │
│ │COMMIT                             1    3319     464    232 │ │
│ │DELETE FROM COMMAND_TABLE WHERE COMMAND_  1  2248  496  4632 │ │
│ │DELETE FROM JOB_COMMANDS WHERE JOBID = :  1  6332  564  4704 │ │
│ │DELETE FROM JOB_QUEUE WHERE JOBID = :b1    1  7241  572  6144 │ │
│ │DELETE FROM JOB_QUEUE WHERE STATUS IN (    1  2284  636  8736 │ │
│ │DELETE FROM TIME_SIGN_TRAIL1 T WHERE T.F   1  6576  768  5072 │ │
│ │DELETE FROM TIME_SIGN_TRAIL2 T WHERE T.F   1  7290  836  5024 │ │
│ │INSERT INTO COMMAND_TABLE( COMMAND_NUMBE   1  2157  548 13080 │ │
│ │INSERT INTO FMS_COMMENTS(COMMENTS,FY_COD   1  6848  820 13120 │ │
│ │                                                            │ │
│ │                              (Restart)  (Hide)  (Quit)     │ │
│ └────────────────────────────────────────────────────────────┘ │
│ └────────────────────────────────────────────────────────────  │
│                                                                │
└──────────────────────────────────────────────────────────────┘
```

FIGURE 12-2.   *Monitor showing contents of the shared pool*

Explain Plan

This utility inspects the indexes being used during the execution of select, insert, update, and delete statements. The output is presented as a list of operations describing the access mode for each table in the statement and the indexes Oracle used during processing. All too often, indexes are created on tables and never get used. Explain plan is the way to detect which indexes are being used and the indexes you could just as well do without.

VIP

Before you can run explain plan, you must own or have access to a table called plan_table. A script called utlxplan.sql in the rdbms/admin directory creates this table for you.

This is how to run explain plan on the following SQL statement:

```
select last_name, first_name, descr
  from person a, classn b
 where pin = 123897
   and a.clssn = b.clssn;
```

1. Save the SQL statement to a file by entering the command **save sql_test replace** (we use the file name sql_test, but use whatever you want).

2. Edit the file called sql_test.sql and insert the text **explain plan set statement_id = 'statement_id' for** in front of your SQL statement. The statement_id is a one-character to 30-character name used to uniquely identify the code. The file sql_test.sql now contains (using a sample statement_id of ST_ID)

```
explain plan set statement_id = 'ST_ID' for
select last_name, first_name, descr
  from person a, classn b
 where pin = 123897
   and a.clssn = b.clssn;
```

3. Run the following SQL script (we call it expl.sql) by entering the command **@expl statement_id**, using the statement_id name from when you loaded your SQL into the plan_table:

```
rem *  File name: expl.sql
spool expl
select decode(id,0,'',
       lpad(' ',2*(level-1))||level||'.'||position)||' '||
       operation||' '||options||' '||object_name||' '||
       object_type||' '||
       decode(id,0,'Cost = '||position) Query_plan
  from plan_table
connect by prior id = parent_id
    and statement_id = upper('&1')
  start with id = 0 and statement_id = upper('&1');
spool off
```

4. Interpret the output in the file expl.lst.

NOTE
The name of the file is based on the spool statement in the code shown in the previous listing. The filename extension .lst may be different on your platform.

The next listing shows the output of the statement loaded in this exercise. Table 12-3 explains the operations in the listing.

OPERATION	MEANING
nested loops	Oracle loops through the column values returned by one set of rows, comparing them against those returned by a second set of rows. The rows that match the selection criteria are displayed; ones that do not qualify are discarded.
table access full	Oracle reads the table from start to finish, one row at a time.
table access by rowid	Oracle reads rows from a table by rowid after obtaining the rowid from that table's index.
index range scan	Oracle retrieves one or more rowids from an index as the index is read in ascending order.

TABLE 12-3.   *Explain Plan Operation Explanations*

```
SELECT STATEMENT    Cost = 13
  2.0 NESTED LOOPS
    3.1 TABLE ACCESS FULL PERSON
    3.2 TABLE ACCESS BY ROWID CLASSN
      4.1 INDEX RANGE SCAN CLASSN_1 NON-UNIQUE
```

VIP

As you become more experienced with explain plan, you will notice that some operations almost always appear with each other. For example, prior to most index range scans, you will find a table access by rowid operation.

SQL Trace and tkprof

These facilities provide performance information on SQL statements. It reports on times spent on the parse, execute, and fetch phases of statement execution. One Oracle technique that allows applications to perform well is the ability to keep significant amounts of data and data dictionary information in memory. As they operate, your applications will find a large part of the information they need in memory. If application-specific information can be found in memory, the I/O involved to retrieve that information can be bypassed. SQL trace also informs you of the percentage of *logical reads* (those satisfied by memory reads) and *physical reads* (those satisfied by reads from disk). To use SQL trace and tkprof:

1. Ensure the timed_statistics entry in your initialization parameter file is set to TRUE.

NOTE
If this parameter is not properly set, set it to TRUE, then you will have to restart the database to activate the changed value.

2. Enter the text **alter session set sql_trace = true;** at the top of your SQL program.

3. Run the SQL program to produce a trace file to be fed to tkprof. For this exercise, the name of the trace file is ora_11277.trc.

NOTE
The location of the trace file is defined by the initialization parameter file entry user_dump_dest. For help finding the name of the trace file, see the next section, "Finding Which Trace File Is Yours."

4. Run the command **tkprof ora_11277.trc output=11277.out explain=/** to produce formatted SQL trace output.

5. Examine the output produced by tkprof. You then begin to see how much time Oracle is spending retrieving your data. When tkprof output is coupled with explain plan, you are presented with formatted output similar to the following.

```
*******************************************************************************
select ename,loc,hiredate
from emp a, dept b where a.deptno = b.deptno

call       count       cpu    elapsed      disk      query   current       rows
-------   -------   -------   --------   -------   -------   -------    --------
Parse          1      0.00       0.06         0         0         0          0
Execute        1      0.00       0.00         0         0         0          0
Fetch          1      0.00       0.06         0        57         2         14

Rows     Execution Plan
-------   -------------------------------------------------------------
      0   SELECT STATEMENT
     14     NESTED LOOPS
     14       TABLE ACCESS (FULL) OF 'EMP'
     14       TABLE ACCESS (BY ROWID) OF 'DEPT'
     28         INDEX (RANGE SCAN) OF 'DEPT_1' (NON-UNIQUE)
*******************************************************************************
```

The technical ins and outs of this output are too much to handle in this book. Suffice it to say, by looking at the Parse, Execute, and Fetch lines that appear in bold type, you can get a grasp of how your SQL statements are performing. Run tkprof, examine the results, and try to get the times for the three processing phases to an absolute minimum.

Finding Which Trace File Is Yours

Picture yourself figuring out which trace file to use for tkprof. You go to the directory where the trace files are deposited and find hundreds of files all starting with ora_ and ending with .trc. You issue the directory command for your operating system, and sit back and watch the show—screens and screens of filenames. Use the following technique to help you find which trace file is yours.

UNIX
At the top of your SQL script, after the line where you entered **alter session set sql_trace = true;**, place the UNIX host character "**!**". The segment of code with the alter session and the host character is

```
alter session set sql_trace = true;
!
```

This will position you at your operating system prompt. Using UNIX, issue the command **ps -fu yourname** to see the activity against your UNIX userid:

```
jrstocks  9824     1  0 15:44:14 tty0p5    0:00 -ksh
jrstocks 11276  2805  0 17:16:21 ttyp7     0:00 sqlplus
jrstocks 11277 11276  0 17:16:21 ?         0:00 oracledev (DESCRIPTION=(LOC)
```

The process identifier in the second column (in this output, it would be process 11277) can be used to build the trace filename for tkprof. The desired trace filename becomes ora_11277.trc.

VMS
In VMS, the SQL script uses the VMS host character $:

```
alter session set sql_trace = true;
$
```

and the VMS command **sh us oracle7/full** yields output similar to

```
VAX/VMS User Processes at 29-FEB-1996 13:40:33.73
Total number of users = 1,  number of processes = 2
Username  Node   Process Name      PID       Terminal
ORACLE7   NCR3   Database Admin.   2020103A  LTA840:  (LAT_AA000400442C)
ORACLE7   NCR3   ORACLE7_1         20201040  (subprocess of 2020103A)
```

The desired trace filename becomes ora_20201040.trc.

VIP

If you turn on sql_trace during testing and program development, make sure the alter session and the host character ARE REMOVED from the programs before they are used by end users. Forgetting to remove them can be disastrous!

What's Next

There is a wealth of information in technical publications, newsletters, magazines, and books on Oracle to help you get the most out of your applications. One of life's golden rules is so applicable when working with Oracle: *Do it right the first time.* In an earlier book, *Tuning Oracle,* the following sentiments were quoted:

You know, one of the things I like so much about Oracle is that it is so tunable.

You know, one of the things I hate so much about Oracle is that it is so tunable.

When it comes to tuning your applications, this is so true.

This chapter wraps up the "Developer Bells and Whistles" portion of this book. By reading the last three chapters, we trust you have become better equipped to write efficient Oracle applications (Chapters 10 and 12) and use some more sophisticated SQL syntax (Chapter 11). You should read on. In the next part of the book, "So You're the New DBA," you will read details on important database administrator (DBA) duties and round out your understanding of Oracle. We touch on database tuning which, alongside application tuning discussed here and in Chapter 10, provides for optimal system performance and efficient use of your computer's resources. Even if "So You're the New DBA" does not apply directly to you, this part of the book contains a great deal of useful information for all.

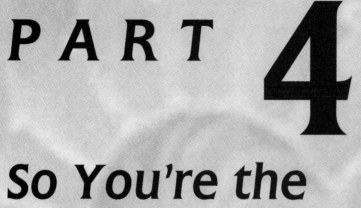

PART 4

So You're the New DBA

CHAPTER 13

DBA 101

In this chapter, we will discuss becoming a database administrator (DBA). The work of the DBA contributes to the effective operation of all systems that run with the Oracle database. The DBA offers technical support to everyone and is expected to become fluent in all technical issues that arise with the Oracle software. The DBA is responsible for the following:

- Day-to-day operations of the Oracle database

- Installation and upgrades of Oracle software

- Performance tuning

- Backup and recovery strategies

- Consultation with data administration personnel

- Consultation with developers

We will show you the tools of the trade: sqldba (pronounced "sequel dba") and Server Manager. Using these tools, we will show you how to do the following:

- Start the database

- Shut down the database

- Give database access to new users

- Revoke database access from existing users

- Create tablespaces

- Add more space to a tablespace

We will lead you through some important concepts and guide you through the DBA job, using code samples. We will cover some new terminology, then we'll use those technical terms as part of the DBA lingo in the rest of the chapter. This is designed to be an introduction, so we will not get into much technical detail. If you have problems, or if procedures do not work as expected, something may be wrong with your configuration or the way the Oracle software has been installed. Personal Oracle7 specifics are covered at the end of the chapter. Chapter 17 covers these and some additional topics in more detail.

Becoming a Database Administrator

You may have already worked with Oracle as a developer, also called a programmer or programmer analyst. Or you may be starting from scratch with Oracle. As you become a DBA, you will start being the focal point for all your installation's Oracle issues. The major components of your new role include the following responsibilities:

 Installation and upgrades of the Oracle Server and all its associated products

- Allocation of resources to support Oracle: memory, disk space, and user account management, to name a few

- Backup and recovery

- Tuning the Oracle database for optimal performance

- Liaising with Oracle Worldwide Customer Support to deal with technical issues requiring Oracle's intervention

- Staying current with Oracle's emerging product line and with new additions that may complement your existing applications

At the end of this chapter, you will have the knowledge to start working as a DBA. We recommend you read this book cover to cover, paying special attention to the following chapters which are of special interest to the DBA:

- Chapter 2

- Chapter 4

- Chapter 15

- Chapter 16

- Chapter 17

We also recommend reading *Tuning Oracle* by Corey, Abbey, and Dechichio (Osborne McGraw-Hill/Oracle Press, 1995) and the *Oracle DBA Handbook* by Kevin Loney (Osborne McGraw-Hill/Oracle Press, 1994). These two works will enhance your understanding of the DBA role and will help you become an effective DBA.

Terminology

The following definitions will arm you with the technical jargon to make it through this chapter.

- When a program operates in *line mode*, it presents output one line at a time; the output scrolls up the screen every time you press the ENTER key. Information scrolls off the screen as room is required for further input.

- When a program operates in *full-screen mode*, it presents information on the screen, and you move around using the TAB key or a mouse and initiate activities based on where you are on the screen.

■ *GUI* (graphical user interface) programs allow the operator to interact by clicking the mouse on an assortment of icons, menus, check boxes, radio buttons, etc. Products such as MS Word 6, WordPerfect for Windows, and Personal Oracle7 are GUI.

■ An *instance* is a set of support processes and memory allocated for accessing an Oracle database. Throughout your experience as a DBA, you will hear the terms Oracle instance and Oracle database. Use these two terms synonymously.

■ *Startup* is the action of placing an Oracle instance in a state that allows users to access the database to carry on their business. Startup initiates processes required for users to access the database, and it reserves a portion of your computer's memory within which Oracle operates.

■ The command *connect internal* logs you onto the database as Oracle user SYS. One accesses the database in this fashion to perform activities such as startup and shutdown.

■ *Shutdown* is the action of taking an Oracle instance from a state that allows users to access the database to a dormant state; when the database is shut down, we say that it is *closed*. Shutdown terminates the processes required for users to access the database, and it releases the portion of your computer's memory within which Oracle was operating.

■ A *job* is a set of one or more computer programs that perform a task. If you use Microsoft Word, you could say that saving your word processing document is a job.

■ *O/S* is a short form for operating system. An operating system is a collection of programs that permit a computer to manage the flow of information between its processor, peripherals (e.g., keyboard, screen, hard disk), and memory.

■ *Batch* is a facility available on most mini and mainframe computers that runs jobs for you unattended; the jobs are submitted to batch using an O/S-specific command. As batch jobs execute, they do not tie up your screen and terminal.

■ A *username* is assigned to people when they require access to the Oracle database. It is also referred to as one's *logon ID*.

■ A *password* accompanies every username and must be supplied to Oracle to connect to the database.

Our discussion of what you need to know when becoming a DBA will start with the line-mode component of sqldba. sqldba comes with Oracle regardless of the hardware platform—from the largest IBM mainframe to desktop.

Line-Mode sqldba

Line-mode sqldba is a tool that is invaluable to any DBA; it is the most commonly used program to start up and shut down the database. It runs on any terminal, regardless of its ability to support graphics. For this reason, we introduce it first and suggest you use it as a starting point on your journey into DBA-land. You can run jobs unattended using line-mode sqldba.

sqldba: Invoking

The command **sqldba lmode=y** starts line-mode sqldba and displays the following output:

```
SQL*DBA: Release 7.1.4.0 - Production on Tue Dec 11 12:34:20 1995
Copyright (c) Oracle Corporation 1979, 1994.  All rights reserved.
Oracle7 Server Release 7.1.4.0 - Production Release
PL/SQL Release 2.1.4.1 - Production
SQLDBA>
```

You are now positioned at the SQLDBA> line-mode prompt, and prepared to work with the database. The basic commands and their output are discussed in the next few sections.

sqldba: connect internal Command

After starting line-mode sqldba, enter **connect internal** and Oracle responds with

```
Connected.
SQLDBA >
```

You must connect to the Oracle database to perform all operations in sqldba. Every session in line-mode sqldba will start with this command.

sqldba: Startup

After starting line-mode sqldba, follow these steps:

1. Enter **connect internal**.

2. Enter **startup**. Oracle responds with the following:

```
ORACLE instance started.
Database mounted.
Database opened.
Total System Global Area        4393640 bytes
               Fixed Size         46112 bytes
            Variable Size       3929736 bytes
         Database Buffers        409600 bytes
             Redo Buffers          8192 bytes
SQLDBA>
```

The database is now started. We also refer to the database as being *open* or the database being *up* after this activity completes successfully.

sqldba: Shutdown

After starting line-mode sqldba, follow these steps:

1. Enter **connect internal**.

2. Enter **shutdown**. Oracle responds with the following:

```
Database closed.
Database dismounted.
ORACLE instance shut down.
```

The database is now closed. Early into your tenure as a DBA, you may run across a situation we have seen many times: You enter sqldba, connect to the database, then issue the shutdown command. For the next few minutes (actually it feels like a few hours when it happens to you), you are looking at the following:

```
SQLDBA> shutdown
_
```

The cursor sits on the next line, flashing for an eternity. When you get tired of waiting, you press the terminal break key (usually mapped to CTRL-C) and get the following message from Oracle:

```
ORA-01013: user requested cancel of current operation
```

Since the shutdown did not complete, the database is left running.

There are two options you may use with the shutdown command when this happens to you: immediate and abort. Why would anyone need to shut down a database while users are connected? Look at the following scenario for one of many reasons:

> An accounts receivable manager inadvertently selects the wrong menu option from her system menu, and invokes a job that initiates year-end processing for a number of accounts. Noticing her error, she phones her IT (Information Technology) contact, who calls you in a panic. If other users are permitted to carry on with their regular business after this has happened, the integrity of the system is in question. You decide the database has to be shut down immediately before more harm is done. You log into sqldba, connect internal, then issue the shutdown command, and guess what—blinking cursor! You return to your O/S and ask for a program status for the machine, and you find out that 17 users are logged onto the database doing various things.

An introductory discussion to shutdown would be deficient without telling you about two of the shutdown options, immediate and abort; they are used in case the "blinking cursor" happens to you.

CAUTION
When any users are logged onto the database, you cannot close that database using the shutdown command without using either the immediate or abort option.

Immediate Option

This is done by entering **shutdown immediate** while connected to your database. The database will not close at once—after Oracle performs some cleanup, the database will shut down. The sessions that were accessing the database are terminated gracefully, and any resources in use by those sessions are methodically freed up. When Oracle completes this work, the database will be shut down. Think of shutdown immediate as a small child's caregiver carrying the youngster up to bed, reading to the child, preparing the blanket and pillow, then putting the child to bed and leaving the room.

NOTE
Shutdown immediate is the most common way you will shut down your database when a normal shutdown does not work. The length of time for a shutdown immediate to complete depends on the number of users on the database when the command is issued. Be patient.

Abort Option

This is done by entering **shutdown abort** while connected to your database. The database will close at once. The sessions that were accessing the database are terminated abruptly. Think of that child in the previous scenario. Shutdown abort is like walking up to that same child, pointing your index finger up the stairs, and saying "GO TO BED, NOW."

CAUTION
Shutdown abort should be used as a very last resort. You may wish to get some advice from colleagues before using this command.

With this advice in mind, there are definitely situations where you will have to use shutdown abort; you will use it from time-to-time when the need arises.

NOTE
After doing shutdown abort, you may wait from a fraction of a minute to 40 to 50 minutes for the database to come up when you issue the next startup command. The 40 to 50 minutes is not common, but it's worth mentioning.

sqldba: Exiting

To exit, type **exit** at the SQLDBA> prompt. Oracle responds as shown here:

```
SQL*DBA complete
```

sqldba: Granting Access to a User

You will need to perform this task as soon as you accept DBA responsibilities. To set up a new user, start line-mode sqldba, then follow these steps:

1. Enter **connect internal**.

2. Enter the command **grant connect to polly identified by gone;** and Oracle will respond with

```
Statement processed.
SQLDBA>
```

3. Enter **exit** to leave line-mode sqldba.

In this example, *polly* is the username and *gone* is the password. Thus, user polly may connect to the database after supplying the password gone.

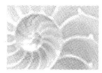

NOTE
The **grant connect** command only allows users to log onto the database; they can work with systems and other users' data, but they have no other privileges. Giving users the capability to have their own data is discussed in Chapter 18.

sqldba: Revoking Access from a User

After starting line-mode sqldba, follow these steps:

1. Enter **connect internal**.

2. Enter the command **revoke connect from polly;** and receive Oracle's response.

```
Statement processed.
SQLDBA>
```

3. Enter **exit** to leave line-mode sqldba.

When this completes, user polly will no longer be able to access the database.

sqldba: Creating a Tablespace

Creating a tablespace is a common activity for the new DBA; almost as soon as you ascend to this throne, someone somewhere will need more space. The specifics for the following exercise are shown in Table 13-1.

TABLESPACE COMPONENT	DETAIL
Name	hold_my_data
Datafile	hmd.dbf
Location	/usr/oradata/disk1
Size	10MB

TABLE 13-1. *Requirements for Tablespace Creation Exercise*

The location specified is a UNIX type; if you are using another O/S, the directory and filename may be different. After starting line-mode sqldba, follow these steps:

1. Enter **connect internal**.

2. Enter the command **create tablespace hold_my_data datafile'/usr/oradata/ disk1/hmd.dbf' size 10m;** and receive Oracle's response.

```
Statement processed.
SQLDBA>
```

3. Enter **exit** to leave line-mode sqldba.

NOTE
The name of the datafile and its location are entered together, enclosed in single quotes. The space requested is mentioned after the filename, using the letter "m" to indicate megabytes (a megabyte is 1,048,576 bytes). The statement is free-form; it appears on two lines here as an example.

Every time you start the database, it will now acquire the hold_my_data tablespace.

sqldba: Adding Space to an Existing Tablespace

We will now add another 10 megabytes (10,000,024 bytes, or 10MB) of space to the hold_my_data tablespace. When this is done, we will have a total of 20MB allocated. After starting line-mode sqldba, follow these steps:

1. Enter **connect internal**.

2. Enter the command **alter tablespace hold_my_data add datafile'/usr/ oradata/disk2/hmd2.dbf' size 10m;** and receive feedback from Oracle.

   ```
   Statement processed.
   SQLDBA>
   ```

3. Enter **exit** to leave line-mode sqldba.

   Line-mode sqldba is an important tool as you go about your DBA business. Some computer programs are referred to as "quick and dirty." Line-mode sqldba falls into this category; it's dependable, easy to learn, and always comes packaged with Oracle.

Full-Screen sqldba

Now we move on to discussing full-screen sqldba. It provides an interface with check boxes and dialog boxes and it allows you to accomplish the same tasks introduced in this section. After filling in blanks and pressing ENTER or the OK button, the SQL commands you have built are passed to Oracle for processing. Thus, the end result of using full-screen sqldba is the same as using the line-mode version.

   Full-screen sqldba is a tool that provides a GUI-like environment with which you can perform all the same tasks as in the previous line-mode sqldba section. When using full-screen sqldba, you'll find a menu at the top of the screen, which you can only access by pressing a key that Oracle calls "Menu" (you will not find a key on your keyboard with the text "Menu"; this is a name Oracle uses). On most keyboards, when Oracle asks you to use the "Menu" key, you press the 0 key on your numeric keypad.

sqldba: Invoking

Enter the command **sqldba** to start full-screen sqldba. You are presented with the screen shown in Figure 13-1.

sqldba: connect internal Command

After starting full-screen sqldba, enter **connect internal**. Oracle responds as shown in Figure 13-2.

You are now connected to the database.

sqldba: Startup

After starting full-screen sqldba, follow these steps:

1. Enter **connect internal**.

2. Enter **startup**. Oracle responds as shown in Figure 13-3.

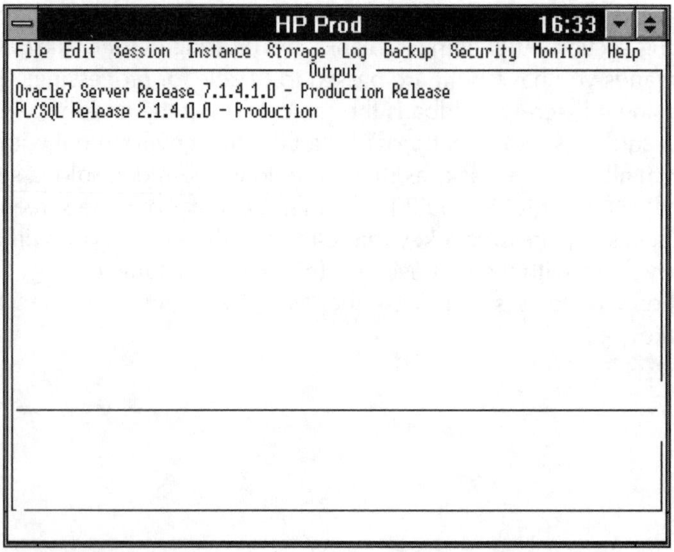

FIGURE 13-1.   *Starting full-screen sqldba*

```
─                         HP Prod                    16:35  ▾  ⬍
File  Edit  Session  Instance  Storage  Log  Backup  Security  Monitor  Help
─────────────────────────── Output ───────────────────────────
Oracle7 Server Release 7.1.4.1.0 - Production Release
PL/SQL Release 2.1.4.0.0 - Production

>connect internal
Connected.
```

FIGURE 13-2. *Connecting to the database using full-screen sqldba*

```
─                         HP Prod                    16:38  ▾  ⬍
File  Edit  Session  Instance  Storage  Log  Backup  Security  Monitor  Help
─────────────────────────── Output ───────────────────────────
Oracle7 Server Release 7.1.4.1.0 - Production Release
PL/SQL Release 2.1.4.0.0 - Production

>connect internal
Connected.
>startup
ORACLE instance started.
Database mounted.
Database opened.
Total System Global Area      5486592 bytes
               Fixed Size       46112 bytes
            Variable Size     4793312 bytes
         Database Buffers      614400 bytes
             Redo Buffers       32768 bytes
```

FIGURE 13-3. *The startup command in full-screen sqldba*

NOTE
Full-screen sqldba awaits your input when the box at the bottom of
the screen is empty and the cursor is available for your input. Usually
this happens just after Oracle has processed your command and
given you feedback on its operation.

The database is now started.

sqldba: Shutdown

After starting full-screen sqldba, follow these steps:

1. Enter **connect internal**.

2. Enter **shutdown**. Oracle responds as shown in Figure 13-4.

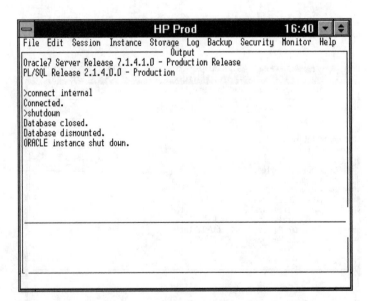

FIGURE 13-4. *The shutdown command in full-screen sqldba*

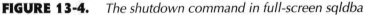

The database is now closed.

VIP
Please refer to the section earlier in this chapter on line-mode sqldba, in which we discuss the shutdown command, which includes some very important and useful information.

sqldba: Exiting

There are three ways to exit full-screen sqldba. The first, and quickest, way is to type the command **exit** and press ENTER. Alternatively, you can do one of the following:

■ Press ESC Q. The Exit dialog box appears as shown in Figure 13-5, with the OK selection highlighted. Press ENTER.

■ Press MENU. Select Quit from the File menu, as shown in Figure 13-6. The same dialog box from Figure 13-5 appears. Press ENTER.

```
┌──────────────────────────────────────────────────────┐
│ ─              HP Prod              16:55 ▼ ◆         │
│ File  Edit  Session  Instance  Storage  Log  Backup  Security  Monitor  Help │
│ ─────────────────────── Output ───────────────────── │
│ Oracle7 Server Release 7.1.4.1.0 - Production Release │
│ PL/SQL Release 2.1.4.0.0 - Production                 │
│                                                        │
│ >connect internal                                      │
│ Connected.        ┌────────────────────────────────┐  │
│ >shutdown         │                                │  │
│ Database closed.  │ CAUTION                        │  │
│ Database dismount │                                │  │
│ ORACLE instance s │ End SQL*DBA session?           │  │
│                   │                                │  │
│                   │                                │  │
│                   │                                │  │
│                   │     (▐K)        (Cancel)       │  │
│                   └────────────────────────────────┘  │
│                                                        │
│ ──────────────────────────────────────────────────── │
│                                                        │
│ ──────────────────────────────────────────────────── │
└──────────────────────────────────────────────────────┘
```

FIGURE 13-5. *Exiting full-screen sqldba*

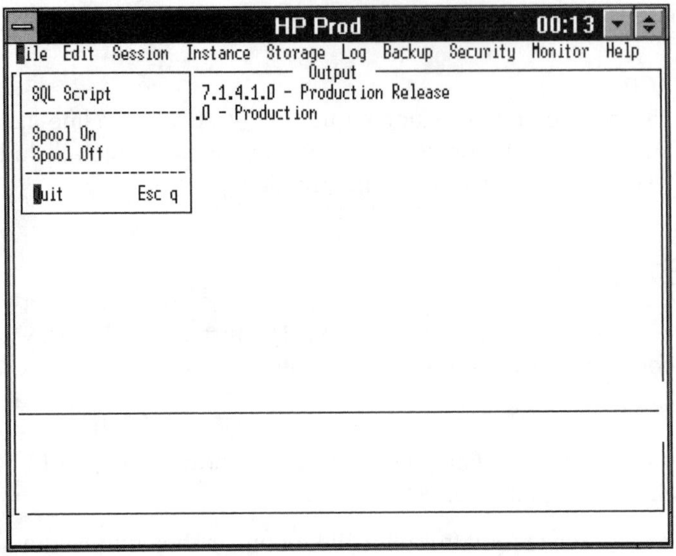

FIGURE 13-6.   *Exiting full-screen sqldba from the menu bar*

sqldba: Granting Access to a User

To set up a new user, full-screen sqldba, then follow these steps:

1. Enter **connect internal**.

2. Press MENU.

3. Select Create User from the Security menu. The Create User dialog box appears, as shown in Figure 13-7.

4. Type **polly** beside the Name prompt, and **gone** beside the Use Password Authentication prompt as shown in Figure 13-7. Move between fields using the TAB key.

5. Tab to OK and press ENTER to complete the command. Oracle closes the dialog box and shows you the command it has just executed.

6. Press MENU once again.

7. Select Grant System Privileges/Roles from the Security menu. The Grant System Privileges/Roles dialog box appears, as shown in Figure 13-8.

8. Fill in **create session** beside Grant and **polly** beside To, as shown in Figure 13-8.

```
┌──────────────────────────────────────────────────────────────┐
│ ─                        Da HP                         ▼ ▲    │
│ File  Edit  Session  Instance  Storage  Log  Backup  Security  Monitor  Help │
│                             Output                            │
│ Oracle7 Server Release 7.1.4.1.0 - Production Release         │
│ PL/SQL Relea┌─────────── Create User ───────────┐             │
│             │                                    │             │
│ >connect int│ Name: polly                        │             │
│ Connected.  │                                    │             │
│             │ (o) Use Password Authentication: gone            │
│             │ ( ) Use OS Authentication          │             │
│             │                                    │             │
│             │   Default Tablespace:              │             │
│             │ Temporary Tablespace:              │             │
│             │            Quota:                  │             │
│             │          Profile:                  │             │
│             │                                    │             │
│             │                                    │             │
│             │                      [OK]  (Cancel)│             │
│             └────────────────────────────────────┘             │
│                                                              │
└──────────────────────────────────────────────────────────────┘
```

FIGURE 13-7.   *Create User dialog box*

```
┌──────────────────────────────────────────────────────────────┐
│ ─              HP Prod                    00:17  ▼ ▲         │
│ File  Edit  Session  Instance  Storage  Log  Backup  Security  Monitor  Help │
│                             Output                            │
│ Oracle7 Server Release 7.1.4.1.0 - Production Release         │
│ PL/SQL Release 2.1.4.0.0 - Production                        │
│           ┌──────── Grant System Privileges/Roles ────────┐   │
│           │                                               │   │
│           │  Grant: create session                        │   │
│           │                                               │   │
│           │    To: polly                                  │   │
│           │                                               │   │
│           │  [ ] Allow grantee to grant the privilege(s)/role(s) to others │
│           │                                               │   │
│           │                           (OK)  (Cancel)      │   │
│           └───────────────────────────────────────────────┘   │
│                                                              │
└──────────────────────────────────────────────────────────────┘
```

FIGURE 13-8.   *Grant Privileges and Roles dialog box*

9. Tab to the OK box and press ENTER to complete the command. Oracle closes the dialog box and shows you the command it has just executed.

10. Enter **exit** to leave sqldba.

User polly can now log onto the database. In Chapter 17 we discuss a number of other user management responsibilities.

sqldba: Revoking Access from a User

After starting full-screen sqldba, you can revoke access by following these steps:

1. Enter **connect internal**.

2. Press MENU.

3. Select Revoke System Privileges/Roles from the Security menu. The Revoke System Privileges/Roles dialog box appears.

4. Fill in **connect** beside Revoke and **polly** beside From, as shown in Figure 13-9.

5. Tab to the OK box and press ENTER to complete the command. Oracle closes the dialog box and shows you the command it has just executed.

6. Enter **exit** to leave sqldba.

```
┌─────────────────────────────────────────────────────────┐
│ ─               HP Prod              00:19 ▼ ▲           │
│ File Edit Session Instance Storage Log Backup Security Monitor Help │
│ ┌──────────────────── Output ────────────────────────┐  │
│ │Oracle7 Server Release 7.1.4.1.0 - Production Release│  │
│ │PL/SQL Release 2.1.4.0.0 - Production               │  │
│ │                                                    │  │
│ │        ┌──── Revoke System Privileges/Roles ────┐  │  │
│ │        │                                        │  │  │
│ │        │ Revoke: connect                        │  │  │
│ │        │                                        │  │  │
│ │        │   From: polly                          │  │  │
│ │        │                                        │  │  │
│ │        │                                        │  │  │
│ │        │                        [OK]  [Cancel]  │  │  │
│ │        └────────────────────────────────────────┘  │  │
│ │                                                    │  │
│ │ ───────────────────────────────────────────────── │  │
│ │                                                    │  │
│ │ ───────────────────────────────────────────────── │  │
│ └────────────────────────────────────────────────────┘  │
└─────────────────────────────────────────────────────────┘
```

FIGURE 13-9.   *Revoke System Privileges/Roles dialog box*

sqldba: Creating a Tablespace

We will use the requirements listed earlier in Table 13-1. After starting full-screen sqldba, follow these steps:

1. Enter **connect internal**.

2. Press MENU.

3. Select Tablespace from the Storage menu. The Tablespace submenu appears, as shown in Figure 13-10.

4. Select Create from the Tablespace submenu. The Create Tablespace dialog box appears, as shown in Figure 13-11.

5. Fill in **hold_my_data** beside Name and **'/usr/oradata/disk1/hmd.dff' size 10m;** beside Data Files, as shown in Figure 13-11.

6. Tab to the OK box and press ENTER to complete the command. Oracle closes the dialog box and shows you the command it has just executed.

7. Enter **exit** to leave sqldba.

```
┌─────────────────────────────────────────────────────┐
│ ─             HP Prod              00:21 ▼ ▲         │
│ File Edit Session Instance Storage Log Backup Security Monitor Help │
│ ┌─────────────────────┬──────────┐                  │
│ │Oracle7 Server Release 7.1.4.1.│Tablespace│         │
│ │PL/SQL Release 2.1.4.0.0 - Prod├──────────┤┌──────────────────────┐│
│ │                     │Rollback Segme│Create │
│ │                     └──────────┤Drop   │
│ │                               │────────────────────│
│ │                               │Set Online      Esc n│
│ │                               │Set Offline     Esc f│
│ │                               │────────────────────│
│ │                               │Add Data File  │
│ │                               │Rename Data File│
│ │                               │────────────────────│
│ │                               │Alter Default Storage│
│ │                               └──────────────────────┘
│ │                                                    │
│ └────────────────────────────────────────────────   │
│                                                      │
│  └─────────────────────────────────────────────     │
└─────────────────────────────────────────────────────┘
```

FIGURE 13-10. *Tablespace submenu*

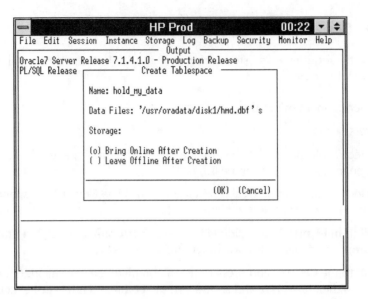

FIGURE 13-11. *Create Tablespace dialog box*

NOTE
The name of the datafile and its location are entered together, enclosed in single quotes. The space requested is entered on the same line as the filename, using the letter m to indicate megabytes (the size is specified at the end of the Data Files line that has scrolled off the screen in the figure).

Every time you start the database, it will now acquire the hold_my_data tablespace.

sqldba: Adding Space to an Existing Tablespace

After starting full-screen sqldba, follow these steps:

1. Enter **connect internal**.
2. Press MENU.
3. Select Tablespace from the Storage menu to open the Tablespace submenu.
4. Select Add Data File to Tablespace from the Tablespace submenu. The Add Data File to Tablespace dialog box appears, as shown in Figure 13-12.

5. Move through the list of tablespaces using the DOWN ARROW key.

6. Press SPACEBAR to select HOLD_MY_DATA.

7. Enter the text **'/usr/oradata/disk2/hmd2.dbf' size 10m** in the dialog box as shown in Figure 13-12.

8. Enter **exit** to leave sqldba.

The hold_my_data tablespace now has an additional 10MB of space within which tables can be stored.

Full-screen sqldba is useful as a learning tool; using the menu system and the dialog box method of data entry, you may find yourself getting more accomplished than when you used line-mode sqldba alone. Always study the commands passed to Oracle when you are finished with a full-screen sqldba dialog box.

Line-Mode Server Manager

Now we move on to discussing line-mode Server Manager, a sister product to line-mode sqldba. If line-mode Server Manager is new to your installation, you will find its look and feel almost identical to line-mode sqldba. The differences between

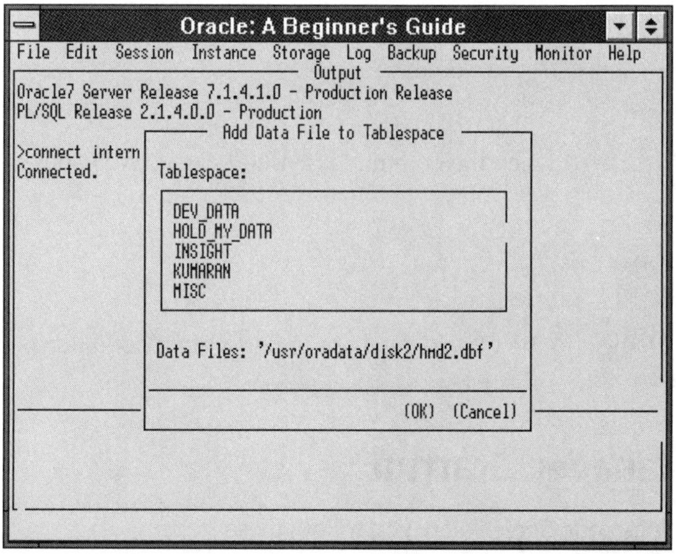

FIGURE 13-12. *Add Data File to Tablespace dialog box*

the two products are minimal and do not affect your use of the product except in one case, which we will discuss in the "Server Manager: Startup" section.

Like line-mode sqldba, this tool runs on any terminal regardless of its ability to support graphics. You can run jobs unattended using line-mode Server Manager. Server Manager first appeared with release 7.1.3.

Server Manager: Invoking

The command **svrmgrl** starts line-mode Server Manager and displays the following output:

```
Server Manager: Release 2.0.3 - Production
Copyright (c) Oracle Corporation 1994. All rights reserved.
Oracle7 Server Release 7.1.4.1.0 - Production Release
PL/SQL Release 2.1.4.0.0 - Production
SVRMGR>
```

Server Manager: connect internal Command

After starting line-mode Server Manager, enter **connect internal** and Oracle responds with one of two responses. If the instance is down when the command is issued, Server Manager responds with

```
Connected to an idle instance.
SVRMGR>
```

If the instance is started when the command is issued, Server Manager responds with

```
Connected.
SVRMGR>
```

You must connect to the Oracle database to perform all operations in Server Manager.

Server Manager: Startup

After starting line-mode Server Manager, follow these steps:

1. Enter **connect internal**.

2. Enter **startup**. Oracle responds with the following:

```
ORACLE instance started.
Database mounted.
Database opened.
Total System Global Area       4393640 bytes
              Fixed Size         46112 bytes
           Variable Size       3929736 bytes
        Database Buffers        409600 bytes
            Redo Buffers          8192 bytes
SRVRMGR>
```

The database is now started. We also refer to the database as being *open* or the database being *up* after this activity completes successfully. Using Server Manager to start your database is actually a three-step process—the startup command performs three distinct steps, as listed here:

```
startup nomount
alter database mount;
alter database open;
```

When starting your database with Server Manager (line-mode or full-screen), if any step in the startup process *abends* (i.e., does not complete successfully), the database is left in the condition it was in when the last step successfully completed. This behavior is different than sqldba (line-mode or full-screen). Using sqldba, if the startup command does not complete, the database is left closed and unmounted.

Following is an example of how this difference can affect your clients and what to do about it. Let's say your production database is shut down every morning at 2:00 for system backups. After the backups complete, you start the database with the command **svrmgrl @startup_prd.sql.** The startup_prd.sql file has the code

```
connect internal
startup
exit
```

In the morning, the users start logging onto the database and receive the following error message:

```
ERROR: ORA-01033: ORACLE initialization or shutdown in progress
```

You attempt to connect to the database, but you get the same message. For some reason, one of the three operations Server Manager has performed during startup has aborted, leaving the database in its previous state. Perhaps the alter database mount operation has failed, and the database has been left unmounted.

NOTE
If you use line-mode Server Manager to start your database, rather than using the command **startup**, you may wish to enter the three commands **startup nomount**, then **alter database mount;**, then **alter database open;** separately.

Server Manager: Shutdown

After starting line-mode Server Manager, follow these steps:

1. Enter **connect internal**.

2. Enter **shutdown**. Oracle responds with the following:

```
Database closed.
Database dismounted.
ORACLE instance shut down.
```

The database is now closed.

VIP
Please refer to the section earlier in this chapter on line-mode sqldba, in which we discuss the shutdown command, which includes some very important and useful information.

Server Manager: Exiting

To exit, enter **exit** at the SVRMGR> prompt. Oracle responds with

```
Server Manager complete.
```

Server Manager: Granting Access to a User

To set up a new user, start line-mode Server Manager, then follow these steps:

1. Enter **connect internal**.

2. Enter the command **grant connect to polly identified by gone;** and receive the response from Oracle:

```
Statement processed.
SVRMGR>
```

3. Enter **exit** to leave line-mode Server Manager.

In this example, *polly* is the username and *gone* is the password. Thus, user polly may connect to the database after supplying the password gone.

Server Manager: Revoking Access from a User

After starting line-mode Server Manager, follow these steps:

1. Enter **connect internal**.

2. Enter the command **revoke connect from polly;** and receive Oracle's response.

```
Statement processed.
SVRMGR>
```

3. Enter **exit** to leave line-mode Server Manager.

When this completes, polly will no longer be able to access the database.

Server Manager: Creating a Tablespace

We will use the requirements listed earlier in Table 13-1. After starting line-mode Server Manager, follow these steps:

1. Enter **connect internal**.

2. Enter the command **create tablespace hold_my_data datafile '/usr/oradata/disk1/hmd.dbf' size 10m;** and receive the following response from Oracle

```
Statement processed.
SVRMGR>
```

3. Enter **exit** to leave line-mode Server Manager.

Every time you start the database, it will now acquire the hold_my_data tablespace.

Server Manager: Adding Space to an Existing Tablespace

We will now add another 10 megabytes (10,485,760 bytes) of space to the hold_my_data tablespace. When this completes, we will have a total of 20MB allocated. After starting line-mode Server Manager, follow these steps:

1. Enter **connect internal**.

2. Enter the command **alter tablespace hold_my_data add datafile '/usr/oradata/disk2/hmd2.dbf' size 10m;** and receive feedback from Oracle.

```
Statement processed.
SVRMGR>
```

3. Enter **exit** to leave line-mode Server Manager.

The hold_my_data tablespace now has an additional 10MB.

You will use line-mode Server Manager from day one. Like line-mode sqldba, it works everywhere and provides a quick method of accomplishing many DBA-related tasks.

Full-Screen Server Manager

We now move on to the latest-and-greatest product in the DBA tools of the trade: full-screen Server Manager. It is possible that your terminal configuration may not support Server Manager in this mode. If you receive the following error message when invoking full-screen Server Manager, check with the system administrator at your installation.

```
TK2-04097: Oracle Toolkit II's connection to the window system was refused
```

Full-screen Server Manager is the graphical companion to line-mode Server Manager. It is a comprehensive DBA tool with an interface that uses familiar check boxes and radio buttons; the look and feel is similar to Windows 3.1. It differs from full-screen sqldba in the following ways:

- The screens look radically different.

- The menus look radically different.

- You can use a mouse with full-screen Server Manager.

- The way it handles database startup as outlined in the startup section of line-mode Server Manager.

Server Manager: Invoking

Enter the command **svrmgrm** to invoke full-screen Server Manager. You will then see the screen shown in Figure 13-13.

Server Manager: connect internal Command

After starting full-screen Server Manager, follow these steps:

1. In the Connect dialog box, click on the Normal drop-down button. A small dialog box appears with the choices Normal, SYSOPER, and SYSDBA.

2. Click on the SYSDBA option.

3. Click on Connect to complete the internal login. When logged in, you will be presented with the screen as shown in Figure 13-14.

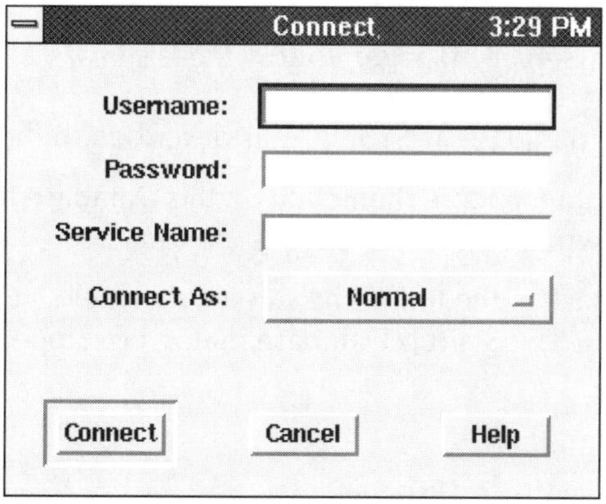

FIGURE 13-13. *Starting full-screen Server Manager*

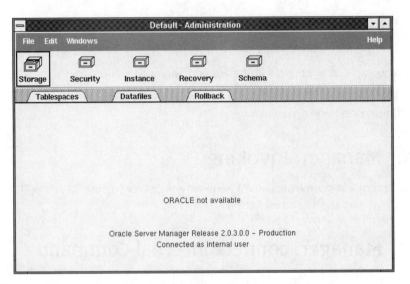

FIGURE 13-14. *Main screen after connecting to the database*

Notice the message near the bottom of the screen, telling you that you are connected as an internal user.

Server Manager: Startup

After starting full-screen Server Manager, follow these steps:

1. Connect to the database as SYSDBA, as described in the previous section.

2. Click on the Instance icon, then click on the Database folder to bring up the screen shown in Figure 13-15.

3. Click on Database at the top of the screen, then select Startup from the Database menu. The Startup Database dialog box appears, as shown in Figure 13-16.

4. Click on Startup Open.

After the database has been successfully started, the screen shown in Figure 13-17 appears, displaying the components in the instance's SGA. We discuss the SGA (system global area) in Chapter 2.

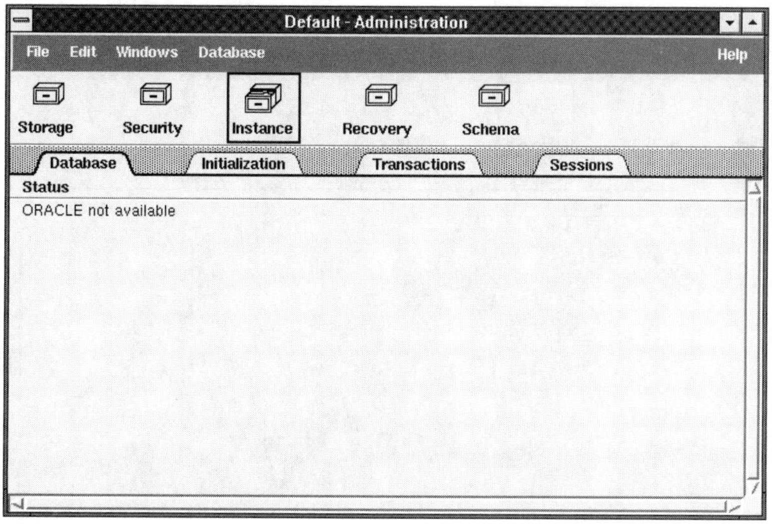

FIGURE 13-15.   *Database folder in full-screen Server Manager*

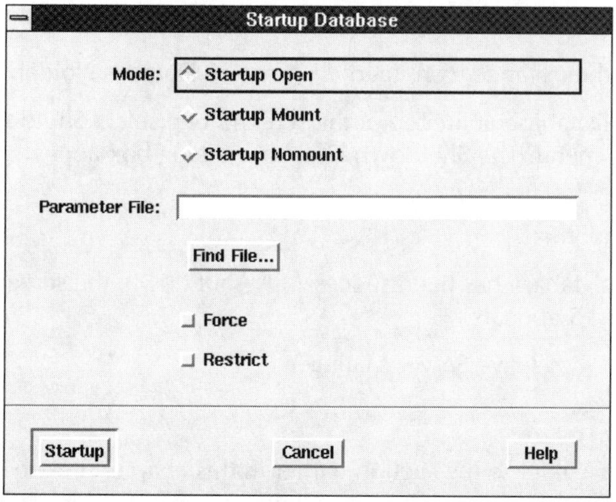

FIGURE 13-16.   *Startup Database dialog box*

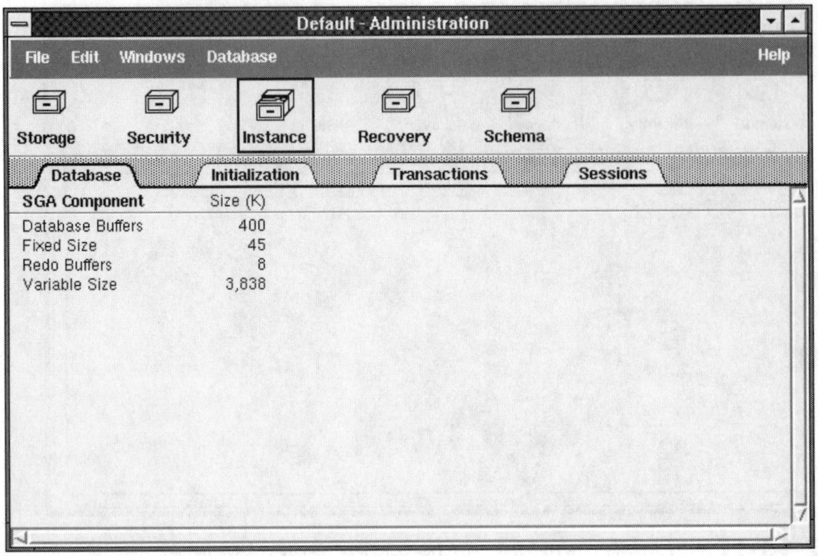

FIGURE 13-17. *Instance started with SGA display*

Server Manager: Shutdown

After starting full-screen Server Manager, follow these steps:

1. Connect to the database as SYSDBA.

2. Click on the Instance icon, then click on the Database folder.

3. Click on Database at the top of the screen, then select Shutdown from the Database menu. The Shutdown Database dialog box appears, as shown in Figure 13-18.

4. Click on Normal.

5. After the database has been successfully shut down, the screen shown in Figure 13-15 appears.

6. Press CTRL-Q to leave Server Manager.

VIP
Please refer to the section earlier in this chapter on line-mode sqldba, in which we discuss the shutdown command, which includes some very important and useful information.

Shutdown Database

Shutdown Mode: ∧ **Normal**

∨ **Immediate**

∨ **Abort**

| Shutdown | Cancel | Help |

FIGURE 13-18.   *Shutdown Database dialog box*

Server Manager: Exiting

There are two ways to exit full-screen Server Manager. The shortcut key combination is CTRL-Q. This will drop you out of Server Manager regardless of what screen you are working with. Alternatively, you can select Quit from the File menu, shown in Figure 13-19.

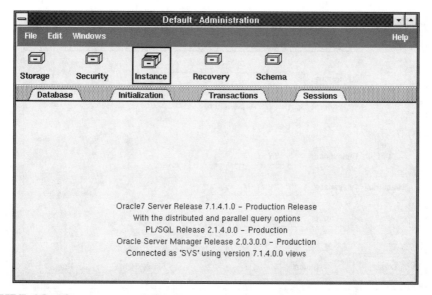

FIGURE 13-19.   *Leaving full-screen Server Manager using the menu*

Server Manager: Granting Access to a User

After starting full-screen Server Manager, follow these steps:

1. Connect to the database as SYSDBA.

2. Click on the Security icon, then click on the Users folder.

3. Click on User at the top of the screen, then select Create from the User menu. The Create User dialog box appears, as shown in Figure 13-20.

4. Fill in the Create User dialog box as shown in Figure 13-20.

5. Click on Create. The Users folder now looks like Figure 13-21. Note that polly is now a valid user.

6. Select Add Privilege to User from the User menu. The Add Privilege to User dialog box appears, as shown in Figure 13-22.

7. Click on CONNECT in the Defined Roles field.

8. Click on Add to complete this activity (the Add button is at the bottom of the dialog box but has scrolled off the screen shown in Figure 13-22).

9. Press CTRL-Q to leave Server Manager.

User polly can now log onto the database.

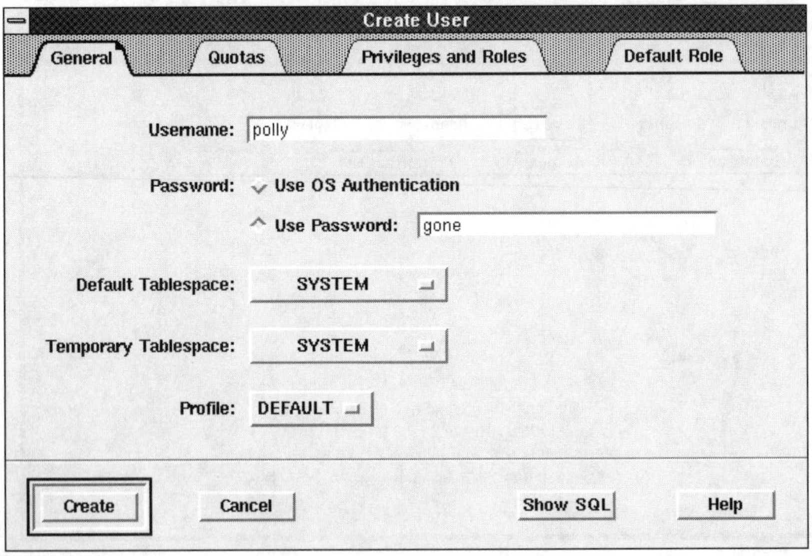

FIGURE 13-20. *Create User dialog box*

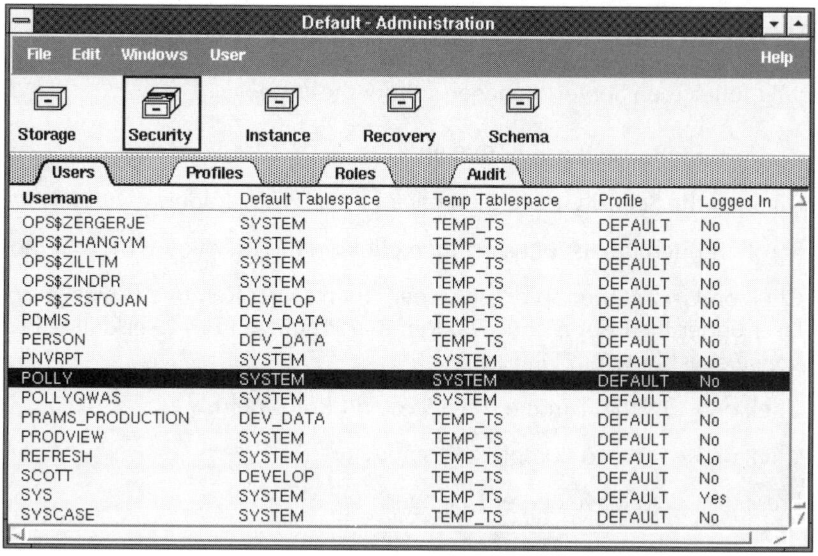

FIGURE 13-21.   *Valid user list showing user polly just created*

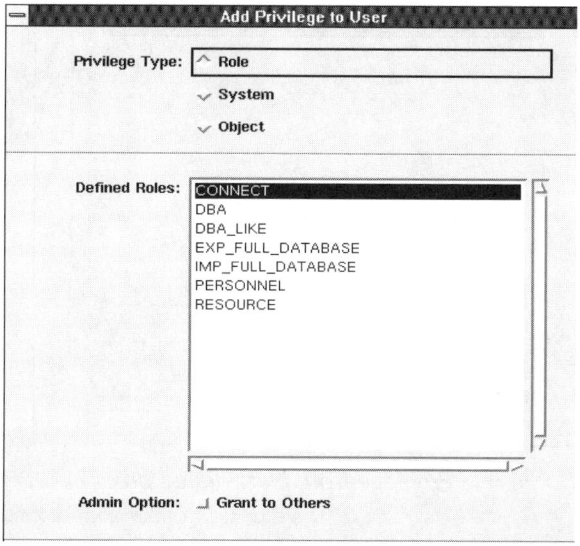

FIGURE 13-22.   *Selecting privilege to give to user*

Server Manager: Revoking Access from a User

After starting full-screen Server Manager, follow these steps:

1. Connect to the database as SYSDBA.

2. Click on the Security icon, then click on the Users folder.

3. Scroll through the list of users, then click on the user you wish to remove.

4. Click on User at the top of the screen, then select Remove Privilege from User under the User menu. The Remove Privilege from User dialog box appears, as shown in Figure 13-23.

5. Click on CONNECT in the Privileges and Roles field.

6. Click on Remove to complete this activity.

7. Press CTRL-Q to leave Server Manager.

User polly can no longer connect to the database.

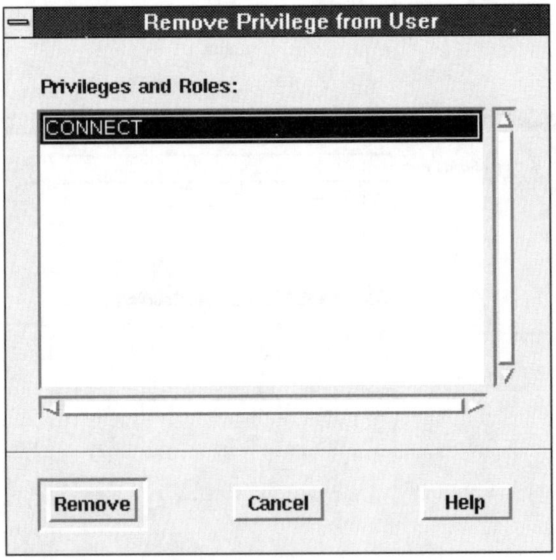

FIGURE 13-23.   *Remove Privilege from User dialog box*

Server Manager: Creating a Tablespace

After starting full-screen Server Manager, follow these steps:

1. Connect to the database as SYSDBA.

2. Click on the Storage icon, then click on the Tablespaces folder.

3. Click on Tablespace at the top of the screen, then select Create from the Tablespace menu. The Create Tablespace dialog box appears, as shown in Figure 13-24.

4. Type **hold_my_data** in the Name box as shown in Figure 13-24.

5. Click on Online in the Status field.

6. Click on New to bring up the New Datafile dialog box, as shown in Figure 13-25.

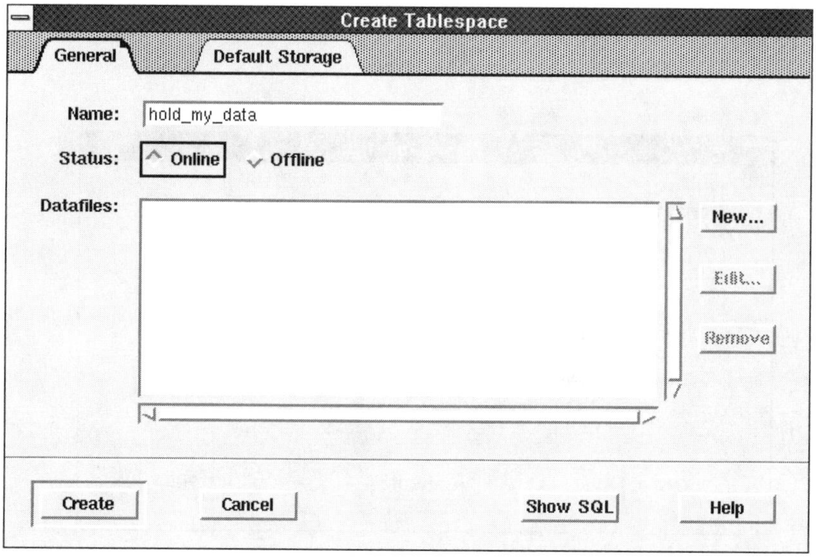

FIGURE 13-24.   *Create Tablespace dialog box*

7. Enter **?/dbs/hmd.dbf** in the Filename box, as shown in Figure 13-25.

8. In the New File Size field, click on the drop-down list, select Mbytes, then enter **10** in the box.

9. Click OK. The Create Tablespace dialog box now looks like Figure 13-26.

10. Click on Create to finish this activity. Notice that when you return to the Tablespaces folder, the new tablespace is displayed, as shown in Figure 13-27.

11. Press CTRL-Q to leave Server Manager.

Notice the Show SQL button in Figure 13-26. To see the SQL that is passed from Server Manager to Oracle, click that button anytime. When the SQL is displayed as shown in Figure 13-28, a Hide SQL button appears, which closes the SQL statement display.

TIP
Use the display SQL facility. It helps you become familiar with the SQL statements that accomplish the DBA's job.

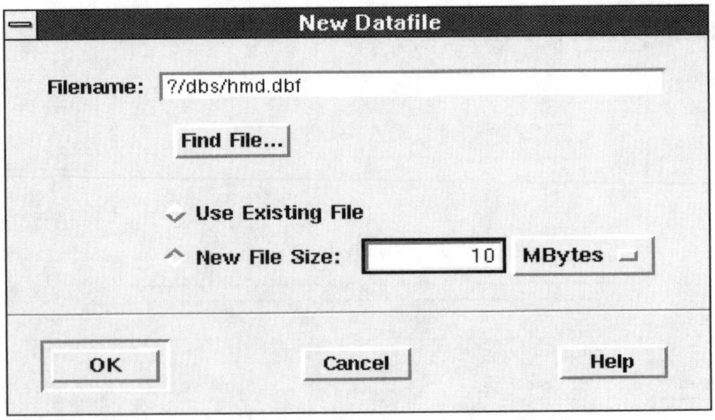

FIGURE 13-25. *New Datafile dialog box*

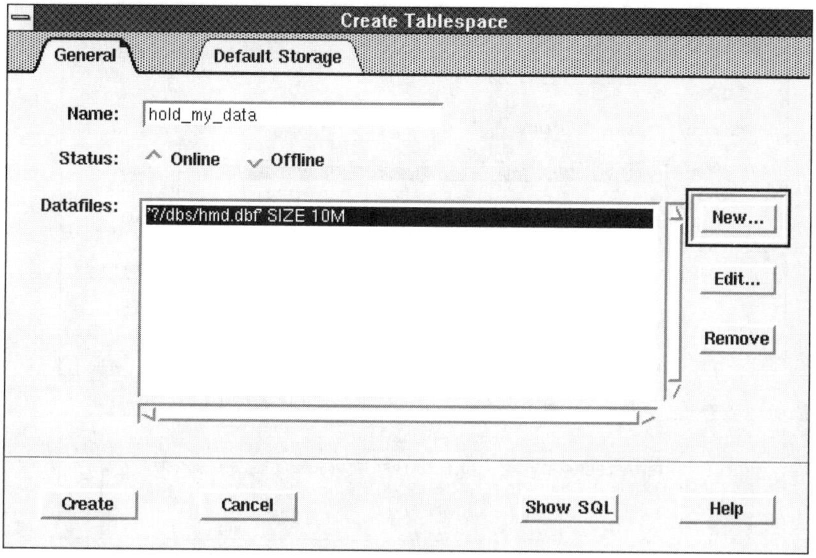

FIGURE 13-26.   *Create Tablespace dialog box filled in*

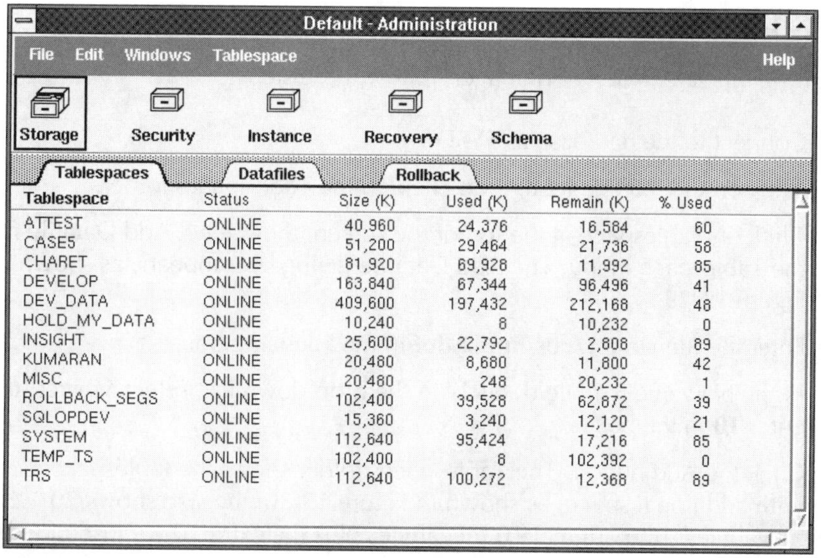

FIGURE 13-27.   *Created tablespace in the Tablespaces folder*

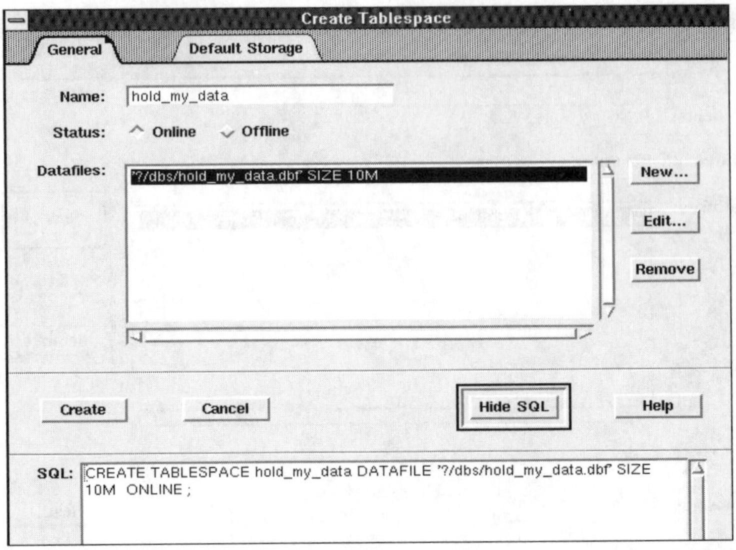

FIGURE 13-28. *Show SQL display*

Server Manager: Adding Space to an Existing Tablespace

After starting full-screen Server Manager, follow these steps:

1. Connect to the database as SYSDBA.

2. Click on the Storage icon, then click on the Tablespaces folder.

3. Click on Tablespace at the top of the screen, then select Add Datafile from the Tablespace menu. The Add Datafile dialog box appears, as shown in Figure 13-29.

4. Enter the filename **?/dbs/hmd2.dbf** in the Filename box.

5. In the New File Size field, click on the drop-down list, select Mbytes, then enter **10** in the box.

6. Click the Add button. The Tablespaces folder shows the tablespace with additional space, as shown in Figure 13-30 (the size shows 20 megabytes—the original 10 megabytes plus the extra 10 we just added).

7. Press CTRL-Q to leave Server Manager.

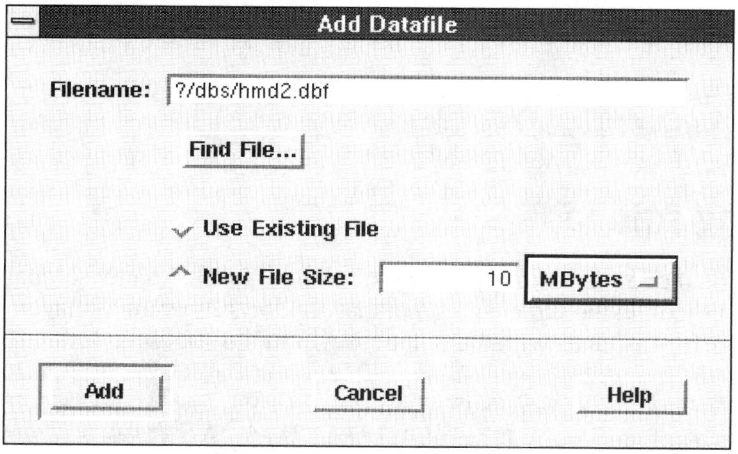

FIGURE 13-29. *Add Datafile dialog box*

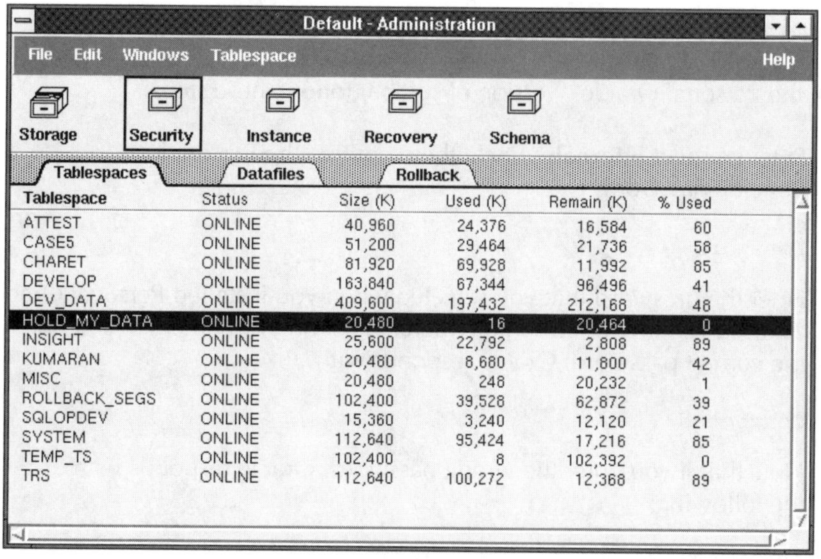

FIGURE 13-30. *Storage folder showing additional space*

Personal Oracle7

We now discuss how to perform the tasks outlined in this chapter with the Windows 3.1-based Personal Oracle7.

Invoking sqldba

There is a line-mode version of sqldba with Personal Oracle7. Enter sqldba by clicking on its icon in the Oracle group of the Windows Program Manager. Personal Oracle7 responds with the output shown in the following listing:

```
SQL*DBA: Release 7.1.4.0 - Production on Mon Dec 18 20:10:29 1995
Copyright (c) Oracle Corporation 1979, 1994. All rights reserved.
Personal Oracle7 Server Release 7.1.4.0 - Production Release
PL/SQL Release 2.1.4.0.0 - Production
SQLDBA>
```

To exit sqldba from Personal Oracle7, type **exit** to return to the Oracle group in the Windows Program Manager.

connect internal Command

Once in the Personal Oracle7 version of sqldba, follow these steps:

1. Enter **connect internal**. Oracle then requests the Personal Oracle7 password.

   ```
   Password:
   ```

2. Enter the password that you selected when you installed Personal Oracle7, as discussed in the "Personal Oracle7" section of Chapter 4. After entering the correct password, Oracle responds with

   ```
   Connected
   ```

   Note that if you enter the wrong password, Oracle responds with the following:

   ```
   ORA-01031: insufficient privileges

   SQLDBA>
   ```

3. Enter the **connect internal** command once more, and reenter the password.

NOTE
Unless you have accessed the database password manager from the
Password Manager icon and reset the Personal Oracle7 database
password, it will still be set to "oracle."

Starting the Database

In this section, you will learn the details on the following tasks:

- Accessing the Personal Oracle7 database manager

- Starting the Personal Oracle7 database

- Entering the database manager password

- Checking the status of the Personal Oracle7 database

With Personal Oracle7, you start the database using the database manager and
the following steps.

1. Click on the Database Manager icon in the Personal Oracle7 group
in the Windows Program Manager. The Oracle Database Manager
dialog box appears, as shown in Figure 13-31. Notice that the host
Status is "Unknown." This is usually the case when the database has not
been started.

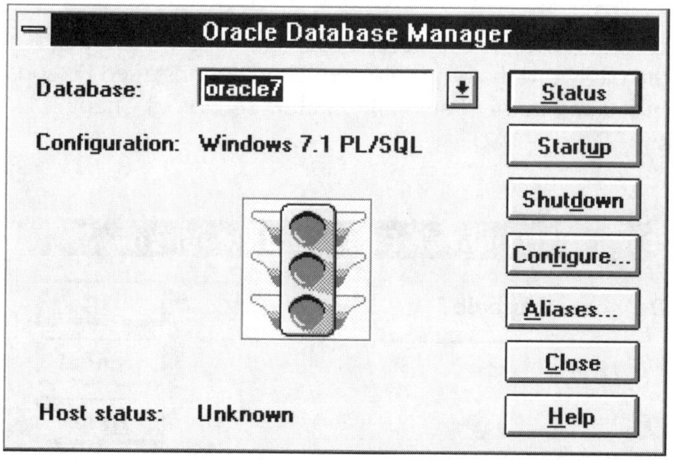

FIGURE 13-31. *Oracle Database Manager dialog box in Personal Oracle7*

2. Click on Startup. The host status field changes to "Getting status" and then "Starting." The Database Password Required dialog box then appears, as shown in Figure 13-32.

3. Enter the password that you selected when you installed Personal Oracle7, as we discussed in the "Personal Oracle7" section of Chapter 4. Click OK to continue. After Personal Oracle7 starts, the host status field changes to "Running" and the green light is lit.

4. Click on Close to exit the database manager.

> **NOTE**
> You can check the status of your Personal Oracle7 database by clicking the Status button in the Oracle Database Manager dialog box. The status will be either "Available: running" or "Available: not running."

Shutting Down the Database

In this section, you will see how to shut down the Personal Oracle7 database. You accomplish this using the database manager and the following steps.

1. Click on the Database Manager icon in the Personal Oracle7 group in the Windows Program Manager. The Oracle Database Manager dialog box appears. Notice that the host status is now "Available: running." This is usually the case when the database has been started.

2. Click on Shutdown. The Database Manager Password dialog box appears. Enter the password that you selected when you installed Personal Oracle7, as we discussed in the "Personal Oracle7" section of Chapter 4, then click on OK.

FIGURE 13-32. *Database Password Required dialog box in Personal Oracle7*

3. When the Database Manager shutdown confirmation box appears as shown in Figure 13-33, click on YES.

4. After Personal Oracle7 closes the database, the host status field changes to "Available: not running" and the red light is lit.

5. Click on Close to exit the Database Manager.

Creating a User

You can create a user with the user manager and the following steps.

1. Click on the User Manager icon in the Personal Oracle7 group in the Windows Program Manager. The User Manager dialog box appears, as shown in Figure 13-34. Before entering user manager, you must enter a DBA account and password.

2. Enter the account and password combination. Unless you have changed the password of the system account, it is "manager." The list of current users is displayed, as shown in Figure 13-35.

3. Click on Create to bring up the Create User/Profile dialog box.

4. The box beside User is highlighted. Leave as is and click OK.

5. When the Create New User dialog box appears, as shown in Figure 13-36, enter the Username **polly** and the Password **gone**.

6. Click OK. Notice the new user in the list of current users.

7. Click on Close to complete this activity.

User polly can now log onto the Personal Oracle7 database using the password gone.

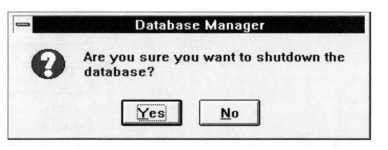

FIGURE 13-33.   *Personal Oracle7 requesting shutdown confirmation*

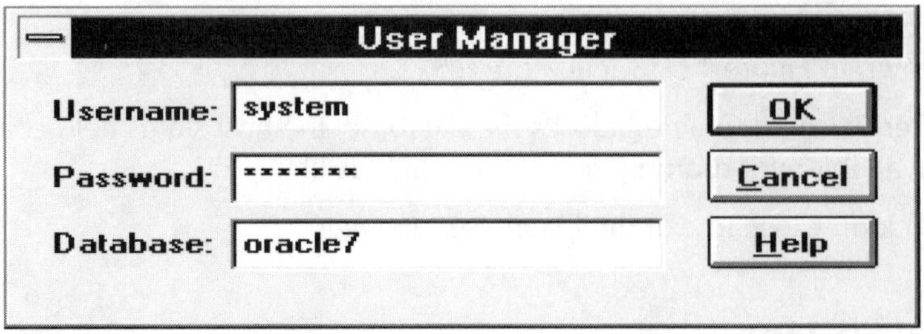

FIGURE 13-34. *User Manager dialog box*

Removing a User

You can remove a user with the user manager and the following steps.

1. Click on the User Manager icon in the Personal Oracle7 group in the Windows Program Manager. The User Manager dialog box appears. Before entering user manager, you need to enter a DBA account and password.

2. Enter the account and password combination. Unless you have changed the password of the system account, it is "manager." The list of current users is displayed.

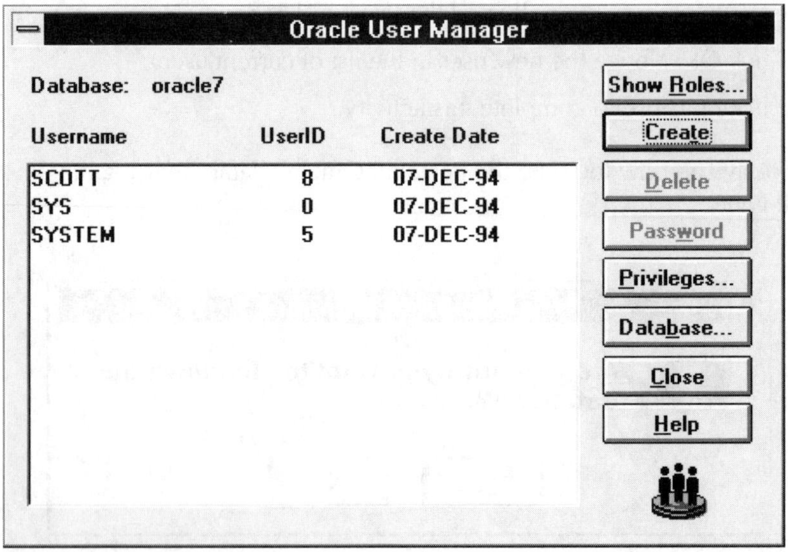

FIGURE 13-35. *Current users display*

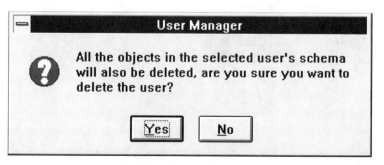

FIGURE 13-36. *Create New User dialog box*

3. Click on the line displaying the user you want to drop.

4. Click on Delete. The confirmation box appears as shown in Figure 13-37.

6. Click YES. Notice that the user is no longer on the list of current users.

7. Click on Close to complete this activity.

User polly can no longer log onto the Personal Oracle7 database.

Adding Space to an Existing Tablespace

With Personal Oracle7, four tablespaces are created during installation. In this section, you will see how to add space to one of these tablespaces. This is done using the database expander.

1. Click on the Database Expander icon in the Personal Oracle7 group in the Windows Program Manager.

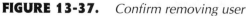

FIGURE 13-37. *Confirm removing user*

2. Click OK to confirm the name of the database. The Database Password Required dialog box appears.

3. Enter the password that you selected when you installed Personal Oracle7, as we discussed in the "Personal Oracle7" section of Chapter 4, "Installation." Click OK. The Oracle Database Expander dialog box appears, as shown in Figure 13-38.

4. Click on the Tablespace drop-down arrow.

5. Highlight then click on the desired tablespace name. We used user_data; enter the name of whichever tablespace you desire.

6. In the Expand by field, enter **500**. Note the number you use is in kilobytes.

7. Click on Expand. The Confirm Database Expansion dialog box appears, as shown in Figure 13-39.

8. Click OK to start expansion. When Oracle is done, you are returned to the Oracle Database Expander dialog box, and Oracle redisplays the database space information showing the space just added.

9. Click on Close to complete this activity.

The requested tablespace now has the additional space.

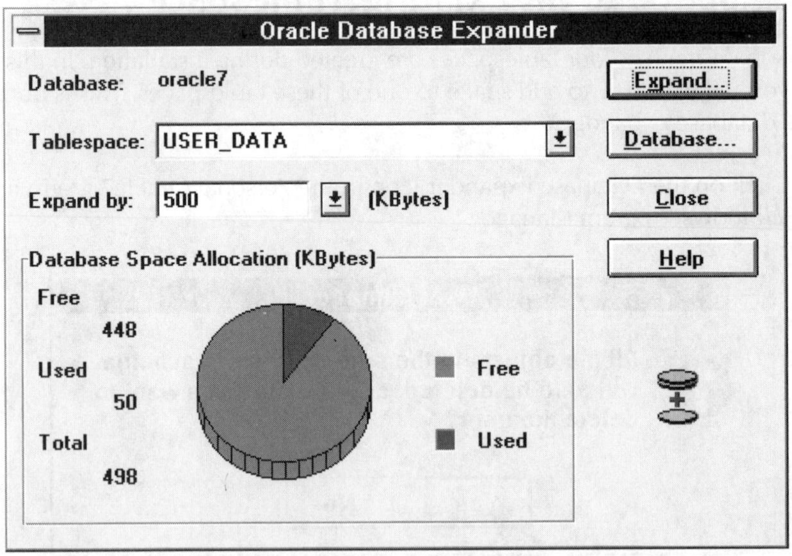

FIGURE 13-38. *Oracle Database Expander dialog box*

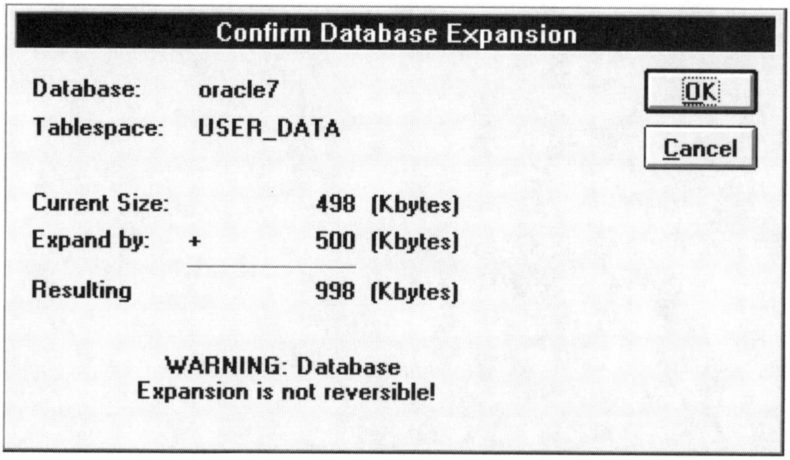

FIGURE 13-39. *Confirm Database Expansion dialog box*

What's Next

Armed with the routines we examined in this chapter, you now know how to work with sqldba, Server Manager, and Personal Oracle7 to perform the following tasks:

- Connect to the database
- Start up the database
- Shut down the database
- Grant access to a user
- Revoke access from a user
- Create a tablespace
- Add space to an existing tablespace

This is enough to get started; this is what you will have to do starting with day one. To find out more about the DBA working with the Oracle database, read Chapter 17. Happy DBAing!

CHAPTER 14

Export/Import

Export and import are the most widely used utilities supplied with the Oracle software. All DBAs, whether seasoned or just getting started, need to be fluent with these two utilities. In Chapter 16, we discuss the role they play in making copies of your Oracle data. Knowing how to use them and why to use them (see the "What Export and Import Can Do for You" section in this chapter) will help your understanding of Oracle as a whole. In this chapter, we will discuss the following:

- Uses for export and import
- Similarities and differences between export and import
- Methods of operation
- Modes of operation
- Error handling and problem-resolution techniques

Terminology

The following definitions will arm you with the technical jargon to make it through this chapter.

- A program runs *interactively* when it enters into a series of questions requiring the operator's response.

- Programs are said to be *parameter-driven* when you code a number of keywords and supply values for each when the program is invoked.

- An *instance* is a separate set of processes and memory structures required to support an open Oracle database.

- An *extent* is a chunk of space in a tablespace that Oracle allocates to tables when they require additional space for new or changed data.

- *Defragmenting* a table is a process whereby you take all the data from all the extents allocated to the table and pack it into one larger extent. Figure 14-1 shows what defragmentation involves.

- *Roles* are used by Oracle to group user accounts together and thereby empower a collection of users to manipulate data or perform restricted activities with the database.

What Export and Import Can Do for You

Export and import empower the DBA and application developers to make dependable and quick copies of Oracle data. Export (invoked using the command **exp**) makes a copy of data and data structures in an operating system file. Import (invoked using the command **imp**) reads files created by export and places data and data structures in Oracle database files. These two handy utilities are used primarily for the following reasons.

- As part of backup and recovery procedures (refer to Chapter 15 for details).

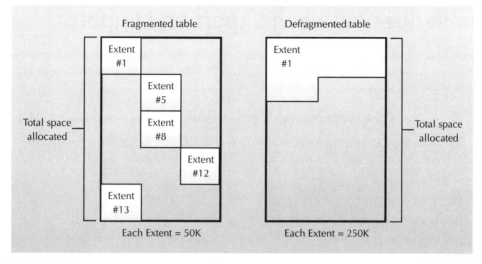

FIGURE 14-1. *Defragmenting extents allocated to a table*

- For moving data between different instances of Oracle. You may export data from your production database and use import to move all or part of the data in that export file into your development database.

- To move all or part of a user's data from one tablespace to another. Suppose userA has data residing in two tablespaces, tablespaceA and tablespaceB. You could move all of the data out of tablespaceB and place it in tablespaceA using export and import.

NOTE
There must be enough space in tablespaceA to accommodate the data being moved from tablespaceB. Import will not add additional disk space to tablespaceA if it is not already there.

- When the need arises to rebuild an existing database, export and import are the only way to preserve the current database data before it is re-created.

NOTE
After performing a full database export, a number of SQL statements and some additional SQL scripts have to be run before the new database is ready for import to reinstate the database's data.

Similarities Between Export and Import

Export and import behave in the same way. Learning one of the two puts you more than 80 percent of the way to mastering both products. These two tools are similar in the following ways:

- Both can be run interactively or can read run-time parameters from a file.

- Both accept keyword (parameters started with **keyword_value=**) or positional parameters (those that mean something based on their order on the command line).

- Both work with Oracle read-only copies of data and data structures.

- Both are used to move data among different Oracle accounts and hardware platforms.

Differences Between Export and Import

Even though export and import are similar, there are some differences. Some parameters are used only with export, others only with import. For example, the **fromuser** and **touser** parameters are only used with import. Likewise, the **compress** parameter is only coded when using export. These parameters are discussed in the "Parameter-Driven Export" and "Parameter-Driven Import" sections in this chapter.

- Import may report on a wide assortment of Oracle errors, since it is creating and loading data into Oracle database files.

- Export is sensitive to the amount of free space on a disk drive to which the export file is being written.

Even though these differences exist, export and import methods and modes of operation are the same. These two areas are the subject of the next two main sections in this chapter.

Methods of Operation

The methods we are about to discuss apply to export and import. Learning and experimenting with different methods is part of your job as a DBA. In this section, we will discuss

- Invoking interactive export with no parameters
- Invoking interactive import with no parameters

- How answers to prompts affect questions Oracle asks later on and the success/failure of import and export
- Running parameter-driven export and import
- Using the **parfile** keyword parameter
- Mixing interactive and parameter-driven methods

When running export and import *interactively,* Oracle presents you with a list of questions. With export, the answers you give to those questions affect what is written to the export file. With import, these answers affect what data is retrieved from the export file. When export and import are *parameter-driven,* you instruct Oracle what you want written to or read from the export file based on values supplied with these parameters. Think of the parameter-driven method as a form you fill out when requesting reimbursement for expenses from a health insurance company; the questions you answer can affect the amount of coverage you are permitted. Later in this chapter, we discuss parameters that can be fed to export and import.

Interactive Export–Invoking with No Parameters

The next listing shows an example of the dialog between export and the user when export is invoked without any parameters.

```
exp
Export: Release 7.1.4.0.0 - Production on Tue Nov  9 11:32:25 1995
Copyright (c) Oracle Corporation 1979, 1994.  All rights reserved.
Username: fin_man/drowssap
Connected to: Oracle7 Server Release 7.1.4.0.0 - Production Release
PL/SQL Release 2.1.4.1 - Production
Enter array fetch buffer size: 4096 > 102400
Export file: expdat.dmp >
(2)U(sers), or (3)T(ables): (2)U > 3
Export table data (yes/no): yes >
Compress extents (yes/no): yes >
About to export specified tables ...
Table to be exported: (RETURN to quit) >e_master
.exporting table                  E_MASTER           122 rows exported
Table to be exported: (RETURN to quit) >
Export terminated successfully without warnings.
```

You are asked to supply the information in the Meaning and Response column of Table 14-1 before Oracle commences the export.

PROMPT RECEIVED FROM ORACLE	MEANING AND RESPONSE
Username	The username and password of the person running export.
Enter array fetch buffer size	The size of the chunk of memory to use as a work area while export writes data to the export file. Normally, one enters values between 10240 (also called 10k) and 10485760 (also called 10m).
Export file	The name of the export file. Defaults to expdat.dmp but can be changed.
(2)U(sers), or (3)T(ables)	Oracle wants to know which method you wish to run. You will be asked for names of one or more users if you choose 2 or the names of one or more of your own tables if you answer 3.
Export table data (yes/no)	Instructions on what to write to the export file. Oracle always writes SQL statements necessary to create exported objects to the export file. Answering yes to this prompt tells Oracle to export the data in the objects as well.
Compress extents (yes/no)	Oracle wants to know if the **create table** statements written to the export file should include an initial space request capable of holding all the existing table data.

TABLE 14-1.   *Dialog When exp Is Invoked with No Parameters*

VIP
When defragmenting a table, answer yes to the compress extents prompt. Figure 14-1 shows what defragmentation involves.

Interactive Import–Invoking with No Parameters

Figure 14-2 shows an example of the dialogue between import and the user when import is invoked without any parameters.

```
imp
Import: Release 7.1.4.0.0 - Production on Tue Nov  9 14:30:48 1995
Copyright (c) Oracle Corporation 1979, 1994.  All rights reserved.
Username: fin_man/drowssap
Connected to: Oracle7 Server Release 7.1.4.0.0 - Production Release
PL/SQL Release 2.1.4.1 - Production
Import file: expdat.dmp >
Enter insert buffer size (minimum is 4096) 30720>
Export file created by EXPORT:V07.01.04
List contents of import file only (yes/no): no >
Ignore create error due to object existence (yes/no): yes >
Import grants (yes/no): yes >
Import table data (yes/no): yes >
Import entire export file (yes/no): yes >
. importing FIN_MAN's objects into FIN_MAN
. . importing table "E_MASTER"                  122 rows imported
Import terminated successfully without warnings.
```

FIGURE 14-2.   *Importing the entire export file*

You are asked to supply the information in the Meaning and Response column
in Table 14-2 before Oracle commences the import.

VIP
If you answer no to the ignore create errors due to object existence
prompt, then Oracle will not bring the table data in for tables that
exist. Almost all the time, you will answer yes to this prompt.

How Answers to Prompts Affect Further Dialog

After using export and import interactively, you will notice that the chain of
questions that follow your responses depend on your answers. For example, when
Oracle asks

```
Import entire export file (yes/no): yes >
```

and you answer no, Oracle then proceeds to ask you exactly what you want to
import, as shown in Figure 14-3.

PROMPT RECEIVED FROM ORACLE	MEANING AND RESPONSE
Username	The username and password of the person running export.
Import file	The name of the file you want import to read. Defaults to expdat.dmp but can be changed.
Enter insert buffer size (minimum is 4096)	The size of the chunk of memory to use as a work area while import writes data to the database. Normally, one enters values between 10240 (also called 10k) and 10485760 (also called 10m).
List contents of import file only (yes/no)	Oracle will list the SQL statements written to the import file if you answer yes. If you answer no, import will bring the data and data definitions into the database.
Ignore create error due to object existence (yes/no)	Oracle wants to know what it should do when it encounters an object in the import file that already exists. If you answer yes, Oracle ignores the fact that an object exists and brings in its data anyway. Answering no causes Oracle to report an error then move on to the next object when it encounters an object that already exists.
Import grants (yes/no)	Oracle wants to know whether to run the grant statements written to the import file after an object is imported.
Import table data (yes/no)	Oracle wants to know if it should bring in the table data (yes) or just run the SQL statements to create objects (no).
Import entire export file (yes/no)	Oracle wants to know if the complete file or only specified portions should be imported. If you answer yes, the import starts at once. If you answer no, Oracle will ask questions about what you wish to import.

TABLE 14-2. *Dialog When imp Is Invoked with No Parameters*

In Figure 14-2, we accept the default yes answer to the import entire export file prompt. The interaction with Oracle is different in the last eight lines of Figure 14-3, since we answer no to the same question. By answering no, we are telling

```
imp /
Import: Release 7.1.4.0.0 - Production on Tue Nov  9 21:47:05 1995
Copyright (c) Oracle Corporation 1979, 1994.  All rights reserved.
Connected to: Oracle7 Server Release 7.1.4.0.0 - Production Release
PL/SQL Release 2.1.4.1 - Production
Import file: expdat.dmp >
Enter insert buffer size (minimum is 4096) 30720>
Export file created by EXPORT:V07.01.04
Warning: the objects were exported by PER_MAN, not by you
List contents of import file only (yes/no): no >
Ignore create error due to object existence (yes/no): yes >
Import grants (yes/no): yes >
Import table data (yes/no): yes >
Import entire export file (yes/no): yes > no
Username: /
Enter table names. Null list means all tables for user
Enter table name or . if done: per_mast
Enter table name or . if done: .
. importing PER_MAN's objects into FIN_MAST
. . importing table "PER_MAST"               2134 rows imported
Import terminated successfully without warnings.
```

FIGURE 14-3.   *Importing part of the export file*

Oracle not to import the complete export file. We then have to supply one or more table names, as shown in the boldfaced lines in the listing.

How Answers to Prompts Affect Success or Failure

As well, export and import behave in different ways based on the responses given to the dialog. In the question

```
Ignore create error due to object existence (yes/no): yes >
```

if you had changed yes to no, the listing shown in Figure 14-4 would have occurred.

In Figure 14-3, accepting yes to the ignore create error due to object existence prompt means that as Oracle encounters the **create table** statement for per_mast, it carries on. In Figure 14-4, when the same **create table** statement is executed, an error condition is raised. As you work more with export and import, you will find

```
imp /
Import: Release 7.1.4.0.0 - Production on Tue Nov  8 22:02:33 1994
Copyright (c) Oracle Corporation 1979, 1994.  All rights reserved.
Connected to: Oracle7 Server Release 7.1.4.0.0 - Production Release
PL/SQL Release 2.1.4.1 - Production
Import file: expdat.dmp >
Enter insert buffer size (minimum is 4096) 30720>
Export file created by EXPORT:V07.01.04
Warning: the objects were exported by PER_MAN, not by you
List contents of import file only (yes/no): no >
Ignore create error due to object existence (yes/no): yes > no
Import grants (yes/no): yes > no
Import table data (yes/no): yes > no
Import entire export file (yes/no): yes >
. importing PER_MAN's objects into FIN_MAN
IMP-00015: following statement failed because the object already exists:
 "CREATE TABLE "FIN_MAST" ("FIN_ID" VARCHAR2(5) NOT NULL, "START_DATE" DATE,
 "END_DATE" DATE, "FY_MAX" NUMBER(4, 0) PCTFREE 10 PCTUSED 90 INITRANS 1
 MAXTRANS 255 STORAGE(INITIAL 16384 NEXT 8192 MINEXTENTS 1 PCTINCREASE 20
 FREELISTS 1 FREELIST GROUPS 1) TABLESPACE "USERS""
Import terminated successfully with warnings.
```

FIGURE 14-4.   *Interactive dialog with import, with a table create error*

there are things you can do with the utilities using the parameter-driven method, discussed in the next section, that cannot be done interactively.

NOTE
When run interactively, export and import suggest a response to most questions. Accept the suggested response by pressing ENTER.

You will find the more you use these utilities that the default answers Oracle suggests are usually the ones you use.

TIP
Use the interactive method when getting started with export and import and experiment with different answers to Oracle's questions. This is the quickest way to familiarize yourself with using these utilities.

Parameter-Driven Export

In the parameter-driven export method, the **exp** command is issued with one or more parameters passed on the command line. This method is the most flexible. We recommend becoming fluent with this method early in your career as a DBA; you will use it from day one. The format of the command is

```
exp keyword1=value1 keyword2=value2 keyword3=value3
```

By using keyword parameters, you instruct Oracle what to write to the export file. A quick list of keywords, their meanings, and their default values can be obtained by issuing the command **exp help=y** from your operating system prompt. The following shows the output from this command.

```
$ exp help=y
Export: Release 7.1.4.0.0 - Production on Tue Nov  9 09:18:01 1995
Copyright (c) Oracle Corporation 1979, 1994.  All rights reserved.
You can let Export prompt you for parameters by entering the EXP
command followed by your username/password:
     Example: EXP SCOTT/TIGER
Or, you can control how Export runs by entering the EXP command followed
by various arguments. To specify parameters, you use keywords:
     Format:  EXP KEYWORD=value or KEYWORD=(value1,value2,...,valueN)
     Example: EXP SCOTT/TIGER GRANTS=Y TABLES=(EMP,DEPT,MGR)
Keyword  Description (Default)        Keyword      Description (Default)
----------------------------------------------------------------------
USERID      username/password        FULL         export entire file (N)
BUFFER      size of data buffer      OWNER        list of owner usernames
FILE        output file (EXPDAT.DMP) TABLES       list of table names
COMPRESS    import into one extent (Y) RECORDLENGTH length of IO record
GRANTS      export grants (Y)        INCTYPE      incremental export type
INDEXES     export indexes (Y)       RECORD       track incr. export (Y)
ROWS        export data rows (Y)     PARFILE      parameter filename
CONSTRAINTS export constraints (Y)   CONSISTENT   cross-table consistency
LOG         log file of screen output STATISTICS  analyze objects (ESTIMATE)
```

Table 14-3 discusses each of the export parameters.

VIP
Use the **log** parameter on ALL parameter-driven exports. If something goes wrong, you need to study the log file to clean up the mess that may be left over by an unsuccessful export.

PARAMETER	MEANING/NOTES	DEFAULT
userid	The Oracle username and password of the account running the utility. If you supply just the username, Oracle will prompt for the password.	None
buffer	The data buffer size in bytes. If you request too big a size, Oracle will carry on with whatever it can obtain.	10240
file	The name of the file being written to. If you do not specify a filename extension, Oracle assumes the .dmp extension.	expdat.dmp
compress	Write storage parameters to the export file that would place all table data in one extent when the data is imported.	Y
grants	Write SQL grant statements to the export file.	Y
indexes	Write SQL create index statements to the export file.	Y
rows	Export the data in the tables' rows as well as the definition of the underlying objects.	Y
constraints	Write SQL statements to the export file needed to re-create declarative integrity when the objects are imported (for example, primary key and references statements).	Y
log	Instructs Oracle to write the screen I/O from the export to a disk file.	None
full	Controls whether Oracle writes SQL statements to the export file to re-create all the system associated datafiles, tablespaces, rollback segments, etc.	N
owner	Provides a list of Oracle accounts whose objects are to be written to the export file.	None
tables	Provides a list of tables whose definitions or data is to be written to the export file.	None
recordlength	Length in bytes of the record written to the export file.	Operating system-specific
inctype	Type of incremental export being performed.	None

TABLE 14-3.   *Export Parameters and Their Defaults*

PARAMETER	MEANING/NOTES	DEFAULT
record	Instructs Oracle to track the type of incremental export being written in some data dictionary views. This information is used when performing an import from an incremental export file.	Y
parfile	The name of a file containing parameters to be fed to export.	None
consistent	Instructs Oracle to maintain cross-table consistency. This ensures that export will make copies of table data as of the time the export started even if tables being exported are being used while the export runs.	N
statistics	Write SQL analyze statements to the export file.	Estimate

TABLE 14-3. *Export Parameters and Their Defaults* (continued)

Parameter-Driven Import

The **imp** command is issued with one or more parameters passed on the command line. Parameter-driven import provides the most flexible and robust method for using import as part of your new skill set. The format of the command is

```
imp keyword1=value1 keyword2=value2 keyword3=value3
```

By using keyword parameters, you instruct Oracle what to bring in from the export file. A quick list of keywords, their meanings, and their default values can be obtained by issuing the command **exp help=y** from your operating system prompt. The following shows the output from this command.

```
$ imp help=y
Import: Release 7.1.4.0.0 - Production on Tue Nov  9 09:17:57 1995
Copyright (c) Oracle Corporation 1979, 1994.  All rights reserved.
You can let Import prompt you for parameters by entering the IMP
command followed by your username/password:
     Example: IMP SCOTT/TIGER
Or, you can control how Import runs by entering the IMP command followed
by various arguments. To specify parameters, you use keywords:
     Format:  IMP KEYWORD=value or KEYWORD=(value1,value2,...,valueN)
     Example: IMP SCOTT/TIGER IGNORE=Y TABLES=(EMP,DEPT) FULL=N
```

```
Keyword  Description (Default)         Keyword     Description (Default)
------------------------------------------------------------------------
USERID   username/password             FULL        import entire file (N)
BUFFER   size of data buffer           FROMUSER    list of owner usernames
FILE     output file (EXPDAT.DMP)      TOUSER      list of usernames
SHOW     just list file contents (N)   TABLES      list of table names
IGNORE   ignore create errors (N)      RECORDLENGTH length of IO record
GRANTS   import grants (Y)             INCTYPE     incremental import type
INDEXES  import indexes (Y)            COMMIT      commit array insert (N)
ROWS     import data rows (Y)          PARFILE     parameter filename
LOG      log file of screen output
DESTROY  overwrite tablespace data file (N)
INDEXFILE write table/index info to specified file
CHARSET  character set of export file (NLS_LANG)
Import terminated successfully without warnings.
```

Table 14-4 discusses each of the import parameters.

VIP
Use the **log** parameter on ALL parameter-driven imports. If something goes wrong, you need to study the log file to clean up the mess that may be left over by an unsuccessful import.

The parfile Keyword Parameter

This parameter deserves special attention. You may feed keyword parameter values to export and import by using this parameter with a filename afterwards. The format of the **parfile** parameter is either of the following:

```
imp parfile=my.parfile
```

or

```
exp parfile=my.parfile
```

You place a list of parameters in the file (in this case, "my.parfile") following the **parfile** keyword. This could be the contents of "my.parfile" being fed into export:

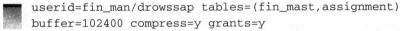

```
userid=fin_man/drowssap tables=(fin_mast,assignment)
buffer=102400 compress=y grants=y
```

PARAMETER	MEANING/NOTES	DEFAULT
userid	The Oracle username and password of the account running the utility. If you supply just the username, Oracle will prompt for the password.	None
buffer	The data buffer size in bytes. If you request too big a size, Oracle will carry on with whatever it can obtain.	10240
file	The name of the file being read from. If you do not specify a filename extension, Oracle assumes the .dmp extension.	expdat.dmp
show	Tells Oracle whether to perform the import or simply show the contents of the export file.	N
ignore	Instructs Oracle on how to deal with SQL create statements in the export file. If set to **N**, Oracle reports an error when trying to create a table that already exists. If set to **Y**, Oracle ignores the error condition raised when attempting to run a **create table** for one that already exists.	N
grants	Execute the SQL **grant** statements in the export file.	Y
indexes	Execute the SQL **create index** statements in the export file.	Y
rows	Import the data in the tables' rows as well as the definition of the underlying objects.	Y
log	Instructs Oracle to write the screen I/O from the import to a disk file.	None
destroy	Instructs Oracle to not overwrite a datafile during a full database import if a datafile contains a tablespace belonging to any database.	N
indexfile	Instructs Oracle to write all **create table**, **create index**, and **create cluster** statements to a user-supplied operating system filename. The table and cluster statements are commented out.	None
charset	The character set of the data in the export file.	NLS_LANG value in initialization parameter file

TABLE 14-4.   *Import Parameters and Their Defaults*

PARAMETER	MEANING/NOTES	DEFAULT
full	Controls whether Oracle executes the SQL statements in the export file to re-create all the system associated datafiles, tablespaces, rollback segments, etc.	N
fromuser	The owner(s) of the data that was written to the export file.	None
touser	The user(s) into which the data should be imported.	None
tables	A list of table names to be imported.	None
recordlength	Specifies the length of each record in the export file. May be necessary when moving data between platforms with different default record lengths.	Operating system-specific
inctype	The type of incremental export being read. Values are either RESTORE or SYSTEM.	None
commit	Instructs Oracle whether or not to **commit** after each array insert. This is very useful when importing large amounts of data that may cause rollback segment errors.	N
parfile	The name of a file containing parameters to be fed to import.	None

TABLE 14-4. *Import Parameters and Their Defaults* (continued)

This could be the contents of "my.parfile" being fed into import:

```
userid=fin_man/drowssap fromuser=fin_man touser=per_man
buffer=102400 grants=y
```

Both parameter files are a free-form format. The export parameter file shows two parameters on the first line, then three parameters on the second. You could as easily have done either of the following.

```
userid=fin_man/drowssap tables=(fin_mast,assignment)
buffer=102400 grants=y
compress=y
```

or

```
compress=y
userid=fin_man/drowssap
```

```
tables=(fin_mast,assignment)
buffer=102400
grants=y
```

Mixing Interactive and Parameter-Driven Methods

You may invoke export and import with a mixture of the two methods by doing the following:

 `exp fin_man/drowssap buffer=102400 compress=n`

As soon as Oracle encounters at least one keyword parameter on the command line, it starts the import or export immediately and does not enter into the interactive dialog. For example, invoking import with the command **imp fin_man/drowssap file=finance** would start import without stopping to prompt for further parameter values. You must be careful when calling export or import this way. Let's say you want to perform a full database export. You call export with the command

`exp fin_man/drowssap buffer=102400 rows=n`

Oracle would not prompt you for any other parameters and would carry on with a user export.

> ***TIP***
> Experiment with export and import so you are not caught off guard by their behavior when you least expect it.

Export and Import Modes

You can run export and import in one of three modes, depending on what you want to accomplish. For example, if you want to create a copy of a table belonging to userA in userB's area, you would use one mode. On the other hand, if you want to preserve a complete copy of userA's data, you would use a different mode. By the end of this section, you will know details on the following:

- Table-mode export and import
- User-mode export and import
- Full database export and import

Table-Mode Export

When using table-mode export, you tell Oracle the names of one or more tables to export. Oracle writes the table data to the export file. The command

```
exp userid=fin_man/drowssap tables=(permast,finmast,stockmast) file=fm.dmp
```

exports the three tables whose names are enclosed in parentheses belonging to Oracle user fin_man. The export file is called fm.dmp.

NOTE
When listing more than one table after the **table** keyword, the names are separated by commas and the whole list is enclosed in parentheses.

User-Mode Export

In user-mode export, Oracle exports all of a user's objects, including views, synonyms, triggers, procedures, database links, and tables. User-mode export is commonly used to defragment a tablespace. After all the user's objects are exported, the tablespace can be dropped and re-created. The command

```
exp userid=fin_man/drowssap owner=(fin_man,per_man,acc_man)
```

exports the three users whose names are enclosed in parentheses. The export file is called expdat.dmp.

NOTE
When listing more than one owner after the **owner** keyword, the owner names are separated by commas and the whole list is enclosed in parentheses.

Full Database Export

When using full database export, all users' data and database support-file (datafiles, tablespaces, rollback segments, etc.) creation statements are written to the export file for every database user except SYS. This export file can be used for a full database import. The command

```
exp userid=system/manager full=y grants=y indexes=y
```

writes the full database export to a file called expdat.dmp.

NOTE
Not every database user will be able to use the full keyword when trying to initiate a full database export. Most full database exports are run using the Oracle SYSTEM account.

Table-Mode Import

When using table-mode import, you tell Oracle the names of one or more tables to import. Oracle writes the table data to the database. The command

```
imp userid=fin_man/drowssap tables=(permast,finmast,stockmast)
```

imports the three tables whose names are enclosed in parentheses belonging to Oracle user fin_man. The export file is called expdat.dmp.

NOTE
When listing more than one table after the **table** keyword, the names are separated by commas and the whole list is enclosed in parentheses.

User-Mode Import

In user-mode import, Oracle imports the specified users' objects, including views, synonyms, triggers, procedures, database links, and tables. User-mode import is commonly used after a tablespace has been re-created during a defragmentation exercise. The command

```
imp userid=fin_man/drowssap fromuser=(per_man,acc_man)
touser=(per_man,acc_man) file=two_users
```

imports the two users whose names are enclosed in parentheses. The export file is called two_users.dmp.

NOTE
When listing more than one user after the **fromuser** or **touser** keyword, the names are separated by commas and the whole list is enclosed in parentheses.

Full Database Import

Full database import runs in two phases. During the first phase, all database support-file (datafiles, tablespaces, rollback segments, etc.) creation statements in the export file are executed. When this phase is complete, the complete structure of the database is in place. The second phase brings users' objects into their appropriate tablespaces. The command

```
imp userid=system/manager full=y file=full_tst
```

performs a full database import from a file called expdat.dmp.

NOTE
Not every database user will be able to use the **full** keyword when trying to initiate a full database import. Most database imports are run using the Oracle SYSTEM account.

VIP
When running a full database import from the system account, the password will be manager, regardless of what it was when the full database export was run.

Switching among Modes

We have devised a hierarchy of export files to illustrate how an export file written using one mode can be used by import in another mode. By assigning a weighting factor to each mode of export (3=full, 2=user, 1=table), you may use a file produced by a higher-numbered mode to run import in a lower- or equal-numbered mode. Table 14-5 summarizes which export files can be used for the three modes of import.

REQUIREMENT	CAN EXPORT FILE WRITTEN BY EXPORT MODE BE USED?		
	Table	User	Full
Table-mode import	Y	Y	Y
User-mode import	N	Y	Y
Full database import	N	N	Y

TABLE 14-5. *Export Modes Used in Different Import Modes*

Thus, a full database export file can be used to do a table-mode, user-mode, or full database import. A user-mode export file can be used to do a user-mode or table-mode import. A table-mode export file can only be used to do a table-mode import.

When to Use Each Mode

Table 14-6 illustrates what export and import can do for you, including a few scenarios and the suggested mode to use with export and import. Although the tasks can easily (and sometimes better) be accomplished using SQL*Plus, we use export and import here.

REQUIREMENT	EXPORT MODE	IMPORT MODE	REASON
Defragment user's tablespace	User	User	We need to get all the user's objects; table mode would ignore view, synonyms, procedures, etc.
Move a copy of the personnel table from development to test	Table	Table	We want one table. This can also be accomplished using the user mode, but table mode is faster.
Move a copy of the salary table from a full database export of production into development	Full	Table	The table we are looking for is in the full database export file. By importing in table mode, we extract only the desired table and data.
Recover the objects belonging to user from last night's full database export after inadvertently dropping a user	Full	User	We need all of the user's objects. Since they no longer exist in the data dictionary, we are unable to collect a list of them and run in table mode. User mode will extract all the user's objects from the full database export file.
Move the personnel system views from one user to another user.	User	User	A table export does not extract SQL view creation statements. You must do this in user mode.

TABLE 14-6. *Export and Import Scenarios*

Requirements for Running Export and Import

As the DBA, you must ensure the two programs exp and imp are accessible to you and your developers. The requirements for a few common environments are outlined in the following table.

OPERATING SYSTEM	REQUIREMENTS
Windows	The executables must be in a directory in the current path and the appropriate values must be set in the oracle.ini initialization file.
VMS	World must have read and execute permissions (W=RE).
UNIX	The executables' file permissions must set to 744 (execute for all users).

Error Conditions and Their Solutions

Yes, you are going to have problems with export and import. We all do! Most of them are a result of coding errors. This section of the chapter will show you how to deal with errors caused by the following situations:

- Trying to run export or import when the database is not open

- Trying to read an export file written by a DBA user

- Trying to run a full database export or import with insufficient privileges

Oracle Not Running

The Oracle instance you are using export or import against must be running: to use these programs. The following is encountered if the instance is not running:

```
imp userid=/ full=y
Import: Release 7.1.4.0.0 - Production on Mon Nov 20 11:39:01 1995
Copyright (c) Oracle Corporation 1979, 1994.  All rights reserved.
IMP-00003: ORACLE error 1034 encountered
ORA-01034: ORACLE not available
ORA-07318: smsget: open error when opening sgadef.dbf file.
```

```
HP-UX Error: 2: No such file or directory
IMP-00021: operating system error - error code (dec 13, hex 0xD)
IMP-00000: Import terminated unsuccessfully
```

Reading Your DBA-Created Export File

When you, as the DBA, create an export file, only other DBA-privileged users may read that file for import regardless of the mode (table, user, or full) used to create the export. The following will occur if a user (no DBA role) tries to read an export file you created as the DBA.

```
imp userid=userx/drowssap full=y
Import: Release 7.1.4.0.0 - Production on Mon Nov 20 11:33:12 1995
Copyright (c) Oracle Corporation 1979, 1994.  All rights reserved.
Connected to: Oracle7 Server Release 7.1.4.0.0 - Production Release
PL/SQL Release 2.1.4.1 - Production
Export file created by EXPORT:V07.01.04
IMP-00013: only a DBA can import a file exported by another DBA
IMP-00021: operating system error - error code (dec 2, hex 0x2)
IMP-00000: Import terminated unsuccessfully
```

Unable to Initiate a Full Database Export

You must start a full database export from your account with the DBA role or an account that you have given the role exp_full_database.

```
exp userid=/ full=y rows=n
Export: Release 7.1.4.0.0 - Production on Thu Nov 9 13:21:02 1995
Copyright (c) Oracle Corporation 1979, 1994.  All rights reserved.
Connected to: Oracle7 Server Release 7.1.4.0.0 - Production Release
PL/SQL Release 2.1.4.1 - Production
EXP-00023: must be a DBA to do Full Database export
EXP-00222:
System error message
(2)U(sers), or (3)T(ables): (2)U >
EXP-00030: Unexpected End-Of-File encountered while reading input
EXP-00222:
System error message
EXP-00000: Export terminated unsuccessfully
```

Relationship Between Parameters

You will soon learn there are certain parameter values with export and import that cannot be coded together. The most common occurrence is with export running in table mode. Suppose you wanted to export one table from userA and two tables from userB in the same export session. The first cut at calling export may be done using the following command:

```
exp userid=fin_man/drowssap owner=(userA,userB) tables=(table1A,table1B,table2B)
```

After pressing ENTER, Oracle responds with

```
EXP-00026: only one parameter (TABLES, OWNER, or FULL) can be specified
EXP-00222:
System error message 2
EXP-00000: Export terminated unsuccessfully
```

and the export aborts.

In the next listing, we are asking Oracle not to export the table data (**rows=n**) and to compress the extents (**compress=y**). Since the **compress** keyword is not on the command line, Oracle defaults it to **Y**, as shown in Table 14-3.

```
exp userid=/ rows=n file=partial
Export: Release 7.1.4.0.0 - Production on Mon Nov 20 12:07:28 1995
Copyright (c) Oracle Corporation 1979, 1994.  All rights reserved.
Connected to: Oracle7 Server Release 7.1.4.0.0 - Production Release
PL/SQL Release 2.1.4.1 - Production
EXP-00035: Cannot specify Rows=N and Compress=Y
EXP-00222: System error message
EXP-00000: Export terminated unsuccessfully
```

In the next listing, you see that Oracle insists you enter the **fromuser** and **touser** parameters in the call to import, issue the keyword **full=y**, or provide some table names using the **tables=** keyword parameter.

```
imp userid=/ file=prod
Import: Release 7.1.4.0.0 - Production on Mon Nov 20 12:07:28 1995
Copyright (c) Oracle Corporation 1979, 1994.  All rights reserved.
Connected to: Oracle7 Server Release 7.1.4.0.0 - Production Release
PL/SQL Release 2.1.4.1 - Production
Export file created by EXPORT:V07.01.04
IMP-00031: Must specify FULL=Y or provide FROMUSER/TOUSER or TABLE arguments
IMP-00021: operating system error - error code (dec 2, hex 0x2)
IMP-00000: Import terminated unsuccessfully
```

UNIX Specifics

We have run across the following UNIX caveats with import and export. Enclosing a list of table names in parentheses when using table mode raises an error, since the operating system interprets rather than reads the leading parenthesis. The solution is to put the keyword and its qualifiers in single quotes or use the UNIX escape character \ (backslash). This forces UNIX to read the parentheses.

```
exp userid=/ tables=(table_q,table_r)
ksh: syntax error: '(' unexpected
```

Either of the following will work.

```
exp userid=/ tables='(table_q,table_r)'
```

or

```
exp userid=/ tables=\(table_q,table_r\)
```

If you code an ops$ account prefix on the command line call to export or import, you get the following error even though, using this example, the account ops$francesl with the drowssap password is valid.

```
exp userid=ops$francesl/drowssap
Export: Release 7.1.4.0.0 - Production on Mon Nov 20 12:07:28 1995
Copyright (c) Oracle Corporation 1979, 1994.  All rights reserved.
Connected to: Oracle7 Server Release 7.1.4.0.0 - Production Release
PL/SQL Release 2.1.4.1 - Production
EXP-00004: invalid username or password
EXP-00222:
System error message
Username:
```

As above, you must either enclose the username and password in single quotes or use the UNIX escape character \ (backslash). Either of the following will solve the problem.

```
exp userid=ops\$francesl/drowssap
```

or

```
exp userid='ops$francesl/drowssap'
```

Examples

We now introduce some real-life export and import situations, and we will present a listing of the parameter file to use with each. As you become more fluent in using these utilities, you will specify the **parfile=** keyword more and more and place the appropriate parameters in a file.

Sample Scenario #1

Export my person, acc_rec, fin_mast, and letters tables into a file called recs. The contents of the parameter file would be

```
userid=/ file=recs tables=(person,acc_rec,fin_mast) buffer=10240
```

Import userA's objects into userB's schema using export file frank. Some of the objects already exist in userB's schema, but we want to bring the data in for existing objects as well.

```
userid=/ ignore=y file=frank buffer=102400 fromuser=userA touser=userB
```

Sample Scenario #2

Export three of userA's tables and two of userB's tables.

```
userid=/
tables=(userA.table_1,userA.table_2,userA.table_3,userB.table_1,userB.table_2)
```

Sample Scenario #3

Make a copy of the tables exported in the previous example in userC's schema.

```
userid=userc/drowssap fromuser=(userA,userB) touser=(userC,userC)
```

Personal Oracle7

We now discuss how to work with export and import with the Windows 3.1-based Personal Oracle7.

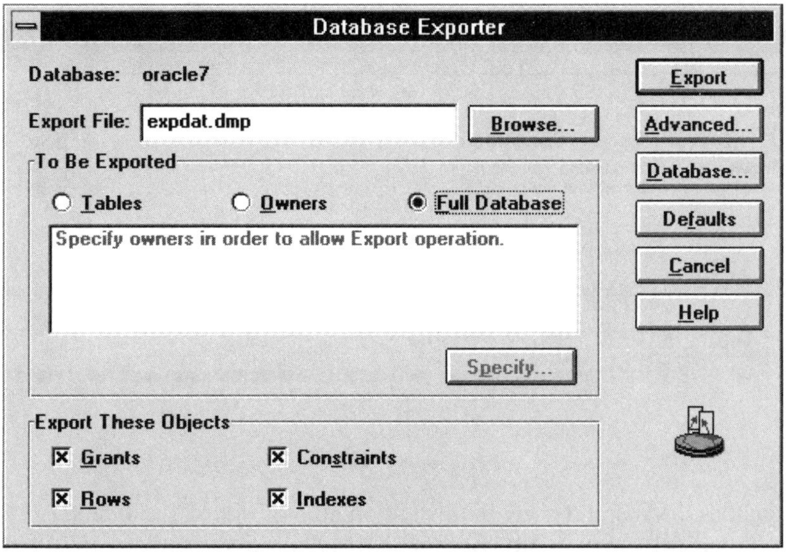

FIGURE 14-5. *Database Exporter dialog box*

Export

We are going to perform a full database export in Personal Oracle7. To accomplish this, follow these steps:

1. Click on the Export icon in the Personal Oracle7 group in the Windows Program Manager.

2. In the Database Logon dialog box, enter **system** for the Username and **manager** for the Password.

3. Click OK to open the Database Exporter dialog box, shown in Figure 14-5.

4. Click on Full Database in the To Be Exported area.

5. Click on Export to begin. Oracle displays the EXPORT Status window, as shown in Figure 14-6.

6. Click on Close to return to the Database Exporter dialog box, then click on Close again to complete this activity.

The full database export has created a file called expdat.dmp in your \orawin\bin directory. It contains all the data and data definitions for your Personal

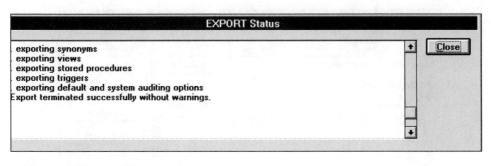

FIGURE 14-6. *EXPORT Status window*

Oracle7 database. Making a copy of this file on tape or floppy diskette(s) is suggested periodically to back up your data. This effort makes a backup of Oracle, just as you do from time to time with your word processing documents.

Import

We are going to show you how to perform a full database import. To accomplish this, follow these steps:

1. Click on the Import icon in the Personal Oracle7 group in the Windows Program Manager.

2. When the Database Logon dialog box appears, enter **system** for the Username and **manager** for the Password.

3. Click OK to open the Database Importer dialog box, as shown in Figure 14-7.

4. Click on the Full Database button in the Import Mode area on the screen.

5. Click Import to start the import. Oracle presents the IMPORT Status window, as shown in Figure 14-8.

6. Click on Close to return to the Database Importer dialog box, then click on Close again to complete this activity.

If you want to perform this activity from the export file created in the previous section, ensure that the expdat.dmp created in the previous section is in your \orawin\bin directory, then use the Database Importer to move its contents back into your database.

Database Importer
Database: oracle7
Import File: expdat.dmp
Browse...
Ignore Creation Errors
Import Mode
Tables
Users
Full Database
Specify Tables before Import or Show can proceed.
Specify...
Objects to Import
Grants
Indexes
Rows
Import
Show...
Advanced...
Database...
Defaults
Cancel
Help

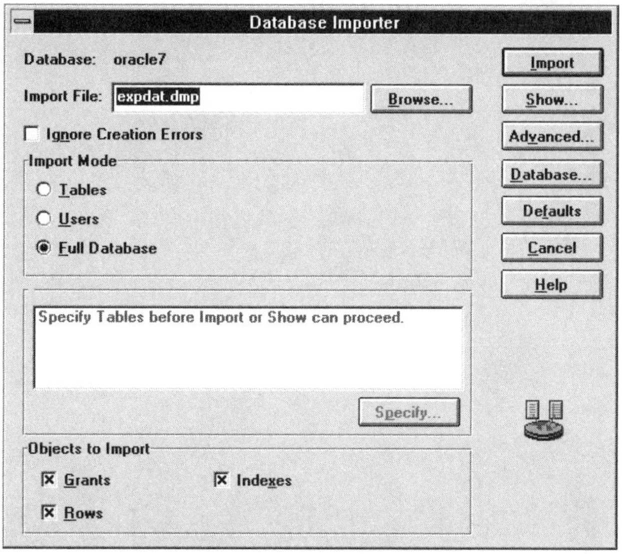

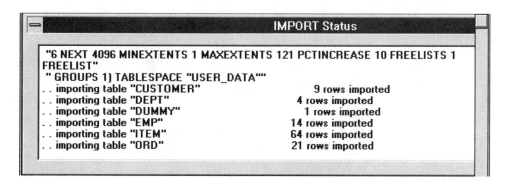

FIGURE 14-7. *Database Importer dialog box*

What's Next

We have stressed throughout this chapter the importance of export and import and how they are integrated into your DBA skill set. In Chapter 15, we will highlight how to use these utilities as part of your backup and recovery procedures. Export and import have been around for years—they are dependable and integral to the set of utilities you receive with the Oracle Server product. Very early in your career as a DBA, you will wonder how you could ever live without them.

IMPORT Status
"6 NEXT 4096 MINEXTENTS 1 MAXEXTENTS 121 PCTINCREASE 10 FREELISTS 1 FREELIST"
" GROUPS 1) TABLESPACE "USER_DATA""
. . importing table "CUSTOMER" 9 rows imported
. . importing table "DEPT" 4 rows imported
. . importing table "DUMMY" 1 rows imported
. . importing table "EMP" 14 rows imported
. . importing table "ITEM" 64 rows imported
. . importing table "ORD" 21 rows imported

FIGURE 14-8. *IMPORT Status window*

CHAPTER 15

Backup and Recovery

Ah yes! Backup and recovery—two of the biggest issues with any system, regardless of the software. Oracle has implemented sophisticated backup and recovery mechanisms that allow you to protect your precious data in case all or part of your database is inoperable. By the time you finish this chapter, you will be able to implement a standard backup and recovery plan for your installation. We include details on the following topics:

- Making image backups of your database

- Leaving the database open and accessible while making backups

- Running the database in ARCHIVELOG mode

- Performing complete and incomplete database recovery

- Integrating backup with export and import

All too often, DBAs look at backup and recovery procedures only when it's too late. One of our clients lost a production database before they "got around" to taking the time to implement routines that would have allowed the necessary protection. Keep in mind, there are two steps to initiating backup and recovery procedures. The first (the backup step) makes copies of the Oracle data; the second (the recovery step) copies the data created from the backup step and restores the database to its operable status.

Terminology

The following definitions will arm you with the technical jargon to make it through this chapter.

- A *checkpoint* causes information to be written from memory to the database files to which they belong. During this activity, the state of the datafiles, redo logs, and control files is synched, and the instance is in a consistent state.

- Oracle keeps an internal transaction log referred to as the *SCN* or system change number. Using an internal set of rules, Oracle assigns an SCN to transactions and, when doing a log switch, records the highest SCN in each redo log as it is archived.

- The Oracle database is in a *consistent state* when the information in the control files (e.g., the last time the datafiles were updated) is the same as the information contained in the datafiles themselves.

Protection Provided by Backup

We need to spend time on some concepts and theory before we discuss how and what to back up. Essentially, Oracle offers two types of backup protection. After we discuss the two and present a complete backup plan, you will know how to secure your installation with bulletproof protection against just about anything.

Protection Against Loss of an Object

Backup using export and import (which will be discussed in the "Export and Import Backup" section coming up) provides protection against loss of objects. How could that happen, you ask? Picture yourself as a developer for a large bank in Germany. You use Oracle's network product called SQL*Net, which allows you to work with databases on a remote machine. You have just finished some cleanup before final installation of a new system in production, and you connect to the production database using SQL*Net. You are called out of the office for a few minutes, and when you come back, you realize that you have forgotten to remove a table from the development database, so you enter the command **drop table account_master;**. Less than five minutes later, your phone rings, and guess what? The account_master table is missing in production (how did that happen?).

VIP

Export and import provide protection against loss of tables that get dropped inadvertently from the database. In other words, they provide protection against loss of all or part of one or more tables.

When a table needs to be recovered from an export file, bring it back using the table mode of import (this is discussed in Chapter 14 in the "Table Mode Import" section). If the export was made at 2:00 A.M. and a table is inadvertently dropped at 3:00 P.M. the next day, any new or changed rows in the table after 2:00 A.M. are not restored as the table is re-created. Sound impossible? Believe us, it happens.

VIP

While import allows protection against losing a table, the import will only restore the table to the condition it was in when the export file was written.

Protection Against Loss of the Database

Protection against loss of the database also means protection against loss of a datafile or tablespace. This protection is related directly to the redo or transaction logs we discuss in many places throughout this book, especially the "Redo Logs" section of Chapter 2. Picture the following situation that happened to us a few years ago. It's morning, and everyone is happily working with the database. There is a phone call to the help desk from a user saying that Oracle is asking her for her username and password. Interesting! When she usually logs onto the machine, the first screen she sees is the main menu for her system. We investigate, and find out that Oracle is not running! We look around and do some exploring, and we receive the following message from Oracle:

```
ERROR: ORA-01034: ORACLE not available
ORA-09243: smsget: error attaching to SGA
```

Panic! Something has gone wrong with one of the disks, and Oracle has shut itself down. This illustrates the second type of backup protection. In this situation, there is a problem with the hardware (disk pack, in this case) and we may have lost the datafiles on the bad disk. Unlike losing one or more objects, here the physical structure of the database is damaged.

Protection for this type of problem is provided by running the database in ARCHIVELOG mode; you then have roll-forward capabilities. The redo or transaction logs record every transaction against the database. By saving copies of the redo logs before they are overwritten, they can be reapplied to the database as if the transactions had been entered by the users. We discuss ARCHIVELOG mode in more detail in the "Recovery" section in this chapter.

VIP

ARCHIVELOG provides protection against an assortment of hardware problems that happen periodically. You can restore a backup of the database and recover all the transactions, since the backup was written using your archived redo logs.

Export and Import Backup

We discuss export and import in Chapter 14 (we thought these two utilities were so important that they warranted their own chapter). If you refer to the "Export and Import Modes" section in Chapter 14, you will see how export and import play a role in most standard backup procedures.

Classically, most backups are done in the quiet hours. When deciding how to use export as part of your backup, examine what we call your "window of opportunity." This window is the amount of time during which everything is quiet on your computer (i.e., there are no reporting jobs or system backups running to interfere with the resources required to do an export), and no users are accessing the database. Most of our clients have a window of between six and seven hours. In some situations, however, that window is as small as 30 minutes or as large as nine hours. We suggest you use export according to the guidelines in the next two sections as part of your backup routines.

VIP
If you can do a full database export within this window of
opportunity, the full database export must be part of your Oracle
backups.

When the Window Is Long Enough

If the window is long enough to accommodate a nightly full database export, run
the command **exp parfile=full_nightly.parfile** and the parameter file contents are
the following:

```
userid=system/manager full=y file=full_sys
buffer=102400 log=full_sys grants=y indexes=y
```

Run this export every night, and you will have all the protection you would ever
want against losing an object.

When the Window Is Not Long Enough

One main question needs to be answered when deciding what to export and when:
"What tables experience the highest activity?" With the answer to that question,
you can decide to export those tables on a regular basis and other not-so-active
ones less frequently. Examine Table 15-1 to see how this could be mapped to the
largest and most strategic data in a communication company's database.

Armed with this information, you then produce the code that will run the export
routines. You always add two more parts to the backup procedures, as shown in Table
15-2. Part 5 exports all the data not done in parts 1 through 4, and part 6 makes a
copy of the makeup of the database but does not export any data.

TABLE NAME	OWNER	APPROXIMATE SIZE	PART
customers	b_cust	8,000,000	1
phones	b_numbers	12,000,000	2
loc_master	b_inventory	615,000	3
interurban	b_ld	7,500,000	4

TABLE 15-1. *Large Objects Part of Export Cycle*

VIP
Based on your configuration, you may have more or less parts after you analyze your requirements.

Use the following guidelines when implementing the procedures (the part numbers referred to are from Tables 15-1 and 15-2):

- Each part (numbered 1 to 4) must complete successfully before the next component runs. Thus, if part 2 does not complete on a Tuesday night, part 2 is run again Wednesday night, and part 3 waits one more night for its turn.

- These procedures must run unattended; thus, export must be run using the **parfile=** parameter (discussed in Chapter 14). Using part 3 from Table 15-1 as an example, the export command would be **exp parfile=sys_part3.parfile** and the parameter file would contain the following:

```
userid=b_inventory/secure file=sys_part3 buffer=102400
grants=y indexes=y log=part3_sys
```

- Part 5 exports all the data not done in parts 1 through 4.

- Part 6 runs every night and writes an export file containing all the SQL statements required to re-create your database. No data is written to the export file during this operation. Assuming the job runs from the Oracle SYSTEM account using the command **exp parfile=full_no_rows**, the contents of the parameter file are

```
userid=system/manager full=y rows=n compress=n file=full_sys
buffer=102400 log=full_sys grants=y indexes=y
```

Keep a log of your export backups. A sample is shown in Table 15-3. Notice how part 3 was scheduled to run June 13, but it did not complete. As a result, part

COMPONENT	PART
Other data not part of 1 to 4	5
Full system no rows	6

TABLE 15-2. *Other Parts of Database to Export*

DATE	PART SCHEDULED	COMPLETED	WRITTEN TO TAPE
June 11	1	Y	Y
June 11	5	Y	Y
June 11	6	**N**	**N**
June 12	2	Y	Y
June 12	5	Y	Y
June 12	6	Y	Y
June 13	3	**N**	**N**
June 13	5	Y	Y
June 13	6	Y	Y
June 14	3	Y	Y
June 14	5	Y	Y
June 14	6	Y	Y
June 15	4	Y	Y
June 15	5	Y	Y
June 15	6	Y	Y

TABLE 15-3. *Export Log*

3 was rescheduled to run June 14. Had part 3 run to completion on the 13th, part 4 would have run on the 14th. Even though parts 5 and 6 run nightly, you still should track their successful completion.

Recovery from an Export File

Once the export files are written as described in the previous sections, restoring one or more objects from the export is done when required. Let's look at a few situations that may come up and how to use import to rebuild one or more missing objects.

NOTE
We recommend doing object restoration from the Oracle SYSTEM account.

Restoring a Single Object

Using the appropriate export file as input, follow these steps to restore the complete contents of the loc_master:

1. Log into SQL*Plus using the SYSTEM account, and enter the command **truncate table b_inventory.loc_master;** to clean out the table. If the table has been dropped, the **truncate** command will return Oracle error "942:table or view does not exist."

2. Leave SQL*Plus, and enter the command **imp userid=system fromuser=b_inventory touser=b_inventory commit=y file=sys_part2 buffer=102400 tables=loc_master ignore=y log=sys_rest**. You will be prompted for the password missing from the command line.

NOTE

Use the parameter **commit=y** to ensure that the import runs to completion. When you are restoring a large table, this ensures Oracle has enough rollback segment space to handle a large import.

3. Log into SQL*Plus as the b_inventory user and verify the grants on the table by issuing the command **select grantee, privilege from user_tab_privs_made where table_name = 'LOC_MASTER';**. If there seem to be some privileges missing, ascertain what they are and give them out again.

Restoring Multiple Objects

This exercise is similar to the previous section, except you have to delete rows from more than one table before bringing the table back from the export file. As well, the command used to invoke import is: **imp userid=system fromuser=(b_inventory,b_cust) touser=(b_inventory,b_cust) commit=y file=sys_part2 buffer=102400 tables=(loc_master,customers) ignore=y log=sys_rest**. You will be prompted for the password missing from the command line. In this command, the Oracle usernames owning the tables are listed with **fromuser** and **touser** in parentheses separated by commas. The tables being brought back are listed in parentheses separated by commas as well.

Image Backups

Let's move from export and import to image backups. Image backups play an important role in your backup and recovery procedures. They make copies of some or all of your datafiles, redo logs, and control files. In this section, we will discuss making consistent (cold) backups and online (hot) backups.

Consistent (Cold) Backups

Cold backups are made with the database closed. Any file, be it datafile, redo log, or control, is part of this backup. Usually, disk space permitting, the files are copied somewhere on a disk, then backed up to tape during the quiet hours in the middle of the night. We recommend running the following program in SQL*Plus; it will create output that can be used to make a cold backup. The **bolded** text in the following listing may change to suit your database.

```
rem You must have select privileges on the v$parameter
rem v$logfile v$dbfile and v$controlfile data
rem dictionary views belonging to SYS to run
rem this program

set pages 0 feed off echo off
col a new_value b
col c new_value d
select value a,sysdate c
  from v$parameter
 where name = 'db_name';
spool cold.backup
prompt
prompt Cold backup for "&b" database on &d ...
prompt
prompt # Redo logs
prompt
select 'cp '||member||' .'
  from v$logfile;
prompt
prompt # Datafiles
prompt
select 'cp '||name||' .'
  from v$dbfile;
 prompt
prompt # Control files
prompt
select 'cp '||name||' .'
  from v$controlfile;
spool off
exit
```

In the listing, the name of the output file is cold.backup; if this does not conform to the filenaming rules on your computer, the **spool** command filename will have to be changed.

Online (Hot) Backups

Hot backups are made with the database running in ARCHIVELOG mode. To find out how to switch your database into this mode, consult the "Tuning Online Backups" section in *Tuning Oracle* by Corey, Abbey, and Dechichio (Osborne McGraw-Hill/Oracle Press, 1995).

Hot backups do not copy the online redo logs, since they are being archived and backed up as part of your nightly backups anyway. The database is open, and an online backup can be performed while the users are working with the database. Hot backups are done by placing a tablespace in backup mode, copying it somewhere else on disk or to tape, then taking the tablespace out of backup mode. After the tablespaces are backed up in this manner, you back up your control file.

VIP

You can provide 24-hour availability of your database by running in ARCHIVELOG mode and making hot backups. Even though the database is open and may be in use, the backup is consistent and may be used for recovery, as discussed later in this chapter.

Sample Hot Backup

Table 15-4 shows a database against which we will be doing a hot backup. The following SQL*Plus script can be used (make modifications where necessary if your operating system is not UNIX):

```
rem   We inform Oracle that we are backing up a tablespace
rem   before doing the copy. This is done one tablespace
rem   at a time. After the tablespace is put in backup
rem   mode, make a copy of its datafile(s). By forcing
rem   a checkpoint after each tablespace is backed up,
rem   we synch the registering of the backup internally
rem   to Oracle.

alter tablespace tools begin backup;
!cp /sys/tools/d1/tools.dbf /sys/backups/repos/tools.dbf
alter tablespace tools end backup;
alter system checkpoint;

alter tablespace temp begin backup;
! cp /usr/oradata/d3/temp.dbf /sys/backups/repos/temp.dbf
alter tablespace temp end backup;
alter system checkpoint;
```

TABLESPACE	DATAFILE(S)
system	/usr/oradata/d0/dbs1.dbf
users	/usr/oradata/d1/users1.dbf
	/usr/oradata/d2/users2.dbf
temp	/usr/oradata/d3/temp.dbf
rollback_segs	/usr/sys/rollback/rbs1.dbf
	/usr/sys/rollback/rbs2.dbf
tools	/sys/tools/d1/tools.dbf

TABLE 15-4.   *Database for Backing Up*

```
alter tablespace rollback_segs begin backup;
! cp /usr/sys/rollback/rbs1.dbf /sys/backups/repos/rbs1.dbf
! cp /usr/sys/rollback/rbs2.dbf /sys/backups/repos/rbs2.dbf
alter tablespace rollback_segs end backup;
alter system checkpoint;

alter tablespace users begin backup;
!cp /usr/oradata/d1/users1.dbf /sys/backups/repos/users1.dbf
!cp /usr/oradata/d1/users2.dbf /sys/backups/repos/users2.dbf
alter tablespace users end backup;
alter system checkpoint;

alter tablespace system begin backup;
!cp /usr/oradata/d0/dbs1.dbf /sys/backups/repos/dbs1.dbf
alter tablespace system end backup;
alter system checkpoint;

alter database backup controlfile to
      '/sys/backup/repos/control_bkp' reuse;
```

Recovery

So far in this chapter, we have discussed export and import, the role they play in
your backup procedures, and how to restore an object from an export file. We
have also discussed image backups. Now comes the meat of this chapter: recovery.
Strap yourself in; this is the heart of Oracle's backup and recovery strategy, and it
can prove quite stimulating!

In this section, we will lead you through some exercises and show you how to perform recovery. You need a "practice" database to do these exercises. Following is a sample **create database** script you can use as a skeleton SQL script to build your own database. It is included to get you started; the text that is **bolded** needs modifications to suit your configuration:

```
connect internal
spool scratch.log
set echo on
startup nomount pfile=?/dbs/initprac.ora
create database prac
        datafile '?/dbs1prac.dbf'                     size 10m
        logfile  '?/log1prac.dbf','?/log2prac.dbf' size 300k
maxlogfiles 20
        maxlogmembers    4
        maxdatafiles    30
        maxinstances     1
        maxloghistory 100;
create rollback segment temp
        tablespace system
        storage (initial 50k minextents 2);
shutdown
startup pfile=?/dbs/initprac.ora
alter tablespace system default storage (pctincrease 0);
set echo off
set termout off
@?/rdbms/admin/catalog.sql
@?/rdbms/admin/catexp.sql
@?/rdbms/admin/catldr.sql
@?/rdbms/admin/catproc.sql
connect system/manager
@?/rdbms/admin/catdbsyn.sql
connect internal
shutdown
```

What Is Recovery?

Recovery is a process whereby an image backup of the database (done, let's say, at 7:00 A.M.) is rolled forward to a later point in time (let's say 2:00 P.M.) using the archived redo logs. Roll forward applies changes recorded in the redo logs, then, using the rollback segments, undoes any transactions that were recorded in the redo log but were not committed. We discuss the redo logs in Chapter 2, pointing out how they record all activities against the database. Say a system had been used by twelve people between 7:00 A.M. and 2:00 P.M. Everything these people did to the database was written to the redo logs; thus, the redo logs are a mirror image of the activities of those twelve people during those seven hours.

Redo Log Types

There are two types of redo logs: online redo logs and archived redo logs. *Online redo logs* are the pool of two or more redo logs written to as the database operates. We discuss in Chapter 2 how Oracle cycles between the online redo logs. When running the database in ARCHIVELOG mode, before reusing a redo log, Oracle copies it elsewhere and adds it to the pool of *archived redo logs*. Every redo log is allocated a sequence number when Oracle does a log switch. In Table 15-5, we show how the status of redo logs cycles between active, being archived, and inactive.

In Table 15-5, after the second log switch, a redo log belonging to group 1 is archived, and that copy is referred to as an archived redo log. Notice that when the fourth log switch occurs, redo log group 1 becomes active once again, and any

	LOG SEQUENCE	REDO LOG GROUP	STATUS
log switch #1	18	1	active
		2	inactive
		3	being archived
log switch #2	19	1	being archived
		2	active
		3	inactive
log switch #3	19	1	inactive
		2	being archived
		3	active
log switch #4	20	1	active
		2	inactive
		3	being archived

TABLE 15-5. *Cycling of Redo Logs Through Four Log Switches*

information in the log is overwritten. This is not a problem, since the previous contents of the redo log have become an archived redo log.

Types of Recovery

Every time you start the database, Oracle looks through its online redo logs to see if there is any recovery it should perform based on the information in those logs. If it finds any information, it applies it to the database before it is opened. This feature is called *automatic database instance recovery*. When you take a mixture of archived and online redo logs and recover all or part of the database, this is called either complete media recovery or incomplete media recovery.

   Complete media recovery can be performed on the database, a tablespace, or one or more datafiles. Recovery stops with the application of the most recent redo log. *Incomplete media recovery* can only be performed on the whole database. The term incomplete is used because, with this type of recovery, not all of the redo logs are applied. You specify when the recovery process is to stop; when Oracle applies enough redo logs to reach that point, the recovery stops. Table 15-6 summarizes what can be recovered using complete and incomplete recovery.

Performing Complete Recovery

We will now lead you through a complete recovery session. The database we are recovering has the following makeup:

TABLESPACE	DATAFILE(S)
system	/oracle/book/dbs1book.dbf
rollback	/oracle/book/rbook.dbf
users	/oracle/book/users.dbf
tools	/oracle/book/tools.dbf
temp	/oracle/book/temp.dbf

   In this scenario, the database is backed up at 4:40 A.M. nightly. The archived redo logs are copied to the directory /oracle/book/arclogs. Image backups are written to the directory /sys/orabkp/backups and written to tape from there at 6:00 A.M. At noon, there is a problem with one of the disk packs, and the database shuts itself down.

	DATABASE	DATAFILE	TABLESPACE
Complete	X	X	X
Incomplete	X		

TABLE 15-6. *What Can Be Recovered Using Complete and Incomplete Recovery*

Before doing the recovery, you must restore the image backup from wherever it resides to the correct location on your disks. Using our sample database, the following five commands copy the image backup to its proper location:

```
cp /sys/orabkp/backups/rbook.dbf /oracle/book/rbook.dbf
cp /sys/orabkp/backups/users.dbf /oracle/book/users.dbf
cp /sys/orabkp/backups/tools.dbf /oracle/book/tools.dbf
cp /sys/orabkp/backups/temp.dbf /oracle/book/temp.dbf
cp /sys/orabkp/backups/dbs1book.dbf /oracle/book/dbs1book.dbf
```

To perform the complete recovery, follow these steps:

1. Invoke line-mode Server Manager with the command **svrmgrl**.

2. Enter the command **connect internal**, followed by **startup mount**.

3. Check the status of the database by entering the command **alter database open;** and receive the following feedback from Oracle:

```
alter database open
*
ORA-01113: file 1 needs media recovery
ORA-01110: data file 1: '/oracle/book/dbs1book.dbf'
SVRMGR>
```

4. Enter the command **recover database;** and receive the following feedback from Oracle:

```
ORA-00279: Change 9964 generated at 12/21/95 14:37:06 needed...
ORA-00289: Suggestion : /oracle/book/arclogs/arch_383.arc
ORA-00280: Change 9964 for thread 1 is in sequence #383
Specify log: {<RET>=suggested ¦ filename ¦ AUTO ¦ CANCEL}
```

5. Press ENTER to accept the log filename presented
(/oracle/book/arclogs/arch_383.arc, in this case).

As Oracle suggests each archived redo log filename, keep pressing ENTER to
accept the suggestions made. When the recovery is complete, Oracle presents you
with this message:

```
Log applied.
Media recovery complete.
SVRMGR>
```

You then issue the command **alter database open;** and the database recovery is
complete! Bravo—nice job.

When presented with the name of the first redo log to apply, you could have
entered the word **auto** (notice it is one of the suggestions in the specify log prompt),
and Oracle would have run the recovery without need for further intervention. The
last log file prompt is shown below, and the recovery complete message follows.

```
ORA-00279: Change 10029 generated at 12/21/95 14:43:13 needed...
ORA-00289: Suggestion : /oracle/book/arclogs/arch_399.arc
ORA-00280: Change 10029 for thread 1 is in sequence #399
ORA-00278: Logfile '/oracle/book/arclogs/arch_398.arc' no longer...
Log applied.
Media recovery complete.
SVRMGR>
```

Performing Incomplete Recovery

Incomplete recovery is one of the most interesting features of Oracle's recovery
mechanisms. Review the exercise we went through in the previous section, in
which Oracle asked for names and locations of archived redo logs, then look at the
following listing:

```
ORA-00308: cannot open archived log '/oracle/book/arclogs/arch_387.arc
ORA-07360: sfifi: stat error, unable to obtain information...
HP-UX Error: 2: No such file or directory
SVRMGR>
```

Uh oh! Oracle wants archived redo log file with sequence number 387—panic
(why did you want to be a DBA anyway!). Confident that Oracle just messed up,
you try the job again and, lo and behold, it happens again. No problem. Just drop

back to the operating system and find the missing log file and all will be well. You issue the command **ls** and receive the following output:

```
arch_382.arc    arch_386.arc    arch_391.arc    arch_395.arc    arch_399.arc
arch_383.arc    arch_388.arc    arch_392.arc    arch_396.arc    arch_400.arc
arch_384.arc    arch_389.arc    arch_393.arc    arch_397.arc    arch_401.arc
arch_385.arc    arch_390.arc    arch_394.arc    arch_398.arc
```

Notice that the file arch_387.arc is not there. This is why incomplete recovery exists.

VIP
Incomplete recovery recovers the database to a point in time in the past. In our example, the database can only be recovered to the transaction at the end of archived log sequence number 387.

There are three ways to perform incomplete recovery: change-based recovery, cancel-based recovery, and time-based recovery. We will run through each one in the next sections. Hold on.

Change-Based Recovery
To do change-based recovery, you need to know the highest system change number (SCN) written to the archived redo log just before the missing log. You can then issue the recovery statement **recover database until change scn_number;** where the **scn_number** is that SCN written to archived redo log file sequence number 386 (i.e., one less than the missing log sequence number 387). You can get that SCN information from a view called v$log_history owned by Oracle user SYS, which looks like the following:

```
THREAD#                                NUMBER
SEQUENCE#                              NUMBER
TIME                                   VARCHAR2(20)
LOW_CHANGE#                            NUMBER
HIGH_CHANGE#                          NUMBER
ARCHIVE_NAME                           VARCHAR2(257)
```

Using the query **select high_change# from v$log_history where sequence# = 386;**, you can find out the desired SCN. The output from this query is the following:

```
HIGH_CHANGE#
--------------------
           9999
```

Now that you know the SCN, let's perform the recovery, using these steps:

1. Invoke line-mode Server Manager with the command **svrmgrl**.

2. Enter the command **connect internal**, followed by **startup mount**.

3. Enter the command **recover database until change 9999;** and receive feedback from Oracle similar to when you started complete recovery.

4. Enter the word **auto** in response to Oracle's suggestion for the first archived redo log. Oracle stops recovery before it looks for arch_387.arc and informs you of the following:

```
ORA-00289: Suggestion : /oracle/book/arclogs/arch_387.arc
ORA-00280: Change 9999 for thread 1 is in sequence #387
ORA-00278: Logfile '/oracle/book/arclogs/arch_386.arc' no...
Log applied.
Media recovery complete.
SVRMGR>
```

The final step in this recovery exercise is to open the database. After we have covered all three incomplete recovery types, we will show you how to open the database in the section called "Opening the Database after Incomplete Media Recovery."

Cancel-Based Recovery

Cancel-based recovery proceeds until you enter the word **cancel** to a prompt Oracle gives you suggesting the name of an archived redo log. So far in our discussions, you have seen the following prompt from Oracle:

```
Specify log: {<RET>=suggested | filename | AUTO | CANCEL}
```

Using the **cancel** option as the prompt suggests, let's do our recovery again. You are logged into Server Manager and have issued **connect internal** then **startup mount**. When you enter the command **recover database until cancel;**, Oracle suggests the name of the first archived redo log it requires. Press the ENTER key to accept the name, and keep going until Oracle asks for log with the sequence number 387. Enter the word **cancel**, and recovery stops, as Oracle tells you the following:

```
ORA-00289: Suggestion : /oracle/book/arclogs/arch_387.arc
ORA-00278: Logfile '/oracle/book/arclogs/arch_386.arc' no...
Specify log: {<RET>=suggested | filename | AUTO | CANCEL}
cancel
Media recovery cancelled.
```

Again, the final step in this recovery exercise is to open the database, which we will cover in the "Opening the Database after Incomplete Media Recovery" section following our discussion of all three incomplete recovery types.

Time-Based Recovery

To use time-based recovery, you need to know the time recorded in v$log_history for archived redo log sequence 387 (the missing redo log). By issuing the query **select time from v$log_history where sequence# = 387;**, you get the following time:

```
TIME
------------------
12/21/95 14:42:04
```

Let's do the recovery now. You are logged into Server Manager and have issued **connect internal** then **startup mount**. When you enter the command **recover database until time '1995/12/21:14:42:04';**, Oracle suggests the name of the first archived redo log it requires. Enter the reply **auto** and Oracle applies archived redo logs until the sequence number 387. You are then told the following:

```
ORA-00280: Change 9999 for thread 1 is in sequence #387
ORA-00278: Logfile '/oracle/book/arclogs/arch_386.arc' no...
Log applied.
Media recovery complete.
```

VIP

When using time-based recovery, the format for the time is YYYY/MM/DD:HH24:MI:SS and it is enclosed in single quotes.

Opening the Database after Incomplete Media Recovery

Before we tell you how to do this, we need to go over some pseudo-legal stuff. The command we are about to show you must **NEVER BE RUN AGAINST ANY DATABASE (OTHER THAN YOUR PRACTICE DATABASE) WITHOUT SPEAKING WITH ORACLE WORLDWIDE CUSTOMER SUPPORT**. Issuing this command against a database after incomplete media recovery will allow you to open the database, however, **THE BACKUP YOU RECOVERED FROM WILL NOT BE USABLE**. If you attempt a recovery again using the same image backup, you will receive the following error:

```
ORA-00283: Recovery session canceled due to errors
ORA-01190: control file or data file 1 is...RESETLOGS
ORA-01110: data file 1: '/oracle/book/dbs1book.dbf'
SVRMGR>
```

The problem is that Oracle knows when the database was last opened with the **resetlogs** option, and any backups written before that time are unusable. We cannot stress this enough. The command **alter database open resetlogs;** is used to get a database open, but it can be very dangerous.

VIP
Do not use the command **alter database open resetlogs;** without speaking with Oracle worldwide customer support FIRST!

You have been warned.

A Complete Backup Plan

We now present an example backup plan, using a combination of export and image backup. The database is running in ARCHIVELOG mode and the window of opportunity is about two hours.

Even though the makeup of the database is fairly static, we use the following SQL and PL/SQL script to write the program to do the hot backup (the **bolded** text may have to be changed if your operating system is other than UNIX):

```
set serveroutput on size 10000
set echo off feed off pages 0
spool hot.backup
select 'File created '||to_char(sysdate,'dd-Mon-yy hh24:mm:ss')
  from dual;
prompt
begin
  declare
    target_dir varchar2(100) := '/data/oracle/bkp/prd/backups';
    source_file varchar2(100);
    ts_name varchar2(100);
    prev_ts_name varchar2(100);
    cursor mycur is
      select file_name,lower(tablespace_name)
        from sys.dba_data_files
        where instr(file_name,'temp') = 0
        order by 2;
  begin
    prev_ts_name := 'X';
    open mycur;
```

```
    fetch mycur into source_file,ts_name;
    while mycur%found loop
        if ts_name <> prev_ts_name then
            dbms_output.put_line ('#######################');
            dbms_output.put_line ('# Tablespace '||ts_name||'. . .');
            dbms_output.put_line ('#######################');
            dbms_output.put_line ('sqlplus '||
            '@/data/oracle/bkp/prd/start.sql '||
                                        ts_name);
        end if;
        dbms_output.put_line ('cp '||source_file||' '||target_dir);
        prev_ts_name := ts_name;
        fetch mycur into source_file,ts_name;
        if ts_name <> prev_ts_name then
            dbms_output.put_line ('sqlplus '||
            '@/data/oracle/bkp/prd/end.sql '||
                                        prev_ts_name);
        end if;
    end loop;
    dbms_output.put_line ('sqlplus @/data/oracle/bkp/prd/end.sql '||
                            prev_ts_name);
    end;
end;
/
```

The program **start.sql** referenced in this listing puts a tablespace in backup mode. It contains the code:

```
alter tablespace &1 begin backup;
exit
```

The program **end.sql** takes a tablespace out of backup mode. It contains the code:

```
alter tablespace &1 end backup;
exit
```

 NOTE
The &1 text in start.sql and end.sql allow passing of a parameter to each program. Since you place a tablespace name after **alter tablespace**, the &1 would translate to a tablespace name.

In the "Substitution Variables in SQL*Plus" section of Chapter 11, we showed how the & character is used. By placing the &1 substitution variable in a SQL*Plus program, you can pass a value to a program. Thus, the command **sqlplus @start system** is expanded into the following:

```
SQL> alter tablespace &1 begin backup;
old    1: alter tablespace &1 begin backup;
new    1: alter tablespace system begin backup;
SQL>
```

Notice how the text **system** from the command **sqlplus @start system** is accepted into the program, and replaces the substitution variable &1.

The complete backup plan we have presented here is to be used as a starting point. As you can see by examining Table 15-7, export, import, and hot backups play a role when developing a full backup strategy. Backup and recovery are two of the most popular topics at Oracle technical conferences. Users and Oracle Corporation personnel present papers and lead workshops on these ever so important topics.

Personal Oracle7

We now move on to Personal Oracle7. Since you are the manager of your own PC, it is your responsibility to ensure you have enough disk space to accommodate backups. We discuss Personal Oracle7 import and export in Chapter 14. They are invoked from the Export or Import icons in the Personal Oracle7 group in the Program Manager. One of the options for import and export in Personal Oracle7 allows you to perform a full database export and import. We will show you how to do an image backup and recovery from that image in the next two sections.

VIP
The Personal Oracle7 database should be shut down before doing an image backup. Use the database manager then the Shutdown button to close the database beforehand.

Backup Using Personal Oracle7

Doing an image backup using Personal Oracle7 is much the same as we have discussed elsewhere in this chapter. All the datafiles, control files, and redo logs are copied to a location on your hard disk while the Personal Oracle7 database is closed.

As the backup runs from Personal Oracle7, it updates a file called vsbackup.ini that Oracle uses later to identify which files belong to which backup. Oracle names the files as it copies them, so it can identify which files belong to which

	COMPONENT	TIME	NOTES
1	Export	2:00 A.M.	Full database export from the SYSTEM account
2	Hot backup	3:30 A.M.	Same as the 12:05 P.M. and 8:00 P.M. backups, except all archived redo logs are moved to another directory
3	Tape copy	5:00 A.M.	Image backup is written to tape as well as the directory to which the archived redo logs were moved at 3:30 A.M.
4	Control file	6:30 A.M.	Control file contents are written to a trace file using the command **alter system backup controlfile to trace;**
5	Export	7:30 A.M.	Full database export with **rows=n compress=n** whose output can be used to create the structure of the database (i.e., the tablespaces, rollback segments, users, etc.)
6	Hot backup	12:05 P.M.	All tablespaces in the database except temp and ones containing objects protected by the nightly export
7	Hot backup	8:00 P.M.	Same as 12:05 P.M. hot backup

TABLE 15-7. *Full Backup Procedures*

backup. For example, when a backup starts, Oracle looks in the directory you specify and builds filenames that start with "tbsp" for tablespaces, "olog" for redo logs, and "cntl" for control files. It builds the file extensions based on how many backups have been performed. For example, if you have three generations of backup files on your disk that have used file extensions 001 through 003, Oracle would use the filename extension 004 to identify the members of the latest backup set.

VIP
You must monitor the disk space consumed by Oracle's backup files on your PC. If necessary, some of the older backup files should be erased or moved offline to tape or diskette.

To perform this type of backup, follow these steps:

1. Click on the Backup Manager icon in the Windows program manager. You are presented with the Backup Manager Logon dialog box, in which you enter the Personal Oracle7 secure database password (usually **oracle** unless you have changed it).

2. You are presented with the Oracle Backup Manager dialog box, shown in Figure 15-1. Click on Files to select the files you wish to backup. To begin the backup, click on Backup.

3. Oracle shows the status of your backup as it is running. When the backup completes, click on OK in the completion dialog box to return to the Backup Manager dialog box. Then click on Close to return to the Personal Oracle7 group.

In Figure 15-1, notice how Oracle fills in the Directory text box for the backup, though you can change it by entering a different directory name beside Directory, or you can click on Browse and select another directory. You are told at the bottom of the screen how much space is required for the backup. Since the database is in NOARCHIVELOG mode, the Backup Type indicates "Offline - Full Database." As the backup runs, Oracle tells you what it is copying, and the name of the file to which the backup is written.

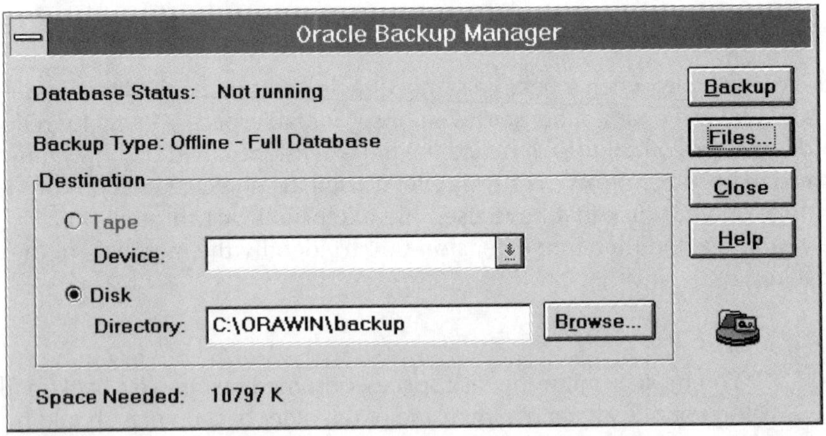

FIGURE 15-1. *Personal Oracle7 Backup Manager dialog box*

Recovery Using Personal Oracle7

Recovery using Personal Oracle7 is similar to our discussions on recovery elsewhere in this chapter. We will show you how to recover from the full database backup you created using the Backup Manager in the previous section. To perform recovery, follow these steps:

1. Click on the Recovery Manager icon in the Windows program manager. You are presented with the Oracle Recovery Manager dialog box, as shown in Figure 15-2.

You are presented with four recovery options. Automatic recovery starts the database and applies any required information from the set of online redo logs. The Restore from full database backup option allows you to specify the backup from which you want a full restore to be done. The Restore datafile, then do recovery option is available on this screen, but if you select this option you will receive the message shown in Figure 15-3, since the database is in NOARCHIVELOG mode. The Restore control file, then do recovery option allows you to bring back online a backup of a control file, then perform recovery using that control file.

2. Click on Restore from full database backup, then click on Recover to bring up the Full Database Restoration dialog box, shown in Figure 15-4.

3. If you want to restore the latest backup, click on OK. If you want an earlier backup, click on the Backup drop-down list for a list of available backups,

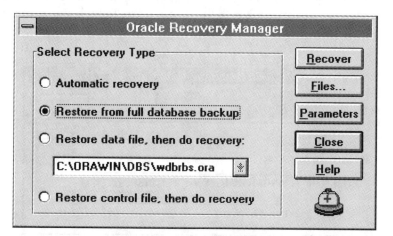

FIGURE 15-2. *Personal Oracle7 Recovery Manager dialog box*

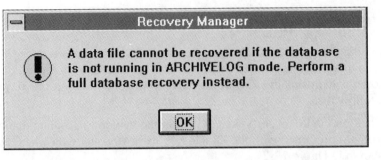

FIGURE 15-3. *Restore datafile error message*

as shown in Figure 15-5. Choose the backup you want, then click on OK to start the recovery.

4. Oracle shows the status of your restore as it is running. When the recovery is complete, click on OK in the recovery completion dialog box to return to the Recovery Manager dialog box. Click on Close to return to the Personal Oracle7 group.

The next time you open your database, it will be in the same condition as when it was backed up. Say it's 1:00 P.M. on January 25. Knowing you have some intricate work to do, you make a backup of your Personal Oracle7 database in case something goes wrong. You do the work, and then on January 30, you discover there is something seriously wrong with the data. You try to fix it, and it gets even

FIGURE 15-4. *Full Database Restoration dialog box*

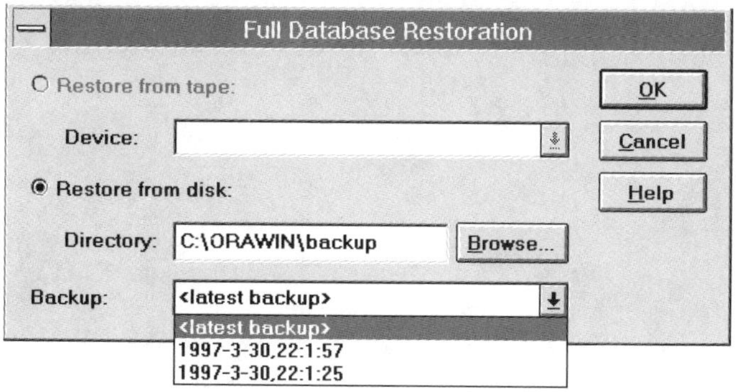

FIGURE 15-5. *List of available backups to restore from*

worse. At that point, you can restore the full backup made on January 25 at 1:00 P.M., fix the problems that messed up your data, then proceed to do the work again.

What's Next

Perhaps you have noticed the amount of ground we have covered in this chapter. We believe that with guidance you can start doing some remarkably intense work with Oracle from day one as a DBA. This is the third chapter in our "So You're the New DBA" section. In the next chapter, we will discuss tuning the Oracle database to help you get the maximum performance from this robust software.

CHAPTER 16

Database Tuning

This chapter deals with tuning your database, not your applications. We will discuss the major items that will allow you, as a database administrator, to get an extra 20 to 30 percent throughput from your Oracle-based systems.

But first, let's discuss what database tuning cannot do. It is not a substitute for good application design—remember that old saying, "Garbage in leads to garbage out." A system that is designed badly will perform badly. The bottom line: good performance out of your database starts with good application design. With this in mind, we will take a look at the key steps you can take to get that extra boost of performance from your system.

In this chapter we will cover the following subjects:

- The initialization parameter file init.ora
- How to determine current initialization parameter file settings
- How to change the current initialization file settings
- Which key initialization file settings to change
- The key input/output stream
- Key tablespaces and their contents
- How indexes work

Terminology

The following definitions will arm you with the technical jargon to make it through this chapter.

- A *database administrator,* or DBA, is responsible for the technical management of a database, including installation, performance tuning, and computer resource management. The DBA classically serves as an advisor on application design to maximize system throughput.

- The *initialization parameter file* (commonly called init.ora) is read by Oracle when starting the database; its values help determine resource utilization. The best analogy to this is your win.ini file in Windows or your autoexec.bat file when you boot your PC.

- A *database instance* is an amount of main memory and a set of support processes required to access an Oracle database.

- *sqldba* is a tool used by database administrators to go about their day-to-day work with an Oracle database. It has been discussed in detail in Chapters 13 and 17.

- A *cache* is a segment of computer memory allocated to holding specific pieces of information. For example, while Oracle operates, it maintains a data cache that contains most recently read data.

- A *table* is defined in Oracle's data dictionary, and it groups rows of information together in the database. A list of your fellow workers' names, numbers, and hire dates is an example of a table.

- An *index* is a structure Oracle uses to permit rapid access to your tables.

Initialization Parameter (init.ora) File

There are many tools available to you for tuning the database; the initialization parameter file is a good place to start. At startup, every database reads its initialization parameter to configure itself. Think of this file as the key to a lock. Before you can enter the room, you must first use the key. Before a database instance can start up, it must read the initialization parameter file. There are over one hundred different changeable entries, all affecting how your database and processes that run against your database work. By making changes to this file, you will change the way your database uses and allocates resources.

VIP

All changes you make to the initialization parameter file only take effect the next time the database is started.

Viewing Initialization Parameter File Settings

Before you begin making changes to the initialization parameter file, it is important you know how the parameters are currently set. The simplest way to see how the entries are set is to use line-mode sqldba. As discussed in Chapter 13, sqldba is a standard utility that Oracle supplies you with to assist with the management of the database.

Invoking

We use line-mode sqldba, since it supports all terminal types. The command **sqldba lmode=y** starts line-mode sqldba and displays the following output:

```
SQL*DBA: Release 7.1.4.0 - Production on Tue Dec 11 12:34:20 1995
Copyright (c) Oracle Corporation 1979, 1994.  All rights reserved.
Oracle7 Server Release 7.1.4.0 - Production Release
PL/SQL Release 2.1.4.1 - Production
SQLDBA>
```

Connect Internal

You are now positioned at the sqldba line-mode prompt. Use the **connect** command to log onto the database. In this example, we use the Oracle account **internal**. We could have used SYS, SYSTEM, or any other Oracle account. After the command executes, Oracle responds:

```
Connected.
SQLDBA>
```

Full Parameter Listing

Now that you are logged onto the database, you have a number of sqldba commands available to you. The command **show parameters** will display all the possible entries and values in the initialization parameter file. The parameters are listed in alphabetical order, and the top of the output resembles the following:

```
NAME                       TYPE              VALUE
--------------------       ---------------   ------------------
audit_trail                string            NONE
background_dump_dest       string            %RDBMS71%\trace
checkpoint_process         boolean           FALSE
cleanup_rollback_entries   integer           20
commit_point_strength      integer           1
```

Partial Parameter Listing

Often, you are only interested in a particular type of parameter. For example, you might be interested in all the parameters that contain the word "buffer." In sqldba, when you type **show parameters** followed by another word, it will do a character match on the word. For example, to see all the parameters that contain the word "buffer" you type the command **show parameters buffer** and receive output similar to the following:

```
NAME                       TYPE              VALUE
--------------------       ---------------   ------------------
db_block_buffers           integer           400
log_archive_buffer_size    integer           127
log_archive_buffers        integer           4
log_buffer                 integer           65596
```

Current Size of the SGA

As you make changes to the initialization parameter file, the changes affect how the database uses resources. One of the things you realize early on in the tuning process is that tuning is all about trade-offs. The more memory Oracle uses, the less memory is available for other processes. Many of the changes to the initialization parameter file affect the size of the SGA and how much memory the current database needs to operate. The command **show sga** tells you the current allocation of memory for the database.

```
Total System Global Area    4817701 bytes
Fixed Size                    28376 bytes
Variable Size               3904532 bytes
Database Buffers             819200 bytes
Redo Buffers                  65596 bytes
```

VIP
The Oracle database is one of many processes that must live, share, and breathe all available resources. With this in mind, the SGA should never take over 50 percent of the available memory of the computer.

Spooling Results

Many times you will find it helpful to spool the results of your sqldba session. We find it especially helpful to capture the output of the **show parameters** command; you can then use this output for your first attempt at customizing an initialization parameter file. By using the captured output as a starting point, you eliminate "fat fingers" (typos).

VIP
A misspelled entry in the initialization parameter file will prevent the database from starting up.

To start recording your actions while in sqldba, do the following:

1. Enter the command **spool file_name** where the filename conforms to the rules of your computer, and receive the following feedback from Oracle.

```
File example.log opened Sat Dec 01 23:04:08 1996.
SQLDBA>
```

2. Go about your jobs in sqldba, then close the file by entering **spool off** and receive the following feedback from Oracle.

```
File example.log closed Sat Dec 01 23:04:20 1996.
SQLDBA>
```

This is the output from the **show sga** command spooled to "example.log":

```
SQLDBA> show sga
Total System Global Area      4767460 bytes
             Fixed Size         36432 bytes
          Variable Size       3846292 bytes
       Database Buffers        819200 bytes
           Redo Buffers         65536 bytes
SQLDBA> spool off
```

Changing Values in the Initialization Parameter File

The initialization parameter file is like any another text file on your computer—pick your favorite editor and make the changes. The order of the entries within the initialization parameter file does not matter.

VIP
If you do not have an entry listed in your initialization parameter file, Oracle configures the missing value to a default setting.

There are three types of initialization parameter file entries:

- Strings: A number of parameters are enclosed in single quotes, some in double quotes, and some need not be in any quotes. Most of the string parameter values you enter will need no quotes. If one requires quotes of either type and you leave them out, Oracle will inform you when you start the database.

- Integer: Some parameters are looking for an integer. There are no quotes.

- Boolean: Some parameters are looking for the value TRUE or FALSE with no quotes.

With this in mind, we now give you an example of each type of entry. We include db_block_buffers (integer type), db_name (string type) and checkpoint_process (Boolean type).

```
db_block_buffers=800
db_name='prod'
checkpoint_process=true
```

It all sounds so simple. Take your favorite editor, change the entry, and you are on your way. Well, almost. Here are the pitfalls:

- Fat fingers (also called typos): If you make one, the entire initialization parameter file is rejected. In other words, your database won't start until the typo is corrected.

- Domino effect: In some situations, a change to one parameter affects other parameters.

VIP
Changing parameter values in the initialization parameter file is no trivial exercise. Look at the effect changes may have on other parameters, and make changes with caution.

With all this in mind, one word describes how you should proceed: **s l o w l y**. Tuning a database takes time. At first, it is best if you make one change at a time. Edit the file, then try to start the database. This way, if you have made a typo, you at least know which entry is causing the database not to start. As you will see, Oracle is not always very gracious in telling you where the problem is. Use sqldba and issue the **show parameters** command to see what changes have occurred. Try to develop your own checklist to help you determine if your changes are improving performance. We refer you to *Tuning Oracle* by Corey, Abbey, and Dechichio (Osborne McGraw-Hill/Oracle Press, 1995) for details on how to tune your database.

Initialization Parameter File—What to Change

In this section, we list the key parameters you should consider tweaking. In our experience, these are the parameters that need changing 99 percent of the time.

db_block_buffers
This is your data cache. Before any process can look at, inspect, correct, or delete a piece of data, it must first reside in this data cache. The higher the value of the cache, the more data blocks Oracle is able to hold in memory. The lower the value, the fewer data blocks it can hold. If the data is not in memory, Oracle issues the needed I/O requests to obtain the data. I/O is one of the slowest operations a computer can do.

To summarize, the larger the number you choose for db_block_buffers, the larger your data cache. A large data cache is a very desirable situation. In fact, in a perfect world, you might want to make your db_block_buffers large enough to hold your entire database. In this situation, the need to go to the actual disk might be eliminated.

VIP
Set the db_block_buffers as high as possible for your operating environment in order to hold as much data in memory as possible.

This parameter is a memory hog. It very quickly increases the size of the SGA. Do not allow the SGA to go beyond 50 percent of the available memory of the computer.

shared_pool_size

This is your program cache and data dictionary cache. The data dictionary is information that Oracle needs to manage itself. For example, when a user logs into the database, a number of data dictionary tables are referenced to determine the validity of the user's request to log onto the database. Before that user can look at a row of information, a number of data dictionary tables are referenced to determine that database user's privileges. The program cache is where Oracle stores programs that work with the database. For example, every SQL statement you run in SQL*Plus must be placed into the program cache before it can be executed. The larger the cache, the more likely your statement will be found in memory. The smaller the cache, the more often Oracle has to place the program into memory. A program cannot make requests from the database until it has been placed into this cache.

VIP

Set the shared_pool_size as high as possible. It is very desirable for performance reasons to have a program cache that is very large.

Again, this parameter is a memory hog. It very quickly increases the size of the SGA. Do not allow the SGA to go beyond 50 percent of the available memory of the computer.

sort_area_size

This is the parameter that controls the allocation of chunks of memory for sorting activities. SQL statements that include the **order by** and **group by** clause generate sort activity. In addition, activities like **create index** also generate sort activity.

When the Oracle database cannot acquire enough memory to complete the sort, it completes the process on disk. An inadequate value for this parameter causes excessive sorts on disk (disk access is very slow compared to memory access).

It has been our experience that the default setting is too low. We typically start off by doubling it.

VIP

Try doubling your sort_area_size parameter value. The default value is much too small.

The value coded for sort_area_size is allocated on a per-user basis. It does not take effect until you restart the database.

checkpoint_process

A checkpoint is an event that happens periodically when the Oracle database writes information from its buffers in memory to the appropriate database files. Refer to the discussion on checkpoints in the "Database Support Processes" section of Chapter 2 for more information. When this event happens, an area in the datafiles is updated to record the event. The writing of this information is done by the log writer (lgwr) or a dedicated checkpoint (ckpt) process.

If the initialization parameter file parameter checkpoint_process is set to FALSE, the checkpoint event is done by the log writer. On systems with a heavy transaction load, having the log writer have the additional job of checkpointing the database may slow down or halt processing momentarily. Setting the checkpoint_process to TRUE instructs Oracle to activate an additional process, whose sole responsibility is to handle checkpoints. It's like being given an additional set of hands. In our experience, there is no down side to activating the checkpoint_process.

VIP
Activate the checkpoint_process by setting its initialization parameter file value to TRUE.

processes

This parameter defines the maximum number of processes that can simultaneously connect to an Oracle database. The default value of 50 is only acceptable for a very small system. Keep in mind that the Oracle background processes are included in this number. In addition, if an application spawns processes recursively, all the spawned processes count toward this number.

The only reason you keep this value low is to limit the number of users for a business reason or because of hardware/software capacity issues. Otherwise, it is highly recommended that you overestimate this value.

open_cursors

This parameter is the maximum number of cursors a user can have open at a time. Think of a cursor as a chunk of memory that Oracle allocates to the user process for SQL statements. The default value for this is much too small. When you run
out of cursors, your application stops. We recommend setting this value to 250 to start with.

VIP
Set this value very high to start. If it is set too low, your application will come to a stop.

db_writers

This parameter controls the number of processes that write information to the database concurrently. On many UNIX platforms, you have the option of having multiple database writers. This greatly improves your ability to write information to the database. If you are on an operating system that supports additional database writers, the first thing you should do is increase the number of database writers that are activated. Many DBAs are under the misconception that this is limited by the number of CPUs; this is not true. In fact, we recommend you set db_writers to two per datafile.

VIP

If you are on an operating system that supports additional database writers, the first thing you should do is increase the number of database writers.

timed_statistics

This parameter tells the database to record additional information about itself as it is running. This is quite useful information in a test environment; in a production environment, we recommend you turn it off. Since this is additional overhead, it has a performance impact on your system.

optimizer_mode

This parameter has a major impact on how your database chooses to execute SQL statements. You have four possible choices for this parameter:

- FULL_ROWS or ALL_ROWS: These two modes instruct Oracle to use the cost-based optimizer approach (discussed as well in the "Cost-Based Approach" section of Chapter 12). With this setting, Oracle takes into account table sizes when you issue SQL statements. For example, your database knows that your customer table has 10,000 rows of information, and your phone_type table has three rows. It takes this into account when executing SQL statements.

- RULE: This is the way Oracle databases have traditionally determined how SQL statements would execute. There is a weighting system that Oracle uses to determine how a SQL statement will execute. For example, a table that contains an index will be favored over a table that has no indexes.

- CHOOSE: This is the default setting. This tells the database to use the cost-based optimization approach when you have the necessary information. Without that information, use the rule-based method.

Approach to Use for Existing Systems   Stick with the rule-based approach. It's been around for many years. Many legacy systems have been tuned to work best under this method. The cost-based approach is a drastic change in optimization; many clients discover a significant drop in system performance after they suddenly switch over to cost-based. Imagine an application with a customer table containing 1,000 rows. A few weeks later, you migrate a legacy system, and in the process add another 2,000 rows to the customer table. Until you analyze the customer table, Oracle's cost-based optimizer still thinks it has 1,000 rows. This would cause problems.

VIP

For systems that were designed and tuned using the rule-based approach, set **optimizer_mode=rule** in your initialization parameter file.

Approach to Use for New Systems   Experiment with the cost-based approach. Investigate using hints when examining this approach. Hints are just that—they are placed in the middle of SQL statements and, even when the rule-based optimizer is the default, instruct Oracle on how to optimize using cost-based. Consult Chapter 7 in *Tuning Oracle* by Corey, Abbey, and Dechichio (Osborne McGraw-Hill/Oracle Press, 1995) for a discussion of using hints.

VIP

Use the rule-based optimizer mode until you feel comfortable with how the cost-based optimizer will work.

I/O Stream

What is a database? A database is a place where information is organized, received, and dispensed. A disk drive is the physical location where a database holds information. To take this one step further, the major task of a database is to read and write data to the disks. The problem you face is that I/O (input/output) from a disk drive is slow. In fact, it is one of the slowest operations a computer can do. Even though CPUs keep getting faster and faster by comparison, I/O has not kept up the pace. Let's now take a look at some things you can do to minimize your I/O.

Tables and Indexes

All the data you place in an Oracle database is stored in an object called a table. Whenever a request is made to the database to read or write information, a record is read from a table or inserted into a table. There is another database object called an index (we also discuss indexes in the "Data and Index Tablespace" section of Chapter 2). As we explained earlier, an index is used to speed up access to particular columns of information in a table. Think of an index as a mini-table. For example, let's say you create an index on the customer table on the column last_name.

There are two major reasons why index access is faster:

■ When you read a record from a table, you must read in every column of information associated with that table. If you had a very large customer table with 300 fields associated with it, even though you just want the last_name column, you are forced into the additional overhead of reading every column of the table. For example, a concatenated index on last_name, first_name only contains two columns. It is faster to read two columns than 300 columns.

■ Indexes are in presorted order. While data in an Oracle table is stored in the order it was loaded, data in an Oracle index is stored in a sorted order. This is part of the requirement of an index.

There are two major things you can do to improve your database's ability to access data. The first is to properly index your tables. In the long run, this will have the greatest impact on performance. The second is to make sure your tables and indexes are stored on separate physical devices. We recommend you create a separate tablespace to hold tables. In addition, you should create another tablespace to hold indexes.

VIP
Put tables on a separate disk from their indexes.

This point is important even if you have a limited number of disks at your disposal (i.e., one to three). Separating tables from their indexes allows for quicker access, since reading and writing to the index and the table may happen simultaneously.

VIP
Large tables in your database should have at least one index on them.

When we say "large," we mean tables with anything over 1,000 rows; our experience dictates that over 90 percent of the tables in an Oracle database are indexed.

VIP
Create separate tablespaces to hold data and indexes.

System Tables

Before an Oracle application can even look at a table or its contents, it must first talk to the Oracle data dictionary. The data dictionary contains information as to what is stored in the database, where it is stored, and who has the privilege to look at it. The tables and database objects that make up the Oracle data dictionary are owned by a database user called SYS. They are stored in a tablespace called system. This is a major I/O stream for the database. In a perfect world, you would place the system tablespace on its own disk drive.

VIP
Do not allow other users to place database objects in the system tablespace.

Temporary Segments

Temporary segments are objects the database periodically creates to help it finish transactions. For example, when you issue a SQL statement with a **group by** clause, the database will likely create some temporary objects to help it in its work. It is very important that you keep temporary objects in their own tablespace. By doing so, you will eliminate the performance problems associated with having temporary segments mixed with other database objects.

VIP
Create a separate tablespace to hold temporary segments.

Rollback Segments

A rollback segment is a database object that holds information when a user does an insert, update, or delete. This rollback information is recorded so that the database can undo or rollback the transaction in the case of failure. Since all transactions are not equal in size, these rollback segments have a tendency to grow and shrink. It is very important that you create a separate tablespace to hold your rollback segments.

VIP
Create a separate tablespace for your rollback segments.

Online Redo Logs

The online redo logs are your transaction logs. Every action that occurs in an Oracle database is recorded into these special files called online redo logs (discussed as well in the "Redo Logs—the Transaction Logs" section of Chapter 2). Since I/O is a very slow operation, it is strongly recommended you place these on a separate physical device.

VIP
Place online redo logs on a separate disk.

Summary

I/O is one of the slowest operations a computer can do. However, it is also one of the most important operations. In a perfect world, you would place every tablespace in a database on a separate disk drive. We don't live in a perfect world, but you should still create these separate tablespaces even if they are on the same disk. Then, utilizing the tools available to you within Oracle and the operating system, balance the I/O load as best you can. If over time you are able to obtain an additional disk drive, then you are ready for them.

Personal Oracle7

Most of what we have said so far in this chapter is applicable to Oracle regardless of the size or type of computer. However, working with the initialization parameter file with Personal Oracle7 is a little different. There is line-mode sqldba with this product; however, you may choose to work with the initialization parameter file as discussed in the next two sections.

Viewing Initialization Parameter File Values

You can view the initialization parameter file from the database manager in the Personal Oracle7 group in the Program Manager. You may wish to view the Personal Oracle7 initialization parameter file before working with one on a bigger machine. To view the current settings, do the following:

1. Click on the Database Manager icon in the Personal Oracle7 group in the Windows Program Manager. The Oracle Database Manager dialog box appears as shown in **Figure 16-1**.

2. Click on Configure to access the Configure Initialization Parameters dialog box.

3. Click on Advanced, then OK in the confirmation box that appears as shown in **Figure 16-2**.

4. Look up the value of any parameter (whether or not it is set in the initialization parameter file) by looking through the Parameter drop-down list and double-clicking on the desired entry. Oracle retrieves the parameter's current value into the Value area.

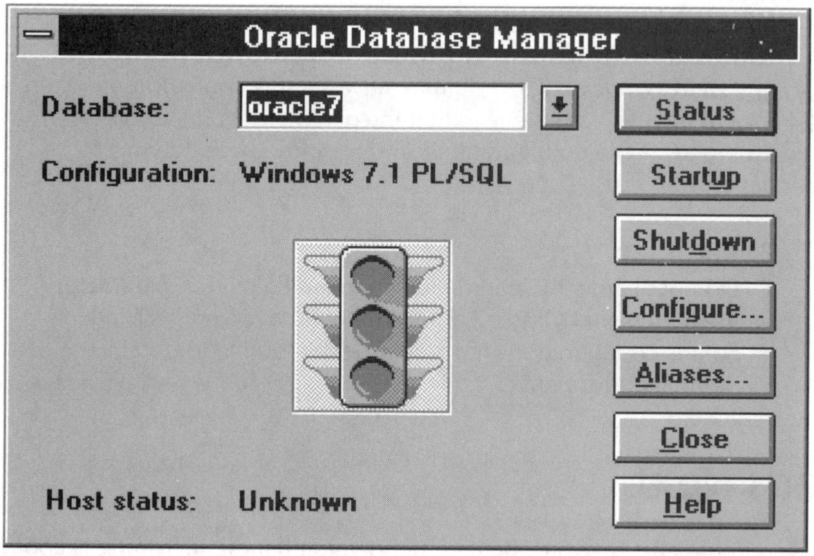

FIGURE 16-1. *Oracle Database Manager dialog box in Personal Oracle7*

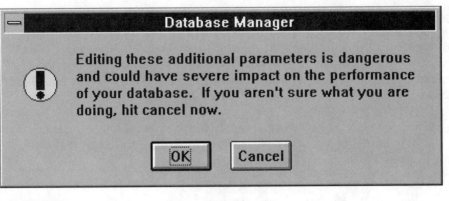

FIGURE 16-2. *Confirming advanced configuration setup*

5. To see the values of parameters set in your initialization parameter file, scroll through the Set Values area on the screen.

Changing Initialization Parameter File Values

As the message in Figure 16-2 suggests, changing values in the initialization parameter file is not recommended unless you know what you are doing. Oracle delivers a number of configurations for Personal Oracle7: NetWare 7.1, NT 7.0 or 7.1, Solaris 7.1, and Windows 7.1. You may have set this configuration when you installed Personal Oracle7. We believe that the parameter values have been fine-tuned for the available configurations, and we offer the following recommendation.

VIP
Do not change the parameters in the initialization parameter file in Personal Oracle7. The Windows, NetWare, NT, and Solaris configurations have been set by Oracle to obtain optimal performance.

What's Next

Tuning is a double-edged sword. Be careful how you handle it. Tuning is about choices. Each choice has its good points and its bad points. If you increase db_block_buffers to expand the data cache, then you are able to hold more data in memory. On the other hand, the system now has less free memory to do its own work. So as you go down the tuning path, you will constantly have forks in the road to consider.

We have introduced you to the two major areas of database tuning: the initialization parameter file and tuning the I/O stream. We talked about the most common items to change in the initialization parameter file. In the "I/O Stream" section, we stressed the fact that I/O is slow. We encouraged you to look closely at indexes and a standard strategy for laying out your database. Now it's up to you. Tune slowly. The tortoise wins this race every time.

Our next chapter, "Advanced DBA," will prove helpful to your expanding knowledge of the Oracle database. We guide you through some advanced tasks you will be responsible for as a DBA and show you how to . . . better still, keep reading!

CHAPTER 17

Advanced DBA

Perhaps, up until now, you have been quite content *not* being a DBA. Somebody stole the DBA and, guess what, you are the new DBA! In Chapter 13, we pointed you in the right direction. We showed you how to do some DBA stuff you will be asked to do from day one (if not sooner). We discussed and walked you through how to start the database, shut down the database, create a tablespace to hold Oracle data, add more space to a tablespace, grant access to a user, and revoke access from a user.

Database administration is pretty much the same regardless of the hardware you are using—Windows 3.1 on a Pentium, an Amdahl mainframe, or a VAX. Oracle releases port-specific documentation that highlights the differences you can expect to run across on different hardware platforms. These manuals are referred to as the port-specific *System Release Bulletin* (SRB) and *Installation and Configuration Guide* (ICG). There is a wealth of information on everything discussed in this chapter in the *Oracle7 Server Administrator's Guide*. Database tuning and installation are two DBA responsibilities that are not discussed in this chapter; they are highlighted in Chapters 3 and 16. By the end of this chapter, you will know more terminology as well as some advanced details on how to do the following:

- Start up the database
- Perform additional user management
- Perform additional tablespace management
- Manage redo log file groups
- Add control files
- Drop control files
- Find your way around the data dictionary
- Classify error messages
- Work with Oracle Corporation's Worldwide Customer Support

In Chapter 13, we showed you how to use sqldba and Server Manager to perform the basic DBA activities. In this chapter, we will concentrate on full-screen sqldba (we will just use the term sqldba rather than full-screen sqldba). There are two interfaces in sqldba:

- The dual window facility: the bottom third of the screen is where you enter SQL commands and the top two-thirds is where Oracle displays then responds to commands.
- The menu dialog box facility: you use the top menu bar with drop-down menus to present boxes that you fill in with SQL statement details.

In this chapter, we will use the dual-window approach—we feel you can learn more by rolling your sleeves up and typing SQL commands manually.

NOTE
You may find that using the dual-window method is many times faster than the menu/dialog box approach.

Terminology

The following definitions will arm you with the technical jargon to make it through this chapter.

■ The *archiving status* of the database controls what Oracle does with redo log files before it reuses them. When this status is ARCHIVELOG, Oracle automatically copies a redo log file to a destination you specify before it is reused. When the status is NOARCHIVELOG, Oracle does not save a copy of each redo log file before it is reused. This is discussed in more detail in Chapter 15.

■ A tablespace is *online* when it is accessible to all users and therefore available for storage of new objects, and for querying and modifying of data.

■ The *system tablespace* is the one that holds all the data dictionary information required to access the database. It must be online and accessible when the database is open.

■ A tablespace is *offline* when its data is unavailable for any access. An offline tablespace must be brought back online before users may access it again.

■ *Backup* is a procedure that makes a secondary copy of Oracle data (usually on tape) and helps provide protection against hardware, software, or user errors; backup minimizes data loss if and when problems arise.

■ *Recovery* is a procedure whereby data is read from a backup in an effort to restore the database to a past or current point in time.

■ *Redo logs* are written by Oracle and contain a record of all transactions against a database. They are written automatically as Oracle operates.

■ The *active redo log group* is the group to which Oracle is currently writing information. All members of the active group are written to simultaneously.

■ *Rollback* is the event that Oracle performs when, for an assortment of reasons, a transaction is not completed. The rollback restores the data to the state it was in *before* the transaction started.

■ A *rollback segment* is a portion of a tablespace that contains undo information for each transaction in the database; this undo information is kept until a transaction is committed or rolled back.

■ An *extent* is a chunk of space in a datafile of an Oracle database; it is measured in bytes, kilobytes (1,024 bytes), or megabytes (1,048,576 bytes). Extents are allocated based on keywords used when objects (e.g., tables, rollback segments) are created.

■ A database is *up* when it has been opened and is accessible to users. A database is *down* when it has been closed and is inaccessible to users.

Startup Options

Most of the time you start your database, you simply start sqldba, connect to the database, and type **startup** to get things going. In this section, we will discuss additional startup options, using these options in sqldba, and when you may need or want to use one of these options.

Startup Normal

This is the default startup mode (you almost always omit the word "normal"). We showed you how to start up the database in sqldba in Chapter 13. Use the output in Figure 17-1 as a reference point for the following discussion on startup options.

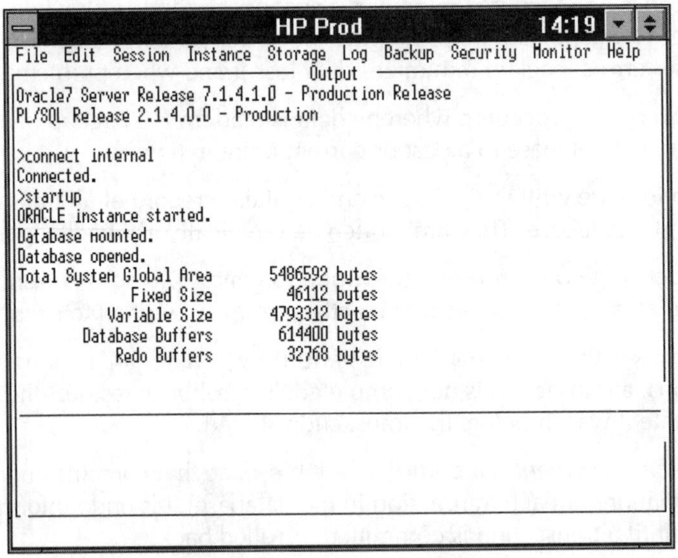

```
                         HP Prod              14:19
File  Edit  Session  Instance  Storage  Log  Backup  Security  Monitor  Help
                           Output
Oracle7 Server Release 7.1.4.1.0 - Production Release
PL/SQL Release 2.1.4.0.0 - Production

>connect internal
Connected.
>startup
ORACLE instance started.
Database mounted.
Database opened.
Total System Global Area      5486592 bytes
             Fixed Size         46112 bytes
          Variable Size       4793312 bytes
       Database Buffers        614400 bytes
           Redo Buffers         32768 bytes
```

FIGURE 17-1.   *Startup normal in sqldba*

Startup Mount

This mode is used to change the archiving status of the database or perform recovery. The database is not open, and therefore access by users is not permitted. After starting sqldba, follow these steps:

1. Enter **connect internal**.

2. Enter **startup mount.** Oracle responds with the output as shown in Figure 17-2.

3. Enter **exit** to leave sqldba.

The database is left in a mounted condition; users are not able to log on in this state. Notice in Figure 17-2 that there is no message about opening the database or the size of the system global area.

Startup Nomount

This mode is used to re-create a control file (discussed in the "Control File Responsibilities" section of this chapter) or re-create the database from scratch.

```
┌─────────────────────────────────────────────────────────────┐
│ ━          HP Prod              14:21  ▼ ◆                   │
│ File  Edit  Session  Instance  Storage  Log  Backup  Security  Monitor  Help │
│ ──────────────────── Output ────────────────────            │
│ Oracle7 Server Release 7.1.4.1.0 - Production Release        │
│ PL/SQL Release 2.1.4.0.0 - Production                        │
│                                                              │
│ >connect internal                                            │
│ Connected.                                                   │
│ >startup mount                                               │
│ ORACLE instance started.                                     │
│ Database mounted.                                            │
│                                                              │
│                                                              │
└─────────────────────────────────────────────────────────────┘
```

FIGURE 17-2. *Startup with the mount option*

The database is not open, and therefore access by users is not permitted. After starting sqldba:

1. Enter **connect internal**.

2. Enter **startup nomount.** Oracle responds with the output as shown in Figure 17-3.

3. Enter **exit** to leave sqldba.

The response from Oracle is similar to Figure 17-2, except the Database mounted message is suppressed.

Startup Restrict

This mode is used to start up the database, but access is restricted to a privileged set of users that you have defined. The output from this command is the same as shown in Figure 17-1. The database is open, but if nonprivileged users attempt to log on, they will obtain the following error message.

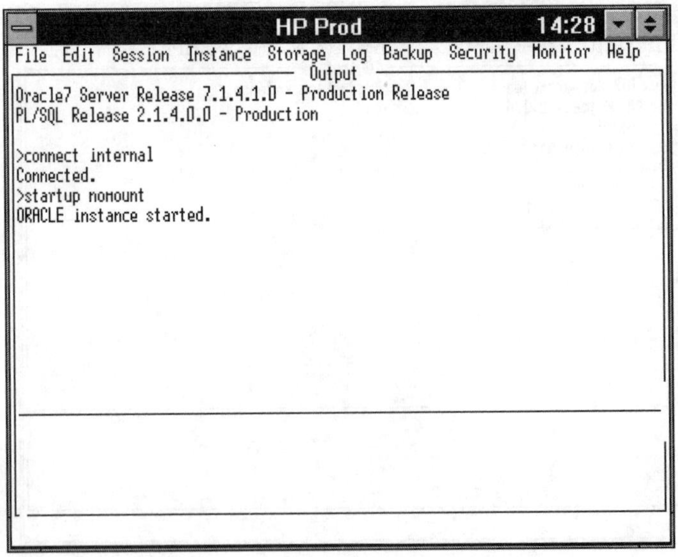

FIGURE 17-3.   *Startup with the nomount option*

```
SQL*Plus: Release 3.1.3.5.1 - Production on Tue Dec 18 22:14:09 1995
Copyright (c) Oracle Corporation 1979, 1994.  All rights reserved.
Enter password:
ERROR: ORA-01035: ORACLE only available to users with RESTRICTED SESSION privileges
Enter user-name:
```

Let's discuss changing the database access mode from restricted to unrestricted. The first is done with the database open, the other by restarting the database.

Change Status with Database Open

After entering sqldba:

1. Enter **connect internal**.

2. Enter **alter system disable restricted session;** and receive Oracle's response as shown in Figure 17-4.

3. Enter **exit** to leave sqldba.

When this is done, the database is running in unrestricted access mode and users will be able to log on once more.

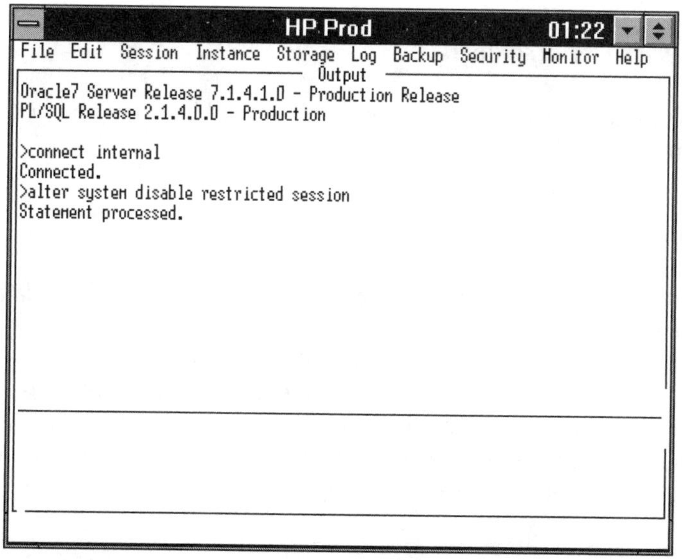

FIGURE 17-4. *Disabling restricted access*

Change Status by Restarting the Database

After entering sqldba:

1. Enter **connect internal**.

2. Enter **shutdown**.

3. Enter **startup**.

4. Enter **exit** to leave sqldba.

Regardless of the method you choose, the database will be open and ready for access by all once the steps are completed.

Startup Force

This option is used in the rare situation when you are unable to shut down a database. It shuts the database, then starts it with no options; the startup operation is the same as having issued the **startup** command alone. After starting sqldba, follow these steps:

1. Enter **connect internal**.

2. Enter **startup force.** You receive the feedback from Oracle as shown in Figure 17-5.

3. Enter **exit** to leave sqldba.

When this operation is complete, your database will be open and accessible to the user community.

Startup pfile

This option with the startup command does not affect the mode of the database operation; it defines the name and location of the initialization parameter file (pfile). As we have discussed elsewhere, the initialization parameter file is read by Oracle as it opens a database. Oracle expects the default initialization parameter file to be in a location and called a name that is dependent on the hardware on which the database operates. In Personal Oracle7, for example, Oracle builds the default initialization parameter filename using the environment variable

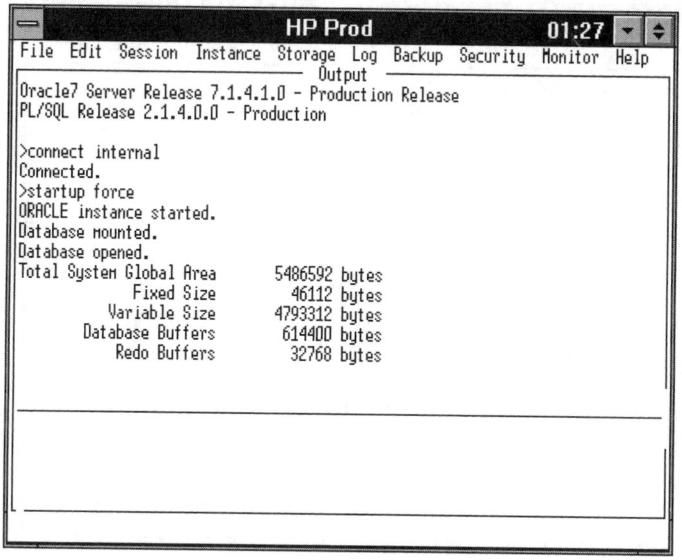

```
 ─                        HP Prod                    01:27  ▼ ▲
 File  Edit  Session  Instance  Storage  Log  Backup  Security  Monitor  Help
 ──────────────────────── Output ────────────────────────
 Oracle7 Server Release 7.1.4.1.0 - Production Release
 PL/SQL Release 2.1.4.0.0 - Production

 >connect internal
 Connected.
 >startup force
 ORACLE instance started.
 Database mounted.
 Database opened.
 Total System Global Area    5486592 bytes
                Fixed Size      46112 bytes
             Variable Size    4793312 bytes
          Database Buffers     614400 bytes
               Redo Buffers      32768 bytes
```

FIGURE 17-5.   *Startup force from sqldba*

"%RDBMS71%\" and appends the text dbaini.ora. To start a database using an initialization parameter file other than the default, follow these steps after starting sqldba:

1. Enter **connect internal**.

2. Enter the command **startup pfile=?/dbs/tstother.ora** and receive feedback from Oracle as shown in Figure 17-6. The text that follows pfile= is a directory name and filename of the initialization parameter file to be used for startup.

3. Enter **exit** to leave sqldba.

From time to time, you may use the pfile option to start your database with some initialization parameter file values different than usual. For example, when running a large data load, you may wish to instruct Oracle to allocate much more memory for sorting than you normally request.

```
┌─────────────────────────────────────────────────────────┐
│ ─          HP Prod              01:31  ▼ ▲ │
├─────────────────────────────────────────────────────────┤
│ File  Edit  Session  Instance  Storage  Log  Backup  Security  Monitor  Help │
│ ─────────────────────── Output ───────────────────────── │
│ Oracle7 Server Release 7.1.4.1.0 - Production Release     │
│ PL/SQL Release 2.1.4.0.0 - Production                     │
│                                                           │
│ >connect internal                                         │
│ Connected.                                                │
│ >startup pfile=?/dbs/tstother.ora                         │
│ ORACLE instance started.                                  │
│ Database mounted.                                         │
│ Database opened.                                          │
│ Total System Global Area    5486592 bytes                 │
│           Fixed Size          46112 bytes                 │
│        Variable Size        4793312 bytes                 │
│      Database Buffers        614400 bytes                 │
│          Redo Buffers         32768 bytes                 │
│                                                           │
│                                                           │
│                                                           │
│                                                           │
└─────────────────────────────────────────────────────────┘
```

FIGURE 17-6.   *Startup with pfile*

NOTE
If you have started your database using the pfile option, remind yourself to shut it down and use the regular initialization parameter file when the job completes.

Nothing will go wrong if you leave your database running with an initialization parameter file other than the file you normally use.

VIP
More than 99 percent of the time, you will start up a database with no options.

Operation Modes

Table 17-1 summarizes the operating modes and indicates what can be accomplished with the database in each mode—open, mount, nomount, and closed. If you attempt to issue a SQL command and the database mode of operation does not support the command, Oracle will inform you.

MODE	ACTIVITIES THAT CAN BE ACCOMPLISHED
closed	■ Add, drop, or move a control file (with modifications made in the initialization parameter file to reflect the changes)
	■ Backup the database—all datafiles, online redo logs, and control files
nomount	■ Create a database
	■ Create a control file
mount	■ Perform database, datafile, or tablespace recovery
	■ Rename any database file
	■ Change redo log archival mode (ARCHIVELOG or NOARCHIVELOG)
	■ Add, drop, or rename redo log groups or redo log file members
open	■ All users can access the database and go about their normal business
	■ Export full database, one or more users, or specific database objects
	■ Import full database, one or more users, or specific database objects

TABLE 17-1. *Tasks with Database in Each Mode*

Shutdown Options

When an Oracle database is not running, we refer to it as *down*. You shut down the database for a number of reasons. Some installations bring the database down for backups. When upgrading or installing some new Oracle software, Oracle must be down during some of the upgrade or installation session. In Chapter 13, we talked about shutdown normal, immediate, and abort (a discussion of shutdown is not complete without mentioning these two extra options). There is nothing more frustrating than being told to shut down your database with the **shutdown** command only to find it does not work!

VIP

Refer to the section on line-mode sqldba in Chapter 13, in which we discuss shutdown—there is some VERY important and useful information there.

VIP

Shutdown immediate will be used more than 90 percent of the time.

As a last resort, you may have to use the **shutdown abort** command. There are situations when nothing else works, and you have no choice.

CAUTION

If you shut down a database with the abort option, start it up immediately, then do a normal shutdown. Experience dictates this is the best way to care for a database shut down with this abort option.

Additional User Management Responsibilities

Coupled with the tasks discussed in Chapter 13, the exercises we highlight in this section will round out your user management skills. By the end of this section, you will know how to do the following:

- Assign a default tablespace for a user's objects
- Give users permission to acquire space in a tablespace
- Point users at a central tablespace for sorting

In the following sections, we'll have a user named polly and the password gone. The examples refer to the tablespace named hold_my_data.

Assign a Default Tablespace

Recall from Chaper 13 (in the "Granting Access to a User" section) that when you allowed a user access to the database, polly was permitted to log onto the database—nothing else. When the time comes to allow polly to occupy space in a tablespace in the database, she will do so by issuing SQL **create table** commands. By assigning polly a default tablespace, all her tables will end up in the hold_my_data tablespace by default. After starting sqldba, assign polly a default tablespace by following these steps:

1. Enter **connect internal**.

2. Enter the command **alter user polly default tablespace hold_my_data;** and receive the feedback from Oracle shown in Figure 17-7.

3. Enter **exit** to leave sqldba.

Oracle assumes that the user (polly, in this case) exists, and the tablespace (hold_my_data) also exists. If either of these is not true, the command will return an error message.

TIP
It is easier to manage user tables when they are permitted to place all of their tables in a single tablespace. You will default tablespace assignment frequently.

```
┌─────────────────────────────────────────────────────────────┐
│  ▬                        HP Prod            01:45  ▼  ▲▼    │
│ File  Edit  Session  Instance  Storage  Log  Backup  Security  Monitor  Help │
│ ┌───────────────────────── Output ─────────────────────────┐ │
│ │Oracle7 Server Release 7.1.4.1.0 - Production Release      │ │
│ │PL/SQL Release 2.1.4.0.0 - Production                      │ │
│ │                                                           │ │
│ │>connect internal                                          │ │
│ │Connected.                                                 │ │
│ │>alter user polly default tablespace hold_my_data          │ │
│ │Statement processed.                                       │ │
│ │                                                           │ │
│ │                                                           │ │
│ │                                                           │ │
│ │                                                           │ │
│ │                                                           │ │
│ │                                                           │ │
│ │     ─────────────────────────────────────────────        │ │
│ │                                                           │ │
│ │   ─────────────────────────────────────────────          │ │
│ │                                                           │ │
│ └───────────────────────────────────────────────────────── │ │
└─────────────────────────────────────────────────────────────┘
```

FIGURE 17-7. *Pointing user at a default tablespace*

Assign Space Quota to a User

This process allows the specified user to occupy space in a tablespace. It differs from the previous process, which points her tables at hold_my_data. That previous command alone does not allow her to occupy space in hold_my_data until this command is executed. After starting full-screen sqldba, follow these steps:

1. Enter **connect internal**.

2. Enter the command **alter user polly quota 10m on hold_my_data;** and Oracle responds as shown in Figure 17-8.

3. Enter **exit** to leave sqldba.

Both the user to whom you are giving the space and the tablespace being assigned must exist when issuing this statement. If either the user or tablespace do not exist, the command will return an error message. The space in this statement is allocated in either megabytes (1,048,576 bytes), kilobytes (1,024 bytes), or the actual number of bytes (e.g., 10240) with no commas.

VIP

Oracle does not verify that the tablespace within which the quota is assigned has that amount of space available. You could (if you wish) assign a user quota of 100m in a tablespace that is only 500k.

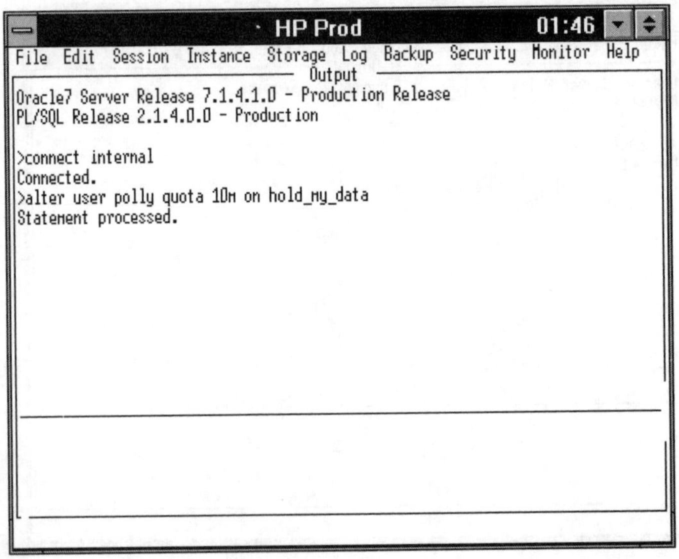

```
┌─                    ·  HP Prod            01:46  ▼  ▲▼ ─┐
  File  Edit  Session  Instance  Storage  Log  Backup  Security  Monitor  Help
  ──────────────────────── Output ────────────────────
  Oracle7 Server Release 7.1.4.1.0 - Production Release
  PL/SQL Release 2.1.4.0.0 - Production

  >connect internal
  Connected.
  >alter user polly quota 10m on hold_my_data
  Statement processed.
```

FIGURE 17-8.   *Assigning quota to a user*

Assign a Tablespace for Sorting

As Oracle runs and users make requests for data, sometimes information needs to be sorted. Most of the time, when there is sufficient memory available, Oracle does this work in memory. When Oracle needs more space than memory can satisfy, it uses work space in a tablespace. This tablespace is referred to as the *temporary segment,* since any objects Oracle creates for the work it does for the user are deleted after the sort completes. After starting sqldba, follow these steps:

1. Enter **connect internal**.

2. Enter the command **alter user polly temporary tablespace temp_ts;** and receive feedback from Oracle as shown in Figure 17-9.

3. Enter **exit** to leave sqldba.

TIP
Create a separate tablespace for sorting and assign it using the above command to ALL users of the database.

Oracle assumes that the user (polly in this case) exists and the tablespace (temp_ts in this case) also exists. If either of these is not true, the command will return an error message.

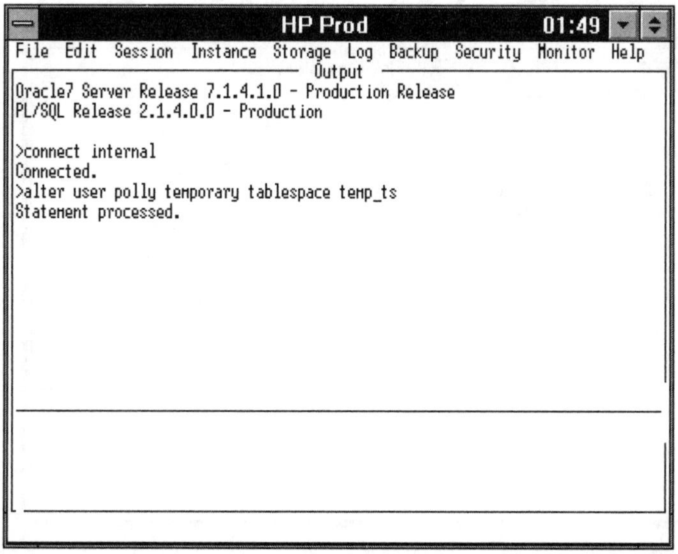

```
┌─                         HP Prod              01:49  ▼ ▲
 File  Edit  Session  Instance  Storage  Log  Backup  Security  Monitor  Help
 ─────────────────── Output ───────────────────
 Oracle7 Server Release 7.1.4.1.0 - Production Release
 PL/SQL Release 2.1.4.0.0 - Production

 >connect internal
 Connected.
 >alter user polly temporary tablespace temp_ts
 Statement processed.
```

FIGURE 17-9.   *Pointing user at a tablespace for sorting*

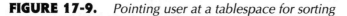

Stacking the Three Previous Commands

The commands in the previous three sections can be stacked together in one statement. After starting sqldba, you can enter the command and then receive the feedback from Oracle as shown in Figure 17-10. There are no rules governing the order of these commands.

Additional Tablespace Maintenance Responsibilities

In Chapter 13, we discussed creating a tablespace and adding more space to one that already exists. By the end of this section, you will also know how to move the datafile that makes up a tablespace (i.e., rename a datafile) as well as drop a tablespace.

Moving a Datafile

Either by plan, or when forced to do so, you may need to move the datafile a tablespace occupies. You may find yourself with one less disk at your disposal and

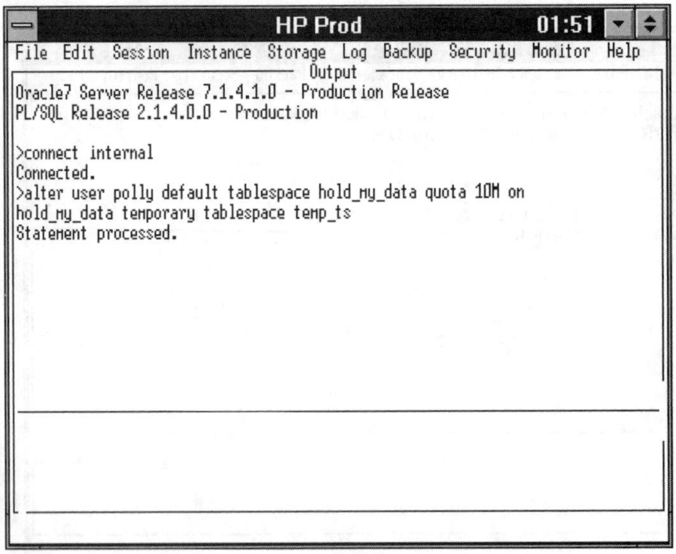

FIGURE 17-10. *Three alter user commands issued together*

may need to move a tablespace to another disk. In the following code, these are the specifications:

Tablespace name	hold_my_data
Datafile	hmd.dbf
Current directory	?/dbs
New directory	?/oracle_dev

After starting sqldba, follow these steps:

1. Enter **connect internal**.

2. Enter the command **alter tablespace hold_my_data offline;** and receive feedback from Oracle as shown in Figure 17-11.

VIP
The tablespace will not go offline if any users are currently using its data.

3. Using your operating system command, copy the datafile to its new location.

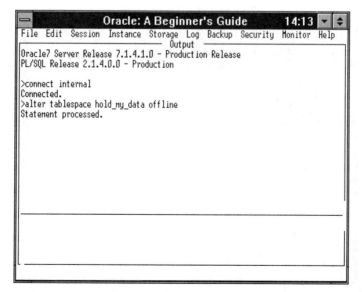

FIGURE 17-11. *Taking tablespace offline*

4. Enter the command **alter tablespace hold_my_data rename datafile '?/dbs/hmd.dbf' to '?/oracle_dev/hmd.dbf';** and receive feedback from Oracle as shown in Figure 17-12.

5. Bring the tablespace online as shown in Figure 17-13.

6. Enter **exit** to leave sqldba.

After you leave sqldba, use an operating system command to delete the old file you are no longer using.

Dropping a Tablespace

Once a user's data is no longer required, you may want to get rid of the data and even the tablespace the data now resides in. After starting full-screen sqldba, follow these steps:

1. Enter **connect internal**.

2. Enter the command **drop tablespace hold_my_data;** as shown in Figure 17-14 and receive feedback from Oracle.

3. Enter **exit** to leave sqldba.

```
┌─────────────────────────────────────────────────────────────┐
│  ─        Oracle: A Beginner's Guide        14:16  ▼ ▲       │
│ File Edit Session Instance Storage Log Backup Security Monitor Help │
│ ───────────────────────── Output ─────────────────────────   │
│ Oracle7 Server Release 7.1.4.1.0 - Production Release        │
│ PL/SQL Release 2.1.4.0.0 - Production                        │
│                                                              │
│ >connect internal                                            │
│ Connected.                                                   │
│ >alter tablespace hold_my_data rename datafile               │
│    '?/dbs/hmd.dbf' to '?/oracle_dev/hmd.dbf'                 │
│ Statement processed.                                         │
│                                                              │
│                                                              │
│                                                              │
│                                                              │
└─────────────────────────────────────────────────────────────┘
```

FIGURE 17-12. *Renaming the datafile*

```
┌─────────────────────────────────────────────────────────────┐
│ ─        Oracle: A Beginner's Guide      14:18 ▼ ◆          │
│ File Edit Session Instance Storage Log Backup Security Monitor Help │
│ ───────────────────────── Output ─────────────────────────  │
│ Oracle7 Server Release 7.1.4.1.0 - Production Release        │
│ PL/SQL Release 2.1.4.0.0 - Production                        │
│                                                             │
│ >connect internal                                           │
│ Connected.                                                  │
│ >alter tablespace hold_my_data rename datafile              │
│    '?/dbs/hmd.dbf' to '?/oracle_dev/hmd.dbf'                 │
│ Statement processed.                                        │
│ >alter tablespace hold_my_data online                       │
│ Statement processed.                                        │
│                                                             │
│                                                             │
│                                                             │
│                                                             │
└─────────────────────────────────────────────────────────────┘
```

FIGURE 17-13. *Bringing tablespace online*

```
┌─────────────────────────────────────────────────────────────┐
│ ─        Oracle: A Beginner's Guide      14:25 ▼ ◆          │
│ File Edit Session Instance Storage Log Backup Security Monitor Help │
│ ───────────────────────── Output ─────────────────────────  │
│ Oracle7 Server Release 7.1.4.1.0 - Production Release        │
│ PL/SQL Release 2.1.4.0.0 - Production                        │
│                                                             │
│ >connect internal                                           │
│ Connected.                                                  │
│ >drop tablespace hold_my_data                               │
│ Statement processed.                                        │
│                                                             │
│                                                             │
│                                                             │
│                                                             │
│                                                             │
│                                                             │
└─────────────────────────────────────────────────────────────┘
```

FIGURE 17-14. Dropping a tablespace

VIP
You are not allowed to drop a tablespace containing any objects. The SQL statement will fail if the tablespace still contains any tables. You must either drop those objects first or use the **including contents** option with the SQL statement as shown in Figure 17-14.

You will find that dropping a tablespace's objects, then dropping the tablespace is much faster than using the **drop tablespace including contents;** statement.

VIP
Dropping a tablespace does not erase the datafile it was using. The datafile must be removed using an operating system command. Erase the datafile from the dropped tablespace immediately. If you decide to do this some other time, more than likely you will forget!

Managing Redo Log Groups

Oracle writes transaction information to redo logs files. Picture a redo log as a passbook that records all changes to the database as if it were a checking account. With Oracle, we speak of redo log file groups. If you define more than one member for a redo log group, Oracle writes to each member simultaneously. This protects you against problems if a redo log file is damaged; Oracle continues to write to another member of the group that is still intact. In this section, we discuss how to do the following:

- Mirror your redo logs
- Add a redo log group
- Drop a redo log group

Mirrored Redo Logs

When instructed, Oracle7 will maintain mirrored copies of all online redo logs. A *redo log group* is made up of one or more equally sized redo log files. Each redo log group is assigned a number when created and Oracle writes to all members of each group at the same time. In the next section, we show you how to add a new redo log group to set up this mirroring. When the database operates in ARCHIVELOG mode, Oracle archives only one member of a redo log group before the whole group is reused.

TIP
Have at least two members in each redo log group. If Oracle ever has difficulty writing to one member of a redo log group, it will carry on, satisfied to write to another member of the same group.

The status of your database redo log groups and members is viewed using the v$logfile data dictionary view and the following query.

```
SQL> select * from v$logfile;
GROUP# STATUS   MEMBER
---------- -------  ---------------------------------------
         1          /lor/prd_log/log1prd_g1.dbf
         1          /data/log_shadow/log2prd_g1.dbf
         1          /picard/log_shadow/log3prd_g1.dbf
         2          /oracle/dbs/log1prd_g2.dbf
         2          /data/log_shadow/log2prd_g2.dbf
         2          /picard/log_shadow/log3prd_g2.dbf
         3          /lor/prd_log/log1prd_g3.dbf
         3          /data/log_shadow/log2prd_g3.dbf
         3          /picard/log_shadow/log3prd_g3.dbf
         4          /oracle/dbs/log1prd_g4.dbf
         4          /data/log_shadow/log2prd_g4.dbf
         4          /picard/log_shadow/log3prd_g4.dbf
         5          /data/log_shadow/log2prd_g5.dbf
         5          /lor/prd_log/log1prd_g5.dbf
         5          /picard/log_shadow/log3prd_g5.dbf
         6          /oracle/dbs/log1prd_g6.dbf
         6          /data/log_shadow/log2prd_g6.dbf
         6          /picard/log_shadow/log3prd_g6.dbf
```

Use the following convention when setting up mirrored redo logs:

1. Ensure there are the same number of members in every redo log group.

2. Ensure each member of each redo log group is the same size.

3. Embed the member number and group number in the name of each redo log file. For example, the third member of redo log group 6 in the previous listing is called log3prd_g6.dbf.

4. Place members of each redo log group on separate disks. For example, the three members of redo log group 6 in the previous listing are on three separate drives: oracle, data, and picard.

NOTE
You may have difficulty when you try to add a third member to your redo log groups. The parameter **maxlogmembers** controls the number of members in a redo log group.

The value of **maxlogmembers** can be increased by re-creating the database control file.

NOTE
If you wish to increase the value for **maxlogmembers**, you can re-create your control file as discussed in the "Building a New Control File" section of this chapter.

Adding a New Redo Log Group

For this exercise, we need to add redo log group 3 with two redo log file members of 1 megabyte each. After starting sqldba, follow these steps:

1. Enter **connect internal**.

2. Enter the command **alter database add logfile group 3 ('log1_gr3','log2_gr3') size 1m;** and receive feedback from Oracle as shown in Figure 17-15.

3. Enter **exit** to leave sqldba.

Notice in Figure 17-15 how the names of the redo log file members are enclosed in single quotes. As well, the two redo log file member names are separated by a comma and enclosed in parentheses. We now have three redo log groups associated with the database.

TIP
When building a redo log file member name, embed the group number and member number in the filename. That is why we named the files log1_gr3 and log2_gr3 in this exercise.

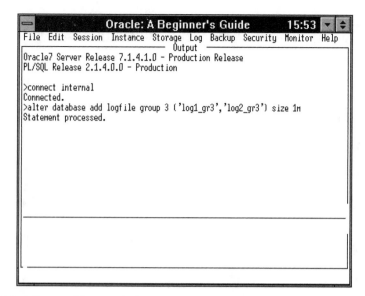

FIGURE 17-15. *Adding redo log group 3*

Dropping an Existing Redo Log Group

You have just upgraded your hardware, and you find yourself with one less disk for Oracle and its associated database files. You used to have three disks, and now you have two. After starting full-screen sqldba, follow these steps:

1. Enter **connect internal**.

2. Enter the command **alter database drop logfile group 3;** and receive feedback from Oracle as shown in Figure 17-16.

3. Enter **exit** to leave sqldba.

Redo log group 3 is no longer part of the database. Note how the SQL statement in Figure 17-16 makes no mention of any redo log file member names as the group is dropped.

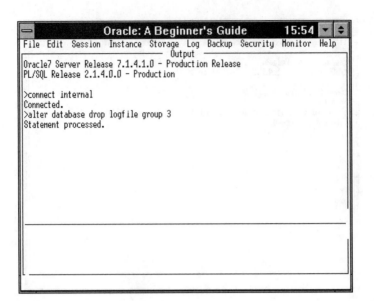

FIGURE 17-16. *Dropping redo log group 3*

Problems Dropping Redo Log Groups

There are two problems that commonly occur when attempting to drop a redo log group. If one of these happens to you, follow our advice and then reissue the command to drop the group.

- You may be attempting to drop a redo log group (let's call it redo log group 2) that would leave Oracle with less than two groups. If this happens, you must add a third group before you can drop group 2. When you drop group 2, that leaves groups 1 and 3, which satisfies Oracle's requirements.

- You may be attempting to drop a redo log group that is active. You must wait until the group is no longer active before it can be dropped.

Rollback Segments

You may remember that these segments are used to store undo information when you update or delete data in Oracle tables. Managing these segments is part of your DBA responsibility. In this section, we show you how to do the following:

- Acquire a rollback segment using the initialization parameter file
- Create a rollback segment
- Change the status of a rollback segment
- Drop a rollback segment

Acquiring a Rollback Segment

When you start up your database, it can be forced to acquire rollback segments by an entry in your initialization parameter file. This is done using a text editor (we use the Windows Notepad as an example) and the following steps.

1. Invoke the Notepad by clicking on its icon in the Accessories group in the Windows Program Manager.

2. Retrieve the initialization parameter file called init.ora. Its current contents are shown in Figure 17-17.

3. Add the entry shown in Figure 17-18.

4. Save the updated initialization parameter file and exit Notepad.

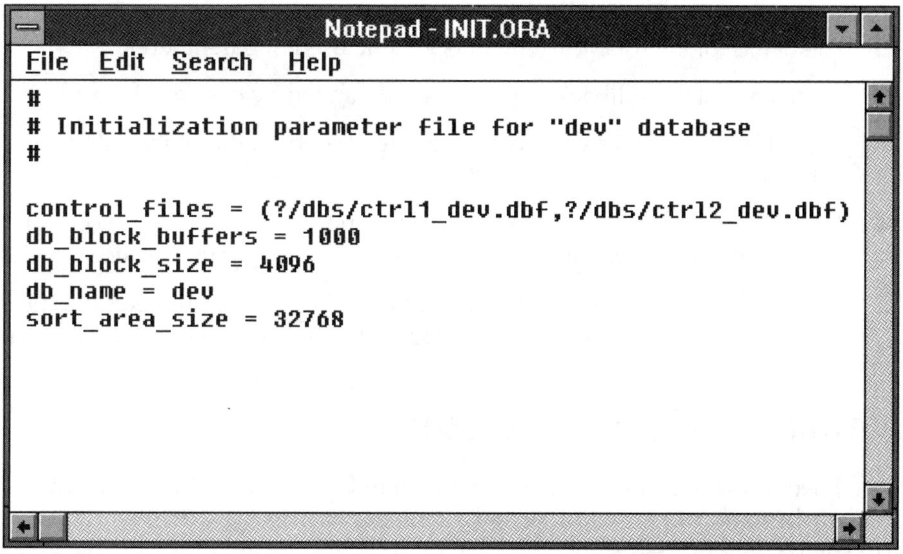

```
                        Notepad - INIT.ORA
 File   Edit   Search   Help
 #
 # Initialization parameter file for "dev" database
 #

 control_files = (?/dbs/ctrl1_dev.dbf,?/dbs/ctrl2_dev.dbf)
 db_block_buffers = 1000
 db_block_size = 4096
 db_name = dev
 sort_area_size = 32768
```

FIGURE 17-17. *Current initialization parameter file*

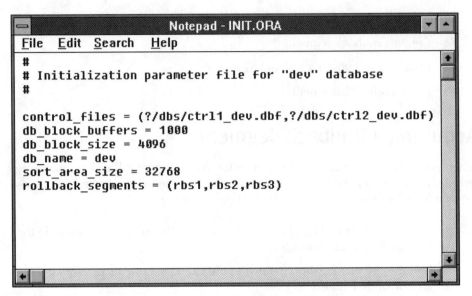

FIGURE 17-18. *Initialization parameter file rollback_segments entry*

To complete this section, note the following points:

■ The names of the rollback segments are enclosed in parentheses.

■ The names of the rollback segments are separated by commas.

■ The rollback segments will not be acquired based on this entry until the database is shut down and started up.

■ The existence of the rollback segments mentioned in the entry is not checked by Oracle when you save the initialization parameter file.

■ If the rollback segments you placed in the initialization parameter file do not exist the next time you start up your database, you will receive an error.

Creating a Rollback Segment

We discussed rollback segments in greater detail in Chapter 3. As the DBA, you will quickly become more familiar with the nuances of working with them. After starting sqldba, follow these steps:

1. Enter **connect internal**.

2. Enter the command **create rollback segment rbs3 tablespace misc storage (initial 100k next 100k minextents 10 maxextents 10);** and receive the feedback from Oracle as shown in Figure 17-19.

3. Enter **exit** to leave sqldba.

The SQL statement is made up of the following parts:

- The name of the rollback segment

- The tablespace in which the rollback segment is placed

- The storage parameters the rollback segment will assume

The name of the rollback segment must be unique and the tablespace you are placing it in must be accessible.

VIP
We recommend you build one or more tablespaces to hold nothing other than rollback segments.

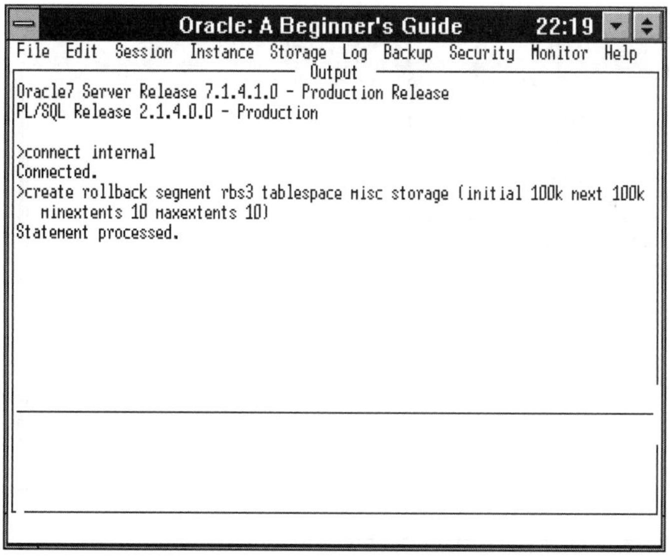

```
┌──────────────────────────────────────────────────────────┐
│ ▬        Oracle: A Beginner's Guide      22:19  ▼ ▲       │
│ File Edit  Session  Instance  Storage  Log  Backup  Security  Monitor  Help │
│ ─────────────────────── Output ───────────────────────    │
│ Oracle7 Server Release 7.1.4.1.0 - Production Release      │
│ PL/SQL Release 2.1.4.0.0 - Production                      │
│                                                            │
│ >connect internal                                          │
│ Connected.                                                 │
│ >create rollback segment rbs3 tablespace misc storage (initial 100k next 100k │
│    minextents 10 maxextents 10)                            │
│ Statement processed.                                       │
│                                                            │
└──────────────────────────────────────────────────────────┘
```

FIGURE 17-19.   *Creating a rollback segment*

Changing the Status of a Rollback Segment

Rollback segments are either online or offline. Suppose the rollback segment rbs1 exists; the status of a rollback segment is changed by doing the following.

1. Enter **connect internal**.

2. Enter the command **alter rollback segment rbs3 online;** and receive the feedback from Oracle as shown in Figure 17-20.

The status of your rollback segments can be obtained from the query shown in Figure 17-21. A rollback segment must be online to be used by Oracle.

Dropping a Rollback Segment

When the need arises, after starting sqldba, do the following.

1. Enter **connect internal**.

2. Enter the command **alter rollback segment rbs3 offline;** followed by **drop rollback segment rbs3;** and receive the feedback from Oracle as shown in Figure 17-22.

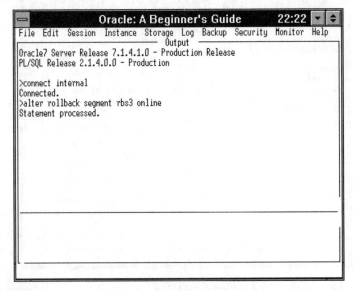

FIGURE 17-20. *Placing a rollback segment online*

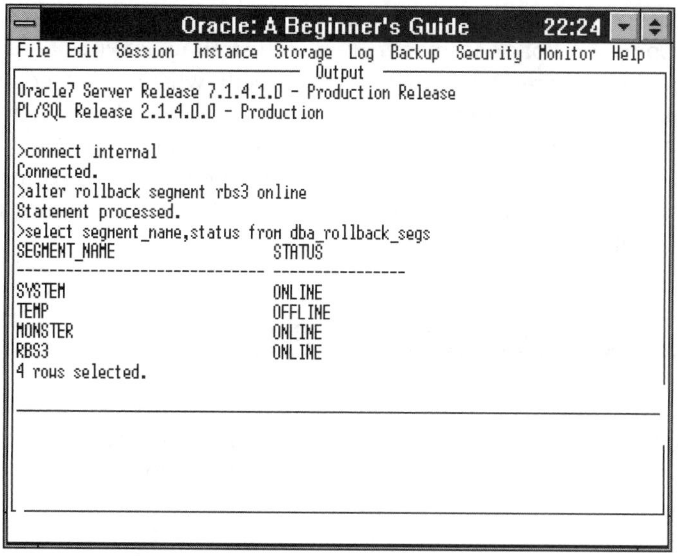

FIGURE 17-21. *Listing status of rollback segments*

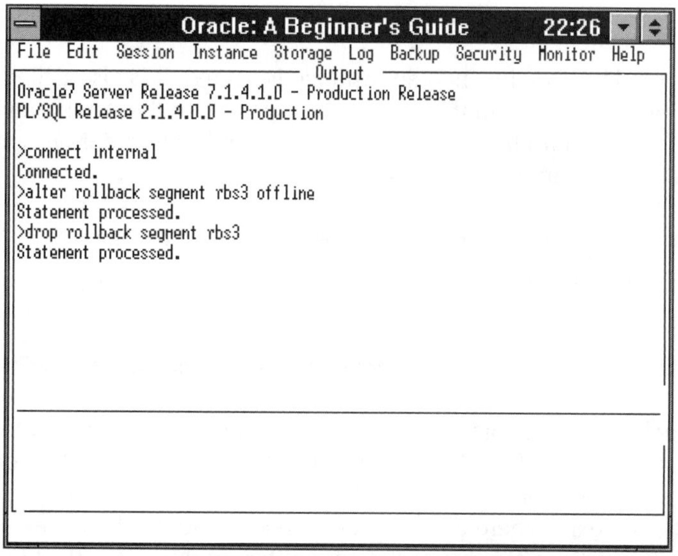

FIGURE 17-22. *Dropping a rollback segment*

Notice how you need to take a rollback segment offline before it can be dropped. Dropping a rollback segment can be a frustrating activity; there are a number of situations where Oracle may not do exactly what you expect. If you try to drop a rollback segment with the online status, then you will receive the error message "ORA-01545: rollback segment 'RBS3' specified not available." As well, if you try to take a rollback segment offline to drop it, and someone is using it when you issue the command, then the rollback segment will not come offline until that user is done with it.

Initialization Parameter File

This file can be one of the most mystifying components of the Oracle database. Many articles in magazines and presentations at technical conferences deal with this file and what it does for the Oracle database. This section will discuss details on the following:

- What the initialization parameter file is used for
- Format of parameters in this file
- Displaying values of entries in this file
- Changing parameters in this file
- Parameters most commonly changed

This file is read by Oracle when an instance is started; it is also called init.ora or the pfile. There are entries in this file that are specific to the database you wish to access, and they control the environment Oracle will set up during startup. The parameters in this file can be used to do the following:

- Define the name and location of files used by the database
- Control the size of portions of computer memory allocated to support the database configuration
- Specify the number of concurrent sessions that may access the database

When Oracle starts the database, much of its operating environment is based on values of entries in this file. When entries list the name and location of files the instance needs to open at startup, these files are checked. Oracle needs to ensure the files mentioned exist where they are supposed to, and can be accessed without error. As well, the settings of some of the parameters in this pfile affect the performance of your database.

Format for Entries in the Initialization Parameter File

There are two kinds of parameters in this parameter file (hereafter referred to as pfile); *explicit* parameters have an entry in the pfile; *implicit* parameters do not appear in the pfile and assume the default until (if ever) you place a value for them in the pfile. In the next listing, all the values except the first (dml_locks) have no entry in the pfile.

```
dml_locks                          integer 1200
gc_db_locks                        integer 75
gc_files_to_locks                  string
gc_rollback_locks                  integer 20
gc_save_rollback_locks             integer 20
row_locking                        string  default
temporary_table_locks              integer 80
```

The format for parameters is

```
pfile_keyword = keyword_value
```

and, for some entries, you need to enclose parameter values in appropriate punctuation such as parentheses () or double quotes "". If parameters span more than one line, they require a continuation character as follows

```
rollback_segments = (rollback_disk1,rollback_disk2, rollback_disk3, \
                    rollback_disk4)
```

Examining Contents of the Initialization Parameter File

A complete list of parameters (implicit and explicit) are available by doing the following in sqldba.

1. Enter **connect internal**.

2. To see a list of the values for all entries, enter the command **show parameters** and Oracle displays a list, the end of which is shown in Figure 17-23.

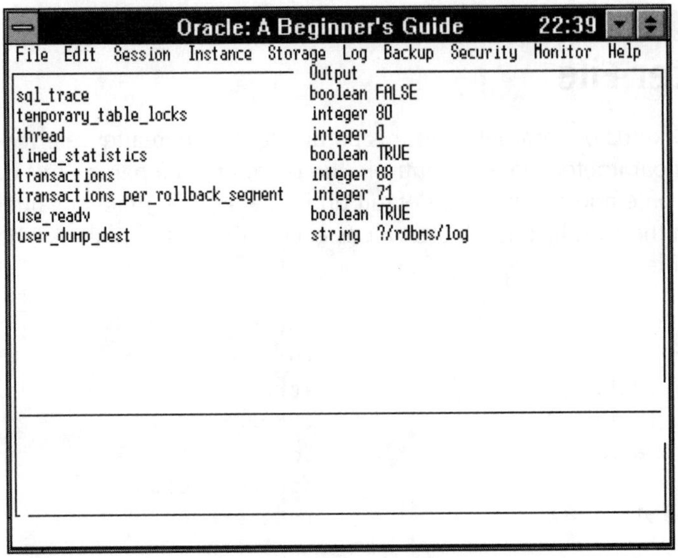

FIGURE 17-23. *Displaying all parameter values*

You can look at a subset of parameters (implicit and explicit). For this exercise, we want all the parameters that contain the word "sort." After starting sqldba, follow these steps:

1. Enter **connect internal**.

2. To see a list of the values for the entries containing "sort," enter the command **show parameters sort** and receive the feedback from Oracle as shown in Figure 17-24.

Changing Parameter Values

When Oracle is first installed on all platforms, it builds an initialization parameter file to start the database. As your knowledge of Oracle grows, you may change some initialization parameter entry values. Some of them can be changed; others must be left as is. Details about changing pfile parameter values are covered in the *Oracle7 Server Administrator's Guide* (commonly referred to as the OSAG). Appendix A in the OSAG discusses the details of the parameter file, and gives advice and recommendations about what can be changed and the acceptable range of values. For example, in this appendix (used with permission of Oracle Corporation), the following advice is given about the shared_pool_size entry.

```
┌──────────────────────────────────────────────────────────────┐
│ ─       .       Oracle: A Beginner's Guide        22:44 ▼ ◆  │
│ File Edit  Session  Instance  Storage Log  Backup  Security  Monitor  Help │
│ ┌──────────────────── Output ──────────────────────────────┐ │
│ │ Oracle7 Server Release 7.1.4.1.0 - Production Release     │ │
│ │ PL/SQL Release 2.1.4.0.0 - Production                     │ │
│ │                                                          │ │
│ │ >connect internal                                        │ │
│ │ Connected.                                               │ │
│ │ >show parameters sort                                    │ │
│ │ NAME                           TYPE    VALUE             │ │
│ │ ─────────────────────────────  ──────  ───────────────── │ │
│ │ nls_sort                       string                    │ │
│ │ sort_area_retained_size        integer 65536             │ │
│ │ sort_area_size                 integer 65536             │ │
│ │ sort_mts_buffer_for_fetch_size integer 0                 │ │
│ │ sort_read_fac                  integer 5                 │ │
│ │ sort_spacemap_size             integer 512               │ │
│ │                                                          │ │
│ │ ┌──────────────────────────────────────────────────────┐ │ │
│ │ │                                                      │ │ │
│ │ └──────────────────────────────────────────────────────┘ │ │
│ │ └──                                                       │ │
│ └──────────────────────────────────────────────────────────┘ │
└──────────────────────────────────────────────────────────────┘
```

FIGURE 17-24.   *Partial list of initialization parameter file entries*

SHARED_POOL_SIZE
Default value:3.5 Mbytes
Range of values:300 Kbytes - O/S dependent
The size of the shared pool, in bytes. The shared pool contains
shared cursors and stored procedures. Larger values improve
performance in multi-user systems. Smaller values use less memory.
Additional Information: Chapter 21 "Tuning Memory Allocation"

Appendix A will also tell you if you are allowed to change the value of an entry.

NOTE
Changes to any entries in the pfile will not take effect until the next
time the database is started.

Parameters Most Commonly Changed

Over 130 parameter values are recorded in the data dictionary view v$parameter.
This view lists the values in effect as the database operates; it serves as the source
for the query output shown in Figure 17-23. Table 17-2 highlights the four entries
in the initialization parameter file you will change most often.

PARAMETER	MEANING	MOST COMMON CHANGES
shared_pool_size	The number of bytes of memory allocated to the shared pool	As the size of your concurrent user community grows, you may increase this value periodically.
rollback_segments	The name of one or more rollback segments to acquire when the database is started	When transaction volume increases or decreases over a period of time, you may add or remove the name of a rollback segment from this list.
sessions	The maximum number of concurrent sessions that may access the database	Needs increasing as more and more users come on board.

TABLE 17-2.   *Most Common Changes in the Initialization Parameter File*

NOTE
When you change an entry in the pfile, comment the old one with the "#" character. This will help you keep track of what changed, why, and when.

Control File Responsibilities

Coupled with the initialization parameter file, control files are read by Oracle every time you start the database. Their file information is vital to opening the database. In this section, you will learn details on the following:

- How Oracle uses the control file
- Adding a new control file
- Dropping an existing control file
- Moving an existing control file
- Building a new control file

As the DBA, you will bear complete responsibility for managing control files. Think of control files as the transmission in your car. When both behave themselves, they require no attention; when both misbehave, they can cause major headaches!

Use of the Control File

Every Oracle database has one or more control files. The control file holds information about the database creation time, the name of the database, and the location and names of all files used when the database is running. You instruct Oracle to maintain as many copies of a database control file (usually two or more) as you deem necessary. The control files are written to as Oracle operates, and they are key to database startup and shutdown. Every time you perform maintenance operations, such as adding a datafile or configuring redo log file groups, the control files are automatically modified to reflect the change. Some control file mainten-ance is performed with the database down; some maintenance is performed with the database in a nomount status. When you start the Oracle database, the control file is opened first. Oracle then verifies the existence and status of all the files needed to operate, and it ensures all redo log files are accessible. As the DBA, you are responsible for ensuring Oracle can open its control files when it needs them. As we discuss in the "Building a New Control File" section of this chapter, making a copy of the control file is included in your backup procedures.

Adding a Control File

You may decide to add a control file when a new disk is added to the disk farm. This is accomplished by following these steps:

1. Shut down the database.

2. Proceed to the directory where the database initialization parameter file is located.

3. Edit the file looking for the entry that specified control_files =. A sample is shown in Figure 17-25.

4. Add the name and location of the additional control file.

5. Save the pfile with the new value as shown in Figure 17-26.

6. Copy one of the existing control files to create the new control file. Using the new control filename from Figure 17-26, you would enter the UNIX command: **cp $ORACLE_HOME/dbs/dev_ctl2 $ORACLE_HOME/dev_ctl3**.

7. Start the database.

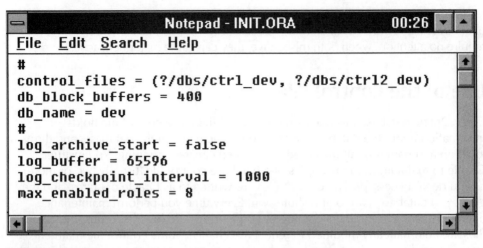

FIGURE 17-25. *Entry in the pfile for control_files*

The additional control file is now part of your database configuration. Once you create the new control file (by copying one of the old ones) and make this change in the initialization parameter file, Oracle will maintain the new set of control files automatically.

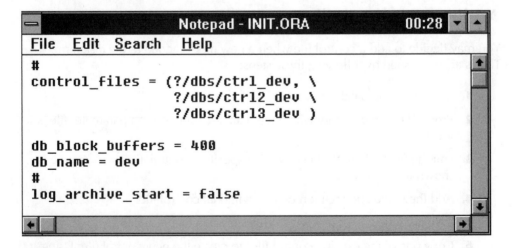

FIGURE 17-26. *Updated control_files entry*

Dropping a Control File

Once in a while, you may find yourself with one less disk at your disposal. This requires you to drop one of your control files that was positioned on that disk. Dropping a control file is accomplished by following these steps:

1. Shut down the database.

2. Proceed to the directory where the database initialization parameter file is located.

3. Edit the file looking for the entry that specified control_files =. The parameter value could resemble the following

```
control_files = (?/dbs/dev_ctl1,?/dbs/dev_ctl2, \
?/dbs/dev_ctl3)
```

4. Remove the name of the control file to be dropped. The parameter value then becomes

```
control_files = (?/dbs/dev_ctl1,?/dbs/dev_ctl2)
```

5. Start the database.

6. Erase the unwanted control file.

Your database is now running with one less file in its pool of control files.

Moving an Existing Control File

If your system administrator needs to change the name of a disk where you have a control file, you too will have to inform Oracle of the name of the new location. This can be accomplished by following these steps:

1. Shut down the database.

2. Proceed to the directory where the database initialization parameter file is located.

3. Edit the file looking for the entry that specified control_files =. The parameter value could resemble the following

```
control_files = (?/dbs/dev_ctl1,/old_loc/dbs/dev_ctl2)
```

4. Change the name of the control file being moved. The parameter value then becomes

```
control_files = (?/dbs/dev_ctl1,/new_loc/dbs/dev_ctl2)
```

5. Move the control file to its new location using an O/S command.

6. Start the database.

Building a New Control File

If and when a control file is damaged, Oracle cannot open your database. This is why in a number of places throughout this book, we recommend you have more than one control file. If the need arises to build a control file, you place the following routine somewhere in your nightly backup procedures.

```
# bcft.sql - backup control file to trace
connect internal
alter database backup controlfile to trace;
exit
```

The step in the nightly backup routine calls this SQL script by the following

```
sqldba @bcft.sql
```

This writes a trace file in the directory defined by the initialization parameter file entry user_dump_dest. The trace file will have the text "ora_" as the prefix and the text ".trc" as the file extension. Embedded in this trace file will be the SQL statements required to build a control file from scratch.

```
startup nomount
create controlfile reuse database "aob" noresetlogs noarchivelog
    maxlogfiles 20
    maxlogmembers 4
    maxdatafiles 30
    maxinstances 1
    maxloghistory 100
logfile
  group 1 '/oracle/oracle_aob/log1aob_g1.dbf'  size 1m,
  group 2 '/oracle/oracle_aob/log1aob_g2.dbf'  size 1m,
datafile
  '/oracle/oracle_aob/dbs1aob.dbf' size 40m,
  '/lor/oracle_aob/prddata.dbf' size 200m,
  '/picard/oracle_aob/prddata2.dbf' size 80m,
```

```
   '/oracle/oracle_aob/temp_aob.dbf' size 100m,
   '/oracle/oracle_aob/fms_audit.dbf' size 70m,
   '/oracle/oracle_aob/misc.dbf' size 1m,
   '/picard/oracle_aob/ruben.dbf' size 30m;
recover database
alter database open;
```

There are three distinct parts to this statement; they give you a better understanding of the use of the control file:

■ The name of the database and its environment, e.g., the database name and the maximum number of members in a redo log group

■ The location and size of all redo log groups and their members

■ The location and size of all the datafiles associated with the instance

TIP
Make this routine part of your daily backup procedure immediately. It can prove a lifesaver many times during your career as a DBA.

We use this routine as part of all backup procedures we have placed at all our clients' installations. We use the SQL statements in the trace file created with this feature regularly.

NOTE
This command only works for Oracle7. It is not available with version 6.

Getting the Most from Your Error Messages

Unfortunately, something will go wrong when working with any software. Oracle feeds an error message back to you with a message number followed by some descriptive text about the problem. Most of the time, you will also get a suggestion or two about how to fix the problem. In this section, we will discuss the following:

■ Ranges of messages you will deal with as a DBA

■ Obtaining error message text online

■ Recognizing Oracle internal errors and what to do with them

As the DBA, you will become familiar with common error conditions, where to look for their resolution, and what to do about them. As time marches on, you will surprise even yourself how quickly you react to common messages. You will begin to spout error text at coffee breaks: "I looked where the clerk told me, and then got 942'ed" or "If I get asked to take on any more responsibilities before vacation, I'm gonna 1547." The *Oracle7 Server Error Messages and Codes Manual* will start following you around.

Popular DBA Message Ranges

As the DBA, you will become familiar with a whole new series of error messages in the following ranges; they relate to your new areas of responsibility. These are the bounds of the assortment of error messages you will spend your time with:

```
00000-00099: Oracle Server
00200-00249: Control files
00250-00299: Archiving and recovery
00300-00379: Redo log files
00440-00485: Background processes
00700-00709: Dictionary cache
00900-00999: Parsing of SQL statements
01100-01250: The database and its support files
01400-01489: SQL execution errors
01500-01699: DBA set of SQL commands
02376-02399: Resources
04030-04039: Memory and the shared pool
04040-04069: Stored procedures
12100-12299: SQL*Net
12500-12699: SQL*Net
12700-12799: Use of multilingual options
```

Online Error Messages

You will become familiar with these ranges, and in a short time period you will know what you have on your hands immediately by where a message number falls in this list. In most operating systems, you can access error text using a program called oerr. When you use oerr, enter the text "ora" followed by the message number of the error, for example, **oerr ora 1547**. You will receive output similar to the following:

```
01547, 00000, "failed to allocate extent of size %s in tablespace '%s'"
// *Cause: Tablespace indicated is out of space
// *Action: Use ALTER TABLESPACE ADD DATAFILE statement to add one or more
//    files to the tablespace indicated or create the object in other
//    tablespace if this happens during a CREATE statement
/oracle:prod>
```

ORA-00600 Internal Errors

Getting one of these errors is the "rights of initiation" to being a DBA, of sorts. The 0600 error is a "catch-all" message returned when Oracle encounters some internal difficulty. It is a generic message followed by up to six arguments enclosed in brackets [ ]. The majority of the arguments in the square brackets are numbers, but sometimes you may find text. The arguments 12387 and 34503 shown in the example below should point Oracle support at the exact reason the error was raised.

```
ORA-00600: internal error code, arguments: [12387], [34503],[],[],[],[]
```

VIP
Almost all 0600 error messages are not fatal. In our experience, the occurrence of an 0600 that impedes the operation of your database is very rare.

Report these errors to Oracle Worldwide Customer Support. They will explain the condition, tell you what to do about it, and reassure you that "yes, you do enjoy being a DBA!"

The Data Dictionary

The data dictionary resides in the system tablespace. Its information enables Oracle to manage its resources as well as track information such as who can log into the database and what files are required to run the database. You need to familiarize yourself with the data dictionary; it's remarkable how much of your DBA work uses the information it contains. In this section, we will do the following:

- Discuss the four types of data dictionary views
- See how objects appear in a different user's snapshot of the dictionary
- Highlight the most important v$ and DBA views

You will become more fluent with the makeup of the data dictionary in a surprisingly short time period. There is no magic in the Oracle database. Just about everything is stored somewhere in a table, or it can be displayed on the screen in some format. The Oracle data dictionary belongs to user SYS. The data dictionary is your friend—get to know it.

Types of Dictionary Views

You now need to concern yourself with types of dictionary views. Their names start with the prefix shown in Table 17-3, and the pieces of their names are connected with the underscore character "_".

The following list shows how the information in these views is related to one another.

```
SQL> select * from dict where table_name like '%OBJECTS';
TABLE_NAME                        COMMENTS
-----------------------------     -----------------------------------
ALL_OBJECTS                       Objects accessible to the user
DBA_OBJECTS                       All objects in the database
USER_OBJECTS                      Objects owned by the user

SQL>  select * from dict where table_name like '%_QUOTAS';
TABLE_NAME                        COMMENTS
-----------------------------     -----------------------------------
DBA_TS_QUOTAS                     Tablespace quotas for all users
USER_TS_QUOTAS                    Tablespace quotas for the user

SQL> select * from dict where table_name like '%_SYNONYMS';
TABLE_NAME                        COMMENTS
-----------------------------     -----------------------------------
ALL_SYNONYMS                      All synonyms accessible to the user
DBA_SYNONYMS                      All synonyms in the database
USER_SYNONYMS                     The user's private synonyms

SQL>
```

Most Useful v$ and dba Views

Unless you put access in place, users do not have privileges to view information in the dba and v$ views belonging to SYS. You need to grant **select** to everyone to allow them to see these views; the information they contain is invaluable to the

DICTIONARY VIEW PREFIX	MEANING
all	Returns information on all objects accessible to a user.
user	Returns information on all objects owned by a user.
dba	Returns a database wide list (for all users) similar to the user category.
v$	Dynamic performance views updated by Oracle as it runs. Performance information and the status of files and memory being used by Oracle is available by querying these views.

TABLE 17-3. *Data Dictionary View Prefixes*

novice as well as the seasoned DBA. These are the most useful dba_views, and the ones you need to become familiar with to get started.

```
TABLE_NAME                COMMENTS
--------------------- --------------------------------------------
DBA_DATA_FILES            Information about database files
DBA_DB_LINKS              All database links in the database
DBA_EXTENTS               Extents comprising all segments in the database
DBA_FREE_SPACE            Free extents in all tablespaces
DBA_INDEXES               Description for all indexes in the database
DBA_IND_COLUMNS           COLUMNs comprising INDEXes on all TABLEs and CLUSTERs
DBA_OBJECTS               All objects in the database
DBA_ROLLBACK_SEGS         Description of rollback segments
DBA_SEGMENTS              Storage allocated for all database segments
DBA_SEQUENCES             Description of all SEQUENCEs in the database
DBA_SYNONYMS              All synonyms in the database
DBA_TABLES                Description of all tables in the database
DBA_TABLESPACES           Description of all tablespaces
DBA_TAB_COLUMNS           Columns of all tables, views, and clusters database
DBA_TAB_GRANTS            All grants on objects in the database
DBA_TAB_PRIVS             All grants on objects in the database
DBA_TS_QUOTAS             Tablespace quotas for all users
DBA_USERS                 Information about all users of the database
DBA_VIEWS                 Text of all views in the database
```

Table 17-4 highlights the most useful v$ views, and the ones you need to become familiar with to get started.

VIEW	CONTAINS
v$datafile	Information on the datafiles used by the database; same as the information in the control file(s).
v$librarycache	Information on management of SQL statements in the shared pool.
v$lock	Information about locks placed on objects by sessions that access the database. Locks are used to prevent users from changing data in the database another user may have already started changing.
v$log	Information extracted from the control file about redo logs.
v$logfile	Information about the location and names of the instance redo log files.
v$parameter	The values of all entries in the initialization parameter file.
v$process	Information regarding current processes.
v$rollname	Rollback segment information.
v$rollstat	Statistics about online rollback segments.
v$rowcache	Information about data dictionary activity/performance in memory.
v$session	Information about active sessions.
v$sesstat	Statistics about active sessions reported in v$session.
v$sqlarea	Statistics about cursors currently help in the shared pool. Cursors are chunks of memory opened by Oracle for the processing of SQL statements.
v$statname	The meaning of each statistic reported in v$sesstat.
v$sysstat	System-wide statistics based on currently active sessions.
v$waitstat	Details on situations encountered where more than one session wants access to data in the database. There can be wait situations when more than one session wishes to manipulate the exact same information at the same time.

TABLE 17-4. *Information in Most Useful v$ Dictionary Views*

Working with Oracle Worldwide Customer Support

As the DBA, you will end up being the central contact point for your organization and technical support requests. To expedite the logging of support calls, Oracle needs the following information when you call.

- Your appropriate customer number for the configuration and tool for which you require support.

- A complete list of version numbers; telling support you are using Oracle version 7.1 is helpful, but knowing it's 7.1.4 is better, and 7.1.4.0 is better still. This is especially true with the Oracle tools: there are significant differences between using Oracle Forms versions 4.0.13 and 4.5.

- A list of any Oracle errors that caused your logging the support request. These can begin with an assortment of prefixes such as ora, frm, or dba.

- Descriptive information about "what was going on" when the error was detected.

Oracle will do one of four things when you call. We prefer the first solution (by far the most frequent).

- Tell you what to do to remedy the situation, and send you on your way a satisfied, enthusiastic customer.

- Keep you online while they search a number of support databases looking for a similar situation and, after finding a match, provide you with a number of workarounds.

- Keep you online while they search a number of support databases looking for a similar situation, and, after finding no match, get back to you in an amount of time that varies directly with the severity of your call (i.e., if the problem inhibits smooth operation of your business, you will be dealt with in a shorter period of time).

- Record pertinent information and call you back at some later time.

Feel free to call and check on the status of your call whenever you feel the need.

"But I Can't See the Forest for the Trees"

You are poised to embark on a journey into the unknown. This DBA job you are starting (or is it "have been saddled with") is not going to wreck your social life. No, contrary to what you have heard, you will not be up until all hours of the night wrestling with the database. Yes, you will have people come to you for answers. Why do you think it's called Oracle? Perhaps they were thinking of you: you are the oracle that sees, says, and solves all.

Become fluent with what we have discussed in this chapter. Read technical magazines. Attend user conferences (ever wanted to go to Japan? Europe? or perhaps Australia?). Frequent Oracle forums and information services on CompuServe, the Internet, and World Wide Web servers. If you don't understand something or you are boggled by a new routine, idea, or concept, just ask! Between the two of us, we have almost 18 years of experience using Oracle. We still learn things from each other. Believe it; we know a developer (thanks Lise!) who showed us some tricks with SQL*Forms version 3 a while back that we had never been aware of. If you figure out how to do something that you are excited about, let everybody know. One of the interesting things about Oracle is that it is such a complex product, you may just have mastered doing something that four other DBAs all over the world have been tearing their hair out trying to figure out for the past two years. Enjoy!

Index

M

P

U

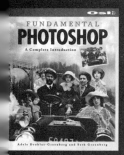

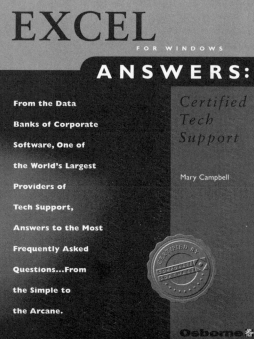

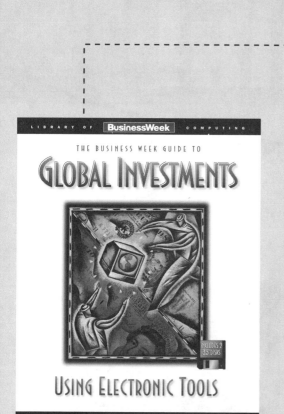

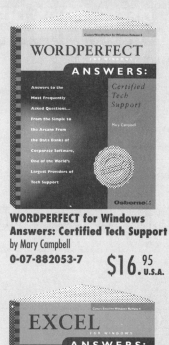

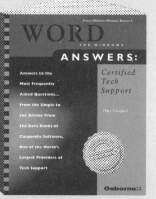

ORDER BOOKS DIRECTLY FROM OSBORNE/McGRAW-HILL

For a complete catalog of Osborne's books, call 510-549-6600 or write to us at 2600 Tenth Street, Berkeley, CA 94710

☎ **Call Toll-Free: 1-800-822-8158**
24 hours a day, 7 days a week in U.S. and Canada

✉ **Mail this order form to:**
McGraw-Hill, Inc.
Customer Service Dept.
P.O. Box 547
Blacklick, OH 43004

📠 **Fax this order form to:**
1-614-759-3644

💻 **EMAIL**
7007.1531@COMPUSERVE.COM
COMPUSERVE GO MH

Ship to:

Name _____

Company _____

Address _____

City / State / Zip _____

Daytime Telephone: _____
(We'll contact you if there's a question about your order.)

ISBN #	BOOK TITLE	Quantity	Price	Total
0-07-88				
0-07-88				
0-07-88				
0-07-88				
0-07-88				
0-07088				
0-07-88				
0-07-88				
0-07-88				
0-07-88				
0-07-88				
0-07-88				
0-07-88				
0-07-88				

Shipping & Handling Charge from Chart Below		
Subtotal		
Please Add Applicable State & Local Sales Tax		
TOTAL		

Shipping & Handling Charges

Order Amount	U.S.	Outside U.S.
Less than $15	$3.50	$5.50
$15.00 - $24.99	$4.00	$6.00
$25.00 - $49.99	$5.00	$7.00
$50.00 - $74.99	$6.00	$8.00
$75.00 - and up	$7.00	$9.00

Occasionally we allow other selected companies to use our mailing list. If you would prefer that we not include you in these extra mailings, please check here: ❑

METHOD OF PAYMENT

❑ Check or money order enclosed (payable to Osborne/McGraw-Hill)

❑ AMERICAN EXPRESS   ❑ DISCOVER   ❑ MasterCard   ❑ VISA

Account No. ☐☐☐☐☐☐☐☐☐☐☐☐☐☐☐☐☐

Expiration Date _____

Signature _____

In a hurry? Call 1-800-822-8158 anytime, day or night, or visit your local bookstore.

Thank you for your order   Code BC640SL

Michael Abbey

Michael Abbey has been working with Oracle since version 3. He is a frequent presenter at conferences in North America and Europe. Michael is the VP of Communications and Director of Publications for the IOUG-A (International Oracle Users Group-Americas). Michael is active as the library sysop on the Oracle User Group forum on Compuserve. He is co-author of *Tuning Oracle* (Osborne-McGraw-Hill/Oracle Press, 1995).

Michael J. Corey

Michael J. Corey is Executive Vice-President of Database Technologies Inc, Newton MA USA, and is currently President of the International Oracle Users Group-Americas. Michael has been using Oracle since early Version 4. He has worked with Oracle on a variety of platforms from PCs to mainframes. Michael's specialties include database administration, performance tuning, and very large databases. Michael has been a presenter on these topics at Oracle user group meetings in Europe and North America. Michael is also one of the original sysops on the Oracle Usergroup forum (ORAUSER) on CompuServe. Michael is a graduate of Bentley college and received his B.S. in computer information systems. Michael brings a very in-depth knowledge of Oracle and its products.